SOUTH AMERICAN INDEPENDENCE: GENDER, POLITICS, TEXT

Liverpool Latin American Studies

Series Editors: John Fisher, *University of Liverpool*, and Steve Rubenstein, *University of Liverpool*

1 Business History in Latin America: The Experience of Seven Countries
Carlos Dávila and Rory Miller (eds)

2 Habsburg Peru: Images, Imagination and Memory
Peter T. Bradley and David Cahill

3 Knowledge and Learning in the Andes: Ethnographic Perspectives
Henry Stobart and Rosaleen Howard (eds)

4 Bourbon Peru, 1750–1824
John Fisher

5 Between Resistance and Adaptation: Indigenous Peoples and the Colonisation of the Chocó, 1510–1753
Caroline A. Williams

6 Shining Path: Guerilla War in Peru's Northern Highlands, 1980–1997
Lewis Taylor

Liverpool Latin American Studies, New Series 7

South American Independence
Gender, Politics, Text

Catherine Davies, Claire Brewster and Hilary Owen

LIVERPOOL UNIVERSITY PRESS

First published 2006 by
Liverpool University Press
4 Cambridge Street
Liverpool L69 7ZU

This paperback edition published 2011

British Library Cataloguing-in-Publication data
A British Library CIP record is available

ISBN 978-1-84631-027-0 cased
978-1-84631-684-5 limp

Typeset in Plantin by XL Publishing Services, Tiverton
Printed and bound in Great Britain by
CPI Antony Rowe, Chippenham and Eastbourne

Fue ése el momento en que Sofía se desprendió de la ventana: '¡Vamos allá!', gritó, arrancando sables y puñales de la panoplia. Esteban trató de detenerla: 'No seas idiota: están ametrallando. No vas a hacer nada con esos hierros viejos'. '¡Quédate si quieres! ¡Yo voy!' '¿Y vas a pelear por quién?' '¡Por los que se echaron a la calle!' – gritó Sofía –. '¡Hay que hacer algo!' '¿Qué?' '¡Algo!'. Y Estaban la vio salir de la casa, impetuosa, enardecida, con un hombro en claro y un acero en alto, jamás vista en tal fuerza y en tal entrega. 'Espérame', gritó. Y armándose con un fusil de caza, bajó las escalera a todo correr…

Alejo Carpentier, *El siglo de las luces*

Contents

Plates

(after page 148)

Acknowledgements

The research for this book was funded by a major Arts and Humanities Research Council award for the research project 'Gendering Latin American Independence: Women's Political Culture and the Textual Construction of Gender 1790–1850' (2001–06), hosted at the universities of Manchester and Nottingham, directed and co-directed by Catherine Davies and Hilary Owen, with Claire Brewster as Research Associate and Charlotte Liddell and Iona MacIntyre as doctorate students. The book is the result of collaborative team-work. Davies was the author of chapters 1–5, 8, 10, 11; Brewster wrote chapters 6 and 7; and Owen wrote chapter 9 and the introductory section on Brazil. The authors would like to sincerely thank the AHRC and following institutions and individuals for their invaluable assistance and encouragement in the various stages of research and writing of this book:

The British Library; The John Rylands Library, University of Manchester; the Hallward Library, University of Nottingham; Senate House Library, University of London; the Bodleian Library and Taylorian Library, University of Oxford; University Library and Centre of Latin American Studies Library, Cambridge; University of Warwick Library; Robinson Library, University of Newcastle; Biblioteca Nacional do Brasil; the Academia Literária Feminina do Rio Grande do Sul; Biblioteca Nacional de Chile; Sala Medina, Biblioteca Nacional de Chile; Archivo Nacional de Chile; Biblioteca Nacional de Perú; Instituto Riva-Agüero, Lima; Biblioteca del Banco Central de Ecuador; Biblioteca Nacional de Argentina; Biblioteca Furt, Argentina; Museo Mitre, Buenos Aires; Museo Nacional de Colombia; Biblioteca Luis Angel Arango, Colombia.

Néstor Tomás Auza, Mercedes Bengoechea, Keith Brewster, Matthew Brown, Sarah C. Chambers, Julie Coimbra, Manuel Díaz, Liz Dore, Rebecca Earle, John Fisher, Raul Flores, Hilda Agnes Hübner Flores, Moacyr Flores, Richard Fardon, Juan A. Fondón, Etelxina Furt, Till Geiger, Charles Jones, John Laidlar, Asunción Lavrin, Jeremy Lawrance, Charlotte Liddell, María Rosa Lojo, David Lowe, Iona MacIntyre, Lilianne Montesinos Rosas, Luis Muñoz, Scarlett O'Phelan, Sergio Otero, Eliana Peña Córdova, Alicia Pololla,

Rossana Pozzi-Escot Subiria, Glynn Redworth, Anna Jean Sánchez, Sarah Sánchez, Rutônio Sant'Anna, Rebeca Sanmartín, Patience Schell, Peggy Sharpe, Wilma Stuardo, Robert Sykes, José Vera and Claire Williams.

Catherine Davies would like to thank the Leverhulme Trust for funding the project 'Hispanic Feminist Thought 1830–1930' (1999–2000), the British Academy for funding research in Argentina in 2001 and the AHRC and the University of Nottingham for sabbatical leave (2005–06), which enabled her to finish her parts of the book.

A shorter version of Chapter 2 was published by Davies as 'Colonial Dependence and Sexual Difference: Reading for Gender in the Writings of Simón Bolívar (1783–1830)' in *Feminist Review*, 79, 2005: 5–19; and a shorter version of Chapter 6 was published by Brewster as 'Women and Spanish American Wars of Independence: an Overview' in *Feminist Review*, 79, 2005: 20–35.

This book will be most profitably read in conjunction with the information, working papers, image bank and, above all, database available on the AHRC project website www.genderlatam.org.uk (see Brewster 2006).

The authors are grateful to the British Library for permission to reproduce plates 2–15, 17, 26 and 27.

PART I

Latin America in 1830

CHAPTER ONE

South American Independence: War, Liberty, Gender, Text

> [D]iscourse is not simply that which translates struggles or systems of domination, but is the thing for which and by which there is struggle, discourse is the power which is to be seized...
>
> Foucault 1970: 52

> Reading for paradox requires a different kind of reading than historians are accustomed to.
>
> Scott 1996: 16

The political status of South American men and women changed radically in the course of the nineteenth century. From subjects of Iberian absolutism without political rights, they became potential citizens of independent republics founded on the principle of liberty. The transition was spasmodic and the outcome assured only in retrospect. For the people living through these turbulent times the political future was uncertain, its resolution largely contingent on where they lived. If, in the 1810s, they lived in areas which acknowledged the legitimacy of the 1812 Spanish liberal constitution, they were governed by a constitutional monarch *in absentia*; in liberated areas controlled by the Spanish American patriots they might be citizens of centralised or federal republics, city states aspiring to autonomy, or provinces incorporated into larger confederations. If they lived in Brazil in 1822, they formed part of an independent monarchy that was not replaced by a republic until 1889 (see below). The name of their homeland might suddenly alter: the Nuevo Reino de Granada on the morning of August 8 1819 was the Republic of Colombia by the evening (Vergara y Vergara 1958: 11). The protagonist of Juana Manso's novel *Los misterios del Plata* (written 1846–50) flees Buenos Aires city for a newly independent country, Corrientes, which was later to be incorporated as a province into the Argentine republic.

Irrespective of national boundaries, the shift from absolutism to republicanism signified one crucial fact: that while absolutism denied political rights to virtually all men and women, the new republican constitutions (and there were many) denied political rights systematically to women only. This included

Brazil, where slavery was abolished in 1888, which, in turn, led to the formation of a federal republic.[1] Women were excluded as a social sector because ultimately gender (rather than class or caste) was the criterion for political exclusion. Indeed, it was on this basis only that the res publica was made possible, in that its functioning was predicated on the separation of the public world and private life; only the public was political, and it was the business of men. In classical republican representation men speak for and in the stead of women. If South American women thought for one moment that political liberty might apply to them, they were sorely deceived; liberty is not democracy. But in the first half of the nineteenth century few South American men and women thought this way; regardless of independence, the idea was not within their horizons of expectations. Women's political rights were not inconceivable (after all, Plato had included women in his *Republic*; and the works of Feijóo and Condorcet, 'le seul grand féministe de la Révolution' (Hoffman 1976: 555), circulated widely), but not even the revolutionaries of France and the United States of America had managed to adequately address the political emancipation of over half their respective populations. As a social sector, South American women recognised, accepted and condoned their political exclusion as a sine qua non of their new societies; it was the consensus, the *doxa,* of their times.

To investigate this complex process, this study explores aspects of the history and culture of South American independence (c. 1800–50) in terms of woman and gender. It consists of two lines of enquiry: the textual constructions of gender categories; and women's writings. Its purpose is to investigate the centrality of gender in the ideological and discursive constructions of South American independence, and the contribution of women's textual production in this process. This involves tracing the gender contradictions in discourses on independence, the gendering of citizenship and the exclusion or ambivalent inclusion of women, and women's strategic complicity and resistance, as is evidenced in their published and unpublished writings.

The historical and political processes known as South American independence mark a critical moment of revolution and constitutional transformation. It was during the first half of the nineteenth century that questions of political rights, nationality and citizenship were most open to debate throughout the continent. This book is a literary and historical study, which examines some of the ideas and activities of the men and women who contributed to the making of public culture and yet, in the case of women, were largely excluded from it. At issue is how gender shaped and was shaped by the political discourses of the independence period. The adoption and reworking of European political thought in South America and the subsequent marginalisation of the subaltern, including the social category woman, in the post-independence quest for national coherence were issues flagged up by John Lynch as requiring further research (Lynch 1999). Since then, much has been achieved (Caulfield 2001; Chambers 2001; Díaz 2004; Blanchard 2004; Gutiérrez Chong 2004; Brown 2005); this book is indebted to the many ideas and insights resulting from this ongoing research.

The book works from the premise that gender, the social relations of sexual difference (Leonard and Adkins 1996: 16), is at the centre of cultural constructions of collective identities (Yuval-Davis 1997), what Pierre Bourdieu would refer to as gender and the symbolic field (Bourdieu 1992). Two aspects of modern political philosophy are particularly problematical for women: determinist theories of human nature (women are inherently different from men); and the public-private distinction (central to political thought). Questions prompting our research include: How was the category 'woman' produced historically and politically in South America at this time? In what ways were those identified as women constructed ambiguously as subjects and objects in contemporary political discourse? How did women living through the social crises detect and respond to these conceptual problems? What were their responses to the republican discourses of individual rights that equated individuality with masculinity? Such questions are rendered complex in South America due to a large mixed-race population, the prevalence of patrimonial authority, patronage and corporate groups (the military and the Church), and the unprecedented rapidity of unforeseen political disruption in a previously stable hierarchical society. The inclusion of the gendered discourse emerging from Brazilian independence affords a significant comparative dimension with the Spanish American case histories, given the specificity of Brazil's accession to independence.

These questions are explored largely on the basis of textual evidence drawing on current debates in gender studies that emphasise the significance of gender as a tool of analysis in literature, history and politics (Scott 1999). We are indebted to Joan W. Scott's reading of French feminist Olympe de Gouges (1745–93) and de Gouge's reworking of Rousseau (Scott 1996), Joan B. Landes's enquiries into gender in Revolutionary France (1988, 2001, 2004a, 2004b) and Linda K. Kerber's into gender and the early Republican United States (1980). Seminal pioneering studies (historical, political and literary) by Asunción Lavrín, Susan Midgen Socolow, Maxine Molyneux, Francine Masiello, Zahidé Lupinacci Muzart, María Inés de Torres and many others have been pivotal in drawing attention to the formation of gender categories in nineteenth-century Latin America and have informed our work. This book aims to complement these findings with gendered critical readings of the rhetorical strategies employed in dominant Latin American discourses and in the resisting or unconsenting discourses that point up gender-specific contradictions. It goes without saying that imaginative literature is a form of resistance, a means by which the dominant order might be contested (de Certeau 1988). The book further develops the work of Jean Franco who, in her critique of the early writings of the Mexican Fernández de Lizardi (1776–1827) (Franco 1989), indicated the need for further exploration of the recodification of gender in this period and the relative accessibility of social, cultural and intellectual capital to men and women.

Women's writings of the first half of the nineteenth century have been largely unexplored. Book-length studies such as feminist journalist Carmen Clemente

Travieso's *Mujeres de la independencia: seis biografías de mujeres venezolanas* (1965), though important in their day, are often no more than domesticated biographies. The diaries of Concepción Lombardo (Mexico), the poetry of Silveria Espinosa (Colombia), Isabel de Orbea (Peru), María Dolores Veintemilla (Ecuador), Hermelinda Garcia da Cunha Mattos (Brazil), Dolores Guerrero (Mexico) and the novels of Rosa Guerra (Argentina) are still relatively unknown, as scholarship has tended to concentrate on later generations of Latin American women writers (Juana Manuela Gorriti, Eduarda Mansilla, Clorinda Matto de Turner, Júlia Lopes de Almeida). Similarly under-researched are the numerous anonymous patriotic (and royalist) chants, hymns, and verses attributed to women such as the *silva,* 'Despedida de las chilenas al ejército libertador del Perú', 1820, which voices women's frustration at not being able to join the patriot men in battle. A few lines are quoted below:

> ...
> Nuestro sexo os envidia:
> Y el alma entera lidia
> Con inútil violencia
> Entre el amor, la PATRIA y la impotencia
> De nuestra débil mano, que esmerada
> Texerá la guirnalda preparada
> A los Héroes de la Libertad.
> Silencio amor ... marchad.[2]

Or the *cielito* 'La Negrita' (1830), apparently written by a Buenos Aires black woman, Juana Peña, which begins,

> Yo me llamo Juana Peña
> Y tengo por vanidad
> Que sepan todos que soy
> Negrita muy federal.
> ...
> He de hacer ver que, aunque negra,
> Soy patriota verdadera. (Lanuza 1941: 22–23)[3]

Literatura menor of this kind, scattered in loose pamphlets and the periodical press of the times, have yet to be collected and examined in depth. Unlike most of the currently available historical studies of the independence years, ours is text-based research involving archival retrieval and discourse analysis.

The chronology of the book extends from the French Revolution (c. 1790) to the mid-1850s, the decade in which the new nation states began to take shape. The geo-cultural scope is continental South America (not Central America, or Mexico, which deserves a book in its own right; and not the Spanish Caribbean (Cuba and Puerto Rico), which remained under metropolitan rule until 1898). The book engages in critical analysis of selected works of selected writers: from the founding fathers of republican patrias (Bolívar, Bello and Echeverría) to the published and unpublished responses of founding mothers (Carrera, Acevedo,

Marín, Manso, Cunha, Barandas). But the detailed study of individual texts, to the degree of wrangling with single words and phrases, demands contextualisation. The historiography on the late colonial and independence period is immense and a comprehensive study of the massive social and political upheavals of the time far exceeds the scope of this book. Nevertheless, an overview of women's participation in the Wars of Independence (see chapter 6) is here provided. Similarly, our study of women's written responses to social change includes their private correspondence, since their letters and diaries were seldom published and scrutinised, unlike those of the men of state. Notable exceptions are Mariquita Sánchez de Thompson (Vilaseca 1952; Villalba 1986) and, for her relationship with Bolívar, Manuela Sáenz (Alvarez Saá 1995; Espinosa Apolo 1996; Poniatowska 1993; Murray 2001; Mizraje 2003). Only recently were the dictated memoirs of Agustina Palacio de Libarona, who was caught up in the civil unrest in Santiago de Estero (Argentina) in 1840, published in a modern edition (Palacio de Libarona 2004).[4] In view of the emphasis on writing, the women featured in this book tend to belong to the educated classes; they are the *letradas* of the emerging bourgeoisie, the former aristocracy and the governing elite.[5]

The book cuts across three broad areas of enquiry: political history, gender studies/feminist critique, and literary analysis, and is underpinned by theories that privilege investigation into the interrelations between society, politics, gender and language. As Angel Rama (1996) indicated with reference to Spanish America, the control of the word is imperative for the transmission and implementation of political will. The political force of the written word during the independence years is indisputable. Words were used as instruments of threat, negotiation and compliance and as signs of condescension or respect. Indeed, the literary field was a site of struggle, with various contending discourses competing for hegemony through the century (González-Stephan 2002). The words of de Certeau are particularly apposite in this respect:

> Revolution itself, that 'modern' idea, represents the scriptural project at the level of an entire society seeking to *constitute itself* as a blank page with respect to the past, to write itself by itself (that is, to produce itself as its own system) and to produce *a new history* on the model of what it fabricates. (de Certeau 1988: 135, emphases as in the original)

The insights of Foucault, Bourdieu, Macherey and de Certeau, of feminist critics concerned with the demystification of belief systems and myths, such as Spender, Irigaray and de Beauvoir, and recent work on gender by Mosse, Dudink, Hagemann, Tosh, McClintock and others, have all been of immense benefit in thinking through these complex issues. Particularly useful have been Bourdieu's concepts of social and symbolic capital (Bourdieu 1977: 1992).[6] In her discussion of the appropriateness of Bourdieu's sociology of culture for feminist critique and textual analysis, Toril Moi draws attention to his 'microtheoretical' approach to social power, which 'allows us to incorporate everyday details of life' in attempting to account for the social construction of gender (Moi 1999: 268). The concept of symbolic capital, that is, the legitimacy or right to speak acquired by playing the game, by obeying the unspoken rules that confer recognition in a particular social field, is especially relevant. Moi's point is that 'in most contexts maleness functions as positive and femaleness as negative symbolic capital' (Moi 1999: 291); being a woman immediately detracts from recognition of social esteem, especially in public life. Neglected women writers, like all neglected writers, have little symbolic power, but the issue here is that this lack is a direct consequence of the gendering of the socially female. However, Moi notes that 'the impact of femaleness as negative capital may be assumed to decline in direct proportion to the amount of other symbolic capital amassed'; women may make up for lack of social recognition in other ways. One of the ways in which women might compensate is to make use of their social capital, that is, 'the power and advantages one gains from having a network of contacts as well as a series of other more personal or intimate personal relations' (Moi 1999: 293). As Bourdieu suggested to Moi, an example would be the hostesses of the literary salons (Moi 1999: 295, n. 33). Another example is, of course, the extended family, which enables 'heavy symbolic investment spread across the whole social field' (Moi 1999: 275). As we shall see, revolutions generally have little impact on these established family networks, which maintain order in their own interests, and this may benefit women.

Spanish America: war

> [I]t is in warlike ages and in warlike countries that women have fared the worst
>
> C.K. Ogden 1915 in Marshall, Ogden and Sargant Florence 1987: 59

The fall of the Spanish Empire in 1826 was of momentous consequence. It resulted in the emergence of a constellation of new nation states and the massive expansion of the United States of America. Although the Spanish Caribbean islands (and the Philippines) remained under Spanish rule until 1898, it was during the 1820s that the Spanish dominions in the Americas, stretching from San Francisco in the north to Patagonia in the south, achieved political autonomy. Spain lost 300,000 square leagues and some 12 million inhabitants. The USA increased its territory by over one-third with the annexation of Texas and the northern half of the United States of the Republic of Mexico in the 1840s. The fall of the Spanish Empire and the independence of Portuguese Brazil (1822) signified the collapse of the European empires in the Americas and the end of the first phase of European expansion, the aims of which had been to replicate the values and traditions of the ancient world (Pagden 1995: 5).

The crisis affected millions of people. On the eve of independence, Spanish America was populated by more than 13,500,000 inhabitants (compared with Spain's 10,500,000 (Sánchez-Albornoz 1984: 34)).[7] This 'elaborate mosaic of peoples' (Sánchez-Albornoz 1984: 33), the product of some 300 years of settlement and miscegenation, was ethnically diverse and racially mixed; just under half were Amerindians, one-third mestizo or mulatto creoles, and a fifth white (or passing as white). The dominant elite, the white creoles, descendants of the Spanish settlers, were mainly urban-based, living in cities. By the eighteenth century, women were in the majority in almost all the cities of colonial Latin America; they constituted 53 per cent of the populations of São Paulo and Quito by the late 1790s, and women dominated in all non-white groups (Socolow 2000: 112–13).

The historiography on Latin American independence is immense and growing, and can only be touched on lightly here (cf. Keen 1992: 158–76; Lynch 1973, 1986, 1999, 2006; McFarlane and Posada-Carbó 1999; Rodríguez 1998; Scheina 2003; Williamson 1992: 195–232).[8] Independence was a complex, messy process that still constitutes 'a serious historical as well as historiographical problem' (Van Young 2001: 225), in Octavio Paz's words, 'un hecho ambiguo y de dificil interpretación' (Paz 1981: 124). Yet to conceive of the Wars of Independence as solely anti-colonial, as a breaking-point conflict between colonies and metropolis, imperial Spain and colonial Spanish America, is to miss the point. There is no doubt that the symbolic and material exploitation of the Americas was of immense benefit to Spain, Portugal and the whole of Europe (not least Britain) (see Hernández Sánchez-Barba 1972: 128–80)[9], but this imperial venture (of conquest and direct rule), theoretically rooted in the Roman imperium, was different from the later, second-wave imperialism (commerce and indirect rule) of Britain and France in Africa and Asia (Pagden 1995). Historians trace the origins of Spanish American independence to the demise of the creole consensus that had existed under the Habsburgs but was disrupted in the mid-eighteenth century by Bourbon reforms. No less significant was the British naval blockade of the Spanish fleet (1796–1802), resulting from Carlos IV's alliance with the French Republic, which cut Spain off from the Americas for over five years. Scheina ends his monumental study of the Wars of Independence with the following 'surprising' observations: the wars started as civil wars between Latin Americans, not against foreigners; they were fought by feudal armies (caudillos and peasants), in which personal loyalty was more important than political ideas; and soldiers who became statesman and politicians owed their preeminence to their martial skills (Scheina 2003: 426–27).

To what extent were the Spanish American wars (encompassing wars between caudillos, against the indigenes, and intra-class wars) primarily a contest between a despotic Crown and popular revolutionaries? The insurgents or patriots, depending on one's perspective, were mainly wealthy creoles, many of whom (for example, General San Martín, who liberated the southern part of the continent) had been trained in the Spanish army. As Lynch points out, 'the ideological origins of the Spanish American revolutions is a book waiting to be written' (Lynch 1999: 36). That there was a strong sense of creole consciousness and identity is undoubted (Zea 1993), but this was by no means uniform throughout the region. Creoles fought to carve out a social and symbolic space that differentiated them from metropolitan Spain, the indigenous Americans and the *peninsulares*. At the outset of independence, the rest of the people – the 'pueblo' – including the indigenous people and the slaves, were usually indifferent and often royalist (for example, the Mapuches in Chile), since the Crown protected them against creole exploitation. Some patriots (notably in Mexico) rose against the Spanish interim liberal governments (1808–14) to defend the Catholic Church.[10] Mexico and Peru toyed in the early years with monarchism; Brazil remained a monarchy throughout this period. Few patriots were persuaded by the radical agenda of the French Revolution; rather more by US republicanism and British and Spanish constitutionalism.

Initially, the uprisings were not ostensibly against the Spanish Crown; there was no Spanish monarch, enlightened or otherwise, against whom to rebel, since the king (Carlos IV and his son Fernando VII) had been deposed during the French occupation of the Peninsula and replaced by Napoleon's brother, Joseph. The catalyst for independence was the crisis in the Spanish monarchy, which prompted in both hemispheres the formation of provincial juntas (emergency representative governments) on liberal principles. In some parts of Spanish America the uprisings were justified as a sign of loyalty to the Spanish Crown against the liberal juntas, or against Napoleon, as discontented creoles took advantage of the power vacuum to establish autonomous rule in the name of the deposed Fernando. The Royal Decree of the Spanish Junta Central of 1809 (the King in absentia) called for elections in the provinces and kingdoms of Peninsular Spain and American Spain, famously declaring that the Indies were not, properly speaking, 'colonias o factorías como las de otras naciones, sino una parte esencial e integrante de la monarquía Española' (Guerra 1999: 61). In the liberal Constitution of Cadiz of 1812, Fernando (still in absentia) is referred to as the 'Rey de las Españas'; Article 1 states 'La nación Española es la reunión de todos los españoles de ambos hemisferios', and Article 5 'Son españoles: todos los hombres libres nacidos y avecinados en los dominios de las Españas y los hijos de estos' (González-Doria 1986: 295). Constitutionalism was thus introduced concurrently to the provinces of both hemispheres; the 1812 Constitution was the first in the Americas, excepting that of Venezuela (1811), probably modelled on an earlier draft (Fernández Sarasola 2004: 18). However, unlike the Constitution of Cadiz, most of the American constitutions incorporated a Declaration of Rights, including the right to liberty, on the model of the Constitution of the United States.

To conceive of the Wars of Independence in terms of what today is understood as nationalism or national emancipation is no less problematical; it could be said that the process was the inverse. This was a movement to disaggregate the existing Spanish nation (the conglomeration of viceroyalties and kingdoms, such as the *reinos* of Chile and Aragón). For this reason Spanish historian Salvador de Madariaga refers to the Wars of Secession (Madariaga 1947). There was little trace of national liberation in Spanish America before 1808; popular rebellions often began with the cry 'Long live the King!' (Lynch 1999: 45). David Brading identifies the transmutation of creole patriotism (classical republicanism) to insurgent nationalism only in Mexico and only in response to the liberal revolution in Spain (1820–23) (Brading 1983: 7–8). On the eve of independence, the Spanish nation was coterminous with one imperial state or, more correctly, 'a confederation of principalities held together in the person of a single king' (Pagden 1990: 3); the Atlantic (indeed, the Pacific) merely flowed through it. After independence, the political boundaries of the new republics largely replicated those of the administrative divisions, the viceroyalties and *audiencias*, of the ancien régime. As late as 1849, Domingo Faustino Sarmiento lamented the persistence of a colonial 'sentimiento nacional' in the Americas: 'en España el aragonés es extranjero en Castilla, el andaluz en Cataluña y los catalanes y los vascos forman dos naciones separadas, odiándose entre sí, se entiende. Lo mismo han hecho las repúblicas americanas' (Sarmiento 1961: 19–20). As John Chasteen indicates in his critique of Benedict Anderson's version of the origins of nationalism in Latin America (Anderson 1991),[11] the problem was not 'how Brazil or Ecuador came to be called nations, but just what 'nation' meant to Brazilians and Ecuadoreans of diverse social, regional, racial and cultural descriptions' (Castro-Klarén and Chasteen 2003: xxi); at issue are the contested meanings of nationalism across the region. *Contra* Anderson, with the exception of Mexico (Earle 2002b), print capitalism did not play a major part in the creole revolution before 1810, but it took on an increasingly important role during the Wars of Independence.[12] In effect, independence in Spanish America became anti-colonial and republican, and national identities were formed and consolidated during the ten years of bloody warfare against absolutism (1815–25) and through the following decades of internecine violence as new republican boundaries were fixed (Castro-Klarén and Chasteen 2003: xv). It was during the Wars of Independence that political ideas were tried out; warfare was the catalyst for revolutionary ideas and practices. Although it may initially have been a response to a power vacuum, Spanish American independence developed into a war of liberation against colonial despotism.

A sequence of events unfolded, often in unexpected, aleatory ways. The first sign of political confrontation was between Peninsular liberal constitutionalists and their American counterparts; for how could the liberals in Spain invoke popular sovereignty and then deny it to the Spanish Americans?[13] The Proclama del Consejo de Regencia de España e Indias a los americanos españoles (February 14 1810),[14] published in the *Gaceta de Buenos Aires* (June 9 1810: 1–7), stated:

> Desde el principio de la revolución declaró la Patria esos dominios parte integrante y esencial de la Monarquía Española. Como tal le corresponden los mismos derechos y prerrogativas que a la metrópoli. Siguiendo este principio de eterna equidad y justicia fueron llamados esos naturales a tomar parte en el Gobierno representativo que ha cesado ... Desde este momento, Españoles Americanos, os veis elevados a la dignidad de hombres libres: no sois ya los mismos que antes encorvados baxo un yugo mucho más duro mientras más distantes estabais del centro del poder; mirados con indiferencia, besados por la codicia, y destruidos por la ignorancia. Tened presente que al pronun-

> ciar o al escribir el nombre del que ha de venir a representaros en el Congreso Nacional, vuestros destinos ya no dependen ni de los Ministros, ni de los Virreyes, ni de los Gobernadores; están en vuestras manos ... (Etchart 1979: 123–24)

This statement not only appeals to the scholastic principle of the reversion to original sovereignty but it also challenges despotism, hence its revolutionary impact (Fernández Sarasola 2004: 19). Yet of the 185 signatories to the 1812 Constitution, drawn up in the midst of the Peninsula's own war of independence against France, just under one-third represented the American *provincias de ultramar*, an anomaly justly criticised by Jeremy Bentham. The Junta apologised for the imbalance,[15] yet in many ways the Spanish liberals were no less colonialist than the royalists (Guerra 1999: 62). Federico Suárez lists the names of 302 deputies, 64 of whom were *americanos* (Suárez 2002: 31–53). The deputies to the 1812 Parliament formed three groups: absolutists, liberals, and *americanos*. The liberals and *americanos* generally worked together, the main point of contention being different interpretations of *nación*. The word was ambiguous, but for the American deputies nation signified both the sum of the provinces which had recovered their original sovereignty (preparing the way for federalism) and also the 'pueblo', the sum of individuals in the Spanish territories (leading to individual rights). The *americanos* argued in favour of equal rights for all, while the Spanish liberals distinguished between *ciudadanos* and *españoles*, conceding rights only to the former. As Fernández Sarasola observes, 'se trataba de evitar que la representación americana fuese mucho mayor que la metropolitana, habida cuenta de la población más extensa de los territorios de Ultramar' (Fernández Sarasola 2004: 23).[16] In short, Spanish men of liberal persuasion did not wish to share power with their liberal American counterparts. As Lynch puts it, 'all Spaniards might be equal before the law ... But the law was not all' (Lynch 1985: 26). And, as will be argued here, just as colonialism denied political rights to Americans, so did masculine hegemony deny political rights to the women of both hemispheres.

Fighting began after independence was declared in Buenos Aires and Chile in 1810 and in Venezuela in 1811. The restoration of Fernando in 1814 and his return to absolutist rule (revoking the 1812 Constitution) caused many creoles to reassess their position, especially Spanish American liberals who had fought for king and constitution. Confrontation became increasingly brutal: in Spain between absolutists and liberal constitutionalists; and in Spanish America between royalists and patriots. Fresh troops were sent from Spain to America under the command of General Pablo Morillo; Fernando attempted a 'reconquest' of the Americas with such cruelty that he provided the patriots with a case for just war and made reconciliation between the two Spains inconceivable. The military contest was in the balance until 1820, when the Spanish liberal troops, which had been in Cadiz for a year awaiting ships, mutinied and refused to cross the Atlantic. Fernando was forced to swear the 1812 Constitution and Bolívar signed a peace treaty with Morillo, which lasted a year.

By 1823 Fernando had reverted to absolutism and all-out war had resumed. The last major battle took place in Ayacucho, Peru, in December 1824. Britain recognised the independence of Mexico, Argentina and Gran Colombia in 1825. Spain did not recognise the independence of Mexico until 1836.[17]

The Wars of Independence produced their own sui generis political and ideological dynamic, which, skilfully presented in print culture and oratory, fortified the symbolic power of the creole elite. The war of arms was packaged in a war of words. Bolívar, taking his cue from Montesquieu, revived the sixteenth-century black legend in his writings while enforcing the War to the Death in Venezuela (1813), according to which all Spaniards were to be put to the sword and all Americans reprieved, irrespective of their political persuasion. Bolívar forced people to take sides, obliging them to assume an American identity. It is in the thousands of written documents produced in these decades that the diverse Spanish American national identities took shape, but boundaries were still in flux – in Argentina, for example, until at least 1860, thirty years after peace with Spain. A second ideological shift is noted from around 1826 with the recrudescence of war between the patriots themselves: notably the war between Chile and the Peru-Bolivia Confederation (1836–41), the War of the Supremes in Colombia (1839–42), and the civil wars in the River Plate region throughout the period leading to the dictatorship of Juan Manuel Rosas (1835–52). Scheina (2003) refers to these as Wars of Separation versus Union. In contention were competing constitutional models: the centralised or federal republic, or the Napoleonic state (as proposed by Bolívar) (Safford 1985: 361).

Material destruction was most devastating in the richer, more populated north (Venezuela, Colombia, Peru), where royalist resistance to independence was strong. Some regions, such as Paraguay, were hardly affected. In others (the River Plate area), hunger was rife. Agriculture, industry and trade suffered and debt mounted. In 1809 the output of the Mexico City mint was 26,000,000 pesos; in 1821, the year of its independence, output was less than 6,000,000 pesos (Bushnell and Macaulay 1994: 55). Long-term effects included the militarisation of society and the institutionalisation of violence (Halperín Donghi 1973). Another was political fragmentation. In Fernández-Armesto's words, Spanish America 'was a Humpty-Dumpty, irremediably smashed by its fall' (Fernández-Armesto 2004: 101). Bolívar compared the fall of the Spanish monarchy with the fall of the Roman Empire, in which 'cada desmembración formó entonces una nación independiente', but with the difference that 'aquellos miembros volvían a restablecer sus asociaciones. Nosotros ni aun conservamos los vestigios de lo que fue en otros tiempos' (Lievano 1983: 168).

Spanish America: liberty

America no es tanto una tradición que continuar como un futuro que realizar
Paz 1981: 123

What was at stake in the Spanish American Wars of Liberation? In what ways were they revolutionary? In theory, independence meant political self-rule, economic self-sufficiency and individual freedom. In 1855 José María Torres Caicedo listed the gains of independence for Nueva Granada (Colombia) as follows: the state guarantee of security, liberty and property; freedom of industry, movement, association, thought and the press; abolition of slavery; separation of Church and state; municipal government; fair taxes; moderate customs duties; fair judiciary, and a small standing army without conscription (Torres Caicedo 1863: 5–6).[18] The Wars of Independence were revolutionary in their pursuit of liberalism (Lynch 1986). The broad complex of ideas known as liberalism, which have been evolving since the seventeenth century, was predicated on the liberty of the individual (equal rights, rule of law, constitutional government). A liberal society is formed of free individuals who are autonomous and equally valuable. From Locke onwards, contract theory stressed the importance of rationality and God-given inalienable rights, equality before the law, and personal freedom; humans were rational and compassionate, but corruptible and in need of moral guidance for self-improvement. Education was seminal to the liberal project: 'the self-dependent man who is not the dupe nor the tool of others and is master of his own resources is an educated man' (Blackman 1968: 182). This emphasis on the rights of individuals extends to the Kantian view that the capacity for 'rational autonomy' is the highest humans possess. The ability to use practical reason or the 'rational will' to create principles of conduct ensures the dignity of the person. Humans are rational agents capable of reasoned choice with free will, enabling them to reach the highest good. In Kantian ethics, moral worth resides in the motivation of duty and good intention.

The concepts of natural rights, liberty and property ownership granted by the state were enshrined in the United Kingdom's Bill of Rights (1689), for example, and the Declaration of Independence of the United States (1776). The French *Declaration des droits de l'homme et du citoyen* (1789) was translated into Spanish by Antonio Nariño, who printed 100 copies in Bogotá in 1793 (he was imprisoned for ten years and the copies destroyed) (Lynch 1985: 44). These rights included freedom of speech, expression, protest, conscience, association, movement, petition, religion and political rights, and freedom from arbitrary arrest, slavery and torture. The US Declaration of Independence added the right to the pursuit of happiness and the premise 'that all Men are created equal and endowed with god-given unalienable rights' as a self-evident truth.

Liberal government derives its power and authority from social contract, the consent of those governed. Laws regulate society for the benefit of the common good, and justice is the exercise of that authority. The Constitution of a state is the corpus of rules that defines how society is organised and sovereign power distributed; these rules for living and working together regulate access to and the exercise of power, but for liberals individual freedom is more important than state interference. From the eighteenth century, liberalism became closely associated with forms of ancient government (classical republicanism) rather than constitutional monarchy (as in Locke and even Montesquieu). The rule of one (a president, for example), with checks and balances, and the absence of hereditary office were thought to be most conducive to securing liberty. The US republic of 1787 stressed the rights of all citizens, but, although it was a republic, it was not democratic. The franchise was eventually extended to all adult males under the presidency of Andrew Jackson (1828–36). Spain, Portugal and Spanish America experienced liberal revolutions. In Spain, the chosen form of liberal government was constitutional monarchy (in which citizenship was a status entailing liberal social rights); in Spanish America it was predominantly classical republicanism (in which citizenship was a practice entailing civic republican rights) (Lister 2000: 98). Portugal and Brazil both became constitutional monarchies.

The tenets of classical republicanism, as practised in ancient Rome and later favoured by Rousseau and Bolívar (Pagden 1990: 146), were liberty, virtue, toleration and active public life (*vita activa*). The virtuous property-owning citizen would need to bear arms to defend the common good, the res publica. Progress could only be achieved through civic virtue, the new religion in post-revolutionary France. By the end of the eighteenth century, republican patriotism was established as 'a language of liberty and a major intellectual tradition' (Viroli 1995: 95). Patriotism was understood as the love of common liberty, charity to fellow-citizens and respect for the republic; the common good was more important than individual freedoms. For Montesquieu, political virtue was the spirit of democracy; a patria cannot exist under despotic rule. Whereas for Rousseau, man could only fulfil himself as a social being as a citizen of a free republic; the violation of liberty of any one citizen constituted an attack on the common liberty of all (Viroli 1995: 87). In both the discourses of liberalism and republicanism, the precise meanings of which are still hotly debated in Spanish America (Aguilar and Rojas 2002), the problem for women lay in the definition of words such as 'human', 'man', 'individual', and 'citizen'. To participate in the polis, women had to make these precepts relevant and applicable to them.

Gender

> Era mi abuela tan femenil como varonil. Lo primero lo prueban sus veinte partos; lo segundo, sus muchos actos de voluntad, de firmeza, de resolución
>
> Lucio V. Mansilla 1904: 32[19]

Since the advent of the 'rights of man' in modern political theory, women have posed a problem. Virtually all modern political theorists see humans as sexually differentiated; 'womanhood and manhood do not have the same political meaning'; 'all men' should not be read as 'all mankind' (Shanley and Pateman 2003: 4–5). In political theory, patriarchalism was the dominant view from the seventeenth century. Hobbes believed that human nature is indeed the same in men and women, but that the subjection of women in the polity follows on from man-made civil law; in Nature, women have the right to dominate in the family, but the overthrow of the mother-right excludes them from civil society as free individuals. Locke, who attacked patriarchy, believed in the 'empirical fact of women's inferiority' (Butler 2003: 82). He incorporated women into his social theory in his *First Treatise of Government,* but in the second he subsumed women under 'persons' without considering how women might act politically, though they might be educated for political life. In the *Social Contract,* Rousseau berated Plato for including women in the Republic as Guardians' Wives (they might turn into men)[20]; women thinkers and politicians he regarded as unnatural. In *Emile* (1762) he allotted them the role of good mothers and wives in the domestic sphere.

More enlightened were Montesquieu and Condorcet. For Montesquieu, civic virtue was passed on to girls and boys by both parents. Only in despotic societies were women badly treated and reduced to servitude. Montesquieu argued that women are not subject to men by nature; women have allowed men to impose their tyranny because they are more gentle and reasonable. Condorcet suggested procedures for including women in the polity in his 1790 'Sur l'admission des femmes au Droit de Cité' (republished in *Oeuvres* in 1847). Women are men's equals other than in physical strength; men claim citizenship on the basis of rational beings with moral ideas, but use the law to create inequalities between the sexes. Condorcet claimed that women are excluded from men's associational life because they are physically weaker and were barred from the military. He argued that a key principle of republicanism was the inclusion of women. Their exclusion was an anomaly because it was 'about the rights of half of human beings, rights forgotten by all the legislators'; its resolution was 'the means of destroying the single objection which could be made to republics and to make between them and states which are not free a real difference' (Kerber 1980: 22). Enlightenment thinkers acknowledged women almost exclusively as wives and mothers, but not as political beings with a stake in the polity. Only Condorcet 'occasionally imagined an autonomous woman' (Kerber 1980: 27; Hoffmann 1976: 555–57).

Olympe de Gouges' *Droits de la Femme* (1791) argued that 'Woman is born free and lives equal to man in her rights' (Hufton 1997: 457); rights for women should include equality with men in the public sphere and equal obligations of citizenship, such as fighting for the state. De Gouges and Wollstonecraft were not only critical of social norms but 'explicit advocates of the political intervention [of women] to redress injustices' (Hufton 1997: 457). They were lone voices; male Enlightenment thinkers included women in the concept of 'man' only implicitly and ambiguously. As Kerber demonstrates with respect to the United States, the women of the American Revolution had no theoretical analyses of their role in society on which to draw for the development of new, radical ideas. As a consequence, other than merely consume Enlightenment ideas, they had to invent their own 'ideology' (Kerber 1980: 32). The women who campaigned for women's rights in antebellum United States made good use of abolitionist arguments for their own cause (Glassman 1979). The First National Women's Rights Convention was organised by US anti-slavery women at the World Anti-Slavery Convention in London in 1840. However, in Spanish America slavery was abolished almost entirely by 1830 and there is little evidence that the issue was raised in connection with women's rights. Even in Brazil, where slavery was not abolished until 1888, there is scant evidence that women appropriated abolitionism for their own cause before the 1850s. De Gouges, de Staël and Wollstonecraft had all attacked slavery in the 1790s, but their ideas did not circulate widely in early nineteenth-century Spanish America, and the trajectory of Wollstonecraft's thinking in Brazil is most curious (see below).

The political fallout of the Spanish American Wars of Independence might have presented an opportunity for women to secure their rights, as it had for slaves; patriot concessions to the pro-royalist slaves (and indigenous population) were necessary to gain their support. As Joan Scott observes in her study of Olympe de Gouges, 'it was in moments of revolution or constitutional transformation that the question of political rights was most open to discussion; and it was under republican governments that the extent and universality of the suffrage could be contested' (Scott 1996: 14). As noted, the work of Montesquieu and Condorcet circulated widely in Spanish America. The Spanish translation of Rousseau's *Social Contract* published in London in 1799 was reprinted in Buenos Aires by Mariano Moreno in 1810. The 'Defensa de las Mujeres', published in 1726 by the Spanish theologian Benito Jerónimo Feijóo (1676–1764), the 'Spanish Voltaire', was reprinted twenty times before the end of the 1780s. Feijóo attacked the Catholic Church for its prejudice against women and the courtly love tradition for its idealisation of women. He held women to be morally superior to men. Like Condorcet, he defended women's intellectual capacity and blamed men's laws for women's exclusion from education (see Feijóo 1774). South American women might have made their support for political change conditional on their inclusion in the polity, but they did not.

The militarisation, violence and destruction experienced during the Wars of Independence resulted in the continuation of the political subjection of women despite (or because of) revolutionary agendas. Three interrelated factors are crucial in this respect: first, the colonial legacy of the paterfamilias (Roman law, Roman Catholicism); next, the militarisation of society, in some places lasting for over half a century; and finally, the institutionalisation of republican politics, in Elizabeth Dore's words, the codification of 'the public authority of elite patriarchs-cum-fathers' (Dore and Molyneux 2000: 16).[21] In recent years the historiography focusing on Latin American women's history and on gender has underscored three major concerns: the diffusion of ideas; the construction of republican citizenship; and the significance of symbolic representation

(Caulfield 2001).[22] Particularly incisive is the exploration of 'the interplay between gender culture and political culture at all levels of the body politic', in other words, 'the politics of gender and the gendering of politics' (Stern 1995: 19, 21) during these years.

Colonial legacy: patriarchalism

> If the 'subject' of discourse is the father, he is the source of all specula(riza)tions
>
> Irigaray 1985: 308

The public actors of South American independence were virtually all men who, in their deeds and words (military and civilian), staged a spectacle worthy of the theatres of war and of the forums in classical antiquity, the written and visual representations of which have provided historians with a wealth of material. In Spanish America there was a constant preoccupation throughout the period and later with the figure of the founding father, the search for original Spanish American paternity (Earle 2002a; Vidal 2004). This was to be expected. The 'two Spains' were governed by one monarch who ruled by divine right, a 'lord of all the world' to paraphrase Pagden (1995). Patriarchalism was replicated at all levels of Iberian colonial society from Holy Roman Emperor, king or pope, viceroys and the heads of churches and towns to the patriarch on his rural estate and the head of the urban household. The Spanish king, the instrument of God the Father, was the head of a family of cities and communities held together by the Bourbon state. Once he was removed, the vertical system collapsed, not randomly like a pack of cards but like a skyscraper reduced, floor by floor, to a flat-pack, each stage accompanied by copious legislation. Having no single head of state, the city councils, some of which aspired to the status of virtual city state or metropolis/mother city (the viceregal capitals, Lima, Caracas, Buenos Aires), vied with each other for local control. Others formed their own *cabildos* or councils. Spanish America was politically fragmented and the patriarchal model was repeatedly replicated in, for example, each head of the provinces of the future Argentine Republic, described by Echeverría as 'ese gigante de catorce cabezas' (Echeverría 1972: 203).[23]

In a time of disarticulation, some semblance of order had to be maintained. Order in the home helped to guarantee the order of the polity as a whole. The history of the struggle for independence is, then, more than military victories and republican legislation. Family history and networks, especially in urban society, and the history of women, a lack of documentary evidence for which makes it difficult to quantify, are indispensable to a full understanding of the period. Asunción Lavrin reminds us that 'Women's history cannot be measured by events or developments of a political character – the marks of distinction of a man-oriented world' (Lavrin 1984: 321).

In the South American ancien régime the legal status of women was 'markedly different from that of men'; consequently 'gender mattered' (Socolow 2000: 178). In official documents, a woman's sex was always already flagged up, whereas class and race might not be. Gender, although inseparable from race and class or caste, was arguably the most important factor in defining a person's social status. Under Roman law, women were recognised as daughters and wives and men as sons and heads of household responsible for dependants (Offen 2000: 52). Under Spanish law, women enjoyed greater rights than in the rest of Europe, particularly with regard to inheritance, which depended on legitimacy, not gender. They could inherit property and control large plantations (Schwartz 1997: 113); they were the linchpins in the perpetuation of the merchant classes, whose marriages cemented business alliances, as, for example in Buenos Aires (Socolow 1978: 53); and non-elite women worked as artisans, sellers, suppliers, market women, and so on (Karasch 1988).

As elsewhere, coverture deprived married women of separate juridical status, as they were legally the wards of their husbands, but widows were considered independent, inheriting *patria potestad* and half the couple's property (Socolow 2000: 9–10). Under Spain's enlightened Carlos III, the aim of educating women to make them self-sufficient in the absence of a husband was encouraged. Public schools, especially for orphan girls, were set up in cities, funded by the municipalities and economic societies. Inasmuch as elite women could exert their influence, they did so in the home, church and socially acceptable urban networks (salons, charitable organisations). They enjoyed a modicum of authority and informal power, but as repositories of their family's honour they were 'protected, cloistered and chaperoned' to maintain white supremacy and regulate interracial and interclass births (Socolow 2000: 178–79). Of the many unpopular Bourbon reforms aimed at curtailing the power of the Church, the two that arguably most adversely affected creole women were the new requirements for permission to marry: parental assent (1778) on penalty of disinheritance (not formerly a requirement of canon law); and royal consent for all government employees, a measure aimed at keeping creoles out of office. Permission in both cases could be denied on grounds of race, class and illegitimacy. Men's control of female sexuality was possibly more harmful to women than property relations. Even more disempowering was the male monopoly and institutionalisation of political power and women's almost total exclusion from the public political sphere (Dore 2000). Despite women's participation in the wars, independence did little to change this situation.

Republican politics

The major effect of the liberal revolutions was to privilege the rational individual above group identities. These privileged individuals might be military heroes, civic leaders or Romantic poets, but they all shared one thing: they were virtually all men. The great task facing women was to reconceptualise the social relations of sexual difference, reformulate gender *doxa* and reshape the way women were perceived legally and politically. Unless they were conceived of as individuals and not just as members of a family, adjuncts to husbands and fathers, they could not merit active citizenship with political rights. Economic dependence meant that women's husbands mediated women's claims to social citizenship rights. Their formal citizenship (the legal status of members of a state) would need to be complemented by the rights and obligations of substantive citizenship, not only in theory but also in practice, what Maxine Molyneux calls 'really existing citizenship' (Molyneux 2000: 122; Lister 2000: 98). As society became more militarised, and military brotherhoods transformed into civic institutions, women found themselves increasingly excluded from the newly invigorated public world. Gender did not become a political issue in Latin America until the 1870s, at the earliest; women were not given full voting rights until the twentieth century, from 1929 in Ecuador to 1957 in Colombia.

Of the three previously mentioned institutions structured on male authority, the family, the army and the law, the most enabling for women was the family. Without wishing to suggest, as does Anne K. Mellor in relation to English women at the time, that 'the doctrine of separate spheres' is 'getting in the way of a richer, more complex and accurate understanding' of men's and women's daily lives (Mellor 2003: 7) (the sheer quantity of women's counter-culture in England bears little comparison with the paucity in Latin America), the public rooms of the family home did provide a liminal space, especially as semi-clandestine centres of conspiracy, in which women exercised political power informally. The public/private divide was fluid to an extent. Women also fought as soldiers. Some patriot women were honoured and commemorated, their contribution to the independence cause recognised with medals (see Chapter 6), but there was no space for women in the legal-political sphere: in the juntas, the constitutional congresses, the town councils. Despite her military credentials, Manuela Sáenz, for example, was severely reprimanded by Bolívar for interrupting his council meetings and barred from the presidential palace (Bolívar and Sáenz 1996: 136, 141). Sarah Chambers identifies the salons, the centres of anti-royalist conspiracy in Spanish America, as interstitial space between the public and private spheres occupied by politically active women (Chambers 2003: 80), and Jorge Myers refers to the 'progresiva politización de todos los ámbitos de la vida común' in early nineteenth-century Buenos Aires, where 'lo público tendió entonces a devorarse lo privado' (Myers 1999: 111). But the only institution outside the home and family in which women were actively encouraged to participate by state and ecclesiastical authorities alike was the Catholic Church.[24] This was important leverage, as almost all the Latin American constitutions recognised Catholicism as the official state religion, and some pledged to protect it. It was in these Church-controlled circles that elite and bourgeois women exercised some power and authority, notably in the management and operation of charitable and educational institutions, especially when the Church worked in partnership with the state. As Erika Maza Valenzuela (1995) has convincingly argued in the case of Chile, Catholics and Conservatives were the first to advocate extending suffrage to women and the delay in Chilean women's suffrage (1949) was due to anticlerical wariness.

Patriarchalism continued in South American republics; in the public exercise of power and authority the male was taken as norm. The common good was regulated by a male elite embodying hegemonic masculine values: order, strength, and the right to enforce obedience. Progress was perceived in terms of the domestication of women in the private sphere, their education and their identification with republican motherhood. For elite women at least, colonial institutionalised gender differences were likely to be exacerbated in the new republican morality (Chambers 1999: 200–14).

Militarisation

Just as social cohesion is founded on normative manliness, so do war and violence impact on gender constructions. During military conflict, warring states need to motivate soldiers and civilians; the boundaries between military and civil society become more porous. Karen Hagemann points out that this symbiosis between nation-building and warfare in the Age of Revolution had far-reaching consequences for the gender order, which also became nationalised and militarised (Hagemann 2004: 399–400). Dudink and Hagemann have argued that 'the conflation of male citizenship and military service increasingly virilised masculinity, differentiating it ever more emphatically from femininity' (Dudink and Hagemann 2004: 11). In Spanish America, soldiering, activism and the association of co-fraternities resulted in the masculinisation of political institutions and practices from the start of the revolutionary process. A public domain of politics can only exist in contradistinction to a private, familial world, so that men's associational life and ideals of masculinity necessitated the exclusion of women and inappropriate men. Ideal masculinity, the 'manly political ideal', was similarly 'virilised' (see Brown 2005, 2006).

However, the broad view that in continental Europe citizenship became masculinised and masculinity militarised during the nineteenth century does not quite fit Spanish America. The French model should not be taken as exemplary of the 'various ways men were integrated into states, militaries and nations' (Dudink and Hagemann 2004: 18). In Spanish America, hegemonic masculinity became militarised and politicised concurrently; in many ways militarisation preceded citizenship. Only Argentina introduced full effective conscription on the Napoleonic model, conflating citizenship with soldiery (Deas 2002: 93).[25] Years later, Article 21 of Alberdi's *Constitución de la Confederación Argentina* (1853) (Alberdi 1942: 332) stated, on the French model, that 'todo ciudadano argentino está obligado a armarse en defensa de la Patria y de esta Constitución', and Article 24 of the *Proyecto* of the Constitution, 'todo argentino es soldado de la guardia nacional' (Alberdi 1942: 303). Women were not soldiers of the National Guard and sexual difference functions here as the most important factor in the exclusion or inclusion of citizenship. In Spanish America, military conscription was not the norm, but the patriots constructed their republics according to classical models. Enlightened despotism was succeeded by militaristic republicanism. In Pagden's words, 'The leaders of the Spanish American independence movements ... were never able to escape from the militarism which was, and remains, an integral part of their political culture' (Padgen 1995: 196). Further, 'Militarism redoubled in the nineteenth century when the post-colonial states failed to make the transition to stable republican rule' (Adelman 1999: 9). The consequences were serious for women. As feministpacifist Catherine Marshall argued 100 years later, in 1915, 'In a state where the social order is based on the power to exercise force, women must always go to the wall' (Marshall, Ogden and Sargant Florence 1987: 45).

But women did fight in the Wars of Independence. There are many testimonies of their courage. In his memoirs of the second Campaña de la Sierra, Peru, 1821, José I. Arenales wrote 'la resistencia que las damas de la Concepción opusieron a la división de [Spanish General] Valdez, en el principio de la campaña, y su defensa del puente del mismo nombre son dignos de los tiempos heróicos de Grecia' (Arenales [1832] 1920: 26–27).[26] There is historical data on at least ninety prominent women soldiers, such as the mestiza Juana Azurduy, who fought with her band of 'Amazonas' against the Spanish in Upper Peru; and Francisca Zubiaga de Gamarra, who was described by a US marine thus: 'Her actions are those of a man. She fires her pistol with great precision and accuracy, handles a sword with agility and is a daring and intrepid horseman' (Basadre 1981: 85). Both women fought alongside their husbands, General Padilla and General Gamarra respectively, the latter allegedly later propelled by his wife to the Peruvian presidency (1829–33) (see Chapter 6). In Brazil, Ana Maria de Jesús Ribeiro da Silva (Anita Garibaldi) (1821–49) famously fought alongside her Italian lover and later husband, Giuseppe Garibaldi, in the Farroupilha War in Rio Grande do Sul (1835–45) (see Chapter 9). These military feats might be recognised publicly, but such examples of supportive wives did little to further the case for the rights of women as individuals; it showed merely that exceptionally virile women might assume the masculinity of men and risk ridicule (as was the case with Zubiaga).

The liberal feminist view of gendered war roles condemns women's exclusion from the army as in other professions (Adie 2003); the essentialist view is that women are naturally peacemaking. The feminist pacifists of the First World War argued that feminism and warfare were irreconcilable. Soldiering might give women new roles, but this was only in the service of militarism. As C.K. Ogden put it:

> Militarism has been the curse of women, as women, from the first dawn of social life ... In war man alone rules: when war is over man does not surrender his privileges ... War and the fear of war, has kept woman in perpetual subjection ... War, militarism, imperialism, in every form they have proved her undoing. (Marshall, Ogden and Sargant Florence 1987: 56–57)

There is little to suggest otherwise in the Spanish American experience. Joshua Goldstein has argued that war is both the symptom and the cause of gender (Goldstein 2001: 401). Although war is global, women's participation in warfare is remarkably consistent across times and cultures; women seldom fight. Goldstein concludes that gender difference is not only reinforced in times of war, but that the constant potential for war in human society produces gender: 'cultures develop concepts of masculinity that motivate men to fight' (Goldstein 2001: 264). Militarised masculinity is reinforced in wartime despite women's participation and it is strengthened by women's claims for peace on essentialist grounds, by 'women's symbolic embodiment of "normal" life and ... women's witnessing of male bravery' (Goldstein 2001: 331).[27] For Virginia Woolf the 'figure in uniform' embodied 'Man himself', the 'quintessence of virility'. She added, 'He is called in German and Italian Führer or Duce; in our own language tyrant or dictator' (Woolf 1984: 266). Women cannot disassociate themselves from that figure 'but are ourselves that figure' (Woolf 1984: 267). It is the complicity and active participation of all adults in the socialisation of men into warriors that shames men into fighting wars.

As stated, patriot republicanism was militaristic, but no less nefarious was the Napoleonic Code (1804), which served as a blueprint across Europe and South America: the family and state were to be governed by the authoritarian patriarch. In her study of European feminisms, Karen Offen concludes that peace-loving countries, such as Scandinavia, are models of egalitarian relations between the sexes. These are contrasted with the 'authoritarian, more militaristic societies' of, for example, Imperial Germany, where women's rights were severely suppressed (Offen 2000: xiii). Fernando López Alves corroborates the 'authoritarian roots of liberalism' in post-independence Uruguay; caudillos 'scoffed' at liberalism, he conjectures, because it threatened patron–client relations in the large estates and smacked of European influence (López Alves 1996: 112). Little is known about how the wars and the constant threat of military conflict throughout the century affected gender relations in Latin America.[28] What was the legacy of this violence for the gender system? How did it impinge on the social and symbolic construction of masculinities and femininities? Did women's participation in warfare further polarise the social relations of sexual difference? What is certain is that any window of opportunity opened up to women by the breakdown of political structures and social norms was firmly closed once republican ideas were implemented in the new constitutions.

Text

The challenge of creating new nation states from kingdoms and viceroyalties was taken up by the men of the creole elite in the midst of continued civil warfare. They were most active in three areas: arms, legislation and letters. The fighters were writers; put another way, the *letrados* took to pen and sword. Bolívar produced thousands of documents, ranging from constitutions to poetry; he was army general and legislator and is included in the *History of the Literature of Nueva Granada* (Colombia) (Vergara y Vergara 1958). In Spanish America the second generation of patriots, the children of the civic and military heroes of independence, were no less industrious. Engaging in intense intellectual labour to systematically produce and disseminate an American lettered culture distinct from and superior to (more modern than) that of Spain, they took over the function of the colonial *letrados* in the *ciudad letrada* (Rama 1996: 32, 40–43). In the River Plate region they were named the 'Generation of 1837'; Esteban Echeverría, writer and radical activist, was one of their most prominent members. These were truly organic intellectuals and a handful of them (Juana Manso, Josefa Acevedo, Juana Manuela Gorriti) were women, the daughters, wives and mothers of patriot soldiers and *letrados*. Paradoxically, many (Bello, Echeverría, Manso) spent large portions of their lives writing and publishing in exile from the nations they endeavoured to create.

This book focuses on the selected writings of a handful of these patriots and intellectuals, men and women, who wrote during the period of warfare. The men (Part 1) would become the founding fathers of Spanish American cultural identity; the women (Part 2) were largely forgotten. Simón Bolívar (1783–1830) and his tutor, Andrés Bello (1781–1865), belong to the first generation caught up in the struggle with Spain; twenty years younger, Colombian Josefa Acevedo (Nueva Granada, 1803–61), Mercedes Marín (Chile, 1804–66) and Esteban Echeverría (1805–51) belong to the second generation, which was embroiled in the civil conflict of the 1830s and 1840s. Bello's longevity enabled him to span the two generations. Marín, Acevedo and Juana Manso (Argentina, 1819–75), the youngest and most radical of this group, were all daughters of patriotic heroes. The Brazilians Delfina Benigna da Cunha (1791–1857) and Ana Eurídice Eufrosina de Barandas (1806-?) wrote during Brazil's period of republican, separatist unrest in the 1830s and 1840s, and it is to Brazil that we now turn.

Brazilian independence and women's literary culture

Brazilian independence followed a markedly different trajectory from that taken by the Spanish empire in South America, in ways one might expect to have had a distinctive influence on gender relations and on women's access to political and cultural agency. Firstly, Brazil remained a monarchy until 1889, sixty-seven years after formal independence in 1822. Secondly, no war of independence was fought against Portugal as the colonising power.[29] The political unity that Brazil ultimately retained, in contrast to the fragmentation of the former Spanish empire, owed much to the monarch's having been actively *in presentia* on Brazilian territory. Brazilian independence arose in a context of significant political, economic and cultural change, which, as in Spanish America, had its roots in the late eighteenth-century events of the Enlightenment and the French Revolution. As the Brazilian economy grew during this period, Portugal became increasingly materially dependent on her colony. At the same time, European liberal enlightenment thinking began to be disseminated among Brazilian-born elites educated at Coimbra University in Portugal (Skidmore 1999: 30–32). The widespread influence of the works of Rousseau in Portugal, despite the power of censorship and the prohibition of foreign philosophical, particularly French, texts during that period, has been convincingly demonstrated (Bishop-Sanchez n.d.: 61–90). Small-scale liberal revolts against Portuguese rule occurred in the late eighteenth century, most significantly the liberal, intellectual and North America-inspired Inconfidência Mineira revolt of 1788–92; and a rising in Salvador, Bahia, in 1798, which was notable for its mulatto involvement. These two revolts were suppressed, however, and the final catalyst in the overcoming of Portuguese rule came by a more circuitous and paradoxical route, bound up with events in Europe and with the transatlantic movements of the Portuguese royalty. In 1808 the Braganças and their entire court travelled by sea to Rio de Janeiro, under British naval protection, in order to escape the Napoleonic invasion of the Iberian Peninsula.

King João VI (ruling as regent for his mother, Queen Maria I, who had been declared insane) made Rio the capital of the Portuguese empire. The arrival of the royal family in Brazil saw the opening of the country's ports, a substantial rise in prestige for the colony, the development of printing presses and university faculties, and a higher degree of Europeanisation among the elites, including women (Hahner 1978: 255). In 1815 Brazil was given a new status as part of the Kingdom of Portugal, Brazil and the Algarves. At the same time, the end of the Napoleonic Wars saw Dom João VI placed under more pressure to return home to Portugal. He was finally drawn back across the Atlantic in 1821, when the post-Napoleonic spread of liberal ideology in Portugal led to a successful military revolt in Lisbon in 1820 demanding a liberal constitution, a representative Cortes to include a specific number of seats for Brazil, and an end to absolutist monarchy. João IV's son, Pedro, was left to rule Brazil as regent. However, Pedro's return to Portugal was demanded by the new Cortes, which appeared intent on restoring Brazil to its former colonial status. Backed by Brazil's elites, Pedro famously refused to leave; his statement, *fico* (I will stay), in 1822 marked the peaceful beginning of Brazil's independence: Pedro was crowned Emperor Pedro I in December of that year. Although some Portuguese military elements who were loyal to the motherland fought on behalf of the crown, these were rapidly defeated and, unlike events in Spanish America, Brazilian independence was not won by military means or prolonged warfare against the mother country. Instead, a part of the mother country simply split off, politically and diplomatically, while both territories, Portugal and Brazil, continued to be ruled by different branches of the same family tree. The physical presence of the Bragança royal family on Brazilian soil marked a significant force for stability, in which the metaphor of the family as the model of nationhood functioned, for certain sectors of society at least, as a literal and concrete source of imagined unity.

The transition to independence from Portugal was marked by a lack of change in the landowning ruling elites and by a substantial economic and military dependence on Great Britain, reflecting Portugal's long-standing history as a client state of Britain. The influence of Britain was to be a major factor in the establishment of political systems and institutions and in the growing pressure to abolish slavery, which dictated much of the course of Brazil's nineteenth-century history. The form and extent of the constitution for the new empire was an important issue for Pedro I from the beginning. Historians frequently summarise the political tenor of his reign in his statement 'I will do everything for the people but nothing by the people' (Macaulay 1986: 213). The first constitution was drawn up on English liberal lines by Jose Bonifácio de Andrada e Silva, Pedro I's chief advisor and First Minister. The Emperor rejected this in favour of a constitution of his own devising in 1824, which granted considerable final 'moderating' or arbitrating power to the monarch (Skidmore 1999: 40). Under this two-house system, the constitution conferred the franchise on the basis of property ownership, but literacy was not a criterion. Women were excluded from the vote, and they acquired no citizenship or political rights under the 1824 Constitution, although a woman could be allowed to rule as monarch in the absence of a male heir (Barman 1988: 123; Costa 2000: 265).

Pedro I's attempt to maintain territorial unity and central government power in Rio was not uniformly successful. The Confederação do Equador revolt in Pernambuco in 1824 was a significant republican rising in the immediate wake of independence. Furthermore, the war with Argentina over the rule of the Cisplatine province in southern Brazil (1825–28) saw Brazil's southern border change, since the border region eventually became the independent buffer state of Uruguay, following British intervention in the dispute. Pedro I's prestige declined somewhat towards the end of the decade, particularly as his scandalous personal life was widely known (Macaulay 1986: 211–12). Growing tensions between Portuguese and nativist Brazilian-born subjects, coupled with liberal republican unrest, notably among the military, led to Pedro I's abdication (Macaulay 1986: 244–53). In 1831, Pedro I returned to Lisbon to support the claim of his daughter, Maria da Glória, to the Portuguese throne, which was now coveted by his conservative, absolutist brother, Dom Miguel. The ensuing civil war in Portugal (1832–34) saw Pedro I's liberal constitutionalism triumph in 1834. Meanwhile, Pedro I's departure for Europe had left his five-year old son, Pedro II, behind in Brazil, which was to be ruled by a regency until he came of age (Barman 1988: 157–59).

Declaring independence had been one thing, but maintaining national unity during the regency was an entirely different challenge, since the liberals moved to the fore in the absence of a unifying monarch (Barman 1988: 160–88). The country's ruling elites were increasingly divided into groups consisting of moderate monarchist liberals, absolute monarchists desiring the return of Pedro I as Brazil's ruler, and extreme liberals or *exaltados*, who propagated republican ideals. The regency period witnessed substantial instability after the passing of the Ato Adicional of 1834, which allowed for greater political decentralisation and devolution to the provinces. The very meanings of 'nation' and 'patria' and the relations between region and central government became a source of material and ideological conflict during this period. The changes in the political system provoked a series of regional republican, separatist risings through the 1830s and 1840s in Ceará, Pernambuco, Bahia, Minas Gerais and São Paulo, Grão-Pará and Maranhão, and Rio Grande do Sul (Barman 1988: 170). These threatened the social order and political unity of the country to various degrees, but it was the last of these risings, the ten-year Farroupilha Revolt in Rio Grande do Sul on the southernmost border, that eventually led to the declaration of maturity of Pedro II early in 1840, in the hope of reuniting the country around a visible symbol of unity. This, and the revocation in 1840 of the powers of the

Ato Adicional brought the country back under centralised control and prevented the splintering of Portuguese America into separate republics in the manner of the perpetually warring former Spanish empire.

As Chapter 9 on women's writing in the Farroupilha Revolt of Rio Grande do Sul (1835–45) will argue, this national experiment with new forms of political participation also saw small numbers of elite women gain a heightened awareness of what it meant to identify nationally and what was at stake in claiming political rights. The Portuguese monarchy in Brazil eventually fell in 1889, when a military coup established the Republic and the Braganças returned across the Atlantic to exile in Portugal more than sixty years after they had first fled Europe. One important element that influenced this occurrence was the fact that Pedro II's daughter, Princess Isabella, was not an acceptable successor because she was a woman. (Skidmore 1999: 73–74). Thus, no woman ever ruled in her own right in Brazil during the imperial era, nor did women possess political rights. Evidently an immense material divide separated the royalty and the Portuguese elites from poor white women, mulattos and black slaves. At the same time, the particular history of the Portuguese expansion and colonial relations in Brazil has meant that racial and sexual politics are inevitably bound up with each other.

White Portuguese women were barely a discernible presence at all in the early days of the Portuguese discoveries, colonial expansion and the captaincies in Brazil, particularly in comparison to Spanish women in South America. As Charles Boxer notes in his women's history of the Iberian expansion, unlike in Spain, there had been no prior tradition in Portugal of a female monarch ruling, except for the regency of the Spanish widow of Dom João IV (1656–62) (1975: 53). Nor did Portuguese women usually accompany their husbands to the New World, though there are a few scant records of women governing the captaincies of colonial Brazil in the sixteenth century, some of them widows and some appointed by their husbands in their absence (Boxer 1975: 54–55). One about whom a relatively large amount is known was Ana Pimentel, a Spanish woman whose Portuguese husband appointed her as *governadora* of his estates in Brazil while he was in India (Boléo 1995, I: 541–47; Klawe 1995, I: 254–55). Exceptions apart, as Boxer remarks, Portuguese women were notoriously closeted at home in virtuous Catholic fashion, leaving the Portuguese menfolk to undertake dangerous sea voyages. The populating of Portugal's imperial possessions was historically the product of white Portuguese male miscegenation with Indian and later black slave women, frequently through concubinage or rape (Boxer 1975: 59). As Boxer notes, during the seventeenth and eighteenth centuries, purity of blood, with no trace of Moorish, coloured or Jewish ancestry, was a key qualifying condition for men (and their descendants) who wished to hold crown or municipal council office, to belong to the powerful Portuguese military orders, or to enter the priesthood (Boxer 1975: 56–57). Thus, the social and political premium on virginal white wives remained high and evidence of their restricted and sheltered lives persists into the nineteenth century.[30]

The history of white women during Brazilian independence cannot easily be read apart from the history of slave women, given the complex calibration of race and colour difference that took place in and through the bodies of black, white and mulatto women. White women lived alongside and depended on the domestic slaves who might also be their husbands' concubines. As Maria Beatriz Nizza da Silva has noted in her study of white women's work and economic survival in early nineteenth-century Brazil, impoverished older women with no family routinely relied on the labours of their slaves to support them (Nizza da Silva 1995, II: 441: 1–9). Furthermore, as Jane-Marie Collins observes, the relationship between mistress and slave was one of the few in which white women exercised power and status and, in cases where the real social or racial distinction between mistress and slave was not great, the mistress would often seek to reinforce power through physical maltreatment of her slaves (Collins 1999: 47).

One important consequence of white women's profound imbrication in Brazil's slavocratic status quo seems to have been the absence of any sustained or significant analogy between African slavery and the subordination of women, an argument, as mentioned earlier, central to the emergence of North American and British women's writings on female emancipation in the context of abolitionism. This does not mean, of course, that Brazilian women did not write critically about slavery during this period. Brazil's best known and most prolific writer on women's rights in the early nineteenth century, Nísia Floresta Brasileira Augusta (1810–85), discussed the issues in several published works and adopted a range of different positions. Maria Firmina dos Reis, a mulatto author from Maranhão (1825–1917), made an abolitionist case in her novel *Úrsula* (1859). Neither, however, established parallels with women's rights, despite the fact that Floresta wrote extensively on both subjects (Liddell 2005). Opposition to slavery was not the stimulus to a collective body of political thought on women's liberation and citizenship.[31] As Skidmore notes, 'monarchy combined with slavery created an atmosphere of deference that was powerfully transmitted to the non-elites. The inculcation of this attitude of subservience, which must be shown toward any superior, was by and large successful in convincing non-elites that there was no way to change their world' (Skidmore 1999: 39). Maria Graham illustrates this in particularly telling fashion, writing about her period of employment as governess to Dom Pedro I's children in 1824. Her stay at court was short-lived, partly because she upset the protocol of royal superiority, and seemed to endorse a somewhat more egalitarian social perspective than the one for which the Crown Princess Maria da Glória was destined. As Graham writes, 'it seems there is a right and a wrong, even in sitting in a single seater carriage and horrible to say, I had been seen perched in the place where a Princess of Braganza ought to have been' (Graham n.d.: 44).[32]

Education remained very limited for girls, often taking place at home, if at all, and the emphasis rested on preparation for motherhood and the production of good patriotic citizens (Hahner 1978: 256–57; Costa 2000: 254, 262). However, during the early nineteenth century, women were also more influenced by European fashions and habits. The extent to which European liberal feminist discourse circulated is difficult to ascertain, but the particular trajectory of Mary Wollstonecraft's thinking in Brazil has given rise to a curious and prolonged intellectual fallacy that remains entrenched to the present day. The debate concerns whether or not Wollstonecraft was ever actually translated into Portuguese in Brazil. In 1832, Nísia Floresta Brasileira Augusta published a text entitled *Direitos das Mulheres e Injustiça dos Homens*, claiming that it was a 'free translation' of Mary Wollstonecraft's *A Vindication of the Rights of Woman*, into Portuguese. There were two subsequent editions, suggesting that the text was popular in its day. However, the problem that has emerged for scholars over the centuries is that the English and the Portuguese texts actually bear almost no relation to each other. A surprise discovery in 1996 by Maria Lúcia Garcia Pallares-Burke proved that the text purporting to be Wollstonecraft's *Vindication* in Portuguese is, in fact, a very precise and exact translation of a much earlier English feminist text, *Woman not Inferior to Man*, printed in 1739 by an unknown author under the pseudonym 'Sophia, a person of quality'. This text, often attributed to Lady Mary Wortley Montagu, in turn borrows many of its ideas from a little-known French Huguenot thinker, François Poulain de la Barre, whose Cartesian tract on women's rights, *Discours Physique et Moral de l'Égalité des Deux Sexes, où l'on voit l'Importance de se défaire des Préjugez* was first published in 1673 (Pallares-Burke 1996: 175–76; Poulain de la Barre 1990). Thus, it is possible to identify in Brazil the influence of the French *querelle des femmes* and the dissemination of those Cartesian debates on women's reason and equality that shaped Wollstonecraft's foundational liberal feminist thinking. However, the direct circulation of Wollstonecraft herself, through Nísia Floresta's translation, did not take place. Indeed, given Wollstonecraft's explicit equation of female and slave emancipation, it is interesting to speculate what the impact of her work in Brazil would actually have been, if it had been disseminated there in an early nineteenth-century, pre-abolition context.[33]

In the final analysis, neither monarchy in its various constitutional forms nor classical republicanism offered discourses of political rights, subjectivity or citizenship for women, although royal women, such as Pedro I's first wife, Maria Leopoldina, did afford models of national female identification as wives and mothers. As Emilia Viotti da Costa points out 'both Catholicism, with its stress on the moral superiority of women and their role as mothers and wives, and the Enlightenment, with its faith in progress and modernisation, and its stress on individual rights and equality before the law, offered women a somewhat contradictory discursive common ground on which to define the meaning of their lives and their identities and the scope of their struggles' (Costa 2000: 258). The absence of a strongly militarised independence process and the lack of a war to unify Brazil against a common enemy put more emphasis on patriarchal family networks of political patronage and influence as an embryonic democratic system emerged. The common image of Brazil's non-violent independence often goes hand in hand with the Portuguese colonial discourse of *brandos costumes* (gentle ways) or what Santos has called Portugal's 'friendly colonialism' (Santos 2002: 12). Yet the private and public distinction becomes crucially blurred in this scenario, so that the patriarch's public political power, in the plantation economy at least, is authorised not so much by excessive militarism as by the extension of his private, familial, domestic, and affective sphere, his dominion over women, children and slaves.[34]

This public/private ambivalence serves to mask the gender imbalances inherent in patriarchal family relations in a way that enhances the political capital of men, rather than affording spaces for women to rethink their roles and possibilities. In this context, the discourse of a 'natural' Portuguese pacificity in the colonisation of Brazil, perpetrated by the men who made love not war, provides a historical alibi for colonialism's suppression of women, on a spectrum that runs from rape of the female slave to the fierce closeting of virginal white bloodstock. Viewed in this light, it would be difficult to argue that the relative absence of militarism and anti-colonial warfare in Portuguese America's independence process necessarily impacted positively on women. If anything, this 'military deficit' may have increased the pressure on men to extend their masculine authority over women in the semi-private, semi-public spheres of their slave plantations and landed estates. Consequently as Chapter 9 on women writers in the Farroupilha Revolt will argue, while Brazil's republican civil wars and revolts of the 1830s and 1840s certainly did not espouse women's political rights, they sometimes did provide a mobile discursive field within which rigidly naturalised gender roles could be challenged by women.

Notes

1 Slavery was abolished in many Spanish American countries by the late 1820s; the only area where the importation of slaves continued on a notable scale into the 1830s was the River Plate region. Abolition was decreed in Argentina, Uruguay, Colombia, Peru and Venezuela by the 1850s. The end of legal discrimination against mixed-race populations and the indigenous was a direct effect of independence (Halperín Donghi in Bethell 1987: 43).

2 Undated pamphlet, believed to be 1820, available on microfilm in the Sala Medina, Biblioteca Nacional de Chile. Reference in Medina 1923: 20.

3 Taken from the pro-Rosas newspaper, *La Negrita*. I would like to thank Robert Sykes for drawing my attention to this text and making it available.

4 First published in 1925 by the Asociación Nacional de Damas Patricias Argentinas de Santiago de Estero. See Mary Berg's introduction (Palacio de Libarona 2004: 181–82 and Lavrin 2006).

5 This book does not extend to studying the writings of nuns, *beatas* and women in convents. For further information see Lavrin 1988; Lavrin and Loreto 2002.

6 For critiques of Bourdieu's work on gender (usually objecting that it is ahistorical and does not admit change) see Hull 2002 and Murray 2002.

7 The heaviest populated areas were New Spain (Mexico) and the two Californias, accounting for 44 per cent of the total population.

8 For magisterial overviews see the essays by Lynch, Bushnell, Halperín Donghi and Safford in Bethell (1985). John Lynch's outstanding and engrossing *Simón Bolívar: A Life* (2006) was published while the present book was at proof stage. Brief references have been included where possible.

9 The most lucrative phase of modern Spanish colonial exploitation was immediately before independence in 1780–96 (Hernández Sánchez-Barba 1972: 177).

10 Napoleon deposed the Spanish King in 1808; a liberal Junta Central governed 1808–10, and a regency of five 1810–12; the liberal Constitution of 1812 was revoked when Fernando VII was restored to the throne in 1814.

11 Anderson argued that the break-up of the Iberian Empires and the shift from colonial dependency to self-government in Latin America was of global significance for the formation of nationalism (Anderson 1991).

12 'The transformation of this vibrant oral culture into the print-based culture of modernity did not *precede* the outbreak of the Wars of Independence in regions such as Nueva Granada. Rather, it developed after independence' (Earle 2002b: 32, author's emphasis).

13 For the question of the significance of the 1812 Constitution in Spanish America, which can only be mentioned briefly here, see the excellent studies in Chust and Frasquet 2004 and especially Chust 1999.

14 Instructions for the elections that were to take place in the Americas and Asia.

15 It was argued that in such an emergency there was no time to bring representatives over from the Americas. The full documentation of the juntas 1810–1812 and the 1812 Constitution are available on-line at Cervantesvirtual.com.

16 The *americanos* also argued that the 1812 Constitution was only applicable to the Americas by consent, and that Article 2 of the Constitution, which stated that the *nación* did not belong to one person or family (so could not be handed over by Fernando to Napoleon) meant that the Americas did not belong to the King.

17 The wars between loyalists and insurgents began in 1811 in the north; by 1813 they had become Bolívar's War to the Death in Venezuela. In 1815 Venezuela and Nueva Granada were reconquered by Spain, but Bolívar resisted with mixed-race soldiers and British veterans of the Napoleonic wars. He defeated Spanish and loyalist troops in 1819 in the Battle of Boyacá. In 1817 San Martín crossed the Andes from the River Plate, where there had been little fighting with Spain, and took Santiago. During the Spanish Liberal government of 1820–23, San Martín captured Lima (1821), after much local resistance. The Battle of Carabobo was won with assistance from the British Legion. By 1821 Venezuela and Nueva Granada were liberated and by 1822, Quito. San Martín and Bolívar met in 1822 in Guayacil, Ecuador.

18 Unfortunately, a note adds, no doubt referring to the conservative Mariano Ospina Rodríguez, 'este artículo se publicó en 1855. Un usurpador ha anulado hoy todas las libertades públicas' (1863: 5).

19 Thanks to Iona MacIntyre for finding this quotation. Mansilla refers to his maternal grandmother Doña Agustina López de Osornio, mother of Juan Manuel Rosas and Agustina Rosas, who famously whipped her surviving ten children, even in adolescence.

20 Plato's idea in Book V is that 'a man and a woman have the same nature if both have a talent for medicine; whereas two men have different natures if one is born a physician, the other born a carpenter' (Plato 1941: 148). He seems to be more taxed by whether women fit to be Guardians should strip naked to exercise, like men (Plato 1941: 151).

21 'the early republics were polities of propertied males who governed their subordinates … in and beyond the confines of their families' (Dore and Molyneux 2000: 16).

22 Caulfield (2001) identifies historiographical interest (since the mid-1980s) in everyday life (microhistory), family history, the history of sexuality and discourse analysis.

23 Stern finds a similar patriarchal structure in late colonial Mexico (Stern 1995: 311).

24 There were numerous *tertulias* hosted by elite women, and much research is needed to further explore their dynamics and networks. Examples are the *tertulias* of Manuela Rábago de Avellafuertes de Riglos and Narcisa Arias de Saavaedra in Lima, and Ana Estefanía de Rigos and Joaquina Izquierdo in Buenos Aires.

25 In European and South American legislation common exemptions were married men, the only sons of widows, priests and miners (Deas 2002: 88).

26 Thanks to Iona MacIntyre for this reference.

27 For a critique of Goldstein see Kiesling 2003.

28 Matthew Brown (2005) examines competing masculinities in his study of the diaries of British soldiers fighting in the Wars of Independence.

29 The events of Brazilian independence have been analysed by a large number of historians and there is broad consensus on its principal events and dates. A good, brief general account is given in Skidmore (1999). Barman (1988) focuses particularly on the political construction of nationhood. Macaulay (1986) approaches the period biographically through the life and reign of Dom Pedro I. These sources have provided the basis for this section.

30 See the diaries of Maria Graham, the British sea captain's wife who travelled to Brazil twice in 1821–22 and in 1823 and acted briefly as governess to the Emperor Pedro I's children in 1824. See Graham 1993.

31 See Chapter 4 of Charlotte Liddell's unpublished PhD dissertation, University of Manchester 2005.

32 The subsequent birth of her younger brother, Pedro II, meant that he became the next Emperor of Brazil and Maria da Glória ruled as Queen of Portugal, 1826–53.

33 For Pallares-Burke's full argument, see Pallares-Burke 1996. For a response by Constância Lima Duarte, see Duarte 1999. It is worth noting that Floresta would have been working from the French translation of *Woman not Inferior to Man*, as she did not speak English. For a detailed and balanced discussion of the Wollstonecraft fallacy, its implications for the study of Nísia Floresta, and its mediation through French, see Charlotte Liddell 2005. We are grateful to Charlotte for bringing this issue to our attention. A long review of Wollstonecraft's *Defensa de los derechos de la mujer* was published in the *Diario de Madrid* by editor Julián de Velasco in September and October 1792.

34 Significant debates on the specificity of gender relations in the Portuguese colonial experience, and in the formulation of Lusophone post-colonial theory, have emerged in the last decade. Most of these focus on the seminal work of the twentieth-century Brazilian sociologist, Gilberto Freyre, and his highly romanticised descriptions of the socio-sexual domain over which plantation owners held power in early nineteenth-century Brazil. Boxer (1975: 54–59) offers an interesting but brief critique of Freyre's ahistorical perspective. Subsequent, post-colonially informed readings of race and sex relations in Freyre include Madureira (1994), Almeida (2000), Santos (2002) and Silva (2002).

CHAPTER TWO

Figuring the Feminine: The Writings of Simón Bolívar (1783–1830)

The mother produces and upholds the subject while she herself remains the matrix, the other, the origin

Hirsch 1989: 168

La imagen del 'dictador hispanoamericano' aparece ya, en embrión, en la del 'libertador'

Paz 1981: 126

The first part of this book examines the rhetorical strategies employed in Spanish American independence discourse, which predicates individual rights on the male universal subject. A strategic rereading of the canonical works of the military and political leaders of the Spanish American revolutions will draw attention to what Bourdieu refers to as 'le mode d'opération propre de l'habitus sexué et sexuant et les conditions de sa formation' in those texts (Bourdieu 1990: 11). Simón Bolívar, the wealthy, white, European-educated, Venezuelan aristocrat (son of a Basque landowner), fought between 1810 and 1824 to emancipate Spanish America from the Spanish Crown. He did this primarily for the benefit of his class, the white, native-born elite. Today, Bolívar is revered as the Liberator, an iconic figure representing the subcontinent's independence from European domination; his name has acquired mythic proportions, above all in the northern republics (Peru, Bolivia, Ecuador, Venezuela, and Colombia).[1] This status is due to his military achievements and political ideas, his oratory and his vision of a united South America. The bibliography about him is immense. Bolívar produced (wrote or dictated) over 10,000 documents during his lifetime (letters, speeches, essays, declarations and constitutions), some 22 tomes of which were published by 1833 (Lecuna 1947: 175). His speeches, writing style and poetry have been studied at length. Venezuelan author and critic Rufino Blanco Fombona described him as 'en punto a letras, lo más alto de su época en lengua de Castilla. Con Bolívar se realiza la Revolución de Independencia en las letras castellanas o, para no salir de casa, en las letras americanas'; he is even included as one of the founders of the Colombian literary tradition (Vergara y Vergara 1958: 136–45, 142).[2]

Bolívar's writings – political, military and personal – are multilayered texts worthy of literary study in their own right. Often turned out on the spur of the moment, in response to specific events, to argue a point and persuade to his cause, they project a self-image that is larger than life: the canny politician, the confident soldier, the frank and faithful comrade-in-arms. In many respects, Bolívar writes himself as the manly ideal (Mosse 1996). This chapter will not focus on the textual representations of masculinity in his work, an undoubtedly rich line of enquiry, but on the less obvious configurations of the feminine which, to be identified and analysed, require attentive reading. Irrespective of his personal views on women, Bolívar's writings are riddled with tensions with respect to gender (Chambers 2006a). As will be demonstrated, his public writings inscribe the feminine as myth, idolised or demonised, but outside historical time. As Bourdieu has argued, such mythopoetic rendering of sexual difference privileges the predominance of a masculine vision of the world (Bourdieu 1990: 15). Deeply engrained as 'schèmes de pensée impensés' or 'inconscient culturel', this kind of symbolic violence, as Bourdieu denotes it, is manifested in the implied meanings and presuppositions inscribed in discourse (Bourdieu, 1990: 11–12). For writers raised in the classic tradition, and Bolívar is no exception, it would be difficult to reconcile the poetic trope of femininity with discursive references to individual women living in real time.

Bolívar, a difficult child, had been educated by a mentor, Simón Rodríguez, much influenced by Rousseau (*Émile*), Pestalozzi and Spanish Enlightenment thinkers (Miller 2006; but see Lynch 2006: 17). Typically for the creole elite of the times, Bolívar's education consisted of readings in the classics (Plato, Aristotle) and Catholic theologians. He was perfectly familiar with the political ideologies and historical feats of the Greek city states and the Roman Republic. Many of his republican ideas may be traced to classical sources (Brading, 1983: 10–11). He was also familiar with the British and US constitutions and the work of Hobbes, Smith, Hume, Locke, Bentham, Paine and Washington. But, through Rodríguez, Bolívar's political inspiration came mainly from Enlightenment France: De Pradt, Voltaire, Bayle, Condorcet, Raynal and, above all, Montesquieu and Rousseau (Lynch 2006: 32–38). In his will, Bolivar stipulated that his copy of the *Social Contract*, which had belonged to Napoleon and was given to him by General Robert Wilson, should be left to the University of Caracas. Locke, Montesquieu and Rousseau are all cited in the 'Discurso de Angostura' (Fitzgerald 1971: 1–9; Guadarrama González 1995: 33–34). Although Bolívar enjoyed the company of women, his view of the social role of the category woman was undoubtedly influenced by Rousseau who, whatever his revolutionary merits, was no philogynist.

Personal correspondence

Not all Bolívar's writings were meant for public scrutiny and dissemination. In his personal correspondence it is possible to detect more varied representations of the feminine than those in the public documents. After all, the letters were addressed to real women, historical subjects with proper names. The discourse of the half-dozen letters addressed to women in the Lecuna collection and others to Manuela Sáenz, ranges from Romantic idealisation to lighthearted mockery.

In the flirtatious love letter to 'mi adorada B...' (written to 'bella Bernardina' in Cali in 1822), the author declares 'lo que veo no es más que la imagen de lo que imagino' (Lecuna 1947: 615), a telling comment indicating intractable idealism and, ultimately, the structure of specularisation (Irigaray 1985) underpinning the public writings (discussed below). The letters addressed to women patriots who supported his cause are conversational, almost collegial, though sometimes patronising. In those to 'las damas Garaycoas, Llagunos y Calderones' (written in Cuenca in 1822) from his unlikely quarters in a church, Bolívar represents women as the tight-laced defenders of virtue, but his tone is humorously ironic. In fact, Bolívar had invited Manuela Sáenz (married to English doctor James Thorne) to spend some days with him in July 1822 on the 'El Garzal' estate owned by the Garaycoa family not long after entering into frivolously amorous correspondence with the Garaycoa ladies (especially Joaquina) (Lynch 2006: 179). Fully aware that his reputation as a womaniser may have frightened off respectable ladies, Bolívar portrays himself as beyond moral reproach: 'mi vida es toda espiritual y cuando vds. me vuelvan a ver ya estaré angelicado' (Lecuna 1947: 683). In a later letter to Manuela Garaycoa de Calderón (written in Lima in 1826) Bolívar writes, jokingly, that he has sent 'Baltita' (Manuela's daughter, Baltasara, age twenty) a copy of his draft Bolivian Constitution and one of his speeches, and that he expects her to read them both carefully and memorise them with her 'feliz memoria', so that next time he visits he may hear from her 'bella boca la reproducción de mis ideas' (Lecuna 1947: 1352), a further indication of an amiable yet condescending rendition of the structure of specularisation. All these letters, published posthumously, contributed to the creation of the Bolivarian legend (the sexually attractive, heroic, manly ideal). At least one passed into oral history. Bolívar's original letter to Eufemia Llaguno de Garaycoa, the elderly mother of the Garaycoa girls (written in Babahoyo in 1823) thanking her for sending him 'dulces ... hechos por esas manos virtuosas' (Lecuna 1947: 774), was lost but remembered by heart by Eufemia's granddaughter, 'Baltita', Baltasara Calderón de Rocafuerte, and then recited to Juan Bautista Pérez y Soto, who gave it to the editors for publication (Lecuna 1947: 774).

Bolívar's notes to his mistress and companion Manuela Sáenz are replete with passion and longing, yet he is forced to deal with her as a spirited individual with a will of her own. His letter of September 13 1823, referring to a rebellion Sáenz had quashed in Quito, the first time she had worn military uniform, shows that he is uncomfortable with the idea of her fighting in armed combat. Bolívar is concerned that she acts 'en detrimento de tu honor y de tu posición' and writes, only partly in jest, 'tu has escandalizado a media humanidad' (Bolívar and Sáenz 1996: 53). He asks her to be prudent 'a fin de que no se lastime tu destino excelso en la causa de la libertad', immediately appointing her to the post of secretary to his personal archive, thus incorporating her into his General Staff as a 'húzar' in a more appropriate administrative capacity. Yet a year later, in 1824, he invites her to join him in the Battle of Junín, to which she replies 'Usted siempre me ha dicho que tengo más pantalones que cualquier de sus oficiales', and she accepts (June 16 1824) (Bolívar and Sáenz 1996: 63). Six months later he reprimands her, again half-jokingly, for 'tu audacia, en que mi orden de que te conservaras al margen de cualquier encuentro peligroso con el enemigo, no fuera cumplida' (December 20 1824) (Bólivar and Sáenz 1996: 70). She had allegedly participated in the Battle of Ayacucho and Sucre wrote to Bolívar asking that she be promoted to 'Coronel de Húzares' (see Chapter 6). Yet when she repeatedly warned him of attempts on his life he ignored her. She wrote, 'Usted no me escucha; piensa que sólo soy mujer' (Bolívar and Sáenz 1996: 142). As is well known, she saved him from several attempts, culminating in that of September 28 1828.

Bolívar's letters to his sisters, on the other hand, are practical in the extreme. He gave his elder sister, María Antonia (a renowned royalist) power of attorney over his property and estates and makes suggestions as to how she should use it, although he would need to countersign any contract she made (Lecuna 1947: 1331; Chambers 2002) (see Chapter 6). Similarly, he advises her on how to protect herself and her family during the wars: to keep her distance from political debate (August 10 1826) (Lecuna 1947: 1421). This sound advice shows that he placed family loyalties far above political differences, particularly as both María Antonia and her royalist son (Anacleto) were disinclined to obey him (see his letter to Santander, 30 May 1826, Lecuna 1947: 1346). On his death in 1830, Bolívar left two-thirds of all his assets, goods and property (mainly the mines in Aroa and jewellery) to his surviving sisters, María Antonia and Juana, and the rest to the children of his deceased brother, Juan Vicente (Fitzgerald 1971: 139–140). The correspondence with the sisters represents women realistically and as rational, propertied, literate individuals almost on an equal footing with, if not superior to, the men of the family. These women fulfilled the formal requirements of citizenship, but formal rights might not translate into substantive rights, especially if women were conceptualised not as individuals, but as the constituent parts of families (therefore dependants defined relative to men) outside the public sphere and historical time. This view would be exacerbated by representations of the feminine as trope.

The remainder of this chapter focuses on a selection of Bolívar's political and legal writings to explore how the symbolic effects of language present the case for continental independence on the basis of deeply embedded gender hierarchies. Four of these, the *Manifiesto de Cartagena* (1812), the *Carta de Jamaica* (1815), the *Discurso de Angostura* (1819) and the Bolivian Constitution (1826), are considered to be founding Spanish American political texts. The others are Bolívar's short speech, the *Alocución a las matronas del Socorro*, delivered in 1820, and the *Carta de Pativilca* addressed to Simón Rodríguez in 1824.

The political texts: the *Manifiesto de Cartagena*

An early example of ambiguities arising from the representations of gender in independence discourse is the *Manifiesto de Cartagena* of 1812, Bolívar's first important public document.[3] In the words of John J. Johnson, the *Manifiesto* was 'northern South America's first great document of hemisphericity' (Johnson 1968: 14). It was written at the very start of Bolívar's military career in the wake of the disastrous reversals experienced in the first wave of fighting against Spain. Bolívar had fled from Venezuela and enlisted with the patriot forces of New Granada (Colombia), which he hoped would liberate his home region. In the *Manifiesto* he examines the failure of the first Venezuelan Republic (1811) and proposes means by which Venezuela might yet be wrested away from colonial rule; he is particularly critical of the attempts to apply the federal system to Latin America.

The *Manifiesto* is in the form of a report addressed to the 'ciudadanos' of New Granada by a native of Caracas. Venezuela and New Granada are both personified as women in need of rescue by Bolívar, the 'hijo de la infeliz Caracas', a feminised city suffering 'ruinas físicas y políticas' (Pérez Vila 1979: 8). Further on in the text, this association through personification of the feminine with weakness is extended to encompass ignorance, insanity and, more worryingly for Bolívar (whose Guerra a Muerte (1813) depended on conflict), leniency and tolerance. The town Coro, for example, which remained loyal to the Spanish, is also referred to in the feminine 'la ciudad subalterna de Coro' (Pérez Vila 1979: 9) in need of subjugation. Bolívar berates the implicitly feminine government or junta because it was too weak to do this. It based its politics on 'principios de humanidad mal entendida' which do not authorise 'a ningún gobierno para hacer por la fuerza libres a los pueblos estúpidos que desconocen el valor de sus derechos' (Pérez Vila 1979: 9). In other words, authority, 'gobierno', must force freedom on to ignorant peoples. Tolerance is ineffective, 'insensata debilidad'; 'clemencia' is 'criminal', and human rights a 'piadosa doctrina' that takes secondary place in the Bolivarian realpolitik (Pérez Vila 1979: 10). The 'hijo' will need to restore masculine values to this lamentable situation: that is, strength, unity and force. The feminine is presented, therefore, both as in need of protection and as a threat to order.

Although the feminine is identified with lack of discipline, 'disolución universal' and naivety, it is nevertheless the domain of human rights, philanthropy and philosophy (here labelled sophistry). The masculine denotes unity, discipline, and leadership, and its sphere is law, tactics and military might, the 'máquina', as Bolívar puts it, that has yet to finish its task (Pérez Vila 1979: 10). The federal government, consisting of civilians not soldiers, has failed because it adhered to 'las máximas exageradas de los derechos del hombre' (Pérez Vila 1979: 12). It has allowed each city to govern itself, that is, it has not imposed control by force. Bolívar complains that each province and city (emphasised as feminine) wants autonomy and self-government:

Cada provincia se gobernaba independientemente; y a ejemplo de éstas, cada

> ciudad pretendía iguales facultades alegando la práctica de aquéllas y la teoría de que todos los hombres y todos los pueblos gozan de la prerrogativa de instituir a su antojo el gobierno que les acomode. (Pérez Vila, 1979: 12)

For Bolívar such caprice (licence rather than liberty) is unacceptable. But in refusing to recognise the right of the feminine cities to independence and self-rule, Bolívar assumes the very tyrannical power against which he himself was fighting, thus undercutting his own legitimacy as liberator. He does not endorse the federal government's view of royalist Caracas as a 'tirana' (Pérez Vila, 1979: 11), but three years later in the *Carta de Jamaica*, he represents Spain in these very terms (the evil, monstrous mother) to justify his own political ambitions. In Bolívar's version, as we have seen, Caracas is suffering and, far from assisting her, the confederation abandoned her and 'le aumentó sus embarazos' by not sending troops in on time (Pérez Vila, 1979: 12). The desired outcome, social order, is perceived in terms of masculine repression: authority, law and suspension of personal freedoms. By contrast, the negative that sustains it, social chaos, is associated with liberty: superstition and tolerance in need of subjection. The subjects or actants in this discourse are the rational (male) elite who also wield the moral force, while the objects or predicates over which moral force is wielded are the (feminised) masses. Underscoring this, Bolívar adds, 'no es siempre la mayoría de la masa física la que decide, sino que es la superioridad de la fuerza moral la que inclina hacia sí la balanza política' (Pérez Vila, 1979: 14). The moral force of the superior male elite rules the dependent feminised masses.

In the second half of the nineteenth century, typically in republican morality, women came to represent the moral fibre of the nation. As Francine Masiello writes of Argentina, 'women were brought into the political imagination of men to represent the virtues of nationhood' (Masiello 1992: 5), though they might still be identified with disorder. In the *Manifiesto*, however, it is the male elite that assumes this moral responsibility. Those who are incapable of governing themselves 'carecen de las virtudes políticas' that characterise true republicans and need to be controlled (Pérez Vila 1979: 12). Here the 'Gobierno' (with a capital 'G') is military government of all those who, inasmuch as they are 'ineptos' and in need of government, fall into the feminine camp. The Government, it is implied, rules his family (of women and minors) like a stern father: 'Si estos son prósperos y serenos, él debe ser dulce y protector; pero si son calamitosos y turbulentos, él debe mostrarse terrible ... sin atender a leyes y constituciones' (Pérez Vila 1979: 12). Paradoxically, then, to be liberated they must submit to the patriarch's authority and discipline.

The *Carta de Jamaica*

Bolívar's independence discourse is structured by this patriarchal family-nation metaphor, which was prevalent at the time in patriotic and nationalist discourse, but with important variations, as seen in his famous *Carta de Jamaica*. The letter was written in Kingston on September 6 1815 and signed 'un americano meridional' in reply to a letter sent to Bolívar by a Jamaican, Henry Cullen, the previous April (Pérez Vila, 1979: 55–75, 55). The context is important. Bolívar had started his military campaigns against the Spanish in 1812 and, despite the dreadful earthquake in Caracas in March 1812, which the royalist clergy blamed on the patriots, had succeeded in defending a Second Venezuelan Republic until 1814. But after Fernando VII was restored to the throne, royalist support rallied and in 1815 Bolívar was ousted from Venezuela. When New Granada (Colombia) refused to give him troops, he resigned from the army and sailed to Jamaica, where he hoped to levy support from the British, a hopeless task while Britain and Spain were allies fighting Napoleon in the Peninsular War. Bolívar reached Kingston in May 1815, just as the Spanish forces reached Venezuela to pacify the region. After Napoleon's defeat at Waterloo one month later, Bolívar lost no time in putting forward the case for independence to the British, using as justification Cullen's letter. In the *Carta de Jamaica* (probably sent to the Duke of Manchester, the British Governor of Jamaica) Bolívar analyses the recent past and sketches the potential future of Spanish America. It is one of his most forceful and rhetorical pieces, 'a mordant attack on the Spanish colonial system' (Lynch 1986: 210), and is widely accepted as 'one of the most prophetic documents of universal political thought' (Pino Iturrieta 1999: 12).[4] Bolívar's argument was, as always, the need for robust centralised government and the union of Latin America. He uses logical reasoning to connote rational thought, as well as a plethora of rhetorical strategies to persuade resisting readers. The prime rhetorical strategy, as we shall see, is to bring into play the dominant cultural phantasy on which Western rational discourse is predicated: the demonised maternal feminine.

The *Carta de Jamaica* represents the struggle against colonial rule in terms of a family narrative; the leitmotif of this document is a family crisis.[5] The crisis is set up in two stages: the first is to do with the mother, the second with her offspring. The embedded narrative is as follows: the Spanish American dominions, who once obeyed their mother blindly, have now grown up and have realised that what they thought was mutual affection is intolerable imposition. The young rebellious adult has entered the age of reason; the bond must be broken to ensure further development. However, although 'padres' implies parents, it is the mother who is cast as demon, though the more logical argument would be the need to break with the father, that is, the absolutist king. Metaphorical figures, including allegories such as this, are anything but logical. A Freudian reading in terms of the phantasy of the phallic, pre-oedipal mother is tempting, especially as emasculation is implicit throughout this text. However, more productive for present purposes is Erich Neumann's structural analysis of the collective archetype The Great Mother, not with a view to subscribing to Neumann's version of analytical psychology but to draw on his insights into the workings of myth (Neumann 1963). Myth naturalises and lends coherence to hierarchies of sexual difference and male domination.

Bolívar writes:

> El hábito de la obediencia; un comercio de intereses, de luces, de religión; una recíproca benevolencia; *una tierna solicitud por la cuna y la gloria de nuestros padres*, en fin, todo lo que formaba nuestra esperanza nos venía de España. De aquí nacía un principio de adhesión que parecía eterno, no obstante que la conducta de nuestros dominadores relajaba *esta simpatía, o, mejor decir, este apego forzado por el imperio de la dominación*. Al presente sucede lo contrario: la muerte, el deshonor, cuanto es nocivo, nos amenaza y tememos, todo lo sufrimos *de esa desnaturalizada madrastra*. El velo se ha rasgado, ya hemos visto la luz y se nos quiere volver a las tinieblas; se ha roto las cadenas, ya hemos sido libres y nuestros enemigos pretenden esclavizarnos. (Pérez Vila 1979: 56–57, my emphases)

The *Carta de Jamaica* represents Spain as the demonised mother figure, no longer the natural mother but the unnatural, denatured, perverse, cruel (all synonyms of 'desnaturalizado') stepmother, who dominates without the legitimate authority of biological family ties (the Latin *matrastra* means 'wife of a widowed father' but, like its equivalent in English, it has accumulated negative connotations). The woman, once respected as mother, has gone mad; she is violent and out of order. The trope family-nation, of course, draws on derivatives of the Latin *natus* (to be born) (cf. nation, native, nature), which in turn derived from the Greek term for 'blood relation'. The *Carta de Jamaica* refers to the Hispanic family-nation, Spain and Spanish America, as one; indeed, Peninsular Spanish and American Spanish were common terms at the time (see Chapter 1). It was this concept of a single Spanish nation that Bolívar aimed to destroy and to replace with the idea of the (Spanish) American family. Thus the myth of origins, the identification of law and legitimation with nature and blood ties, is broken; Spain is imaged not as mother but as a stepmother, who is legitimated by human law rather than nature and whose authority is unnatural. In the *Carta de Jamaica* the Hispanic family-nation still exists but is shown to be deeply troubled. 'Desnaturalizado' means not only unnatural but also 'to give up one's nationality' (whereas to naturalise is to admit to citizenship). Spain, then, in no longer fit to be a mother of the family-nation and all ties must be severed. Despotic, enraged and overpossessive, she has become animal-like, a barbaric, bloodsucking monster, an old serpent about to devour her offspring:

> *insaciables de sangre y de crímenes* rivalizan con los primeros *monstruos* que hicieron desaparecer de la América su raza primitiva... [Spain is] *una vieja serpiente*, por sólo satisfacer su saña envenenada, devore la más bella parte de nuestro globo... Qué *demencia la de nuestra enemiga*, pretender reconquistar la América. (Pérez Vila 1979: 58–59, my emphases)

Here, Spain fits the description of the archetypal Terrible Mother, the monstrous feminine inspiring repugnance. According to Neumann's scheme, the positive elementary character of the Feminine is the mother-child dyad, and the negative elementary character of the Feminine is this Terrible Mother, an archetype found in myths and religions across the world: the 'dark side of the

Terrible Mother takes the form of monsters', in which the 'generative nourishing, protecting' aspects of Femininity turn to 'death, destruction, danger and distress, hunger and nakedness'. The Terrible Female has phallic attributes, such as the teeth and tusks of the Gorgon, and snakes: the 'terrible aspect of the Feminine always includes the uroboric snake woman, the woman with the phallus'; the earth's womb becomes the 'hungry earth, which devours its own children' (Neumann 1963: 149).

This progression of Mother Spain from cradle-protector to child-eater is made explicit in the *Carta de Jamaica*. Monstrous caricatures were used widely in eighteenth-century political debate. Queen Marie Antoinette, for example, was repeatedly portrayed by the French revolutionaries as a bloodsucking monster, ravenous for the people's blood, a tiger, a she-panther and a hyena (Landes 2004b: 155–58). Bolívar may have taken this particular figure from classical myth in order to impress his classically educated British and creole readers, familiar with Hecate, Medea and the Gorgon. But the text also draws on local religious symbolism and arguably alludes to the Aztec goddess of death and earth mother Coatlicue, the dreaded 'lady of the skirt of snakes', the Great Mother with Serpents. Coatlicue, one of whose aspects was Tonantzin (the mother redeemer) was acculturated into Mexican sixteenth-century Catholicism as Mary, the Virgin of Guadalupe, who is mentioned in the *Carta de Jamaica* (Pérez Vila 1979: 73). The reference is of interest. Bolívar dismisses the idea that the Aztec god Quetzalcoatl might serve as a symbol to rally the Mexicans in the struggle for independence: the god is hardly known in Mexico, he objects, and as divine legislator (reminiscent of divine rights) does not serve the purpose. The Mexicans' religious fanaticism has been channelled 'felizmente', by the 'directores de la independencia' towards veneration for the Virgin of Guadalupe, the 'reina de los patriotas', who thus symbolises the mother-nation, Catholicism and liberty. Equally, Coatlicue, the mother goddess, could only be accepted into nationalist discourse as the sanitised Catholic version, rendered an unthreatening virgin mother by the fathers of the Church (Anzaldúa 1999: 49–50).[6]

Coupling Mother Spain to Coatlicue as the epitome of female savagery clearly presents a paradox and a curious reversal of perspective. Throughout the *Carta de Jamaica*, Bolívar panders to the British by citing Bartolomé de las Casas and the Black Legend, propagated by Enlightenment thinkers such as Montesquieu. He thus equates Spain with barbarism and the rest of Europe with civilisation. Spain and its 'raza de exterminadores' (Pérez Vila 1979: 58) is denounced for wiping out the indigenous populations and oppressing the modern creoles. Yet in order to underline Spain's primitive savagery, the text implicitly draws an analogy with Aztec sacrificial rites by means of references, for example to the bloody crimes and 'sacrificios humanos' wrought by Spain, so that 'este suelo [que] parece destinado a empaparse con la sangre de sus hijos' (Pérez Vila 1979: 58). In the *Carta de Jamaica,* neither Spain nor the Aztecs signify rational civilisation: both are cast as the Terrible Mother, thus carving out and legitimating the discursive space occupied by the rational, male, creole elite. This way Bolívar effects a neat textual manoeuvre: the post-conquest association of the New World with the monstrous is at once confirmed (the indigenous) and reversed (Spain) but disassociated from the enlightened creoles. Bolívar perpetuates the Black Legend but at the same time counters the thesis of De Pauw, Buffon and Abbé Raynal (in the *Histoire des Indes*, 1770, 'which enjoyed almost Talmudic status' (Adelman 1999: 4) among Latin American reformers), according to which the creoles were degenerates incapable of governing themselves.

For Neumann an archetype such as the Great Mother is 'an image at work in the human psyche' (Neumann 1963: 3). The negative Feminine originates not in actual women or their attributes but in the inner 'anguish, horror and fear of danger' produced by the unconscious in consciousness. Human consciousness, he adds, 'is experienced as "masculine" ... the masculine has identified itself with consciousness and its growth wherever a patriarchal world has developed' (Neumann 1963: 148). Conversely, the unconscious is experienced (in relation to consciousness) as maternal and feminine:

> The phases in the *development of consciousness* appear then as embryonic containment in the mother, *as childlike dependence on the mother, as the relation of the beloved son to the Great Mother, and finally as the heroic struggle of the male hero against the Great Mother.* In other words, the dialectical relation of consciousness to the unconscious takes the symbolic, mythological form of a *struggle between the Maternal-Feminine and the male child, and here the growing strength of the male corresponds to the increasing power of consciousness in human development* ... the liberation of the male consciousness from the feminine-maternal unconscious is a hard and painful struggle for all mankind. (Neumann 1963: 148, my emphases)

The narrative Neumann employs in his analysis of the archetype is remarkably similar to that inscribed by Bolívar in his *Carta de Jamaica* some 150 years earlier (Neumann signed his foreword in 1954), indicating the persistence of the patriarchal paradigm or deep myth structure. The process of transformation and rebirth, of maturity leading to separation and independence, recurs in this symbolic representation: 'A male immature in his development ... perceives the feminine as a castrator, a murderer of the phallus' (Neumann 1963: 172). The narrative of the *Carta de Jamaica* points to a similar deep structure strategically employed to indicate the political relationship between the Spanish metropolis and the developing Spanish American republics.

Having established the illegitimacy and unnaturalness of the Terrible Mother, the *Carta de Jamaica* develops the family trope with reference to the children or wards of the 'desnaturalizada madrastra' (Pérez Vila 1979: 57), who have broken the umbilical cord/maternal bond, 'el lazo ... está cortado' (Pérez Vila 1979: 56), and wish to go their separate ways. The text lists the new states/offspring one by one, caught in the fracture between monarchy and republic. Although the words 'república' and 'nación' are gendered feminine in Spanish, all these children are gendered masculine: 'el belicoso estado' River

Plate; 'el Reino de Chile ... lidiando'; the 'virreinato del Perú' (Pérez Vila 1979: 57). If they are worth their salt, they are fighting for their independence rather than giving in. The one exception is 'la heroica y desdichada Venezuela' who is reduced, like a poor woman, to 'una absoluta indigencia y a una soledad espantosa' (Pérez Vila 1979: 58). This view echoes the *Carta de Jamaica*'s opening sentence, in which Cullen is thanked for his interest in Venezuela and for commiserating with her on account of 'los tormentos que padece' (Pérez Vila 1979: 55). The gender distinction, and resulting attributes, is repeated throughout the text: masculinity signifies revolutionary combat and femininity passive suffering. Such difference is inscribed subtly, not by reference to men and women, but in the symbolic effects of language.

There is only one mention of 'mujeres' in the *Carta de Jamaica* (compared to half a dozen references to 'hombres') but it is a significant one. Bolívar describes the situation in (pacified, feminised) Venezuela: those who remain are 'tristes restos ... algunas mujeres, niños, y ancianos... Los más de los hombres han perecido por no ser esclavos y los que viven combaten con furor' (Pérez Vila 1979: 58). In other words, adult men who are not children or elderly have died rather than give in, or are still fighting. Women, children, old people do not fight; they need to be protected and if they survive and are dominated they are slaves. Apart from this reference, the *Carta de Jamaica* ingeniously avoids any mention of women as a distinctive group by denoting the peoples of Spanish America with an array of collective nouns, mostly in the masculine, in which women are subsumed: inhabitants, population, souls, people, residents, Americans, indigenous, slaves, shepherds and peasants. 'Hombres', as a category, appears more often; 'ciudadanos' is employed three times, with reference to republicanism and synonymous with 'hermanos' (Pérez Vila 1979: 66, 63).

The second part of the *Carta de Jamaica* continues to put forward the case for independence in terms of unjustly arrested development and infantilisation, thus reconfirming the narrative of the Terrible Mother:

> Un pueblo es esclavo cuando el gobierno, por su esencia o por sus vicios, huella y usurpa los derechos del ciudadano o súbdito. Aplicando estos principios, hallaremos que la América no sólo estaba privada de su libertad sino también de la tiranía activa y dominante ... *nos dejaban en una especie de infancia permanente con respeto a las transacciones públicas* ... si hubiésemos siquiera manejado nuestros asuntos domésticos en nuestra administración interior, *conoceríamos el curso de los negocios públicos y gozaríamos también de la consideración personal que impone a los ojos del pueblo cierto respeto maquinal* que es tan necesario conservar en las revoluciones. (Pérez Vila 1979: 62–63, my emphases)

According to this paragraph, both the republican citizen and the subject of a monarchy have rights that entail a degree of autonomy or self-governance, which in turn command respect from the people. Who are the 'nosotros' on whose behalf Bolívar speaks and among whom he includes himself? He is clearly not one of the 'pueblo', those who give respect and publicly recognise the worth and honour of the dominant elite. The 'nosotros' here is the white, male, creole elite, who since early colonial times acted as 'padres de familia', patriarchs of the great family of subservient masses who were guided by their paternalistic benevolence (Pino Iturrieta 1999: 36). The 'pueblo' refers to the subaltern, to all dependents, that is, slaves, indigenous peoples, mestizos, *pardos* and women. As Sarah Chambers notes in her study of the Peruvian Constitutions of the 1820s, 'only slaves and women were excluded [from citizenship] as groups, regardless of conduct or status'; 'the assumption that women were by nature dependent on patriarchal authority was a powerful political fiction' (Chambers 1999: 199). In the new republican morality, as exemplified in the Napoleonic Code of 1804 (the model for the Codes of Law for many South American republics), the husband/father ruled the household and women were made dependants legally and economically and strictly subject to patriarchal control (Socolow 2000: 178–80; Smith 1989: 120–23).

Dependence, presented in the *Carta de Jamaica* in terms of the infancy of humanity ('in-fans' meaning 'not speaking', or 'without speech') means specifically dependence on the mother, uncertainty and error:

> ¿Se pudo prever cuando el género humano se hallaba en su infancia rodeada de tanta ... incertidumbre y error, cuál sería el régimen que abrazaría para su conservación?... Nosotros somos un pequeño género humano ... nuevo en casi todas las artes y ciencias. (Pérez Vila 1979: 62)

It follows, then, that to be certain and right is to follow the father. According to the *Carta de Jamaica*, if the creoles, 'un pequeño género humano' (used metonymically to signify the entire Spanish American population) do not break with the overbearing mother they will become: passive consumers, politically naïve, excluded from public life, absent from the world of government and state administration, obedient, and ruled by custom. In other words, it is inferred, they will become like women:

> Pretender que un país tan ... rico y populoso sea meramente pasivo ¿no es un ultraje y una violación de los derechos de la humanidad?... Estábamos ... abstraídos y ... ausentes del universo en cuanto es relativo a la ciencia del gobierno y administración del estado. (Pérez Vila 1979: 63–64)

Here lies the ambiguity. To be excluded from public life, to be forcibly rendered passive (like weak women) is considered a breach of human rights. Human in this context therefore signifies man. Obedience and ignorance is the domain of woman. The desired alternative – violent resistance, aggression, revolution and enlightenment – is the remit of fighting men and masculinity. A powerful woman/mother is an aberration. Moreover, according to the *Carta de Jamaica* (as in the *Manifiesto de Cartagena*) it is the warring, enlightened men who provide the 'fuerza moral', the moral strength of the struggle, while those who submit to established power relations (such as women) provide the mere 'masa física' (Pérez Vila 1979: 74). Women represent substance or corporality rather than idea. This equivalence brings to mind Luce Irigaray's concept of mother-matter, the unacknowledged, unrepresentable maternal-feminine that makes possible rational discourse (Irigaray 1985: 301–02), and such might be a reading of the *Carta de Jamaica*'s reference to Plato's allegory of the cave ('el velo se ha rasgado, ya hemos visto la luz y se nos quiere volver a las tinieblas; se ha roto las cadenas, ya hemos sido libres y nuestros enemigos pretenden esclavizarnos'), quoted above (Pérez Vila 1979: 57; Plato 1941: 222–30 Irigaray 1985: 243–58).

To recap, maturity, growth and self-fulfilment are stymied by the Terrible Mother, who keeps her sons (the male creole elite, the states, viceroyalties and kingdoms) in a state of permanent infancy, that is, in oedipal terms, castrates them and reduces them to the weak position of women (such as Venezuela). To develop into mature republics they have to make the break. In these anti-colonial circumstances, the myth of the Mother Nation ('madre patria'), so powerful in Europe, needed to be demonised and rejected. Bolívar ends the *Carta de Jamaica* by suggesting that what the American territories require is the paternal (rather than maternal) care of government to cure their wounds, 'los cuidados de gobierno paternales que curen las llagas y las heridas' (Pérez Vila 1979: 68). The imperious mother is divested of power by the neonate, the newly born, independent father.

Having sanctioned the ancient tenets of patriarchy – inculpating the unreasonable, phallus-wielding mother, equating mindless submission with the feminine and, on the other hand, future progress, self-fulfilment and legitimate authority with macho bravado and the father, the *Carta de Jamaica* might well strike a chord with its readers (included among which, it was hoped, were British politicians), who would immediately recognise and sympathise with this deeply felt mythic structure or cultural phantasy. But it raised uncomfortable problems for revolutionary independence discourse.

The *Alocución a las matronas del Socorro*

The clash of discourses is further illustrated with reference to another of Bolívar's political texts, an example of performative discourse, the *Alocución a las matronas del Socorro*, read out in public in February 1820 (Pérez Vila 1979: 136–37). Socorro, a town in New Granada (Colombia), was famous for the 1780 Comuneros rebellion against the Spanish Crown, in which women played a part, and had recently fought the Spanish once again. Several women patriots had been executed by the royalists, including the iconic 'La Pola' (see Chapter 6). The word 'matrona' was usually used only for married women or housekeepers and denoted great respect. In this context, the term stands in contradistinction to the barbaric stepmother. 'Mujer', like 'hombre', occurs only once in the text; it is avoided by reference to 'socorreñas' and a string of family terms that position women in relation to men: wives, daughters and mothers. When it does appear, the word 'mujer' is qualified significantly. Bolívar employs a phrase that crops up repeatedly in nineteenth-century Spanish American discourse: 'mujer varonil', virile or manly woman.[7] Later in the century it was used derogatively to denote unfeminine (unnatural) women and, in the twentieth century, feminists. Here it is used positively, drawing on a long tradition of celebrated feisty women, in classical myth (Athena, Diana, etc.) and in colonial writings (the Amazons in Las Casas, and in Gaspar de Carvajal's chronicle of the Orellana expedition, and so on) (Clément 1997, 1: 101). The speech reads:

> A las ilustres matronas del Socorro:
> Un pueblo que ha producido mujeres varoniles, ninguna potestad humana es capaz de subyugarlo. Vosotras, hijas del Socorro, vais a ser el escollo de vuestros opresores. Ellos, en su frenético furor, profanaron lo más sagrado, lo más inocente, lo más hermoso de nuestra especie; os hollaron. Vosotras habéis realzado vuestra dignidad endureciendo vuestro tierno corazón bajo los golpes de los crueles.
>
> Heroicas socorreñas: las madres de Esparta no preguntaban por la vida de sus hijos, sino por la victoria de su patria; las de Roma contemplaron con placer las gloriosas heridas de sus deudos; los estimulaban a alcanzar el honor de expirar en los combates. Más sublimes vosotras en vuestro generoso patriotismo, habéis empuñado la lanza; os habéis colocado en las filas y pedís morir por la patria. Madres, esposas, hermanas, ¿quíen podrá seguir vuestras huellas en la carrera del heroísmo? ¿Habrá hombres dignos de vosotras? ¡No, no, no! Pero vosotras sois dignas de la admiración del Universo y de la adoración de los libertadores de Colombia. (Pérez Vila 1979: 136–37)[8]

These women are not domesticated, put under the yoke, or 'subyugadas'. They are praised precisely because rather than send their male loved ones into battle, that is, participate by means of affective solidarity with a man, they have wielded the (phallic) lance in their very own hands. Bolívar makes good use of the traditional association of New World women with uncommon strength and valour. Such symbolism was, nevertheless, risky; after all, these women might end up as dreaded phallic mothers, despots illegitimately daring to assume authority. But any such suggestion is neatly sidelined in the *Alocución* by means of four textual strategies. First, as mentioned, women are referred to only in relation to men: full autonomy is not conferred on them. Second, they are shown to be worthy of praise, and thus contributing to the revolution, only in as much as they adopt masculine attributes: they have done this by hardening their hearts, so rejecting purportedly inherent feminine feelings. Third, it is implied that their aggression was for self-defence against the profanation of the innocent, echoing resistance to the Spanish imperial 'rape' of the Americas and subsequent rescue by the liberators, mimicking what Anne McClintock refers to as the 'erotics of imperial conquest' (McClintock 1995: 24). In this way sanctioned gender categories are not disturbed. In fact, sexual difference and hierarchy is reinforced by means of a fourth strategy: the displacement of the significance of these women from historical time into epic and myth. They are compared to the mothers of Sparta and Rome; they are to be adored as goddesses, admired by the entire universe. They are sublimated from solid individuals to gaseous fantasy. Through the *Alocución* to virile women, masculinity is still predicated on heroism and enlightenment, and femininity on beauty, innocence, the sacred, the tender and the family. Women will be excluded from the polis unless they act, unnaturally, like men in these 'unnatural' circumstances (in the *Carta de Jamaica* Bolívar stresses the uniqueness of the historical context) to disarm the phallic mother (Pérez Vila 1979: 63).

To sum up so far, Bolívar brings into play a dominant cultural phantasy, the demonised mother, on which Western rational discourse is predicated (Irigaray 1985). Progress is represented as movement away from the dark threat of the maternal unconscious and submission to the light of male reason and action. The rejection of the maternal-feminine is shown to make possible Enlightenment thought. But this would pose great problems for the future, when Bolívar no longer wanted Spanish Americans to fight like men, but to be submissive and obedient like women, not to the mother Spain, of course, but to patriarchs like him, to the newly legitimated fathers, authorised by republican constitutions of their own making, rather than by birth and lineage. In official documents and letters of the time Bolívar was often referred to as the 'padre de la patria' (Bolivia) and Bolivia as his daughter. He was also the 'padre de Colombia'; Antonio José de Sucre, for example, Bolivia's first president (1826–28) and Bolívar's most loyal commander, wrote 'Yo amo a Bolivia como la hija querida del padre de Colombia' (Lecuna 1975: 163, 165, 587, 588).[9]

Bolívar's writings carefully avoid undermining the father figure. However, legitimacy and stability were not achieved in Spanish America. As Edwin Williamson observes, 'only in retrospect was it possible to perceive that the colonial pact which had kept the creoles loyal to the Crown for centuries had involved the exchange of precious metals for the intangible but no less precious benefits of legitimate royal authority' (Williamson 1992: 232). Once the all-powerful father-King-Crown and its unifying myth, Mother Spain, were removed, there was no strong rule of law to take their place. It would take time for the denatured Mother to be replaced by the myth of the legitimate Father; until then, boys would be boys, and the 'liberators' fell to fighting their 'jeux de pouvoir' (Bourdieu 1990: 25) among themselves. Bolívar wrote prophetically, 'Many tyrants will arise upon my tomb', and he was right (Pendle 1990: 125).

The *Carta de Pativilca*

The mother symbol is given a further twist in the *Carta de Pativilca*. As stated, woman was often figured as a source of private purity in the midst of public political corruption. This is the case in Bolívar's enthusiastic letter to his tutor, Simón Rodríguez, on learning of Rodríguez's return from Europe to Colombia. Written in Pativilca on the Peruvian coast in January 1824, the letter entreats Rodríguez, somewhat optimistically, to join Bolívar and climb the great Andean volcano Chimborazo, a symbol of the primitive grandeur of the New World. From the peak he may contemplate the liberated lands beneath him: 'Venga vd. al Chimborazo, profane vd. con su planta atrevida la escala de los titanes, la corona de la tierra, la almena inexpugnable del Universo nuevo' (Pérez Vila

1979: 173). Bolívar was recovering from an illness at the time, but within a year was sufficiently fit to win the Battle of Junín (August 1824), which with the Battle of Ayacucho in December of that year, waged by José Antonio Sucre, finally liberated Spanish America from Spanish rule. The letter to Rodríguez exudes confidence.

Of particular interest is the way Bolívar represents nature to his former tutor, who was a keen naturalist. Nature is referred to, conventionally, as 'la próvida Madre', but Rodríguez, writes Bolívar, has only seen her in Europe. He has only seen her leftovers and remains, her 'reliquias' and 'desechos'. In Europe, Mother Nature is old, crooked and ill; she has been weighed down by the 'hálito pestífero de los hombres', that is, by the pestilent breath of degenerate men. In America, however, she is young and pure, a beautiful virgin, adorned not by the hands of men but by God, 'doncella, inmaculada, hermosa, adornada por la mano misma del Creador' (Pérez Vila 1979: 173). She is unsullied by the 'tacto profano del hombre', which has not yet withered her divine attractions, her 'gracias maravillas', her 'virtudes intactas'. In other words, in the Americas Mother Nature (the topography, the land) is cast as an immaculate Virgin (suggesting again the Catholic Virgin Mother) while in Europe, Nature is a whore.[10] But the agent of her corruption is man.

Again, this inscription of the archetypal virgin/whore, Eve/Mary dichotomy is paradoxical. Nature in America is a girl untouched by man; in Europe she is an old woman poisoned by man; hence, as in Rousseau, men are agents of corruption and destruction. Nature is god-given and divine, but once worked on or developed by men, it becomes corrupt. Civilisation, as the product of man's labour, is necessarily impure. Men's relationship (as subjects) with the object Nature is inscribed in terms of their relationship with the feminine, which, in turn, is sublimated into myth (Mother Nature) and religion (Immaculate Virgin). Real, living women are again excluded from the picture, yet as part of his strategy to persuade Rodríguez to meet him, Bolívar does not hesitate to resort to whetting his tutor's sexual appetite for the immaculate maiden (though Rodríguez was arguably rather old for such capers): 'Amigo, si tan irresistibles atractivos no impulsan a vd. a un vuelo rápido hacia mi, ocurriré a un apetito más fuerte. La amistad invoco' (Pérez Vila 1979: 173). Ultimately, male bonding or homosocial republican friendship was more important. On a more personal note, it is the tutor Rodríguez who has replaced the mother figure in this text. Bolívar images himself as the mature plant that Rodríguez sowed as a seed, and as Rodríguez's instrument; the 'buril victorioso de los libertadores' has sculpted the patria out of the stone of despotism, he writes, but the hands that guided it were Rodríguez's (Pérez Vila 1979: 173).[11]

The *Discurso de Angostura*: 'Project for Establishing a Chamber of Censors in the Republic'

Despite the above considerations, mothers are referred to as potential citizens in historical time in Bolívar's hare-brained scheme 'El proyecto para instituir un Poder Moral de la República', part of the proposed Venezuelan Constitution (based on the British Constitution), presented to the Constituent Congress of Angostura on February 15 1819 (see Chambers 2006 for an illuminating comparative study of the Poder Moral). The scheme was rejected by Congress as entirely impracticable and reduced to an appendix to the Constitution, on which the 'sabios del mundo' were invited to comment.

Bolívar aimed to establish a unitary state with a strong executive, checked by a hereditary senate and an elected lower chamber. He emphasised the urgency of educating the people in civic virtue, and set out his plans for creating a branch of government (complementing the executive and legislature) to safeguard high moral standards and public decency and to promote republican civil religion, as proposed by Rousseau (Johnson 1968: 91). Citizens were to act publicly as moral agents. The Poder Moral (Chamber of Censors), would be formed by the President and four members named by Congress, to be known as the Areopagus (a term taken from Montesquieu, based on that of the city state of Athens), to exercise 'una autoridad plena e independiente sobre las costumbres públicas y sobre la primera educación'. These members were to be 'padres de familia', over 35 years of age, distinguished for their 'virtudes públicas'; their names would be drawn from lists of the most virtuous 'ciudadanos' i.e. male citizens. After twenty-five years' service they would earn the title 'padre benemérito de la patria', but all the members would be known as 'padres de la patria' – indeed, their persons would be sacred ('sus personas son sagradas') and all the authorities of the Republic would owe them 'fraternal', or brotherly, respect. Because the Areopagus would be 'esencialmente irreprensible y santo', above blame and above the law, they would be installed in their posts with such ceremony as to inspire 'la más alta y religiosa idea de su institución' (Pérez Vila 1979: 128).

In short, in this plan the moral authority of the state is invested in male heads of family recognised for their good deeds benefiting the republic, their own families standing metonymically for the fatherland, whose father they are also. Such men are endowed with semi-divine attributes, raised to the level of immortal gods and sustained there by mutual adoration.

If ever there was a concrete political plan to put into practice the law-of-the-father, the structure of specularisation, or what Irigaray refers to as the male ego's 'hom(m)osexual' economy of 'the self/same', this is it (Irigaray 1985: 137, 141).[12] If a member failed to live up to the expectations of his saintly condition and fell into disgrace, he would be dismissed and forced to wear mourning for three days. As a sign of opprobrium his seat would be covered for fifty years by a black cloth, on which his name was to be written in large white letters. Should three members be dismissed over a period of twelve years, the entire Republic would have to wear mourning for a month. A member who was good and declared 'eminentemente virtuoso, héroe o grande hombre' (Pérez Vila 1979: 130) might be commemorated with a statue.

Women are positioned as the object, the 'other-of-the-same', the reverse side of the mirror that makes possible this specular relationship. But is there no place for them in the Poder Moral? Bolívar divided his Poder Moral into two chambers or houses, one dealing with public morals and the other with education. With reference to the Chamber of Censors or Morals ('cámara moral'), women are mentioned twice. First, it is stated explicitly that teachers of both sexes, 'institutores e institutrices' (Pérez Vila 1979: 130) should be publicly praised for their good works. This singling out of a woman's profession is rare, and there is an explanation, as we shall see. Usually, women are implicitly included in collective nouns such as 'familias', but the fact that in this plan they are named explicitly in connection with education indicates that their inclusion in collective masculine nouns such as 'ciudadanos' and 'individuos' should not be taken for granted. The 'policía moral', for example, would watch out for infractions of moral standards such as ingratitude and lack of respect towards 'los padres, a los maridos, a los ancianos, a los institutores, a los magistrados, a los ciudadanos ... virtuosos' (Pérez Vila 1979: 131). Might these nouns referring to social groups deserving respect apply to women? 'Padres', possibly, but certainly not 'magistrados' or 'maridos'. Are women included in 'ancianos', 'ciudadanos virtuosos', and 'institutores'? Might you be punished for ingratitude towards an 'institutriz'? There is no mention of being punished for lack of respect to one's wife. A list would be published naming those who have committed 'vicios públicos' and a citizen thus named would be barred from employment in public service or administration. 'Ciudadano' cannot here refer to women other than 'institutrices'. If women were unambiguously included in collective nouns such as 'ciudadanos', there would seem to be no reason for Bolívar to add one final article to this section, Article 13, which states that the proposed legislation, commendations and punishments apply just as much to women as to men: 'las mujeres igualmente que los hombres están sujetas a la jurisdicción de la Cámara y reciben de ella premios o castigos, según su mérito' (Pérez Vila 1979: 132).

It is in the Cámara de Educación, however, that women are referred to as historical subjects, but only as mothers and as wives of 'institutores'. This Chamber was be in charge of the physical and moral education of children from birth up to 12 years of age. Schools and curricula would be established and pedagogical research encouraged. The Poder Moral recognises the importance of the early years of a child's education and recognises that the cooperation of mothers is indispensable in this respect. But the Chamber (of men) would not trust women to educate their children appropriately. It would publish instructions to be distributed to women by priests and local government officials. Every mother would have to state that she had received these instructions and had memorised them on registering her child's birth or on the day of its baptism. Bolívar writes, 'la Cámara cuidará muy particularmente de publicar y hacer comunes y vulgares en toda la República algunas instrucciones *breves y sencillas acomodadas a la inteligencia de todas las madres de familia* sobre uno y otro objeto' (my emphasis), that is, instructions on men's views of mothers' roles in the education and care of their children, worded simply for the not so bright.

As for schools, again the sexes were to be differentiated: schools were to be built 'tanto para niños como para niñas', as boys and girls should be separated 'desde que la razón empieza a obrar en ambos' (Pérez Vila 1979: 133). Each school would be run by an 'institutor'. It is the wife of the 'institutor' who would be the 'institutriz': the 'institutriz ... de las niñas, aunque *bajo la dirección de su marido*'. This class of 'ciudadano', who would be loved and respected 'como los primeros y más preciosos ... de la República' (Pérez Vila 1979: 134) does include women, therefore. The collaboration of women was needed in the public civilising process, but women (all women, including the indigenous and the poor) would be issued with instructions on how to behave, how to raise their children, by the men of the Church and state. Women are not considered autonomous rational subjects, and can only assume a public presence when dependent on men.

Women citizens? The 1826 Bolivian Constitution

The issue of women and citizenship is central to the Bolivian Constitution of May 1826, written by Bolívar, whose patronymic was now used to designate an area and population newly distinguished as a nation.[13] One of the features of the 1826 Constitution was the provision of elections through electors; an elector was to be chosen by ten citizens, so that the nation should be represented by one-tenth of its population. Strictly speaking, it was possible for women to stand as electors. The requirements were capacity ('capacidades') rather than property, literacy, and to profess a science or art that assured an honest living. The only explicitly disenfranchised were criminals, illiterates, the completely ignorant and the unemployed ('ociosidad'). According to Bolívar, wisdom and honesty are all that is needed for the exercise of Public Power (Pérez Vila 1979: 232). However, a closer study of the 1826 Constitution in comparison with later reformulations throws up the textual ambiguities that made it possible to interpret the Constitution as having not included women in the concept of active, meaningful citizenship. Women were not explicitly excluded, but neither were they unambiguously included.

In the section 'La persona humana y el estado', the 1826 Constitution referred to 'todos los bolivianos'. That this might not mean all Bolivians is demonstrated in the various permutations (more or less restrictive) later made to clarify this point: in 1843 'los habitantes de la República'; in 1851 'todo hombre'; in 1861 'todo hombre que goza en Bolivia de los derechos civiles'; in 1938 'toda persona que goza de los derechos civiles', and finally, in 1967, explictly all Bolivians:

> todo ser humano tiene personalidad y capacidad jurídicas ... goza de los derechos, libertades y garantías reconocidos por esta constitución, sin distinción de raza, sexo, idioma, religión, opinión o de otra índole, orígen, condición económica o social, u otra cualquiera. (Galindo de Ugarte 1991: 18, 19)

Similarly, in the section 'Derechos fundamentales de la persona', the 1826 Constitution refers to 'todos los bolivianos'; in 1851 this becomes unambiguously 'todo hombre', and in 1938 'toda persona' (Galindo de Ugarte 1991: 21, 24, 27). The 'Requisitos de ciudadanía' in 1826 were, tautologically, 'ser boliviano', which included foreign men married to a 'boliviana' (the only occurrence of the feminine form of the noun), while a Bolivian woman married to a foreign man lost her Bolivian nationality (until 1938). To clarify what was meant by 'to be Bolivian', the Constitution of 1861 stipulated 'haber nacido en Bolivia', but this was then changed back to 'ser boliviano' until 1967, when the inclusion of women was again made explicit: 'son cuidadanos los bolivianos varones y mujeres mayores de 21 años de edad, o de 18 años siendo casados' etc. The fact that citizenship depended on nationality and that this was in turn ambiguously defined meant that the rights of citizenship were also unclear. In 1826, only those who were 'ciudadanos en ejercicio' could obtain 'empleos y cargos públicos'. In 1851 this was clarified to an extent, so that all Bolivian citizens 'por nacimiento' were 'igualmente admisibles' to public employment with preference given on merit (Galindo y Ugarte 1991: 102). That women did not take up public employment in the 1850s (other than as teachers) suggests they were not unambiguously counted as citizens. This fudging was, of course, deliberate and may be contrasted with the articles on taxation. Article 153 of the 1826 Constitution stated clearly 'las contribuciones se repartirán proporcionalmente sin ninguna excepción ni privilegio' (Galindo y Ugarte 1991: 65). As in post-revolutionary France, the citizenship rights and obligations of women (including the right to fight defending the Republic) were included in the political agenda ambivalently. Male citizenship was predicated on active armed service; the role of the *citoyenne* was to produce and nurture citizens (Hufton 1992: 3–4).[14]

Reading for gender in the networks of meaning that constitute political discourse exposes the tensions and ambiguities in these liberal, anti-colonial texts, which made them susceptible to diverse and contradictory interpretations. The political discourse of the nascent Spanish American republics remained profoundly 'patricentric' and patriarchal; as elsewhere, masculinity was taken as the norm in the exercise of power. Institutionalised colonial gender differences were confirmed in the new republican morality (Chambers 1999: 200–14). The moral welfare of the collective was regulated by a male elite embodying masculine values: order, strength and the right to enforce obedience. For Hernán Vidal there is a clear continuity between the misogynistic writings of colonial satirist Terralla y Landa (1798) (see Chapter 5), Bolívar ('Carta de Jamaica') and Mexican José Joaquín Fernández de Lizardi's *El Periquillo Sarniento* (1816), in that they each represent the degeneracy of colonial rule in the figure of the debased mother who obstructs paternal authority and the emergence of the enterprising young man (Vidal 2004: 193, 198–203). Progress entailed the subjection of feminine threat to the light of male reason and action.

Although it is generally agreed that Bolívar was more of a constitutionalist than a dictator and that he aimed for government through institutionalised power rather than personal caprice (Lynch 1992: 60), his words in the 1812

Manifiesto on the weakness of tolerance and the pious doctrine of human rights will sound uncomfortably familiar to Spanish Americans today. This chapter ends with a quote taken from Chilean semiologist Giselle Munizaga's analysis of a corpus of political speeches delivered by an authoritarian leader. She concludes:

> El gran eje estructurador ... es el Orden desdoblado en un plano mítico, trascendental y utópico ..., y en un plano de operación instrumental (mantención del orden público, disciplina social ... principio de autoridad, respeto a la jerarquía etc). El orden preexistirá a cualquier voluntad individual o colectiva ... Es un principio universal. (Munizaga 1988: 88)

The speeches in question are not those of General Simón Bolívar, but of General Augusto Pinochet for whom 'la Patria ... es como una virgen que no conoce la maldad y el pecado' and must therefore be defended (Munizaga 1988: 85). The patriarch embodies the principle of (his) irrefutable Order imposed on those thus made dependent on him. Munizaga's analysis is not gendered but her conclusion on the role of woman in Pinochet's texts, 'la mujer ... no es por lo tanto un sujeto de la historia, sino un objeto en ella' (Munizaga, 1988: 30) is predictable. Domination on the basis of sexual difference underpins all such dictatorial phantasies.

As suggested, it could be argued that the writings studied here are further instances of the structure of specularisation, the dominant cultural phantasy, in which 'the male projects his own ego onto the world' and in which the maternal body, woman matter, functions as the tain of that mirror, the other of the same (Irigaray 1985: 302; Whitford, 1991: 34). Masculine rationality is predicated on the demonised maternal-feminine who, reduced to physical mass, is subordinated to the autonomous male, whose effective use of reason enables him to govern those who are not fully men and therefore not fully entitled to human rights (Bonilla 1990). These are the discursive traces of the *libido dominandi* identified by Bourdieu in male-dominated societies, in which social relations of sexual difference position women as 'spectatrices' in order to publicly recognise and ratify the male ego, political power and symbolic capital (Bourdieu 1990: 24). Unresolved ambiguities, such as those in the *Alocución a las matronas del Socorro*, would later be exploited by Spanish American women for their own purposes (Craske 2005). Ultimately, colonial relations of dependency would prove easier to break than dependencies resulting from essentialisms such as sexism, 'sans doute le plus difficile à deraciné' (Bourdieu 1990: 12), essentialisms employed strategically by the Spanish American male creole elite to justify and secure their own political hegemony.[15]

Notes

1 For the process leading to Bolívar's apotheosis, his 'viaje al Olimpo' (2003: 59), see Elías Pino Iturrieta 2003 and Lynch 2006: 299–304.

2 Vergara y Vergara (1958, vol. 3: 143) cites the following: José Joaquín Ortiz, *Bolívar,*

orador militar, Anuario de la Academia Colombiana, vol. 1, 1874; Luis Febres Cordero, *Los versos de Bolívar, El Nuevo Tiempo Literario*, vol. 12, Bogotá 1912.

3 For further discussion of gender and revolutionary/republican discourse see Kerber 1980, Landes 1988 and Scott 1996.

4 Quoted from Venezuelan Rafael Armando Rojas. Pino Iturrieta (1999) offers a radical rereading of the *Carta de Jamaica* identifying the class and race (though not gender) prejudices informing the text.

5 As noted by Rebecca Earle in her discussion of Republican motherhood (Earle 2000: 131). See also Hernán Vidal's incisive analysis (2004: 202–05). On the use of familial and parent-child relationships in independence discourse in the American Revolution see also Kerber 1980: 28. The analogy of national independence/a boy reaching maturity is widespread in Enlightenment writing, as are other biological, evolutionary and genealogical metaphors throughout the nineteenth century. See López 2003.

6 The statue of Coatlicue was discovered in Mexico City in 1790 and buried again soon after. It was unearthed for Alexander von Humboldt in 1803 and quickly reburied until after independence in 1824. The cult to Tonantzin (Our Mother) was transferred to the Virgin by early missionaries. Tonantzin's temple is now a shrine to the Virgin of Guadalupe (Vaillant 1950: 180).

7 Popular in Golden Age Spanish drama. See Johnson 1983: 13.

8 A tradition emphasised by Benito Jerónimo Feijóo in his *Defensa de las mujeres* (1726), in which he draws attention to the 'valor y fortaleza' and 'heroyco valor' of New World women. Feijóo contested the eighteenth-century French depiction of women in the Americas as pathological and lascivious Malinche figures. See Leitner 2003 and Vargas Martínez 1992.

9 Colombia is also referred to as 'madre de la República Bolívar' and the latter 'su hija primogénita', suggesting that Bolívar fathered Bolivia through a relationship with his own daughter, Colombia (Lecuna 1975: 332). Nation-building had to be kept in the family. See Earle 2002a.

10 A similar polarisation is found in Bello's poetry, see Chapter 3. This idealisation of a pure New World was prevalent in eighteenth-century European discourse on the noble savage, notably in France (Voltaire, Rousseau, Chateaubriand, Bernadin de Saint-Pierre and so on).

11 Bolívar was himself identified with the Mountain of Potosí (the Virgin or pachamama), the symbol of the nation and guarantor of Indian rights, by the Bolivian Indians in their interpretation of independence. See Platt 1993: 169–73.

12 For Irigaray, in Western philosophy woman is conceived as similar to man but different, that is, as excess and/or lack. In Christine Battersby's words 'The male has acted as both norm and ideal for what is to count as an entity, a self, or a person', Battersby (1998: 50). In her feminist critique of philosophy from Plato to Freud, Irigaray argues that all culture and discourse of the West 'displays the structure of specularisation'; the world is a mirror in which he sees his own reflection everywhere. Woman is the body of which the mirror is made, which prevents her from ever seeing reflections of herself (Irigaray 1985: 301–03, 315–16; Whitford 1991: 34). See Hennessy (1993: 93) for the need to historicise Irigaray's readings.

13 Bolivia's first constitution, which abolished slavery, prohibited torture, gave back to the Indians their lands and suppressed tributes, was ratified by the General Constituent Congress, November 11 1826, in Chuquisaca, and promulgated by José Antonio Sucre later that month. However, neither Sucre not Simón Rodríguez, who were left to implement the constitution, could bring the utopian vision to fruition. Bolivia was governed by a succession of eleven constitutions during the nineteenth

century. As in most other Western countries, it was not until the twentieth century that both partners in marriage had the same rights and duties, and that children (born to married parents or otherwise) were equal before the law.

14 The politicians of the French 1789 Constituent Assembly excluded three types of people from suffrage: the poor and servants (after much debate) and women (without a murmur). (Hufton 1992: 3). Hence the impact of Olympe de Gouges' *Droits de la femme* (1791).

15 I would like to thank Sarah C. Chambers for her insightful comments on an early draft of this chapter.

CHAPTER THREE

Troped Out of History: Gender Slippage and Woman in the Poetry of Andrés Bello (1781–1865)

What is truth if not the unspoken of the spoken?

Kristeva 1986: 153

El la clara belleza os revelaba
Del idioma de León i de Cervantes,
I con labores serias e incesantes
La senda de la gloria os allanaba ...

Lumbrera fue de Chile peregrina,
Jenio de orden, de paz i de cultura,
De lo recto i lo justo la hermosura,
Idealizó su inspiración divina.

Mercedes Marín 'A la muerte del ilustre sabio Don Andrés Bello', *Poesías* 1874: 262

Although clearly not averse to rhetoric, Bolívar was sceptical of literary mythification where he and his generals were concerned. He disapproved, for example, of José Joaquín Olmedo's epic poem 'La Victoria de Junín' (1825), which depicts him and his officers as the semi-divine heroes of Greek myth. In a letter to Olmedo he objected 'Vd. nos hace a su modo poético y fantástico; y para continuar en el país de la poesía, la ficción y la fábula, vd. nos eleva con su deidad mentirosa'. Myth detracts from reality and devalues the efforts of real-life men; 'vd. pues, nos ha sublimado tanto, que nos ha precipitado al abismo de la nada' (quoted in Vidal 2004: 214–15; Conway 2001). The mythification, or mystification, of woman in literature functions as perniciously (de Beauvoir 1997: 171–292).

This chapter examines the woman-trope in the poetry of Andrés Bello, but first traces the slippage from gender as a grammatical category to gender signifying sexual difference in his *Gramática*. Bello's *Gramática de la lengua castellana destinada al uso de los americanos* was published in 1847, but prepared in the 1810s. His two most celebrated *silvas*, 'Alocución a la poesía'[1] and 'La agricultura de la zona tórrida', were published respectively in the *Biblioteca Americana* (1823) and *El Repertorio Americano* (1826). [2] The poems were to form part of an unfinished 'Canto' entitled 'América' and were written while Bello lived in London, during and immediately after the Wars of Independence. He was reluctant to publish them at the time and considered them no more than 'fabulitas' (Rodríguez Fernández 1981: 41). What do they tell us about Bello's conceptualisation of the nation in terms of gender at this critical moment of social and political transformation? This chapter explores the construction of the myths and tropes of sexual difference underpinning these texts and the resulting ideological and political implications. As will be seen, Bello's poetry perpetuates a conservative gender ideology, legitimated by a neoclassical and republican appropriation of the rhetoric of classical antiquity. As a consequence, women are troped out of nation-building in historical time.

Andrés Bello is without doubt one of the most forceful intellectuals in the ideological formation of Spanish American independence (Fontaine Aldunante 1981). Educated in the classics and philosophy, his poetry adheres to neoclassical convention, with notable shifts towards a Romantic aesthetic (Rodríguez Fernández 1981). Two of the best-known early poems written before the Wars of Independence were 'Oda a la Vacuna' and the sonnet 'A la Victoria de Bailén', celebrating the Spanish victory over Napoleon in July 1808. Like the *silvas* of his Spanish liberal contemporary, Manuel José Quintana, 'A la Expedición española para propagar la vacuna en América' (1806) and 'A España después de la revolución de marzo' (1808) (Quintana 1958), they mark an Enlightenment concern with scientific progress and Romantic nationalism. By 1810, Bello had reached the position of senior official in the Venezuelan colonial government, a position confirmed by the newly formed Junta of Caracas. He was sent to London that same year, at the age of 29, with Bolívar, aged 27, to seek support for an independent Venezuela. Independence was declared in 1811 and Bello stayed in London as an emissary for the new government. But the Spanish regained control of Caracas and he was forced to stay in London without government support.

Bello remained in London for nineteen years (1810–29), eking out a living by teaching and writing, while making full use of the British Library (in Montague House at the time) and the magnificent library of Francisco de Miranda (in whose house he lodged with López Méndez after Bolívar's departure) for his studies on international law, philosophy and literature. While in London, Bello witnessed the fallout of the abdication of Napoleon (1814), Waterloo (1815), and the Congress of Vienna. He was married twice (in 1814 and 1824) to women of Irish descent, was introduced to Lord Holland and his circle, and met some of the most influential thinkers of the day, such as James Mill, who shared his love of Greek civilisation. It is said he collaborated with Mill on the transcription of Jeremy Bentham's almost illegible manuscripts (Murillo Rubiera 1982: 15). Certainly, Bello was much influenced by utilitarianism, which informed his mammoth twenty-year undertaking, the Civil Code of the Chilean Republic, *Proyecto de Código Civil (1841–45)* (1846), later adopted by Colombia and Ecuador. London was the city where many Spanish exiles took refuge from Fernando VII's absolutism between 1814–1820 and

1823–1833, and the destination of several Spanish Americans, some of whom were sent by the new republican governments to negotiate with the British, or were fleeing repressive regimes at home. Among Bello's closest friends were Spanish liberal exiles José María Blanco White and Bartolomé José Gallardo, and Guatemalan Antonio José Irisarri (Murillo Rubiera 1982). While in England, Bello co-edited two periodical publications, the *Biblioteca Americana* (1823) and the *Repertorio Americano* (1826–7), published by Rudolph Ackermann (Roldán Vera 2003; Pratt 1992: 172–73), in which he published his poems.

In 1829, aged 47, Bello finally left for Chile, where he remained until his death, aged 84. He was appointed to a senior position in the Chilean Ministerio del Interior and took Chilean nationality. From then on, as a senator in the government, he was instrumental in the foundation of the Chilean state and the setting up of educational institutions, in particular primary schools and the University of Chile (of which he was the first Rector), which was founded in 1842 on British and German models. His Grammar was considered the most important Grammar of the Castilian Language and he was the first to write in Spanish on modern international law; his *Principios del derecho de gentes*, 1832, was the first treatise of its type in Spanish. These major works, which include *Filosofía del entendimiento* (1881), inspired by Locke, and his practical contribution as, for example, tutor to Bolívar, Senator in the Chilean Republic, and founder of the University of Chile, attest to an outstanding contribution to the formation of the Chilean nation state and to Spanish American cultural independence (Cussen 1992; Jaksić 2001).[3]

Grammatical gender

As critics have noted, the purpose of Bello's literary and philological work was to establish Spanish America as a centre of independent, post-colonial cultural production. An initiative such as a Spanish Grammar undertaken by a former Venezuelan colonial subject and bureaucrat, now nationalised Chilean, who dared to instruct the Spanish metropolis on how the language of the former empire worked and should be employed just twenty-five years after independence, was audacious. Bello was well aware of his position and famously wrote in the Prologue to his *Grammar*, 'No tengo la pretensión de escribir para los castellanos. Mis lecciones se dirigen a mis hermanos, los habitantes de Hispano-América' (Bello 1928: vi). His intentions were patriotic and conservative: to retain the linguistic unity of Spanish America, to bind together the disparate peoples of the Americas, to make them mutually intelligible, and to resist the flood of neologisms introduced by modernity. The greatest danger, he wrote, was that each country might revert to its own mutually incomprehensible 'barbaric' dialect, as did the Europe of the Dark Ages after the fall of the Roman Empire. A continental language unified the patrician creoles and ensured them cultural and political domination as the new republican elite; Bello's didactic mission similarly ensured the transmission of the dominant ideology through education and journalism. His *Grammar* was conceived as an instrument of power and a central element of the independence process.[4] As he wrote in *Indicaciones sobre la conveniencia de simplificar y uniformar la ortografía en América* (1823), paraphrasing Rousseau's *Emile* (1762), 'Se forman las cabezas por las lenguas,… y los pensamientos se tiñen del color de los idiomas' (quoted in Alonso 1951: x); ideas are shaped by the language in which they are formulated. In this view, linguistic fragmentation was equivalent to deculturation. Bello wanted to retain Americanisms, as long as they had developed from Castilian roots and were endorsed by the educated elite: 'Chile y Venezuela tienen tanto derecho como Aragón y Andalucía para que se toleren sus accidentales divergencias, cuando las patrocina la costumbre uniforme y auténtica de la gente educada' (Bello 1928: ix).[5]

What did Bello understand by *género*? As a language specialist, he was fully aware of the distinction between grammatical gender and sexual difference. That language is neither transparent nor neutral, but shapes ideas, encodes values and meanings and mediates access to social reality, as Bello believed, is axiomatic for feminist critical enquiry today. But the (lack of) symbolic representation of women in language was not an issue in Bello's time, and would not be until the 1970s. Since then, research across languages and cultures has demonstrated the asymmetrical representation of men and women in discourse and the historical exclusion of women from cultural forms (Spender 1985: 52–75). 'Gender is at the heart of the construction and classification of systems of difference' (Haraway 1991: 130) and, as feminist linguists argue, language sustains gendered inequality (Cameron 1985). For Monique Wittig, 'gender is the enforcement of sex in language, working in the same way as the declaration of sex in civil status' (Wittig 1986: 65). Historically, women have been excluded not only from the production of language but also from its public dissemination, legitimation, codification and institutionalisation. Masculinity was the norm; as Dale Spender succinctly puts it, 'Masculinity is the unmarked form: the assumption is that the world is male unless proven otherwise. Femininity is the marked form: it is the proof of otherwise' (Spender 1985: 20). In Spanish, the so-called 'masculino genérico' subsumes the feminine within the masculine, thereby gendering mixed-sexed groups masculine (as in the sentence 'Cansados, llegaron los tres al pueblo', which might refer to three men, or to two women and a horse (Bengoechea 2000: 36)). It also substitutes the masculine for the feminine: in 'el jazmín es una flor', jasmine is included in the generic 'flower', but in 'María es un hombre', María cannot be included in the generic 'hombre' (cf. 'persona'), unless 'hombre' is identified with universal humankind (Bengoechea and Calero Vaquera 2003: 39). The effect is cumulative, with lasting repercussions on the self-image and interpretation of men and women in society, a situation which has only started to be redressed (Bengoechea and Calero Vaquera 2003; Bengoechea 2000; Lorenzo 1994).

In Spanish (and other Indoeuropean languages) the root cause of what is sometimes referred to as sexism in language may be identified as the slippage between grammatical gender and sexual difference. This results from the semanticisation of morphology and syntax, that is, the attribution of sexual difference to language forms (e.g. to endings in 'o' or 'a'). The blurring originates in the conflation in Greek and Latin between classification (cf. genus [kind] and genre) and sex (cf. *generare* L. [to beget]). Such slippage is long-standing and prevalent even today. The entry on gender in the *Shorter Oxford Dictionary* (1944, reprinted 1972) reads:

> Gender: Each of the three (or two) grammatical 'kinds' [sic] corresponding more or less [sic] to distinctions of sex (or absence of sex), into which substantives are discriminated according to the nature of the modifications they require in words syntactically associated with them.

Classical and early modern grammarians notoriously conceived of grammatical gender in terms of biological sex. For Nebrija (who identified seven genders of nouns in Spanish), gender in the noun is that which distinguishes 'macho' from 'hembra' and 'neutro' from both (Nebrija 1980: 175).[6] The first edition of the *Gramática* of the Real Academia Española (1771) states that nouns are divided into two genders: the first masculine and the second feminine. The masculine refer to men and male animals, and the feminine to women and female animals; gender classification 'distingue los dos sexos' (quoted in Bengoechea and Calero Vaquera 2003: 29). Whether gendered inequality is inherent in particular languages, such as Spanish, or a product of pragmatics and language use, is still much debated. Gender for some linguists is no more than 'un accidente gramatical ... la capacidad de una palabra de presentar variación formal para expresar las relaciones sintagmáticas' (quoted in Bengoechea and Calero Vaquera 2003: 32; see also Roca 2000). Aníbal García Meseguer argues that each Spanish speaker makes an unconscious connection between grammatical gender and biological sex and that this false idea, or false consciousness, is the effect of patriarchy ('la cultura patriarcal es culpable y la lengua es inocente', quoted in Bengoechea and Calero Vaquera 2003: 35). Patrizia Violi, writing in 1991, takes a different view: 'El género no es sólo una categoría gramatical ... sino que, por el contrario, es una categoría semántica que manifiesta dentro de la lengua un simbolismo profundo ligado al cuerpo: su sentido es precisamente la diferencia sexual' (quoted in Bengoechea and Calero Vaquera 2003: 27), an opinión shared by Mercedes Bengoechea:

> Por mucho que se niegue, lo cierto es que las reglas de utilización del género gramatical de nuestra lengua [española] han formado parte del sistema sexo-género por el cual las diferencias biológicas han justificado diferencias culturales y diferencias de poder entre los colectivos definidos como femenino y masculino. (Bengoechea 2000: 54)

Bello's concept of gender, in contradistinction to that of Nebrija, does not solidly identify sexual difference with grammatical gender although, as I will argue, slippage does occur. Like the sixteenth-century grammarian El Brocense, who wrote that if adjectives did not exist, 'nadie podría encontrar el género gramatical' (Bengoechea and Calero Vaquera 2003: 30), Bello conceived of gender as adjectival (to do with attributes) rather than substantive (to do with things). Feminist linguist María Luisa Calero Vaquera applauds Bello as 'el maestro en el manejo coherente de los criterios morfosintácticos' (Bengoechea and Calero Vaquera 2003: 31). He broke with the centuries-old authority of Nebrija by presenting gender as a morphosyntactic phenomenon unrelated to sexual difference. Bello's thinking was so influential that the Real Academia Española altered its entry on gender in the *Esbozo de una nueva gramática de la lengua española* (1973) to similarly privilege formal rather than semantic properties. As Amado Alonso points out, Bello's *Grammar* is surprisingly modern, and unlike any other European grammar of the time. In the prologue to his 1951 edition, Alonso wrote 'sigue hoy mismo siendo la mejor gramática que tenemos de la lengua espanola' (1951: ix). This may be due to the influence of the Mills, and Bello's knowledge of Berkeley, Hume, and Locke as demonstrated in his *Filosofía del entendimiento*, or, more likely, his encounter with Alexander von Humboldt and Aimeé Bonpland during their residence in Caracas from November 1799 to February 1800. Bello, aged 18, may well have conversed with Alexander about his brother, the philosopher and pioneer in historical comparative linguistics, Wilhelm von Humboldt, then aged 32. Humboldt claimed in *On Language: The Diversity of Human Language-structure and its Influence on the Mental Development of Mankind*,[7] the Introduction to his monumental unfinished *Die Kawi Sprache* (Berlin, 1836), that each language imposes on thought its own structures and formal laws, only tangentially connected to logic, and that morphology and syntax reveal the differences between languages, making possible their comparison and classification (Alonso 1951: xxvi–xxvii). Nevertheless, confirming Bengoechea's remarks above, even in Bello's *Grammar* grammatical gender spills over into sexual difference, and gendered inequality is firmly inscribed in the symbolic field that is Bello's literary work. As we shall see, Bello would not hesitate to use gender for ideological purposes.

In Chapter IV of his *Filosofía del entendimiento* (1843), 'De la semejanza y la diferencia', Bello employs 'género' correctly to mean 'class, species, genre' (Bello *Filosofía* 1951: 92). He adds,

> Llamemos cualidades de los objetos las que percibimos, y atributos o predicados los signos con que las representamos en el lenguaje: es fácil echar de ver que no hay entre las unas y los otros la correlación o paralelismo que han figurado muchos filósofos. (Bello *Filosofía* 1951: 95)

In other words, there is no necessary link between the signified (the qualities we perceive in objects) and the signifier (the linguistic sign or word – adjective or predicate – employed to represent those perceived qualities), no necessary connection between the word 'femenino' and the object described. Bello thus deconstructs the binaries of Enlightenment rationality (Cussen 1992). The meaning of the word 'género' shifts from 'genre' to what we understand in English today as 'gender' in the *Gramática*. Through his detailed study of the Spanish language, Bello could not fail to note – and make explicit – the arbitrary attribution of gender (masculine and feminine) to labels denoting a binary classification system to do with word formation and inflexion, the arbitrary relationship between biological sex and linguistic gender, and the slippage that occurs between the two in discursive practice. It could be said that he identifies 'woman' as a sign in discourse. In describing and attempting to account for the laws of the language, his reasoning is as follows. The first mention of gender in the *Grammar* is in the section entitled 'Classification of Words' (Chapter 2), subsection 'Adjectivos'. Here Bello states that there are two classes ('clase') of adjective in Castilian Spanish, depending on the word endings.[8] Adjectives are labelled, 'llamamos' (Bello 1928: 12), of the first 'terminación' if they end in 'o', and of the second if they end in 'a'. In effect, this establishes an a priori hierarchy in words denoting attribution, but not as yet related to sexual difference. However, some nouns will only admit adjectives with the first ending, and some only adjectives with the second ending. It follows, then, that nouns (words denoting objects, things, people) must also be divided into two classes. Until this point there is no mention of gender (either grammatical or sexual) as word or concept. The key sentence follows: 'Los [sustantivos] que se construyen con la primera terminación del adjetivo se llaman *masculinos* [sic] ...' Having distinguished the classification of adjectives according to inflexion, and the classification of nouns according to their concordance with adjectival inflexion, a label is found to identify and differentiate each of the two classes. The label denotes gender difference. Why? – 'porque entre ellos [the nouns] se comprenden especialmente aquellos que significan sexo masculino como *niño, emperador, león*' (Bello 1928: 12). Similarly, nouns that take the second adjectival ending are called feminine 'a causa de comprenderse especialmente en ellos los que significan sexo femenino, v.gr. *niña, emperadora, leona*' (Bello 1928: 13). Bello adds, 'Son, pues, masculinos *árbol, palacio*, y femeninos *planta, casa*, sin embargo de que ni los primeros significan macho ni los segundos hembra' (Bello 1928: 13). It is important to note here the 'pues', the logic of reasoning: gender (masculine or feminine) is attributed to a noun on the basis of the ending (i.e. class) of the adjective it takes, a gender (masculine/feminine) which may or may not correspond to a sex (male/female). Bello shows awareness of the distinction, which he makes explicit, between sex and gender. In effect, he identifies the sex/gender system.

Having established in his discussion of concordance the two classes or genders of nouns, he then proceeds to desconstruct the binary masculine/feminine and the misleading correlation between sex and gender in three stages. First, some nouns 'significan ya un sexo, ya el otro' with just one ending, that is, the nouns denote either sex (*el testigo, la testigo*) irrespective of the noun's class/gender: 'se llaman comunes, que quiere decir, comunes de los dos géneros masculino y femenino' (Bello 1928: 13). Here we have the first mention of the word 'género', meaning class and also sexual difference, as noted in the slippage between sex and gender in this explanation. *Testigo* is 'common', not because its ending in 'o' is invariable, but that despite its ending in 'o' it denotes either sex. Second, some nouns, the 'unigéneres', denote one sex and take ('emplear en') only one gender e.g. *rey, mujer*; among these are the epicenes, words that belong to a gender that apparently contradicts the sex of the being referred to, e.g. '*una persona discreta*' – feminine gender/male sex: 'Pero ... hay sustantivos que denotando seres vivientes, se juntan siempre con una misma terminación del adjetivo, que puede ser masculina, aunque el sustantivo se aplique accidentalmente a hembra, y femenina, aunque con el sustantivo se designe varón o macho' (Bello 1928: 13) e.g. *la liebre macho, el buitre hembra*. The gender of the adjective thus arbitrarily contradicts the sex of the noun; for this reason, 'epicene' means 'for or having the characteristics of both sexes'.[9] Third, some nouns vary in gender ('mudan de género') irrespective of the sex they denote, 'sin que esta variedad de terminación corresponda a la del sexo, del que generalmente carecen'. These are labelled, 'los llamamos', 'ambiguos' e.g. *el/la mar* (Bello 1928: 14). To summarise,

> La clase a que pertenece el sustantivo, según la terminación del adjetivo con que se construye, cuando este tiene dos en cada número, se llama GENERO. Los géneros, según lo dicho, no son más que dos en castellano, *masculino* y *femenino*. Pero atendiendo a la posibilidad de emplear ciertos sustantivos, ya en un género, ya en otro, llamamos *unigéneres* (a que pertecenen los epicenos) los que no mudan de género; como *rey, mujer, buitre; comunes* los que varían de género según el sexo a que se aplican, como *mártir, testigo*; y *ambiguos* los que mudan de género sin que esta variación corresponda a la de sexo, como *mar*. (Bello 1928: 14)

In Castilian Spanish there are two genders, masculine and feminine. Some nouns never change gender, irrespective of the sex denoted. Others vary in gender corresponding to the sex denoted. Others vary in gender irrespective of the sex denoted. Words are attributed to a gender that serves as a label for classification; gender does not necessarily correspond to sex, and sometimes contradicts the sex of the being referred to. In other words, there is no direct correlation between language and the world, or between gender and sexual difference; the Spanish language does not divide (name and describe) the world neatly into masculine and feminine, there is no clear-cut masculine/feminine distinction; there is no necessary sex/gender identification; and any sex/gender identification that exists may be arbitrary, in that it does not fit the logic of the classification system of which it forms a part.

In the section 'Gender of Nouns', however, Bello further develops the concept of gender in relation to sexual difference. Here he states that in order to determine the gender of the noun we must look at both the meaning (semantics) and the ending (morphology) of the word. In consideration of meaning, 'masculine' will refer to 'varón o macho o seres que *nos representamos como* de este sexo' (my emphasis), e.g. *Dios, ángel, patriarca, monarca*, rivers, mountains, and every word that refers to itself (metalinguistic commentary). Feminine will refer to nouns that 'significan mujer o hembra o seres que *nos representamos* como de este sexo', e.g. *diosa, ninfa, hada*, cities, villages, and letters of the alphabet (Bello 1928: 42). 'Nos representamos' means that it is in the use of Spanish (rather than in the language itself) that classificatory endings 'o' and 'a' are attributed to (represented as) sexual difference. Further, Rufino José Cuervo repeats that there are only two genders in Castilian, and although some nouns are apparently neutral, 'esto es ni masculino ni femenino', they are nevertheless masculine, because 'se construyen con la primera terminación del adjetivo' (Bello 1928: 14). In this way the universal masculine subsumes all that is not specifically marked feminine. The slippage from grammatical gender to sexual difference occurs in the very codification of the language (the grammar), which in turn responds, at least in part, to language use.

Gender and trope

How do these two concerns, gender and Spanish American cultural autonomy/authority, come together in Bello's work? The use of gynomorphic stereotypes prevalent in the writings of, for example, Bolívar and Echeverría, is not so striking in Bello's non-literary public writings. Even so, in the speech he wrote for Chilean President Joaquín Prieto, delivered in September 1841 (the last speech of Prieto's administration) the 'revolución chilena' is described as an unsullied maiden, with strong connotations of the Immaculate Virgin; it is 'la menos mancillada de crímenes' among the Spanish American revolutions due to the 'pureza' and loyalty of its statesmen. Similarly, the Chilean people have proved to be 'modesto y sensato' as becomes a woman, it is implied, in the domestic sphere (Bello 1976: 60, 62).[10] In his article 'Modo de escribir la historia', published in *El Araucano* (February 1841) he argues (following Michelet, Thierry and other French historians) for inductive, bottom-up methodology ('inducción sintética') rather than the application of any a priori theoretical model, 'sistema falaz que impuesto a la historia la adultere' (Bello 1976: 189) and, in agreement with François Villemain, criticises William Robertson for failing to mention the subaltern in his History of the Emperor Charles V (1769), the women and children who weep as their fathers and sons depart for battle. In this article, which urges young Chileans to think independently, the collective history of the (Chilean) nation is represented as 'el hombre chileno de la Independencia' (Bello 1976: 199), 'las masas de hombres', 'cada hombre-pueblo', and the history of prominent individuals as 'el hombre-individuo' and 'un solo hombre', as was the norm of the time. But Bello also refers frequently and more inclusively to 'personas' and 'poblaciones' (Bello 1976: 181, 182, 199). Science may be 'lozana y florida' and 'la América', when tethered to European thought, still in chains (Bello 1976: 201), but there is little sense of devaluation or disparagement of the feminine.

However, literary discourse presents a different picture. Simone de Beauvoir raised the question of why virtually all verbal or pictorial allegories (in Western culture) are women: 'Not only are cities and nations clothed in feminine attributes, but also abstract entities, such as institutions: the Church, the Synagogue, The Republic, Humanity are women; so also are Peace, War, Liberty, the Revolution, Victory'. The reason is that 'Man feminises the ideal he sets up before him as the essential Other, because woman is the material representation of alterity' (de Beauvoir 1997: 211).[11] The result is that 'we see woman no longer as flesh but as glorified substance ... woman is no longer an animal creature but is rather an ethereal being, a breath, a glow' (de Beauvoir 1997: 211). This chapter develops these ideas by focusing on Bello's two *silvas* that, like the versed fables of the 'Poemas menores', are representative of his neoclassical (rather than his more intimate) style.[12] In the fable 'La Cometa' (1833), for example, the threat of the reckless 'pueblo insensato' (Bello 1952: 236) is inscribed in terms of the dangers of uncontrolled woman. A 'bella cometa', who longs to be free from 'ese tiranuelo, / que, según se le antoja, / o me tira la rienda, o me la afloja' (Bello 1952: 235) breaks her string only to plunge head first into a thorn. The explicit moral is that the fickle populace should be restrained by law, which it refers to as 'servil cadena', but the analogy with the need to control (fickle) woman is obvious.

'Alocución a la Poesía'

In the hortatory address to Poetry, 'Alocución a la Poesía', acknowledged 'como el manifiesto de la Independencia intelectual del continente hispanoparlante' (Pérez Vila 1979: 361), the Poet or maker, conventionally gendered masculine, urges Poetry to leave decrepit Europe and fly to the Americas where she will find new inspiration (Bello 1952: 5–35):

> Divina Poesía
> tú de la soledad habitadora,
> a consultar tus cantos enseñada
> con el silencio de la selva umbría,
> tú a quien la verde gruta fue morada,
> y el eco de los montes compañía:
> tiempo es que dejes ya la culta Europa,
> que tu nativa rustiquez desama,
> y dirijas el vuelo adonde abre
> el mundo de Colón su grande escena. (Bello 1952: 5)

In this allegory, 'la Poesía', an abstract noun, is gendered feminine and represented as a female figure in the allegorical tradition of classical antiquity: the trope personifies the gendered noun and attributes to it qualities considered feminine, divine and human. Poetry is a 'diosa', a 'ninfa', and a 'maestra' 'de los pueblos y los reyes' (Bello 1952: 6). The feminine is thus identified with ideal and divine knowledge, in contrast to the historical reality of men.

America, the gendered noun denoting a territory and a political entity, is also personified in allegory and a sex is explicitly attributed to it. America acquires a family, a genealogy, and reproductive and nurturing functions: she is the young wife of the sun, the daughter of the ancient ocean, and gives birth to and nurtures riches. The analogy identifies America as land, emerging (implicitly like Venus) from the seas, which, in conjunction with the sun produces abundant natural growth. America is the end product of complex geological and biological processes, neatly encapsulated and simply communicated by means of the familiar family trope. Thus the female functions as a metaphor for nature which (pace Rousseau) signals primitive freedom, creation and the unlearned, which are applauded in that they are untrammelled by culture and civilisation, not yet subjected to man ('do viste aún su primitivo traje / la tierra, al hombre sometida apenas' (Bello: 1952: 7)).

A third abstract noun, 'la filosofia', is gendered feminine and given a human shape and female sex, perhaps contrary to expectations in view of the association of reason and intellect with masculinity, but still within the norms of classical antiquity. Yet Philosophy is figured as a negative feminine, as Poetry's 'ambiciosa rival', for having firmly established herself in Europe. In quick succession Philosophy is identified with decadent monarchy, slavery, crime, flattery and barbarism. Philosophy is not American; she is the 'coronada hidra', a courtesan in the royal courts of Europe, synonymous with servility. According to the poem, Philosophy, insofar as she is European has sold out to the monarchies of the ancien régime and, like them, has become tarnished, uncultured and mercenary: 'la virtud al cálculo somete' (Bello 1952: 6). As well as the rivalry between idealised Poetry and debased Philosophy, a further contrast is set up between the young wife (America) and the old courtesan (Philosophy), thus further identifying America with poetry and motherhood, and Europe with materialism and female sexual promiscuity. The entire panorama of the nineteenth-century clash of ideas, systems of government, including Enlightenment versus Romanticism, nature versus society and civilisation versus barbarism, is reduced to a domestic scenario: a young mother dominated by an old whore. The Poet exhorts Poetry to leave prostituted Philosophy's den of iniquity and to emigrate to America, where she can move in with a younger, much healthier, family, have lots of children and sing to her heart's content.

The figurative predominance of the feminine leaves little space for the masculine which, following classical *doxa,* should be at the centre of all things. Poetry and thought, nature and the city, Europe and the Americas, the virtuous and immoral are all here figured in terms of competing femininities. Where does the poem locate the masculine and what might it represent? An indication is found in a second-level genealogy embedded in the poem that refers to indigenous myth which, according to Bello's footnote, is taken from Alexander von Humboldt's *Vues des Cordillères*. Huitaca, goddess of the waters, was jealous and caused the river Bogotá to flood, killing many people. Nenqueteba, 'legislador de los muiscas' (Bello 1952: 9), the son of the sun (and presumably the son of America, who in the poem is married to the sun), broke open a gap in the mountain peaks and allowed the river to flow away, thus saving the population. He then gave the people law and art. The indigenous feminine, Huitaca, represents disaster, while the indigenous masculine, Nenqueteba, law and art forged out of catastrophe. Nenqueteba then turns Huitaca into the moon, to be forever in his shadow. This indigenous myth dispenses with Europe and European America entirely; reason, law and art are identified with the indigenous masculine that restrains feminine irrationality.

Having rejected the European Enlightenment, posited reason (authentic, uncorrupted) as indigenous and masculine, and Poetry and America as feminine, the Poet now embarks on a long imaginative journey, a lyrical travelogue, across the continent to recreate for his readers (many of whom would be acquainted with little more than their *patria chica*) the stunning landscapes where America/Poetry might find true inspiration, that is, conditions appropriate for their fulfilment. The text presents the landscape loosely in terms of the nation or city state, so that each is exhorted to display his or her assets: Buenos Aires, Chile, Quito, Ecuador, Monte Avila (Caracas), 'la ciudad' (Mexico) (Bello 1952: 8); any ambiguity is clarified by Bello in footnotes. The poem weaves a continental unity in the collective imaginary while at the same time carefully respecting political borders, where these existed.[13] The landscapes described are selected to match the republican polities and the poem is divided so that each is addressed in turn and given a proper name. Geographical personification thus encapsulates a collective Spanish American identity, distinctive from that of Spain. When Bello employs the word *nación* in an American context he uses it in the sense of people: the Aztec nation of indigenous people (for whom nation is not synonymous with republican state), or the nation (people) who fought for Mexican independence; this is contrasted with the oppressive Spanish nation state (25).[14] The landscapes are selected for their aesthetic and historical value; they are significant on account of the events that took place there. The poem thus marks out these recent events and their locations as historical and significant in the formation of new national identities; they are newly known places or, if old, no longer significant as repositories of colonial culture. The poem inscribes the landscapes of place as landmarks in historical time. Geography and topography (countries, cities, rivers, mountains) are gendered (e.g. El Ecuador, la Quito) but not generally personified or sexed (except the town Cundinamarca, which is attributed with a 'fértil seno'). I will return to this point.

A third of the way through the poem, the Poet changes tack. He invokes Marón, the cognomen of Virgil,[15] whose eclogues praised the beauty of the Italian countryside and whose georgics celebrated agricultural husbandry – in this respect Virgil was one of the models for Bello's 'La agricultura de la zona tórrida'; the sixteen lines following the invocation to Marón are glossed and repeated in the later poem (the line 'el ananás sazona su ambrosía' occurs in both (Bello 1952: 37)). Virgil, and the other Latin poets who Bello translated (Tibullus and Horace) represent the Augustan Age, the restoration of peace and tranquillity after a century of civil disorder and massacres (Cussen 1992: 126).[16] But Virgil was also the epic poet who, in the *Aeneid*, described and celebrated the origin, growth and destiny of the Roman Empire. The Poet offers Poetry a choice: will she sing pastoral poetry in praise of the countryside, natural and cultivated, or will she sing epic verse in praise of human endeavour? The answer is both, as the American landscape is scarred with the signs of the ongoing, momentous epic, the Wars of Independence.

The shift from pastoral poetry to epic panegyric denotes a reformulation of the gender categories, and the masculine is now more overtly marked. The feminine provides a matrix of imagined cultural abstractions (Poetry, Philosophy and so on), which sustains and gives meaning to the real business of nation-building, the heroic enterprise of individually named men. From this point, the dominant gender is masculine. The protagonists of history are men. Each 'provincia' has its 'varón' and they are named individually (Gamero in Chile, Moreno, Balcarce, Belgrano in Argentina, and so on) and collectively (the Regiment of Coquimbo, that 'tantos héroes contó como soldados', each individual man being a hero) (Bello 1952: 13). The collective nouns of significance are masculine: 'granaderos', 'campeones', 'soldados', and 'hijos', groups from which women are implicitly excluded. Collective nouns gendered feminine refer to the masses, 'gallarda gente', 'pobre, inculta, desarmada plebe', or to the demonised Spanish army 'veteranas filas' (Bello 1952: 14, 15). Individual women are included in the epic in supportive roles, but not individually named. The 'tierna esposa' of 'Chamberlen' prefers to die with her husband than be left to suffer 'ignominiosa servidumbre' (Bello 1952: 18); Baraya is executed by Morillo despite the pleas of his sister and 'cien matronas' (Bello 1952: 23). However, of the fifty or so named heroes (including indigenous leaders) and their enemies, two are women, the celebrated exceptions to the rule: Luisa (Luisa Cáceres de Arismendi) and Policarpa (Policarpa Salvatierra/Salavarrieta (see Chapter 6).[17] That these women's names are known to readers and inscribed in the collective imaginary is suggested by Bello's omission of an explanatory footnote for them unlike, for example, Gual, Boves and Monteverde, for whom brief details are provided. Otherwise, women are tacitly excluded from the collective nouns, gendered masculine, denoting the revolutionary fighting forces. This is signalled with the reference to the Battle of Margarita, Venezuela, in which women did take part, 'donde hasta el sexo blando / con los varones las fatigas duras / y los peligros de la Guerra parte' (Bello 1952: 19). The political struggle is between men: Pablo Morillo, who is directly addressed, commander of the Spanish army, on the one hand, and the 'inexperto campesino vulgo' on the other (Bello 1952: 19). The poem ends with a reluctant panegyric to 'el liberador' himself, Bolívar.[18]

What is the gender subtext in this poem? All symbolic systems are represented as feminine: ideas, inspiration, imagination, nationalism, morality, nature, civilisation and lack of it, government and lack of it, and so on. In as much as a symbol represents something else and the symbolic makes present something that is not, it could be said that in this poem the feminine is meta-symbolic, the mother of all symbols. Here femininity 'becomes the necessary support and signifier', not so much of rationality (Moi 1999: 357) but of history. The masculine, on the other hand, marks events, facts and reality. The distinction is between myth (f) and history (m), theory (f) and practice (m), immanence (f) and contingency (m). This subtle slip from the gendered noun, through prosopopoeia, allegory and myth to the discursive representation of woman is predicated on the empirical exclusion of women from historical time. Apart from the two exceptions mentioned, women are not sovereign individuals; they have no part in the nation-building process, save as appendages of men or as defined by their family function. Le Doeuff claims that a discipline can only exist if defined against something else; in philosophy the 'man/woman difference is invoked ... to signify the general opposition between definite and indefinite, that is to say validated/excluded' (quoted in Moi 1999: 357). Similarly, historical discourse is recognised as historical only when defined against timeless myth and symbol. The feminine serves this purpose. As a consequence, women are troped out of existence. Moreover the symbolic system underpinning the poem's historical discourse subsumes a dichotomy virtue/infamy, figured as controlled good wife/uncontrolled prostitute. In his pursuit of doxic stability, Bello, the 'liberal conservador', 'partidario de un autoritarismo evolutivo y renovador' (Fontaine Altunante 1981: 126) appears, like his contemporary, Hegel, to condemn woman to an ahistorical mode of existence 'outside the realms of struggle, work and diremption [forcible separation] which in his [Hegel's] eyes are characteristic of human consciousness as such' (Raven, quoted in Benhabib 1991: 131).

'La agricultura de la zona tórrida'

Gendered difference is more starkly marked in 'La agricultura de la zona tórrida' (1826), which opens with a panegyric not to the heroic warrior, epitomised by Bolívar, who was then at the height of his glory, but to the life-giving American land:

> ¡Salve, fecunda zona,
> que al sol enamorado circumscribes
> el vago curso, y cuanto ser se anima
> en cada vario clima,
> acariciada de su luz, concibes! (Bello 1952: 36)

The poem is a fervent plea for peace in the Americas, to leave off the sword and take up the plough; to find glory not in war and destruction but in husbandry. Unlike the earlier poem, the conflict is no longer between colonies and metropolis (the Wars of Independence having ended by 1825), but internecine – between the new republics, the cities and the provinces. If 'Alocución a la poesía' celebrated the warring heroics of virile men, this is certainly not the case in 'La agricultura de la zona tórrida'.

The poem, opening with the famous address, is an allocution to a zone, one of the five encircling regions into which the surface of the earth is divided, a geographical subdivision, a scientific measurement. By 1826, it is a region of politically independent states. The allegorical, abstract 'zona' is not only gendered feminine but also sexed female, as is evidenced in the erotic imagery indicating gestation and genealogy. She is fertile and attracts the masculine sun, who caresses her and creates new life; she conceives all kinds of beings. The zone symbolises procreation, synonymous with Mother Nature. Not only is she sexed, but as such, she is given a social role throughout the poem: she weaves, cooks, arranges flowers, makes drinks, gives food, provides, feeds, dresses and perfumes. She raises, nurtures and works on her offspring, her 'hijos', the raw materials of nature, to produce products of social use and consumption. The vocabulary is almost entirely domestic. The process of gestation, nurturance and genealogy is developed throughout the poem so that the offspring of this mother, irrespective of their gender, also nurture and produce in their turn. So the potato educates its flowers, the cotton unfolds its buds, the pineapple seasons its sweetness, the passion flower hangs out its fruits, the maize swells its grain, and so on. The verbs here (Bello 1952: 37–63) 'cría', 'sazona', 'educa', 'despliega', 'cuelga', 'hincha' and 'desmaya', all pertain to the semantic field of feminine domesticity.

After these first pages of celebration of activities associated with the mother and wife in the homestead, the Poet, addressing the fertile zone, declares: if only your 'indolente habitador' had looked after you properly; if only there had been good husbandry. Who might this lazy male inhabitant be? He is certainly not the 'labrador sencillo' who is praised for his work.[19] The target of criticism is the class for whom Bello wrote, the educated, wealthy elite – 'aquellos que fortuna hizo señores' (Bello 1952: 39) – who, he laments, have abandoned the countryside for the city. As in 'Alocución', a contrast is drawn between the pure country and the corrupt city, the main victims of which are young men. The source of urban corruption is money, emphasising the instrumentality of resources rather than their uses, rational calculation, impersonal social relations and the rise of the capitalist mode of production, referred to famously by C.B. Macpherson in his study of liberal thought as 'possessive market society' to which 'possessive individualism' is most appropriate (Macpherson 1962: 271). Bello shows a keen awareness of the workings of capitalism and consumerism: 'el mercader que necesario al lujo / al lujo necesita' (Bello 1952: 41). Modernity, urban culture and European influence are anathema and to be avoided. As in Romance fiction, industrial capitalism is symbolically erased in images of countryside retreats, fulfilled love and women's entrepreneurship (Fowler 1991).

From a gender point of view, it is significant that the agents of corruption in the city are prostitutes (as in Terralla y Landa's satire, see Chapter 5). However, it is not so much women who represent depravity in this poem, but rather sex for money. Venality, 'fe mercenaria', is the greatest sin; it commoditises love and sexual relations and corrupts the established moral order.[20] The city is marked as the locus in which established gender categories break down, and where gender difference becomes dangerously sexual, that is, where sexual relations take place for pleasurably erotic rather than reproductive purposes. Such desire and dissipation, resonant of the foppish 'petimetres', make men effete. The city itself is figured feminine on account of its 'lujuria' and conspicuous consumption. Reason is tied to the triumphal carriage of fashion, personified as a global feminine phenomenon: 'de la moda, universal señora, / va la razón al triunfal carro atada' (Bello 1952: 41). The result is that the city, figured as negative feminine, provides not freedom but constraint, as all its inhabitants are subject to keeping up appearances. Urban society, functioning on the basis of the circulation of money, not only leads men to gambling, seduction and drink but incites them to civil disorder or, and here is the nub, to so-called patriotism: 'sopla la llama de civiles bandos / o al patriotismo la desidia enerva' (Bello 1952: 39). In contrast to the earlier poem, urban conflict is not synonymous with heroic patriotism; it denotes the opposite, social chaos.

If the moral fabric of society, the wholesome farmland and the vice-ridden city, is figured as competing femininities (respectively good and bad), where does the poem locate the site of desired masculinity? As stated, the masculine ideal is not associated with war; those who glory in warfare deserve 'vituperio' (Bello 1952: 48). The new post-independence heroes will be farmers who till the land, hard-working young men identified with the traditional (that is, colonial) rural order, but who now make the land productive. In short, culture is cultivation, and citizenship is farming. Men should display their heroism by domesticating and taming the (feminine) land, by sowing, planting and harvesting; while women should convert natural raw materials into domestic products to be consumed, as did the fertile zone and Mother Nature in 'Alocución'. The identification of women with nature is reinforced by trope. Men, for their part, as in Virgil's georgics or Rousseau's *Emile*, are urged to 'honrad el campo, honrad la simple vida / del labrador' (Bello 1952: 48). All of which points to the domestication of the masculine.

What gender pattern emerges from this reading? The collective identity of America, an identified territory and self-governing society, is figured as the Mother, Mother Nature and motherland. The structuring principle of the poem is the Mother, the point of origin, the symbol of blood ties and social cohesion, emblematic of the family and the affective relations that bind citizens to the state. In Lange's words, 'Without a feminine role grounded on motherhood, the family ... loses its unique quality of being a human artificial institution which incorporates natural relations' (Lange 1991: 105). The mother-family provides a natural base for the development of civil virtue. The purpose of the poem is to insert or subsume a new post-colonial masculinity in this collective imaginary. Possessive individualism and self-interest need to be replaced by the ties (to the land, to the polity) figured as mother. Thus, following Rousseau, men may be free, yet ruled by law and affect.

In this way, the maternal symbolic secures the new doxic order. Order is threatened by war, inscribed in terms of masculinity, and by the city, represented as feminine, effeminate or epicene and marked as the site of a threatening gender ambiguity, as in colonial satire. Neither aggressive masculinity nor effeminacy is the answer. It is not that men should take on the attributes of women, but that men (with their essential virility intact) should be inserted into a new maternal imaginary. Masculinity should change its style; male citizens should nurture, not kill. As Rousseau wrote in *Emile*, 'one must choose between making a man or a citizen, for one cannot make both at the same time' (quoted in Lange 1991: 111). Put more bluntly, men should mother. Here is the irreconcilable contradiction resolved in trope, arguably no less contradictory than 'la madre patria'. Both poems reject Rousseau's 'société civile' of personal interest and 'amour propre'. They posit another version of modernity: an ordered, autonomous society founded on agricultural production, autarky and virtue, that is, the conformity of the individual to the collective will. Thinking about this further, gender appears to be configured in a triangular structure: the 'genetrix' at one apex, out of time (myth), and the epic soldier at another, relegated to the past and to memory (history). At the third apex is the real of everyday life, the poems' here and now, the contemporary social and geographical map, which is gendered ambivalently. It is here that worldly tensions are detected between urban and rural, and between foreign exploitation and autonomy. Gender promiscuity in the modern urban world and the uncontrolled activities of women as historical subjects outside the confines of myth and trope disrupt order and signify threat.

It is possible to identify the poet's sleight of hand, the textual process by which gender *doxa* infiltrate these poems. The poems inscribe gender of necessity, in that the Spanish language is gendered. But once tropes (allegory, prosopopoeia) come into play, once abstract concepts take human bodily form, grammatical gender slips into representations of sexual difference. Only the feminine is represented figuratively in this way; the mythical and allegorical figures are almost entirely female in form. Moreover, marked attention is paid exclusively to female sexuality and reproduction. In the earlier poem the ideal feminine symbolises the myth of national unity, while history is firmly inscribed as the domain of men; yet there is some concession to the idea that real women might contribute to the nation-building process. In the later poem, however, which presents an imaginary post-colonial order in terms of mothering and domesticity, real women do not appear. The tilling of the soil, the husbandry needed to consolidate the new society, is the work of 'el labrador sencillo', 'el hombre americano' (Bello 1952: 39). Although mothering is a central concern in the poem it does not provide women with a tangible nation-building role. Rather, men are exhorted to assume this role too.

Literature as an ideological form is a powerful tool in nation-building. As Bourdieu explains, every established order tends to naturalise 'its own arbitrariness', resulting in a stable society in which the natural and social worlds are rendered self-evident *doxa* (Bourdieu 1977: 164; Moi 1999: 277). A close reading of the poems shows how gender is naturalised in myth and trope and put to work for the purposes of stability and nation-building. From a gender perspective the consequence is a highly doxic order, which allows little room for transformation. In Bello's poetry the feminine is sublimated, while the masculine represents historical reality. Macherey argued that literature is the production of fiction effects, a language of figured compromise, by means of which irreconcilable contradictions may be rendered natural and inevitable (Balibar and Macherey 1974; Macherey 1978: 61). This is also the language of illusion and myth. In Bello's poems the feminine takes on the work of representing the post-colonial continent to the collective imaginary as a coherent system of signs signifying origins, belonging, social, moral and political order, eliciting attraction and affect; the citizen may then embrace the nation 'as one would a lover' (Landes 2004a: 104). The salient trope is prosopopoeia, by means of which the abstract (the ideal and theoretical) is rendered concrete in the female bodily form. The result is to naturalise a historical and political reality and the conservative gender order it subsumes. The feminine functions as the vehicle by means of which the realpolitik of post-colonial political realignment is represented as self-evident. More detrimental, particularly to women readers of the time, are the ideological effects of gender difference as inscribed in the poems. Woman is conceptualised in terms of nature so that, in the words of Colette Guillaumin, 'all human beings are natural, but some are more natural than others' (Guillaumin 1996: 94), the political implications of which are significant.

In Bello's poems there is no space for women in historical time. Men are the doers and movers in everyday life, while woman supports the fabric. There is nothing new in this. And this is the point. For as Claude Lévi-Strauss argues, 'Mythology is static, we find the same mythical elements combined over and over again, but they are in a closed system, let us say, in contradistinction with history, which is, of course, an open system' (Lévi-Strauss 2002: 34). This leads Lévi-Strauss to ask, 'What is the difference between the conceptual organisation of mythological thinking and that of history?'(Lévi-Strauss 2002: ix). This reading of Bello's poetry suggests that history is teleological and myth recursive, and that the difference is gendered: the sign woman denotes the organic, immanent, and mythic, the division of humanity into two somatic groups, one appropriated by the other and immured in nature. Only to those in dominated groups (women, slaves, serfs) are attributed eternal essences and anatomical and physiological difference. As Guillaumin writes:

> The political consequences of this ideology are incalculable. Apart from the prescriptive aspect of such discourse (the dominated are made to be dominated; women are made to be submissive ...) this Naturalist discourse attributes all political action and all creative action ... to the dominant group alone. All political initiative on the part of the appropriated individuals will be rejected or severely repressed. (Guillaumin 1996: 102)

The future progress of the post-colonial nation states depended on stability. In these poems, order is secured by perpetuating and indeed exacerbating the gender *doxa* of classical antiquity and republicanism. Literary representations of the feminine make possible the naturalisation of the new social and political order as inevitable and self-evident. Any struggle against this order will appear as unnatural, or 'as a natural process *without political meaning* and will be presented as *regression* towards the dark zones of instinctive life. And it will be discredited' (Guillaumin 1996: 102, her emphasis). In resisting, yet imitating, the cultural paradigms of the metropolis, the intellectuals of the New World replicated those of the Old. The terms of their resistance were always already configured in the paradigms of what continued to be the dominant culture and language, the axis of which was gender.

Notes

1 Originally entitled 'Alocución a la poesía en que se introducen las alabanzas de los pueblos e individuos americanos que más se han distinguido en la guerra de independencia'.

2 *Silva* is a free metrical composition of heptasyllabic and hendecasyllabic lines, most of which are unrhymed. There is no strophic arrangement.

3 On the 'efecto Bello', the institutionalisation of Bello's *Grammar* and authority on language in Chile well into the twentieth century, to the extent that he was identified with a pedagogy based on memorising and learning by rote (precisely contrary to his own views on learning by observation and independent thought), see Poblete 2003: 241–49, 247.

4 Bello was, of course, familiar with Antonio Nebrija's *Gramática de la lengua castellana*, the first grammar of the Romance languages written according to humanist principles. Nebrija's prologue was finished after the fall of Granada in 1492, although he had shown Isabel I a copy in 1486. In the prologue, dedicated to the Queen, Nebrija writes, with reference to Greek and Latin, 'que siempre la lengua fue compañera del imperio, y de tal manera lo siguió, que juntamente començaron, crecieron y florecieron, y después junta fue la caida de entrambos' (Nebrija 1980: 97). The *Grammar* was to be employed as an instrument of Castilian imperial power; when the Queen asked 'para qué podía aprovechar' the book, the Bishop of Avila answered, 'que después que vuestra Alteza metiese debaxo de su iugo muchos pueblos bárbaros y naciones de peregrinas lenguas, [y] con el vencimiento aquellos ternían [sic] necesidad de recebir las leies qual vencedor pone al vencido, y con ellas nuestra lengua' (Nebrija 1980: 102).

5 The *Grammar* was to be used as a textbook, particularly in Santiago, as Bello points out. Bello wanted to free Spanish grammar from the constraints of Latin models and terminology. The grammars available at the time were that of the Real Academia Española, based on the Latin model for spelling, verb conjugation and declension of nouns, and that of his Spanish Liberal friend, Vicente Salvá, published in 1830, 1835, 1837. Iván Jaksić writes, 'Bello's departure from the Grammar of the Spanish Academy was a political statement of freedom from cultural dependence on the mother country' (Jaksić 2001: 150).

6 The seven genders are: male, female, neutral, common to two, common to three, doubtful and mixed. Nebrija adds that gender does not always denote sex in those nouns 'en que la naturaleza no demuestra diferencia entre machos y hembras por los miembros genitales, como el milano, la paloma, el cielo, la tierra ...' (Nebrija 1980: 183).

7 The English title is taken from the translation by P. Heath (Cambridge: Cambridge University Press, 1988).

8 All references are to Bello 1928. Bello published his *Principios de la ortología y métrica de la lengua castellana*, in Santiago de Chile, 1835; his *Análisis ideológica de los tiempos de la conjugación castellana*, in 1841. Rufino José Cuervo's first edition of the *Grammar* (Paris, 1918) was the nineteenth edition. See also Rafael Trujillo's 1981 annotated edition of the *Gramática*.

9 'Epicene' (deriving from Greek, meaning 'common', as in 'common noun') denotes either sex without change of gender; used by or of both sexes; with characteristics of both sexes; with no characteristics of either sex; and effete.

10 'Exposición que el presidente de la república Joaquín Prieto dirige a la nación chilena el 18 de septiembre de 1841', published in *El Araucano*, September 24 1841. See Bello 1976.

11 She adds that 'Philology is rather mystifying on this question' (de Beauvoir 1997: 211, note 16).

12 Compare, for example, representations of gender in the more intimate 'La oración por todos', addressed to the poet's young daughter.

13 In 1823, a year before the final battles of the Wars of Independence (Junín and Ayacucho), the borders of the new republics were still in flux. For example, Argentina and Bolivia did not exist as such, and Gran Colombia incorporated today's Colombia, Venezuela, Ecuador and Panama.

14 Note also the two readings of the signifier 'Manzanares', marking the symbolic value of the rivers Manzanares (towards the end of the poem): the Colombian Manzanares (de 'aguas bellas') signifies the beauty, peace, purity, and fertility of the American people; the Spanish Manzanares (in Madrid) ('de ondas pobre') signifies the exhaustion, poverty and arrogance of the Spanish people, who are proud to be subjected to the King (Bello 1952: 16).

15 Virgil was born in a small village near Mantua named, curiously, Andes. Menéndez y Pelayo stated that Bello was the most Virgilian of poets writing in Spanish (Ménendez y Pelayo 1893: cxlii).

16 The Augustan period in Rome established peace and order but also strong centralised rule and, by analogy, Absolutism, compared to the less orderly freedom of Republican Rome. Cussen argues that in 'Alocución', Bello shifts from an Augustan vision to one in which agricultural production predominates, the balance is thus tipped towards republican values, away from monarchy (Cussen 1992: 126).

17 María Luisa Cáceres de Arismendi (1799–1866) was captured in Venezuela and exiled to Spain; Policarpa Salvatierra (or Salavarrieta) (1795–1817), known as 'La Pola', was executed in Bogotá (see Chapter 6).

18 The poem praises Miranda, who was betrayed by Bolívar and handed over to the Spanish authorities. Such 'perfidia' is explicitly mentioned. It also praises Manuel Piar the *pardo* leader who Bolívar executed in 1817. Bolívar was outraged when he read the poem (see Jaksić 2001: 57, and Cussen 1992: 140–41).

19 For a post-colonial reading of this poem and the influence of Humboldt see Pratt 1992: 172–80. Pratt asks who is doing the agricultural work and suggests that Bello fails to acknowledge the labours of the anonymous multitudes (Pratt 1992: 180). However, the poem does explicitly refer to the 'labrador sencillo', the 'fatigado agricultor', 'la gente agricultora del Ecuador' and so on (Bello 1952: 39, 45), and makes clear that these labourers are not the degenerate city-dwellers.

20 Cussen reads this reference to 'fe mercenaria' (mercenary faith) as a reference to the Church's monopoly on official credit in the colonies and its improper intrusion in civil society (Cussen 1992: 120–21).

CHAPTER FOUR

Competing Masculinities and Political Discourse: The Writings of Esteban Echeverría (1805–51)

De la amada patria nuestra
Escudo fuerte es tu diestra
¿Y qué vale una mujer?
Huyamos, tú de la muerte,
Yo de la oprobiosa suerte
De los esclavos ...

María to Brián, 'La Cautiva', *Obras Completas:* Echeverría 1972: 462

The writings of Esteban Echeverría, like those of Bolívar and Bello, tend to mythify the feminine and historicise the masculine, which, in turn, extend to troped representations of man and woman in imaginative literature, as we shall see. This chapter draws on recent work on war, gender and the history of masculinities, in particular the concept of hegemonic masculinities (Tosh 2004: 54), as mobilised by historians, to explore the development of contradictory or competing masculinities (including revolutionary masculinities) in nineteenth-century politics and war. Joan B. Landes's discussion of heterosocial desire in French republican culture highlights the symbolic significance of the female body as the object of patriotic love, the 'site for men's patriotic investments' (Dudink 2004: 103). This usefully complements Mosse's work (1996) on homosocial desire in the discourses and visual culture in the age of nation-building, when the 'manly ideal', signifying national progress, was modelled on the young Greek male. The view that citizenship became masculinised and masculinity militarised throughout the nineteenth century is a valid one, but this is only true if we take the French model as exemplary (Dudink and Hagemann 2004: 18). In other words, historical specificity is paramount. War and violence are recurrent elements in the constructions of masculinity. As noted in Chapter 1, Goldstein claims that gender difference is reinforced by war and that the constant potential for war produces gender. It is important to enquire into the effect of the legacy of violence on the gender system and how it affects the social and cultural construction of masculinities and femininities and the meanings attributed to 'man' and 'woman'. For Goldstein gender is the symptom of war and ultimately the source of conflict (Goldstein 2001: 264).

It is in the light of this research that Echeverría's work will be considered.

The reconfiguration of the colonial Viceroyalty of the River Plate (1776–1810) into the state that is today called the Argentine Republic (known variously before 1860 as the Provincias Unidas del Río de la Plata and the Confederación Argentina) was a long and complex process of conflict. Since its inception in 1810, Argentina has been what Shumway refers to as a 'house divided against itself' (Shumway 1991: 299). Paraguay seceded in 1811; Bolivia in 1825; the Banda Oriental Province, renamed Uruguay, in 1828. The main conflict, not resolved until 1880, was between the city of Buenos Aires and the other provinces. A strong, modern, centralised state, with its capital in Buenos Aires, was the liberal Unitarian programme; a loose confederation of semi-autonomous states was the more conservative federal option. In the 1820s, an ambitious programme of economic reform, modernisation and education was initiated by Unitarian Bernadino Rivadavia (governor of Buenos Aires province 1821–1827) and the United Provinces seemed well on the way to becoming an emerging but credible nation state. But Rivadavia's uncompromising attitude towards the other provinces and his privileging of the city Buenos Aires, to the extent that in 1826 he proposed a Unitarian constitution, with Buenos Aires as the federal capital of a newly named Argentina, led to his downfall. He resigned in 1827 and it was his elected federalist successor, Manuel Dorrego, who signed the peace treaty with Brazil, ensuring the independence of the newly formed Uruguay. The unlawful execution of Dorrego by Unitarian General Lavalle in December 1829 resulted in a federalist uprising led by Juan Manuel Rosas and Estanislao López. Thus it was that federalist army leader Rosas came to be appointed by the Provincial Legislature to the position of Governor of Buenos Aires, shortly before Echeverría's return from Europe. His first term lasted three years, from December 1829 until November 1832. Rosas brought Rivadavia's reforms to an end, introduced press censorship, tightened political control and increased support for the clergy and the army. But he restored order, which earned him the title 'restaurador de las leyes'. In his second term, from March 1835 until his defeat in 1852, he ruled as a tyrant. He persecuted his enemies, many of whom fled to Montevideo, and set up a paramilitary death squad, the Mazorquera, to terrorise his opponents. His regime was even more repressive in the 1840s, after Lavalle's unsuccessful attempt to unseat him. For many, the late 1830s and 1840s were years of terror.[1]

The texts studied in this chapter were written and/or published in the 1830s, a time of acute political crisis and conflict. Echeverría had spent most of Rivadavia's period of reform studying in Paris. He had travelled to Europe at the age of 20, and stayed there for five years (for the influence of European Romanticism on Echeverría see Roggiano 1977 and Mercado 1996). By the time he returned in 1830, a convinced progressive with a political mission, Rosas was in his first term. Echeverría was one of a group of young liberal revolutionaries, known as the Generation of 1837, who opposed what they considered to be the barbarism of Rosas and the anachronistic intransigence of the old Unitarians. They were, according to Alberdi, 'hombres de estilo', men of style in their clothes, manners, walking, talking, writing and thinking (Halperín Donghi 1951: 14), a group 'de constructores que se confiere la verdad y el poder de ser jueces' (Demaria 2002: 71). In 1837, Echeverría inaugurated the Asociacíon de la Joven Generación de Argentina, modelled on Mazzoni's Young Italy and the Young Europe movements, which resulted in the publication of the *Dogma Socialista de la Asociacíon de Mayo*, one of Argentina's most influential political texts, the following year. It is fair to say that Echeverría's life was crippled by Rosas, but the experience turned him from a dissatisfied idealist to a committed political thinker and theorist. In Halperín Donghi's words, 'La más breve, la más sumaria de las historias del pensamiento argentino será inconcebible sin el nombre de Echeverría' (Halperín Donghi 1951: 13).

The majority of Echeverría's writings are as much political as literary texts, influenced by French republican ideas. The early collection of lyrical poetry, *Los Consuelos* (written 1830–31) was published in 1834, in the interregnum between Rosas's two terms, but by the time *La Cautiva* appeared in 1837, Rosas was well into his second term and the situation in Argentina was fast becoming intolerable. In 1839, Echeverría took part in an aborted attempt to unseat Rosas, after which, like so many other Unitarians, he fled to exile in Montevideo. That same year he wrote 'El Matadero', according to author and critic Juan María Gutiérrez, his close friend and editor. Echeverría remained in exile for the rest of his life, until his death in 1851, the year before Rosas was defeated. He spent half of his life under the Rosas regime, and his last twelve years exiled by federalist persecution.

Early poetry and post-colonial cultural independence

Echeverría returned to Buenos Aires from Europe aged 25. This was a period of rapid transformation in the American nation-building process and during his time abroad much had changed. He had left Buenos Aires during Rivadavia's progressive government, a period known in mainstream Argentine history as the 'feliz experiencia' (Shumway 1991: 83). When he returned, Rosas was in his first term. However, Echeverría was appalled by what he found, hence the tenor of his early poetry, ranging from melancholy and frustration to suppressed anger, a *mal de siècle* more profound than a pose.

'Elvira, o la novia del Plata' (1832) was published anonymously in the press two years after Echeverría's return from France. In the dedication (to José María Fonseca, signed June 28 1832). Echeverría stresses that the poem is not modelled on implicitly backward Castilian poetry but, rather, inspired by the more modern 'poesía del siglo', the Romantic poetry of France, England and Germany. He adds that he has always tried to avoid the 'vías trillados por nuestros poetas' (Echeverría 1972: 444). This statement indicates the continuation of a process of rupture with Spanish literary and cultural tradition, with which he aspires to break, but to which he feels he and Fonseca still belong, and an aspiration to imitate northern European Romantic paradigms. Three years later, Echeverría's Spanish contemporary, José de Espronceda, having also returned (to Spain) from exile in France, published his first overtly Romantic poem, 'La canción del pirata', in *El Artista* (1835).

'Elvira' is a Gothic romance characterised, like Espronceda's poetry, by emotional lyricism, metric variation and, above all, fatalism. An allegory of frustrated desire, it tells the story of the star-crossed lovers Lisandro and Elvira; just before they are due to be married, Elvira dies. As Juan María Gutiérrez comments, the poem dramatises the triumph of the forces of evil over hope and happiness. The protagonists represent goodness: Lisandro, the man, 'es la virtud y la ciencia encarnadas en un alma joven y viril sedienta de amor'; Elvira, the woman, 'es la esencia candorosa de la belleza, bajo la forma de una mujer, prometida a las ardientes aspiraciones de aquella alma de hombre'. Their union represents 'la ventura suprema' (Gutiérrez, 'La Vida y la Obra de Echeverría' in Echeverría 1972: 26); their separation, by a diabolical hand, merely confirms the ephemerality of happiness, love and beauty. As the final verse states, 'así se desvanece la esperanza / que dio un instante a la existencia. / Y el encanto de amor y la hermosura / como flor del desierto solo dura' (Echeverría 1972: 450). In another poem, written for Fonseca in September 1831, Echeverría described the theme of 'Elvira' as 'dos amantes / Víctimas tristes del destino adverso' ('A D.J.M.F. Dedicatoria de Elvira' (Echeverría 1972: 770). In the words of the Duque de Rivas in his famous play, *Don Alvaro*, staged in Madrid in 1835, these are the tragic consequences of 'la fuerza del destino'.

This is poetry of transition, as Echeverría acknowledges with the two epigraphs taken from Moratín (neoclassical Spanish) and Wordsworth (Romantic English). 'Elvira' is written in an innovative arrangement of traditional Spanish *silvas,* hexasyllabic, and octosyllabic verses. The metric scale, initiated by Hugo in 'Los Djins' and later favoured by Romantics such as Espronceda, Zorrilla and Gómez de Avellaneda, and by Bello (in 'Los duendes'), is certainly one of the first in Spanish. The poem is set in an unidentified location and tells a traditionally (western European) story of tragic love. What characterises the poem as Romantic, rather than Renaissance or neoclassical, is not so much the theme of a malevolent universe or even sentimental love, but the passages of Gothic horror. The title suggests that the subject of the poem is Elvira, the bride of the River Plate, but as we shall see in the European Romantic imaginary this was not likely to be so without substantial qualification. This is a poem of a man's frustrated desire.

The poem is narrated by a third person, and the direct dialogues between Elvira and Lisandro are fairly evenly distributed. Lisandro has been studying and exploring 'el campo de las ciencias' and, on his return, he and Elvira fall in love. But then Elvira experiences a nightmare, a surreal 'triste y fatal presentimiento' (Echeverría 1972: 446) in which two hearts are separated by a skeleton's black arm. Lisandro, too, has a nightmarish premonition, followed by a grotesque vision of death and hell with serpents, larvae, devils and so on, and a horrific encounter with Elvira's ghost – for she has, of course, died. Elvira, though given a modicum of characterisation in the poem, is finally eliminated; the subject of the poem is the desiring Romantic hero who is left to mourn.

However, and this is the crux, he could not be a Romantic hero without an Elvira, a feminine other, to frustratingly desire. She constitutes the object's resistance to his self-fulfilment; she is constitutive therefore of male Romantic subjectivity (Kirkpatrick 1989: 118–29). As Kirkpatrick writes;

> while [Spanish] liberals and Romantics pursued a cultural revolution that would support and facilitate the transformation of public power and economic structures, they preserved traditional gender hierarchy as carefully as they did the hierarchy of class, developing new ideologies to hide the inherited inequalities. In the end, identifying female subjectivity with family love amounted to the same thing as conceiving woman as the object rather than the subject of consciousness. (Kirkpatrick 1989: 60)

As the incarnation of the unattainable object of love, the Elvira trope symbolises moreover the classic European feminine ideal: young, pure, fair skin, golden hair, likened to jasmine and purple rose. She is the hero's muse, his inspiration, and at the same time the desired (European, classic) ideal: 'un mundo de risueños ilusiones / de esperanzas felices y ambiciones' (Echeverría 1972: 445). In other words, the female character Elvira embodies the feminine ideal, which in turn symbolises both the source (the generation of) and the object of male heterosexual desire, as well as its potential attainment and frustration. What prevents this realisation is uncontrollable, random fate. The woman-object of desire symbolises Providence ('astro benigno') in the face of death and man's adverse fortune; she is the means by which man can arrest his bad fortune 'que contraria fue desde la cuna'. She is thus worshipped ('cuando miré tu perfección divina y consagré a su culto mi albedrío' (Echeverría 1972: 446, 447)).

A similar pattern is noted in the poem 'El y Ella', published in the collection *Los Consuelos* (1834), a dialogue between a man and a woman on the carpe diem theme. The anonymous speakers express their mutual love. He is associated with subjectivity, experience, autonomy, imagination and memory (of past passions and violence). She, on the other hand, is there to reanimate, soothe and cure him of his world-weariness, 'La aciaga memoria / de mis pasados desdichas', the 'terribles borrascas' that have agitated his life (Echeverría 1972: 733). He sings and She, his angel, is his inspiration. Again 'Ella' is given a modicum of subjectivity, in that she expresses in direct speech the joy at being able to dedicate her life to loving him. But He is the sun that lights her. He is 'de mi alma claro espejo'; in other words She is reflected through and in him, and without him her life is meaningless. He has a life without her; She has none without him. She is his facilitator, enabling his self-fulfilment which, in turn, is hers. He is the poet, She his inspiration and his poetry. He is the artist, She the art. Having each established their relative roles and status, He then tries to persuade her to help him enjoy life's pleasures and quench his 'amor sediento'. Although She demurs, saying 'modera tus transportes', He insists, 'no, apuremos temprano, querida' (Echeverría 1972: 735), and their happy union is ensured.

As in most Romantic poetry, woman is here positioned outside subjectivity.

It must have been difficult for women readers of the time not to assimilate this message, not to identify with these female fictions of sentimental romance. Juan María Gutiérrez, writing in 1874, notes that *Los Consuelos,* possibly modelled on Sainte-Beuve's *Les Consolations* (Mercado 1996: 41), was extremely popular and received favourable reviews, including by Mariquita Sánchez's son, Juan Thompson (Mercado 1996: 41). Gutiérrez makes a point of differentiating between men and women readers. Women read the poems, he writes, 'en busca de las páginas que hablan de amor y en donde dialoga la pasión entre *él* y *ella*, dejando en blanco los nombres propios', whereas 'los ardientes rayos que destellan las composiciones consagradas a los recuerdos patrios tentaban a su lectura a los hombres maduros testigos de la revolución' (Echeverría 1972: 29). Women readers looked for love; men for war and patriotic verse.

Nevertheless, although the poems in *Los Consuelos* may be classified thematically in this way, in a gendered reading the distinction is not so clear. What the feminine stands for in this early poetry is not just male erotic desire, or even the fulfilment of a young man's life ambitions, but the realisation of a much greater collective project: the realisation, the constitution, of the new nation and a new collective post-colonial identity. That this was the raison d'être of 'Elvira' is indicated in Echeverría's letter to Fonseca, included as a prologue to the poem (Echeverría 1972: 444), in which he again draws attention to his poetry's originality and the fact that it is not modelled on Castilian verse forms. For this reason, in the note that precedes *Los Consuelos,* he seems to apologise for having imitated Spanish metrical form, particularly in 'La Profecía del Plata': 'las escribí preocupados aun del estilo y formas usadas por los poetas españoles, cuyas liras rara vez han cantado la libertad' (Echeverría 1972: 716), although this poem is written in quintets, a form not common in neoclassical Spanish poetry and developed more fully in its 11/7 variation in the Romantic period by, for example, Echeverría's Cuban contemporary, José María Heredia (1803–39). But even his poem 'A la Independencia Argentina' (signed July 1831) is written in the classic Spanish *silva.* Echeverría was dissatisfied with his efforts and aimed to create entirely original poetic forms that owed nothing to the colonial Spanish cultural tradition: 'Si, recobrando mi patria su [pre-Rosas] esplendor, me cupiese la dicha de celebrar otra vez sus glorias, seguiría distinto rumbo; pues solo por no trillados senderos se descubren mundos desconocidos' (Echeverría 1972: 716). By writing a new type of poetry in Spanish that consecrates the object of man's desire in feminine-nationalist terms, the poet could contribute to the collective labour of creating a distinctively post-colonial literary and cultural national tradition. Echeverría explains further, true to German Romantic thought, that in order for 'la poesía' (personified in the feminine) to fully acquire her influence and authority 'entre nosotros' (in Buenos Aires), as in the 'cultas naciones europeas', she needs to have ('si se quiere conquistarla'):

> un carácter propio y original, y que reflejando los colores de la naturaleza física que nos rodea, sea a la vez el cuadro vivo de nuestras costumbres, y la expresión más elevada de nuestras ideas dominantes, de los sentimientos y

> pasiones que nacen del choque inmediato de nuestros sociales intereses, y en cuya esfera se mueve nuestra cultura intelectual. Sólo así campeando libre de los lazos de toda extraña influencia, nuestra poesía llegará a ostentarse sublime como los Andes: peregrina, hermosa y varia en sus ornamentos como la fecunda tierra que la produzca. (Echeverria 1972: 716)

His views (new words, new cultural forms, make for new worlds) echo those of Bello (see Chapter 3). Echeverría aimed to create a nation with the pen, if not the sword, and in order to do so he needed to dream up a new object of man's collective creation and desire, 'la poesía' y 'la patria', a poetry born of the native land. The product of men's creative ability, agency, thought, and subjectivity is the feminine other.

Several poems in *Los Consuelos* indicate frustrated patri(er)otic desire (Landes 2004a: 104) figured as the polyvalent feminine: 'en vano busco la mujer hermosa' ('Recuerdo', Echeverria 1972: 716). In pursuit of hope the eponymous hero of 'Lara o La Partida' (1831) leaves 'mi patria y mis amores' (Echeverria 1972: 718). In 'Estancias' (1831) love of woman/the homeland are intermeshed in an elusive Argentine ('estancias') domestic ideal: 'Feliz aquel que de su patrio suelo / contempló solo el halagueño cielo / y libre de pesares / vivió seguro del cariño amante / de la beldad que idolatró constante / en sus quietos hogares' (Echeverría 1972: 718). In 'Imitación del inglés' (signed January 1832), repeating the theme of 'La Ida', the silver connotations of the River Plate (which throughout the collection signifies Buenos Aires, Argentina, and 'la patria' indistinctively) likens the 'argentino' river to pure, white flowers ('rozagante lirio' and 'cándida azucena') which in turn are personified (having 'hermosos ojos, belleza rara, candor divino') as a young maiden. The death here, though, is not that of the flowers or even the maiden, but the river, 'la flor malograda / del Argentino río' (capital A), that is, the patria (Echeverria 1972: 721).

The relational complexities of gender in *La Cautiva*

The narrative poem *La Cautiva* was published in *Rimas* during Rosas's second term, in the momentous year of 1837, when the Joven Generación de Argentina, captained by Echeverría, inaugurated the revolutionary Asociación de Mayo. The poem was written to question the apparent success of the 1833 Desert Expedition led by General Juan Facundo Quiroga, Rosas and others, and the subsequent document *Relación de los cristianos salvados del cautiverio* (1835) (Rotker 2002: 81).[2] It is set in Indian territory, and tells the story of how the captured María attempts to rescue her wounded soldier-husband, Brián.[3] The author explains in the preface that his purpose was to describe the desert, but in order to avoid mere description, he created the story of 'dos seres ideales' (Echeverría 1972: 451). This is, as in 'Elvira', a typically Romantic plot of tragic heroes and star-crossed lovers. However, there is one significant difference. The story and the characters are carefully contextualised; their milieu is the Argentine plains and their adversaries the southern Indians. They are described physically in some detail. In Echeverría's words, the story may be fiction but it is also verisimilitude, 'entra en los posible' (Echeverria 1972: 451) and, as such, verges on reality. The characters, then, are lifted out of timeless myth into history. Although the dramatic effect is deliberate, there is a strong element of *costumbrismo* in the poem; indeed, the description of the desert, though not entirely accurate, suggests the writings of naturalists such as Humboldt; and that of the Indian camp, though by no means objective, might be considered an early form of ethnography. Echeverría is of the opinion that the desert, 'nuestro más pingüe patrimonio' could be put to good use in the economic sense and, more importantly, as cultural capital. He draws an explicit analogy between 'La Cautiva', the protagonist of the poem, and the poem itself, *La Cautiva*.[4] The art form and its fictional heroine, he writes, represent passion that, in its intensity, consumes itself. As we shall see, the passion of the poem and of the protagonist is to liberate the captive love object, the husband and son, the Christian family, in short, the spirit of Argentina.

There are considerable grounds for reading *La Cautiva* as a feminist text. First, it features a feisty female hero, a veritable superwoman, who frees her wounded husband from the Indians, saves him from a bush fire by carrying him on her back across a river, defends him against two tigers and keeps him alive in the desert for four days. María is not only physically strong, brave and active but she is also an autonomous individual, intelligent, resolute and self-liberated.[5] She (not He) embodies the aspiring Romantic hero who strives against nature, fate and death to realise her ambition. She is the desiring subject and her love object is her husband. She is endowed with agency and subjectivity, self-reflexive consciousness, reason, willpower, and ideas, and she has the strength of purpose to carry them through. The poem presents her in an entirely positive light, not as a monster or abnormal, but with traditional feminine attributes: she is compassionate, honourable and dutiful. She is even compared to a flower, though trampled, and a water nymph. María represents the perfect woman for the new nation or, as Fernando Operé argues, Argentine creole identity (Operé 2003: 551). In *La Cautiva* the feminine ideal is not merely one of beauty, purity and feeling but it also incorporates autonomy, industriousness, strength and decisive action. It would seem, then, that in María, stereotyped gender differences are blurred.[6]

There are, nevertheless, problems with this reading. The most important objection is that María's understanding of self-fulfilment is dependent on another, her husband. María's life project is to save her husband and be with her family, rather than fulfil herself; or rather, as She in 'El y Ella', fulfilling herself is concomitant with fulfilling the lives of others. She is not a woman in her own right, but a wife and mother. Although she is virtually alone in the middle of a desert, making decisions and carrying them out, she acts entirely for the benefit of her husband. As such she is inscribed not as an individual but as a self-sacrificing wife and mother, as indicated by her Christian name. The text represents her trials in the wilderness in Christian terms: the bound husband is associated with Christ on the cross, and María with Mary

Magdalene, who frees him; she is his guardian angel, who delivers him. She is, literally, his support: 'mi brazo y poder divino / te servirán de sostén' (Echeverría 1972: 444). The clinching argument against a feminist reading is the manner in which María finally dies. She survives the rigours of Indian captivity and the desert (wild animals, drought, fire, heat) successfully. What kills her is news that her surviving son has been murdered.[7] This, according to the sympathetic narrator, signifies for her the end of all hope. Her death is instantaneous. She had transferred her love object from her dead husband to her child. Without either there is no reason for her to exist; she is eliminated from the text. Without her husband and son she is a tree without a root, 'en la tierra ya no afianza / su pompa y florido ornato' (Echeverria 1972: 475). María then, defined above all as a mother and wife, is a heroic martyr to conjugal and motherly love, love of the family and the nation. The poem inscribes an ideal femininity: no longer passive, or merely beautiful, but a strong and valiant mother and wife who aspires to peaceful domesticity. The poet praises María, 'Oh María. Tu heroísmo / Tu *varonil fortaleza* / Tu juventud y belleza / Merecieran fin mejor' (Echeverria 1972: 475, my emphasis).

This ideal femininity is contrasted with another in the text, the juxtaposition of which demonstrates how racial relations of power may be expressed in terms of sexual difference. The sine qua non of the ideal femininity represented by María is not only family love but also a white, Christian, creole identity. A competing femininity is represented by the indigenous women who are carefully differentiated in the poem from the indigenous men. A sign of the depravity of the Indian men is their harsh treatment of their women, and although Indian men and women are usually referred to as an undifferentiated mass, the women are distinguished from the men in a crucial scene. Following the festivities, described as a scene from hell, the men, drunk and violent, are contrasted with the women who attempt to placate them, thus demonstrating a degree of reason and compassion. The women (who are never individualised) and María, despite differences of race, religion and culture, share a compassion for their menfolk. This reading discerns a social hierarchy: on the lowest rung are the wild beasts (tigers), followed by, in this order, beast-like savages, the less savage indigenous women, María, the Christian, white wife and mother and, at the top of the evolutionary scale, Brián the (white, Christian) wounded male hero. The sign of civilisation in women is their care of men.

With reference to masculinity, at a first reading the competing masculinities seem to be more polarised. One is predicated on animal savagery and the other on patriotism and human civilisation. To what extent does Brián, the dying warrior, represent hegemonic masculinity? (Tosh 2004: 48–51). Is it that hegemonic masculinity is no longer identified with heroic combat and military values? Brián is emasculated masculinity; he is wounded, barely able to move and entirely dependent on his wife. He has no physical strength; he is not an autonomous individual; he is not rational but delirious. Brián symbolises the demise of the hegemonic masculinity of the 1820s and 1830s. Yet he still constitutes the love object of a woman. The signs of his masculinity are his reputation and glory, his honour (which is dependent on his wife's virtue, her sexual purity), and his resistance and passive fortitude. His heroic deeds are now relegated to the past; he remembers them and they are conjured up for the reader, but they are anachronistic.

The masculine ideal as proposed by the text is made more explicit if we consider the competing masculinity of the indigenous men. These are represented in two ways, which undercut the above arguments that advocated a positive reading of the feminine. When represented en masse, not as individuals, the Indians (men and women) are almost always referred to in the feminine as 'la tribu', 'la chusma', 'la caterva estulta' and so on, that is, as animal-like, mindless brute force. The feminine is associated in this way with the sub-human other, the enemy. However, when the Indian men are named as individuals in this section of the poem (Quillán, Callupán, Quitúr and so on), bravery and heroism are attributed to them; they fought with valour in order to be free. As critics have noted, the poem indicates a certain respect for individual Indian men. Masculinity therefore denotes bravery and combat, but, again, relegated to the past. In the poem the Argentine troops find the camp and slaughter all the Indians, men, women and children. This episode is not represented as brave or masculine, but neither is much sympathy shown for the Indians. What comes across most clearly in the poem is that irrational violence for its own sake, fighting and, in particular, self-inflicted infighting, is the culmination of savagery. Disorder, lack of control, lack of reason (exacerbated by drunkenness) and lack of compassion equate the Indians en masse not only with savagery but also with the devil and superstition. The savagery and mob mentality of the Indian masses connote that of the federalists. In *La Cautiva* there is no place for masculinity as traditionally understood in a militarised society. Violence, which is shown to be perpetrated entirely by men, is to be commemorated if necessary, but brought to an end. As Brián acknowledges, his ambition to be remembered as a glorious hero was 'insensato'. In his place the text proposes a new concept of manly femininity: a heroism motivated by love (of man, family, community) that is active, compassionate, strong and family-oriented.

The desert may be read metaphorically as an empty space, a tabula rasa, on which the creole men and women of the new patria make their mark. It is María's intelligence and skill that shape the desert into a shelter rather than a death trap. This is the survival of the fittest, and the fittest is a woman. María is a heroic republican citizen (autonomous, rational and active), whose epic story takes mythical proportions as she attempts to tame wild Nature. But María does not succeed in saving Brián; she survives, but she does not live to tell the tale. Again, María represents (the ideal version of) Argentina, the patria figured in the feminine. She incarnates the valiant maternal, not confined to domestic space but acting out her destiny on the open plains. The character María stands for is 1830s Argentina, the Argentina of the here and now, struggling for liberty in a hostile environment (the barbarism of the Indians, the desert and the federalists) that needs to be eliminated (Indians), or managed (desert), if not domesticated (federalism). Brián represents the (old, Unitarian) Argentina of the previous twenty years (since May 1810); once given to glorious warfare, now immobilised as a consequence of internecine violence. Citizenship and national independence, understood as martial masculinity, have failed. What keeps the spirit of liberty alive is faith and hope in the future, in Providence, as represented by María. The feminine still stands for ideal perfection, but also the agency whereby the ideal is achieved. Gender polarities are deconstructed in this textual alternative to war. *La Cautiva*, the mother who is committed to the service of her family and community and hence serves a political purpose, is the nearest Echeverría comes to imagining a republican femininity. However, true to Romantic paradigms, María fails too. This is a pessimistic appreciation of the then current situation in Argentina; the new nation, by this model, is fated to fail. Past violence has led to present defeat and there is no hope for the future.

The feminine in 'El Matadero'

The short narrative 'El Matadero' was probably written in 1839, the year Echeverría left Argentina for exile in Montevideo, and was published posthumously in the *Revista del Río Plata* in 1871, twenty years after his death. It was presented by Gutiérrez, who also later edited Echeverría's *Obras Completas* (1874). Set on the outskirts of the city of Buenos Aires in Lent 1839, during the mourning period for Rosas's wife (October 1838–October 1840) at the start of the decade of terror, the sketch or story (Pupo-Walker 1973) describes a scene in which bullocks are being slaughtered for meat. There is a scarcity of food in Buenos Aires, due to floods, and the populace is hungry; for this reason Rosas has made an exception and allowed the slaughter to go ahead, despite the Church's prohibition of meat consumption during Lent. A series of dramatic episodes occasioned by a bull's escape (the accidental beheading of a child, an Englishman knocked from his horse), recounted with macabre black humour, culminate in mob aggression against a young Unitarian who has wandered into the area unawares. Gutiérrez presents the sketch, possibly the first of its kind written in post-independence Argentina, to the 1870s reading public in terms that today would identify it not as fiction but as *testimonio*. According to Gutiérrez, had the sketch fallen into the hands of Rosas, Echeverría would have disappeared instantly (Echeverría 1972: 310). He repeatedly insists on its historical, political and documentary value: 'es una página histórica, un cuadro de costumbres y una protesta que nos honra'. The final confrontation between the Unitarian and the federal Judge, he adds, 'no es una invención sino una realidad que más de una vez se repitió en aquella época aciaga' (Echeverria 1972: 313). The story, then, is mobilised as a national political text, an act of cultural and political memory, a warning for future generations, for as Gutiérrez stated in 1874, a nation has to face up to its criminal past in order not to repeat the experience:

> Hemos pasado por una verdadera época de terrorismo que infundió admiración y escándalo en América y Europa. Pero si se nos pidieran testi-

> monios y justificaciones escritos para dar autenticidad a los hechos que caracterisan aquella época, no podríamos presentarlos, ni siquiera narraciones metódicas y anecdóticas, a pesar de oírlas referir diariamente de boca de los testigos presenciales. Cuando éstos dejen de existir estamos expuestos a que se crea que no hemos sido víctimas de un bárbaro exquisitamente cruel, sino de una pesadilla durante el sopor de una siesta de verano. (Echeverría 1972: 313)

The *testimonio,* the witnessing in 'El Matadero', is that of the narrator; the voice of this heavily intrusive and opinionated first-person narrator oozes corrosive irony and sarcasm and might easily be conflated with that of Echeverría.[8] The story was meant to be read as the narrator/Echeverría's account of a scene that he himself witnessed and experienced, which at a symbolic level constitutes a scathing attack on Rosas. In one interpretation, the objective is the representation of reality (the slaughter fields) as it is, in all its gruesome and grotesque detail. As such, the sketch is an early form of realism or naturalism, resonant of the work of Echeverría's contemporaries Eugene Sue (1804–75) in France (*The Mysteries of Paris,* 1842) or Dickens (1812–38) in England (*Oliver Twist,* 1838). However, 'El Matadero' is not only intended as *testimonio* or historical documentary; it is also a rich and complex literary work, social and political satire at its most biting and effective, a multilayered text that constantly slips away from the narrator's control and undoes his credibility (Lojo 1994: 126). The narrator overstates his case and the fissures and unresolved paradoxes of the account merely confirm his unreliability.

At the crux of these tensions is a mismatch between the political and gender discourses inscribed in the text. The political ideal may be Unitarian, but the manly ideal is not. The most striking feature of the text from a gendered point of view is the erasure of the feminine. At most, the feminine may be said to signify the disavowed abject other, the horror of engulfment, which must be repressed. The text also foregrounds the relational complexities of gender, that is, how other relations of power pertaining to race and caste are constructed in terms of sexual difference and hierarchy.

The overt aim of the narrator is to demonise and ridicule the federalists, Rosas and the common people from whom he drew his support. This political confrontation is played out in terms of masculinity. In a conventional reading, the liberal, progressive option is represented by the Unitarian, and pre-modern retrogression by the pro-Rosas mob, including the Judge of the Peace and the chief slaughterer, Matasiete. The Argentina of Rosas is symbolised as a bloodbath, a quagmire of mud, guts and excrement. But despite pressure from the narrator and editor, a resisting reader will want to question such Manichean polarisation and query any straightforward equivalence between the killing of bullocks for meat and the political violence in Buenos Aires. The slaughter of animals for food is a perfectly legitimate occupation and certainly not violence. Violence usually denotes illegitimate physical harm committed intentionally by one person against another (not against an animal); it denotes unacceptable moral impropriety (Riches 1986). Whether an act is considered violent depends on the cultural and political values and norms in play. What is legitimate for the performer will not be for the victim, but of crucial importance in the attribution of violence to an act is the point of view of the witness. David Riches refers to this as the 'triangle of violence' (Riches 1986: 8). In 'El Matadero', the witness is the narrator, who attempts to persuade the reader that the killing of animals is equivalent to the arrest of a Unitarian, and that both are instances of cruelty and violence. If the reader takes the role of dissenting witness, however, the actions of the slaughterers and the federalists are neither unacceptable nor violent. At the end of the day, no physical harm is caused to the Unitarian; he is not attacked arbitrarily, thanks to the intervention of the federal Judge, who merely enforces the law, although whether the law of Rosas, 'el Restaurador de las Leyes', is deemed legitimate is the nub of the question. After the Unitarian's death, the Judge laments 'Pobre diablo: queríamos únicamente divertirnos con él' (Echeverría 1972: 324) suggesting surprise at the outcome (Folger 1999: 47).

Resisting a unidimensional political reading of the slaughter fields opens up exploration of the text in terms of public space. The space, the text, is criss-crossed by close-up scenes of groups of people engaging in various tasks. This is a working environment dedicated to domestic meat production, typical of the urban slaughterhouses of the time.[9] The scene is one of movement, dynamism and activity on an almost industrial scale. The bullocks are quickly killed and converted into meat; the Judge is there to prevent thieving; the poor convert the discarded residue (offal) into useful products. This is an early nineteenth-century Argentine industrial scene, in which the characters are the workers and the dispossessed. Central to a political reading of these social and economic practices is an understanding of the way gender works in the text.

The text constructs at least two masculinities; one is the 'manly ideal' (Mosse 1996: 4) associated with the Enlightenment, liberalism and modernity, represented by the Unitarian; the other is that of the pre-modern federalists, represented by chief slaughterer Matasiete, who, employed presumably by the government, is identified by his clothes as a gaucho. In the story, and at the time of Rosas (late 1830s), Matasiete's masculinity is hegemonic, that is, he represents the masculine norm to which the dominant federalist majority subscribe, and by which it maintains its authority. Indeed, this dominant masculinity stands as a metaphor for the whole political community. Liberal, Unitarian masculinity is marginalised and oppressed. The preferred manly ideal of the narrator should be the liberal type; but the text belies this assumption. Certainly, the Unitarian youth is mounted on a horse (denoting status and hierarchy); he is clean, elegantly dressed, courageous, and of 'gallarda y buen apuesta persona' (Echeverría 1972: 321). His appearance proclaims his status. As such, he fits the liberal, nationalist image of acceptable manhood; for Locke and Rousseau outward appearance was a symbol 'of inner worth, a sign for all to see and judge' (Mosse 1996: 27). Yet this image is fatally flawed. For the narrator, the blood-spattered, cut-throat Matasiete is the Unitarian's countertype, but this is clearly not the view of the crowd, who hold Matasiete in great esteem and regard the Unitarian as a fop. Although these two masculinities, emblematic of apparently unresolved cultural and political differences, seem to be competing, it could be argued that they are in fact complementary. Given that the narration undercuts the narrator's authority, there is some ambiguity as to which of the two characters embodies dominant masculinity and which the countertype. From the point of view of the power relations of gender underpinning the text, each type of masculinity (and each political option) is arguably but an extension of the other.

The story draws no sharp distinction between gender and sex, that is, between biological sexual difference and the social relations of sexual difference; in fact, what is under threat due to this lack of differentiation are precisely 'social relations', social cohesion. The text represents society on the verge of collapse or degeneration. Put another way, it presents a series of masculinities (a sign of society and culture) that textually coalesce with maleness (a sign of nature) and are hence downgraded from the human and cultural to the level of the animal and biological. This fits the narrator's view that Rosas is reducing society to savagery; or, rather, that without civilised government, culture (masculinity) is reverting to its natural state (maleness). Male sexual difference and potency, marked by the presence or absence of 'cojones', the unmentionable 'c…' in the story (Echeverría 1972: 318), is a central structural principle and is raised explicitly as a topic of discussion in the story in relation to the bull. The bull, at the male end of the male-masculine spectrum, stands for male sexuality in its most brute form. Yet the bull, an undomesticated animal, is out of place (indeed prohibited) in the slaughter fields and rightfully makes a bid for freedom. It is this resistance and decision to break free from unjust captivity that earns it respect and leads to the speculation that it does indeed have 'órganos genitales' (Echeverria 1972: 318), as the narrator politely puts it, which are hidden from view. Although the bull is eventually killed, its sexual organs represent power and defiance when threatened with death: 'Aquí están los huevos'; 'dos enormes testículos, signo inequívoco de su dignidad de toro' (Echeverria 1972: 320). The bull, though a beast, is invested by the crowd and by the witness-narrator with a certain honour and nobility. These are human characteristics, pointing to a degree of anthropomorphisation, that is, the personification and naturalisation of sexual potency.

The masculinity associated with the federalists is, like the bull's maleness, fierce, courageous and determined (pre-modern male attributes). The epitome of federal masculinity is Matasiete, who is 'hombre de c…' and also 'degollador de unitarios' (Echeverria 1972: 318). He is ugly and dirty, but his upright bearing and unrivalled skill at killing and dismembering bullocks, a work ethic, command respect. The narrator does not portray Matasiete as entirely negative; unlike most of the other deformed and grotesque characters, including, arguably, the Unitarian, he is certainly not ridiculed. He is at least an individual, the only named character, who completes his task, takes his earnings and is disposed to move on. It is the crowd that urges him to attack the Unitarian.

Nevertheless, for the narrator his filth and lack of finer sensibilities approximate him to the brute. Thus Matasiete and the bull, two males with 'cojones', together represent the overlap between the human and the animal, dominant masculinity and the male, the cultured and the wild. But the text also explicitly links the Unitarian and the bull, in that they both resist captivity, exercise free will and desire freedom (cf. Lojo 1994: 114–15).

The masculinity of the Unitarian is presented as the more desirable, but it is subordinate and proscribed. The Unitarian is an individual but, unlike Matasiete, he is not named; in addition, he has little opportunity to fight or to show physical strength. He is tied up, like the bull, and taken to be tormented, though not necessarily killed. He is described by the federalists as effeminate, a countertype to their ideal: he sits on his horse like a 'gringo', with a saddle (rather than bareback, like the gauchos). He is described by the narrator as 'la víctima' (Echeverría 1972: 321), compared to an ox set upon by tigers, suggesting castration, and even to Jesus Christ. Yet the Unitarian displays his masculinity not by brute strength, but in his conduct. If the mob expected him to behave 'manso', or passively, he proves them wrong (Marvin 1986: 128); his defiance commands respect. Honour is self-respect recognised by others, the opposite of shame and humiliation (Johnson and Lipsett-Rivera 1998: 2–3). The Unitarian's major concern is to maintain his honour and this is signified by his resistance to having his clothes (his status and humanity) removed. Removing his trousers (to whip his backside) would humiliate him, by treating him as an animal or a child, and reveal his sexual organs: cowardice or effeminacy would taint his reputation. From the crowd's perspective, however, his resistance is that of a 'salvaje unitario' and as such he is seen to behave like a wild animal ('está furioso como toro montaraz', 'rugiendo de rabia', which they will domesticate, 'ya lo domaremos' (Echeverria 1972: 322, 323)). For the narrator there is no need for the Unitarian to prove his masculinity by revealing his sexual organs for, unlike the bull, he proves his honour by cultural rather than biological means: his determination to avoid being treated like an animal. If, as it seems, it is his willpower that causes his death, his decision not to be dishonoured and to die in the way he chooses, then he does maintain his self-respect as an autonomous individual by non-violent means and self-inflicted death. The narrator's view is that he dies a martyr to the cause, sacrificing himself on moral principle for the greater good. As such he represents masculine civic virtue.

Although the Unitarian embodies the progressive manly ideal, he nevertheless displays features associated with an older type of aristocratic and chivalrous masculinity, a 'flattering fiction that the elites of colonial Latin America found convenient to believe' (Johnson and Lipsett-Rivera 1998: 8). He wanders into the melee like a knight errant on his horse. His strong sense of personal worth is predicated on his noble blood, his elite caste. He is furious because he is denied the respect he considers due to his rank. The mob does not recognise his status or share his culture codes and pulls him off his horse. In other words, this liberal image of manhood incorporates an aristocratic code of honour, yet it is the manly ideal of the revolutionary progressives. In this respect, the Unitarian resembles the eighteenth-century gentleman rather than the republican citizen (Smith-Rosenberg 2004). The text further unravels the liberal ideal in the connections it makes between the bull and the Unitarian, already mentioned, and above all in the strange ending. According to George Mosse, one of the most salient attributes of Enlightenment and bourgeois nationalist manly virtue is self-control or 'quiet strength' (Mosse 1996: 50). The virtuous man is imaged as the statue of a young Greek male: beautifully proportioned and emotionally contained. But the Unitarian's angry, abusive spat with the Judge and loss of self-control, indeed hysteria, when disarmed and tied down, so that he lashes out more like a tethered bull than a hero stoically meeting death, jars with the masculine ideal of civic virtue. According to Pitt-Rivers, a man should only respond to impugned honour in public and to the challenge of an equal, suggesting that the Unitarian should not have responded at all (Pitt-Rivers 1965: 29). In short, he lets himself down. His lack of self-mastery causes his death. And it is in the death scene where implied author and narrator part company.[10] Matasiete, on the other hand, the man of action and few words, shows perfect restraint throughout, the 'virility, courage in battle and manly self-control' expected of the republican citizen (Smith-Rosenberg 2004: 62).

The masculinities of both the Unitarian and Matasiete are overtly underpinned by maleness, yet neither embodies the flawless ideal of masculinity that might be mobilised in social relations. It could be argued that the three characters, the bull, Matasiete and the Unitarian, though positioned on either side of the political divide and at each end of the nature-culture, dominant-dominated spectrum, share a common feature: they all, to some degree, command respect from the characters, the narrator and the reader. This respect is earned by their actions and decisions as individuals, their sense of purpose and determination, here predicated on the common denominator: the male sex. Over and above their differences (of culture, politics and, indeed, genus), this individualism is the most important factor in the masculinity that the text posits as exemplary. Reading against the grain, then, it is not that the masculinity of the federalists stands for barbarism, and that of the Unitarian for civilisation. The Unitarian could be said to be unreasonable, the Judge rational and Matasiete noble, in his way. The text constructs different versions of masculinity, but they run almost as a continuum between the human and the animal, the cultured and uncultured, rather than as competing alternatives.

If these masculinities do not function in the text as type and countertype, then arguably their 'foil', using Mosse's (1996: 24) term, is the feminine. It is here that the structures of sexual domination operating in the text and in the political order may be identified. Where is the feminine located in 'El Matadero'? There are many secondary characters in the story, men and women. All, bar the Judge, are feminised as mass, 'la chusma' (Echeverría 1972: 316). There are also several female characters, all minor, and only partially picked out by the narrator from the masses as groups. These are the 'achuradoras', women tripe-makers, who take the offal of the slaughtered beasts and prepare it for consumption.[11] These women have one thing in common; they are marked as much by race as gender (the words 'negra' 'mulata' 'africana' fuse the two categories) and, as a corollary, by class and caste. They are described by the (patronising, sarcastic) narrator, who does not belong to their class, by their job; their work determines their being. These coloured women are associated from the start of the story with low life, animals and other sub-human forms of existence, to the extent that the narrator purposely elides the differences between the women's (deformed) bodies and the body parts (the innards) of the dismembered animals they are handling.[12] The women unravel not 'ovillos' of wool, but of entrails; they are even mockingly compared to Penelope (318). They are marked not by their femininity (cultural attributes) but their biological femaleness, here presented as surreal and grotesque. To this extent they do not participate in the human world, but slip indistinctly between the human and animal life; they defy classification.

In these passages, the narrator slips into the satirical genre, deforming women as objects of ridicule and scorn (see Chapter 5). Two other brief references are made to women: 'beatas' leaving the Church, and the women of the Rosas family and other 'señoras federales'. Both groups symbolise non-reason, obscurantism, fanaticism, obedience to the Church and family; servility and dependence; they are products of the retrogressive Church and the Rosas state machinery. It is these women, semi-submerged like a form of aquatic life in sludge and slime, that constitute 'El Matadero', who populate the space of 'el matadero' and provide the substratum of the text, against which all other cultural constructs are measured. They are the dehumanised, absolute 'Other' (Folger 1999: 51). Arguably, there is no feminine in this story and certainly no ideal feminine to complement the various masculine ideals. The black and mulatto women signify the naturalised, objectified female; a product of nature, not culture, indicating a resemanticisation of the feminine. As such, the women represent the abject, chaos, the absence of bodily containment, all that needs to be eliminated or rather disavowed from the purview of the rational elite, but against which the rational elite has to define itself.[13] This categorisation may be extended to the feminised masses in general ('La chusma'; Echeverría 1972: 316), as mentioned earlier, which are also referred to as vultures and tigers. For the narrator, savagery is concomitant with chaos and anarchy. The black women are the undifferentiated mass from which cultural and social relations emerge. It might be objected that the text presents their activities as more social, collaborative and productive than those of the male individuals, but these movements take place in a filthy public space from which woman, as conceptualised by the narrator (white, respected), is proscribed. From the point of view of the narrator, the 'negras' and 'africanas' cannot be considered women. They serve as a foil to individualism, which is predicated on masculinity and the male.

The political contention and power struggle taking place in the story between competing moral codes and values, the linchpin of which is gender, takes place entirely within the realm of the masculine. The debate is between Unitarian or federal, urban or marginal, elite or popular, traditional or progressive masculinities. Those who have no part in this debate, the women and the masses, are feminised and bestialised as the gruesome abject. The dichotomy between, on the one hand, human/science/reason/free will/control and, on the other, animal/body/superstition/appetite/dependency is signified by the gender binary: the individual is gendered male. In 'El Matadero', sexual difference is dramatically polarised, whereas apparently contradictory masculinities coalesce. If woman signifies feminine, then on the eve of the decade of terror, there can be no place for her in the public space of liberal discourse.

Reiterating the point that social cohesion is founded on normative manliness, if 'El Matadero' is a proto-nationalist text, the feminine cannot symbolise the nation, neither as the alluring object of heterosocial desire that constitutes patri(er)otic love nor as the 'genetrix', the mother/matron representing the motherland and natural origins (Kerber 1980). If there is no ideal feminine, how might the nation be signified? There is no homoerotisim in this story, either, no symbol of moral virtue exemplified by ideal, manly, classic beauty. In short, there is no nation, no solution for Argentina.

Reading for gender in this selection of Echeverría's works points to 'El Matadero' as symptomatic of the moment of greatest despair, for the author and for Argentina, when the political order was at its most inchoate. This is apparent in the marked shift in the representation of gender in his writings after 1834, at the outset of the second period in government for Rosas, and the further polarisation of gender differences as violence intensified after 1839. In the early lyrical poem 'Elvira', Elvira is, to paraphrase Gutiérrez, the essence of pure beauty in the form of woman (Echeverría 1972: 26). In *Los Consuelos* the feminine stands as the source and object of male desire, as well as the realisation of a greater collective project: the new nation. In *La Cautiva* there is an inkling of what is to come in Echeverría's work, as La Cautiva's ideal femininity (white, Christian, creole) is contrasted with the countertype of the Indian women who, like the 'achuradoras' in 'El Matadero', are figured as subhuman mass. In contrast to Echeverría's early poetry (*Los Consuelos*), there is no Romantic lyricism in 'El Matadero'. The author does not need to imagine visions of hell, as in his Romantic poem 'Elvira'; rather, he presents the reader with hell on earth, not in the liminal space of the wilderness, as in *La Cautiva*, but in the suburbs of Buenos Aires, on the edge of the so-called centre of civilisation.

Hegemonic masculinity ('sons of the fathers of the fatherland') and women between the lines in *El Dogma Socialista*

The above reading of gender in 'El Matadero' is borne out by Echeverría's political manifesto, *El Dogma Socialista de la Asociación de Mayo*, signed August 1837. Echeverría read out the 'Palabras Simbólicas' at the inaugural session of the Asociación de Mayo in 1837. The text, entitled 'Código', was later published by Juan Bautista Alberdi in *El Iniciador*, Montevideo, in January 1839 and in *El Nacional*, Montevideo, in February and March 1839, while Echeverría was writing 'El Matadero' in the country estate Las Talas. The *Dogma* was later published as a book in 1846. with a short introduction by Echeverría (Echeverría 1972: 124).[14] Consisting of a series of paragraphs or statements modelled on those of Young Europe, as noted by Gutiérrez, it is written in the first person plural, 'nosotros'; its targeted audience is a group of young men (the Asociación de Mayo or Generation of 1837) to which the author belongs. Thus the opening address, 'a la juventud Argentina y a todos los dignos hijos de la patria' who wish to 'vestir la toga viril' (Echeverria 1972: 125), refers to young men. What is considered to be virile? From the start of the *Dogma*, gender is employed to differentiate between the good and the bad, between the 'la ciega muchedumbre', the feminised masses on the one hand and on the other 'los hijos de los héroes de mayo y julio', the 'jóvenes hijos de los padres de la patria', who must 'fraternizad y obrad' (Echeverria 1972: 126). Although for Echeverría the laws of democracy must not copy European models but develop bottom-up, from the collective Argentine will, there is no place here for women, mothers or daughters, as individuals or as political subjects (Didier 1966: 141).

The manifesto is also a call to arms, a 'cruzada de emancipación'; virtue is equated with action; freedom can only be regained with blood; 'el reino de la verdad no vendrá sino con guerra' (Echeverría 1972: 127). This is another instance of the militarisation of masculinity and citizenship noted across Europe, particular France, at the time (Dudink and Hagemann 2004: 19). The *Dogma* is invaluable for its systematic codification and explanation of the political beliefs and ideals of Echeverría and his circle. Association, Equality, Freedom, Honour, Glory and Democracy in this context are all gendered concepts.

In Echeverría's *Dogma* there is no explicit mention of the social category women (that is, over half of the Argentine population) yet, reading between the lines, it is possible to identify the discursive strategies of exclusion and hence to acknowledge some trace of women's presence by default. Briefly, three discursive strategies are in operation: first, the social relevance and symbolic meaning of giving birth is invalidated; second, citizenship is predicated on subject positions that may only be ascribed to women (and certain categories of men) ambiguously (so that not all men are patriots but all patriots are men); third, certain inequalities are justified. As mentioned, Echeverría addresses other young Argentine men inclusively ('nosotros'). Theirs is an association of equals; young men who are patriots and citizens in as much as they are not dependent on or subservient to others (as are slaves); young men bonded by human fraternity, who share mutual love. They are sons of the fathers of the fatherland. Belonging to the republican patria, the homeland, is no longer predicated on birth and mothers (Argentina is not described as a nation, the word is never used) but on citizenship and the rule of law (of the father), as is evidenced in paragraph 26 of the *Dogma*: 'los esclavos o los hombres sometidos al poder absoluto no tienen patria; porque la patria no se vincula a la tierra natal sino en el libre ejercicio y pleno goce de los derechos de cuidadanos' (Echeverría 1972: 126). Thus an exclusively male genealogy is established, in which women have no part. It is men who give birth, 'partos', to ideas and activities in what might be again described as a hom(m)osexual economy of the self/same (Irigaray 1985: 137, 141).

The Association is made up of patriots, that is, of individuals who are rational and independent in body and mind. Society is composed of such individuals and social contract guarantees freedom, independence and equality. But not all people are considered to be rational, independent individuals; some are irrational and/or dependent on others, and they must be tutored and educated correspondingly. Some people are unequal by nature; they are essentially, irreparably, different and subordinate. This is underscored by presenting the natural as an extension of the divine, so that in the hierarchy of creation, God rules man and delegates man to rule over 'las demás criaturas', those who are not rational individuals and who are not independent in body or mind. Men (rather than mankind) are thus attributed with divine right of rule over 'criaturas', which, as we shall see, does not refer to animals but the subaltern: the divine right of absolute monarchs to subject men and women is here traduced into the divine right of dominant men (who consider themselves individuals, a status defined a priori by them) to govern subordinate men and all women, all those who fall outside the individual/independence category that dominant men constructed in the first place. The subaltern includes all those to whom reason and independence are not attributed, who are ignorant and/or inactive and/or governed by instinct (here identified as vagabonds). Only rational, independent individuals are worthy of public life, yet to ensure this status among their confrères, they must maintain their honour and respect. Honour is earned in society, in the public arena; the private domestic space is regulated by moral codes pertaining not to the state but to the Church. Thus, what goes on in the home is of no business of the state; glory and honour, conversely, cannot be gained in the home. In this way the 'grandes hombres' of a particular society come to symbolise, for eternity, the glory of the patria.

Women, generally confined to the home and inactive in the public political arena, made (by the state) legally dependent on men (fathers and husbands), and to whom emotions, feelings, and instincts are attributed, rather than reason, according to these definitions of citizenship and, indeed, humanity, cannot be considered rational, independent individuals. Their inequality is ratified and naturalised by their God-given biological difference. By inference women, as a category, are grouped with boys and girls (minors), with men and women who are uneducated or insane, men and women who depend on others for a living, and men and women slaves and vagabonds. Together, they constitute the feminised 'masas ignorantes' (Echeverría 1972: 153), in short, the vast majority of the population.

Nevertheless, the discursive ambiguity arising from the fact that women are not mentioned, nor are they explicitly excluded, so that the document may be read (as it is normally) as referring to enlightened men and women, provided educated, elite women with some space for manoeuvre. According to the *Dogma*, in order for women (and the subaltern) to become citizens and patriots, they first need to be educated (to be rational and independent of mind). Many elite women were perfectly well educated. Second, they would need to earn honour and social equality by demonstrating their valour, their active public spirit, and their sacrifice to the collective good. A woman might show her independence of mind, for example, in the sphere of art, with the pen rather than the sword, in civil society rather than in public life (from where she was largely excluded). Above all, women must do this for themselves; they must 'emanciparse'. Educated women could at least be written into citizenship, as Juana Manso attempted to do in her novels of the time. Echeverría's *Dogma* had a long-term impact; it was used by Juan Bautista Alberdi in the formulation of his *Bases y puntos de partida para la organización política de la república argentina* (1852), which formed in turn the basis of the 1853 Argentine Constitution, the substance of which remained in place until Carlos Menem's reforms of 1994.

Manual de Enseñanza Moral. Para las escuelas primarias del estado oriental: woman connoted

Echeverría's *Manual*, signed 1844 and published in Montevideo in 1846, is addressed familiarly to 'niños' in the second person plural. Despite the gender ambiguity of the plural noun, Echeverría addresses boys only (implying that girls do not receive primary education). Again, women, as a social category, are virtually erased from the Manual proper, but are explicitly referred to at the end of the marginal 'Advertencia preliminar' (Echeverría 1972: 231–39). Here, Echeverría underlines the importance of the family in social life and observes that his *Manual* should be supplemented by a book, 'un *libro* por hacer' [sic], on the Family. This is where woman would have appeared, though the book was never written. Nevertheless, by 1844 Echeverría had identified in the 'Advertencia preliminar' a significant social role for Argentine women, by now represented as intelligent, therefore rational, beings: the role of the mother of sons. De Tocqueville, he writes, attributes the prosperity of the 'Unión Americana' (the United States) to the 'superioridad de sus mujeres', and adds, '¿Por qué las nuestras, tan inteligentes como bellas, no podrán igualarlas'? (Echeverria 1972: 238). The one time the word 'mujeres' is used in the *Manual* is to denote the women of the USA. Echoing Rousseau, Echeverría stresses the importance of early upbringing in the family for the formation of the young citizen, that is, the boy:

> ¿Qué importa que el niño aprenda en la escuela buenas doctrinas, si al volver a su casa no oye del labio del padre, y especialmente de la madre, palabra alguna que las fecunde o si ve ejemplos que las contraríen? ¿No es el hogar donde su tierno corazón recibe las impresiones más eficaces y las ideas que lo dominan en su vida y deciden su porvenir de hombre? (Echeverría 1972: 238)

His definition of citizenship excludes women, but he concedes that good mothers make good sons and good citizens: 'Formad buenas madres para tener buenos hijos: formad buenos ciudadanos si queréis tener patria: he aquí todo el problema de la educación' (Echeverria 1972: 238).

In the *Manual* proper there is one further mention of woman (rather than 'madre'), and this is as a wife whose purpose is the reproduction of the species: 'Así como el amor aproxima a los seres racionales y produce el bien, el amor es como el *verbo* [sic] que engendra la unión física y moral del hombre y la mujer, llamada matrimonio, destinado a perpetuar la especie' (Echeverria 1972: 251). Woman is considered a rational being, although this is undermined somewhat by the subsequent statement that the father is the head of the family and the mother the heart, thus aligning woman/mother with feelings and emotions. There is no other mention of women or girls in the *Manual*. Moreover it is difficult to see how girls could read the *Manual* as addressed to them, despite the so-called neutral 'niño' or 'niños' employed throughout. The paragraphs on honour, valour, fraternity, sacrifice and, as a consequence, citizenship emphasise the need to actively achieve independence and personal freedom: 'Debéis trabajar para vivir de vuestro trabajo, no ser onerosos a nadie y adquirir independencia personal' (Echeverria 1972: 247). Liberty is gained rather than given; pupils should learn to be hard-working, 'hacer uso de la libertad'; otherwise they will be like slaves or colonised peoples, 'siempre sometido[s] a la dependencia indirecta de otros más civilizados y más poderosos' (Echeverria 1972: 255–56).

The paragraphs on democracy also stipulate the need for personal and political liberty and it is difficult to see how this too could apply to women. Personal liberty entails the right to gainful employment, to dispose of property, form associations with others and express one's thoughts freely. Political freedom is the right of citizens, here defined as free men, to vote, to be elected (as judge or magistrate), and to be politically represented, 'y ningún ciudadano puede ser privado de esa prerogativa sin justa causa' (Echeverria 1972: 260). The *Manual* states that to be a citizen a person has to be twenty years old and literate; what it does not state is that a person also has to be a man. It is inferred, but not made explicit, that women's debarment from political rights precludes them from citizenship. There is some attempt at justification, though again implicit. Echeverría stresses the existence of natural inequalities and that although all men are equal before the law (as written in the constitution), some men, the virtuous and talented, are naturally better than others. Other natural inequalities are 'origen' and education. 'Origin' here means born in the countryside 'el habitante de la campaña'; the non-urban populace is 'condenada por su ignorancia a una inferioridad de condición indigna de su rango soberano' (Echeverria 1972: 261). Women form part of the rural population, of course, but there is no suggestion that urban-born women are superior to country women. Inequalities are naturalised scientifically: in the natural world the 'astros subalternos' circle around the 'astros reguladores'; large masses of matter dominate smaller masses; in the animal world strong, fierce animals (such as the lion) rule over inferior species; and among rational creatures the centre is dominated by 'el hombre y solamente el hombre, comprendiéndolo todo sometiendo a la ley de su inteligencia o de su fuerza todas las cosas creadas y descollando, como rey, en medio del Universo' (Echeverria 1972: 262). As in the *Dogma*, man (the King of the Universe) is made in the image of God. There is no place for woman in this universal hom(m)osexual hierarchy. Yet it is possible, reading between the lines, that Echeverría might refer elliptically to women, almost as an afterthought:

> El conjunto de pueblos o naciones que puebla la tierra es lo que constituye la Humanidad. La Humanidad es el género humano, cuyo padre celestial es Dios. En este sentido, todos los hombres, *o más bien todas las criaturas racionales*, son hermanos en Dios. (Echeverría 1972: 267, my emphasis)

The interpolated phrase 'or, rather, all rational creatures' is ambiguous. Does it mean 'all men, that is, all rational creatures', or 'all men (or rather, all rational creatures because women, the only other rational creatures on earth, must be included in the brotherhood of God)'? It is as if Echeverría cannot bring himself to write the word 'mujeres'. Women are discursively wiped from the plot. Yet there is a strong sense of disavowal in this text, the sense that the author knows full well that he is erasing half the Argentine and Uruguayan population. Their traces remain in the gaps between the lines, to be written into another future story, another book that was never begun.

Notes

1 John Lynch estimates that between 250 and 6,000 political executions took place during Rosas's 20-year regime. Two of the most notorious were the executions of the nineteen-year-old Camila O'Gorman and her priest lover. The couple had eloped and Camila was eight months pregnant (Lynch 2001: 116, 118).

2 *Relación de los cristianos salvados del cautiverio por la División Izquierda del Ejército expedicionario contra los bárbaros al mando del señor brigadier general D. Juan Manuel Rosas* (Chacabo: Imprenta del Estado 1835).

3 There is nothing to suggest that Brián is English as Mary Lousie Pratt suggests (Pratt 1992: 185). The name is Irish, referring to the eleventh-century warrior king, Brian Boru, an Irish national hero, and was possibly familiar to Echeverría due to a mania for all things Celtic in early nineteenth-century western Europe.

4 The title of the poem will be italicised to avoid confusion.

5 Rotker (2002: 90–91) suggests that María was a *fortinera* or *cuartelera*, a woman who accompanied the troops.

6 Operé's interesting article points to María as an androgynous figure (Operé 2003: 550) who assumes the masculinity of Brián. However, in my view the alleged 'barbarización de María' (552) is more than tempered by her Christian connotations and her representation of the power of love, both human and divine.

7 There is a reference earlier in the poem to another son who was killed.

8 There have been various studies of the narrator. See Alazraki 1995.

9 Not to be confused with the export livestock industry. The *saladeros*, who produced salted or jerk beef from the 1810s on, accounted for more than 80 per cent of River Plate exports by 1836 (Lynch 1987: 319–20, 324). The meat-canning industry began around the mid-century.

10 Halperín Donghi's reading of this ending is that the Unitarian represents an ideal and for this reason is not a convincing character (Halperín Donghi 1951: 115).

11 With reference to the slaughterhouses of Rio, Mary Karasch (1988: 267) explains that the dirtiest and most dangerous tasks, considered vile occupations, were given to women, slaves and Indians.

12 Bauzá (2000: 197) comments in a note that the 'achuradoras' are located on the 'plano narrativo' of the rats, stray dogs and scavenging birds.

13 Folger (1999) also refers to the 'abyección del otro'. Folger draws on Bakhtin's theorising of the carnivalesque to argue that the 'chusma' are deformed and grotesque and that the text itself disrupts the monological version of the narrator. Folger refers to the 'chusma' as anonymous, whereas I see it as gendered feminine. María Rosa Lojo (1994) also draws attention to the carnival aesthetic in the story and to the threat of hybridity.

14 The *Dogma* was not widely distributed but was read by Domingo F. Sarmiento in San Juan. Urquiza read the copy he was sent and realised he had the support of the exiles, which encouraged him to successfully challenge Rosas. See Echeverría 1999.

CHAPTER FIVE

Satirised Woman and Counter-Strategies

> Colonisation almost invariably implies ... discursive or political suppression of the heterogeneity of the subject(s) in question
>
> Chandra Talpade Mohanty 1988: 65

> [G]ender dynamics were, from the outset, fundamental to the securing and maintenance of the imperial enterprise
>
> McClintock 1995: 7

The final chapter of the first part of this book explores representations of the feminine in satire, one of the most successful literary genres in late colonial Spanish America, and further enquires into the relational complexities of gender (vis-à-vis class and race), as is evidenced so far in the work of Echeverría. It then goes on to suggest how women writers might resist.

Satire flourished in neoclassical Spain and the Americas between the sixteenth and nineteenth centuries, and has continued until today. As we have seen, it appears in Echeverría's writings and to some extent in Bolívar's. A principal structural device of satire is misogyny: Quevedo, 'master of grotesque female portraiture' (Johnson 1993: 130), provided a model of notoriously virulent representations of women for later writers. Satirists were keen to criticise the women of their societies, as well as other social sectors (primarily blacks, mestizos and indigenous), although their main concern was not women per se but society at large. Satire used as a political weapon aims to undermine discourses of power and authority by drawing attention to discursive strategies and incongruities. As Johnson has convincingly argued, colonial Spanish American satirical writings constitute a counter-discourse employed to contest the sacrosanct official image of the New World utopia, which was shaped and controlled by metropolitan Spain. Satirists pinpointed what they viewed as the appalling disparity between appearance and reality, myth and history. The effectiveness of their writing depended on the skilful use of literary techniques (irony, parody, understatement, hyperbole, punning and so on) and a competent public able to read between the lines and identify both the official version and the counter text.

Central to this agenda and literary discourse was the figure of woman as trope. If in the bucolic and Petrarchan traditions, which continued throughout the colonial period, woman signified ethereal beauty and harmony, in satirical writings woman denoted the obverse: the grotesque and monstrous. In colonial texts written by educated male creoles and visiting *peninsulares,* the figure of woman, functioning metaphorically (directly or indirectly) as image for the source of corruption and social decay, encapsulates the physical and moral dissolution of colonial society. Idealised femininities such as the matriarch, the aristocratic wife, the holy nun, the female warrior and the Indian maiden were consistently derided to delegitimate colonial courtly love and heroic frontier conventions (Johnson 1983: 107–109). Hybridity (of gender or race), the blurring of boundaries of caste and class integral to the carnivalesque, also undermined the social order. Satire became an effective means of subverting the authority of the Crown, its colonial representatives and institutions. During and after independence the practice continued, as we have seen. Depending on the political views of the satirist, the monstrous or ridiculed female figure might symbolise metropolitan rule (as in Bolívar's writings) or internecine political dissidence still needing to be resolved (for example, the lampooning of the Rosas women in Mármol's *Amalia* or Echeverría's distortion of black women in 'El Matadero'). In any event, satirists were unlikely to face reprisals from women. Although they were the subject of most satire, women rarely published satirical works (Sor Juana Inés de la Cruz was the great exception). Two potential counter-strategies that women might adopt are flagged up in this chapter: one is to write satire which does not single out women as figures of fun; the other is to provide a sympathetic counter-version of the object of satire's ridicule.

Colonial satire in Peru

The grotesque woman is not used in colonial satire merely as metonym (signifying reprobate women or all people) or even as metaphor (meaning the city, the patria, evil, corruption and so on) but as a strongly recurrent symbol of the threat of chaos, which needs to be contained. The trope extended to women of all castes and races, from workers, servants, and whores (black, white, mulatto, indigenous, mestiza) to ladies of the elite. In these writings, the objective was not only or even primarily women's improvement, but the reform of the colonial polity and society. Woman as satirical trope represents the unacceptable social order that needs to be disarticulated and exposed. The ridicule of women in satirical discourse suggests that women wielded substantial social and economic power, which was seen by the satirist to pose a threat to stability. In what follows, I will discuss representations of Lima women in the satirical writings of the 1790s.

A long tradition of satirical writing existed in Lima, from Mateo Rosas de Oquendo, Juan del Valle y Caviedes and Alonso Carrió de la Vandera in the early and mid-colonial periods, to Felipe Pardo (1806–68) and Joaquín Larriva (1780–1832) in the first half of the nineteenth century, and Ricardo Palma (1833–1919) in the early twentieth century.[1] Palma was influenced by Quevedo, but his *costumbrista* pieces, which mock women in hyberbolic encomium and suggestive allusion, are gentle and light-hearted compared to the caustic earlier works. In *Poesías varias y jocosas* by Caviedes, published in the late seventeenth century, Lima's prostitutes are inscribed as a symptom of social disease (the spread of syphilis) and (as in Bello's 'Alocución') the commercialisation of love (Johnson 1993: 99). The Petrarchan idealisation of noble women is parodied and inverted, so that whores are referred to as 'damas' and so-called shepherdesses as ugly hags. Particularly grotesque and salacious is the poem 'A una dama que rodó del cerro de San Cristóbal', in which a prostitute's private parts (rotten fruit), are displayed as she rolls down the hill. The poem is full of coarse double entendres referring to farting, urinating, defecating and copulating:

Al caer mostró por donde
Suele el pepino amargar,
Que es por donde el melón huele
Y las damas hieden mal.
En tanto cielo mostró ... (Johnson 1993: 100)

The purpose of the poem is political; 'moral degradation is tied to the forfeiture of political power' (Johnson 1993: 101). Caviedes, born in Spain but brought up in Lima, was not well known until his poetry was published by the Sociedad de Amantes del País in the *Mercurio Peruano* in 1791, 1792.[2] No less shocking is his satirical portrait of a woman camp follower, 'Pintura de una fea buscona en metáfora de guerra', in which, as the poem's title indicates, the female body parts are employed metaphorically as the instruments of war. Parodies such as these undermine the view (as in Feijóo's *Defensa de las mujeres*) that American viragos, such as the feisty Amazons, were admirable due to their masculine courage and fighting spirit (Johnson 1983: 96–7).[3]

By the time Esteban Terralla y Landa (pseudonym Simón Ayanque) published in Madrid his infamous ballad *Lima por dentro y fuera* (1797), the City of Kings was already 'a prime target for satirists' (Johnson 1993: 126). Terralla was born in Spain and had resided in Peru for ten years before writing the poem. He was dissatisfied with Lima society and had caught syphilis. The poem is a guide to Lima women, addressed to the narrator's friend, whose patria is Mexico (Terralla y Landa 1798: 1). The narrator, a Spaniard who was fully acquainted with Lima's horrors, is astounded that his friend wishes to leave Mexico, 'del Orbe la maravilla', for Lima. He writes as a European to denounce the vices of the creoles 'de aquel continente' (Terralla y Landa 1798: v), although recognising that such foibles are found in Spain and all over the New and Old Worlds. Lima is symbolic of general human perversion. *Lima por dentro y fuera* subverts works such as Pedro Beralta Barnuevo's *Lima fundada,* which presented Spanish America as a paradise. It attacks an inflationary economy caused by people living beyond their means (Vidal 2004: 198–202). Yet although the narrator denounces most sectors of Lima society (not the government or public administration) his target is women. As the title announces, Lima women are emblematic of womanhood at large, the 'madamitas' of Peru,

Spain and elsewhere; the poem is to be used as a defence against the 'madamitas del nuevo cuño', the modern women of the day (Terralla y Landa 1798: iv).

Contemporary Lima women personify the moral and physical deterioration of the virtuous society of men. Hence the poem's insistence on filth, broken drains, mud, flies, sewage, rubbish tips, fleas and dogs. Terralla depicts Lima as a hell on earth, a place where social order has collapsed entirely and the world is truly turned upside down. As in Menippean serio-comic satire, a journey to Lima is a virtual trip to the underworld.[4] The colonial capital is a city of duplicity and affectation, dominated by women and the racially mixed (that is, not by white, elite men), who are motivated solely by material interests. The most harshly criticised sector of society is mulatto women and prostitutes who, as the agents of social decay, are blamed for the exploitation of men and of the Americas. The text parodies the courtly love idealisation of women and presents them as artificially created monsters of sin:

Verás muchos albayaldes (white lead)
Dientes postizos y pelos
Cejas de aciete de moscas
Y un tizne de caldero,
Pantorillas de algodón,
De la misma especie pechos,
Los zapatos embutidos
Y los carnillos rellenos (Terralla y Landa 1798: 113)

As Johnson comments, 'feature by feature the poet dissects his victim and reassembles her in random fashion with artificial substitutions' (Johnson 1993: 131). Certainly the reader's reaction to these rag dolls is one of horror and disgust. But the text also berates the deformation of an allegedly ideal colonial establishment. The object of scorn is not colonial government, but the society and customs of creoles (in effect, creole women), who have perverted the social order to this extent. The two most obvious signs of depravity in Lima society/women are grasping materialism (thieving, commercialisation of sex) and miscegenation. Hybridity, or 'mixtura' of races and castes, to which the poem repeatedly refers, has dissolved the social fabric and undermined the colonial enterprise:

Que ves muchas cocineras,
Muchas negras, muchos negros,
Muchas indias recauderas,
Muchas vacas y carneros.
Que ves a muchas mulatas
Destinadas al comercio,
Las unas al de la carne,
Las otras al de lo mesmo.
Que ves indias pescadoras
Pescando mucho dinero,

Pues a veces pescan más
Que la pesca que traxeron. (Terralla y Landa 1798: 10–11)

The mulatto woman's hybrid body, circulating disguised and unchecked, breaks down the political economy from within. The mulatto women purchase the most expensive stockings on credit, ruining the *peninsular* shopkeepers, 'con que las viene a pagar / El comerciante europeo' (Terralla y Landa 1798: 32), who are forced to bear insults from slaves. But outer apparel cannot disguise the inherent race or status of the mulatto woman/prostitute who is reified as furniture or social mobility ('mueble', signifying movement):

De una que fue de continuo
Mueble inútil, floxo cuerpo,
Parte por no haber crianza,
Y parte por tanto negro.
Pues no teniendo destino
Las niñas de fundamento,
Pierden por necesidad
Aun de la vergüenza el velo.
...
Causa de la perdición
De aquel dilatado imperio,
En el qual las densas nubes
Llueven natales de prietos.
Y si esta casta faltara,
O fuera en tanto exceso,
No hubiera tanta miseria
Ni tan escaso comercio.

No hubiera tercera tanta,
No hubiera tal mezcla en ellos,
No se viera tal desgarro
Ni tan vil atrevimiento.
Hubiera más humildad
Más sanos procedimientos (Terralla y Landa 1798: 33–34)

Mulatos, born of *mulatas*, are the source of recividist degeneracy. The breakdown of the caste system is due to dissemblance and misrepresentation. All *limeños* are duplicitous, women in particular. Fine clothes and manners are not a sign of honour, but a device for beguilement and trickery. The motivation is materialism. This is an essential attribute of women, irrespective of their age and caste:

Que te pones a observar,
Que ves bellísimos cuerpos
Con las almas de leones
Y las pieles de cordero.
Que son ángeles con uñas (Terralla y Landa 1798: 28)

Verás con muy ricos trages
Los de baixo nacimiento,
Sin distinción de personas,
De estado, de edad, de sexo.
Verás una mujer blanca
A quien enamora un negro,
Y un blanco que una negra
Tiene embebido su afecto.
Verás un título grande,
Y al más alto caballero,
Poner en una mulata
Su particular esmero. (Terralla y Landa 1798: 55)

Recklessly extravagant women squander their husbands' and fathers' wealth. High-class *tapadas*, pulled in carriages by slaves, are mocked by punning on 'cara', meaning face/expensive/lacking in (money) and cheeky:

Jamás las verás las caras
A las caras que van dentro
Porque son caras muy caras
Con mil encarecimientos (Terralla y Landa 1798: 20)

Young girls marry old men for their wealth, and old women marry 'mozos / Porque les den alimentos'. Old women, 'de siglo y medio', wear 'barrigas postizas' to make them look pregnant and younger; to avoid poverty in later life, due to their own improvidence, they strive to look young, 'ninguna quiere ser vieja / por no ver su menosprecio'. In short 'a muger alguna quieras / por que te pondrán en riesgo' (Terralla y Landa 1798: 112, 160, 157).

Finally, the analogy between women and government/public administration and the need for control is made explicit in the following lines:

Verás un gran predominio
En el femenino sexo
Porque todo lo gobiernan
Sin que ellas tengan gobierno
...
Verás que ninguna de ellas
Se ocupó en más ministerio
Que en la visita, en la calle,
Y en un continuo bureo (Terralla y Landa 1798: 74)

Creole women of all races and castes are caricatured to such an extent that they meld into homogeneous perfidious womanhood. Lima woman symbolises social and economic disorder, and mixed-race woman social degradation. The perspective is masculinist, racist and Eurocentric; the vices of colonial society are feminised, aberrant and monstrous. This hegemonic view entails the suppression of heterogeneity. As elsewhere in Spanish America, notably slave-holding Cuba and Brazil, the female hybrid body stands for disruption and contamination (Martínez-Alier 1974).

The Lima colonial press

A less embittered satire is found in the late eighteenth-century Lima press, which was replete with articles, editorials and poems about women. The majority of the items about women are not satirical and focus on the education and health of women and their children. Some articles are signed by or attributed to Peruvian authors; others are lifted from books and newspapers published in Spain. In addition, the press published numerous thematically varied stories and anecdotes that centre on women. Some of these are anonymous, while others are pseudonymous, signed by men or, apparently and less frequently, women. A signature means little, since editors often included their own writings under a fictitious woman's name in order to attract women readers or to attribute what might be considered a ridiculous proposition to a woman's pen.[5]

In view of the problem of fixing the authorship of these texts, this chapter, following Iser (1976), will also consider the reader and the rhetorical strategies the texts put into operation to appeal to a particular reader and elicit response. Who is the implied reader of these publications? What kind of reader is constructed by the text, and what kind of dialogue does the text initiate with the reader? How does the reader participate in textual interpretation? An indication of the attractiveness of the periodical press, its circulation and readership in 1790s Lima is provided in the 'Prospectus' of the short-lived weekly, *Semanario Crítico* (June 5 to September 18 1791), founded by Spanish-born Fray José Antonio Olavarrieta. This was the first Lima periodical publication specifically oriented towards women (Rosas Lauro 1999b: 145):

> un papel periódico vuela con facilidad desde la prensa a manos de una madama, de un negociante, de un artesano: el poco valor de su costo, los estrechos límites de sus hojas, y la brevedad con que se desprende de la variedad hermosa de sus materias, le hacen digno objeto de las atenciones de muchos, y aun de la curiosidad de todas aquellas personas imposibilitadas por su oficio, profesión, ocupaciones falta de medios y principios, a emprender la lectura de libros, y volúmenes cuya vista sola las horroriza y aturde. Finalmente un papel periódico se lee con facilidad en un sarao, en un almacén, en una tienda, en un paseo, en una tertulia, en un café y en un pórtico, sin detrimento de las honestas labores en que suele ocuparse el bello sexo, sin interrumpir el despacho de los negocios públicos, sin contravenir a la necesidad del placer y del recreo, sin temor de molestar a sus amigos, sin acalorar la cabeza, agriar el estómago, ni faltar al respeto de los santuarios. Todos hallan en su lectura un pasto racional proporcionado a su talento, medios y ocupaciones, con que insensiblemente y sin experimentar trabajo alguno, resultan ilustrados. (*Semanario Crítico*: 1–2)

The *Semanario Crítico*, which explicitly rejected satire (*SC*: 3), was dedicated to the dissemination of information and opinion on children's education, 'la educación física, moral y político de los hijos', from birth until they enter 'la luz pública' (*SC*: 4) (Dunbar 1943). Unlike its chief competitor, the *Mercurio Peruano* (1790–95), the *Semanario*'s target readership was not 'sabios maestros y eminentes doctores' (*SC*: 8), but women, particularly mothers, whose alleged ignorance with respect to children's welfare and education needed to be corrected. Important, too, were critical reviews of the theatre and public entertainment in Lima. Less significant was news about fashion, dances and *tertulias*. The style was to be plain and everyone – men and women – was invited to contribute with letters, news or criticism of Olavarrieta's views (Prospectus, *SC*: 1–9) (see Chapter 7).

The more successful and intellectual *El Mercurio Peruano*, subtitled *de historia, literatura y noticias públicas*, was the official organ of the Sociedad Académica de Amantes del País, Lima, founded by José Rossi y Rubí and José María Egaña in 1790 and formalised in 1792. The motives for founding a newspaper were patriotic; the aim was to disseminate Enlightenment thought in the Viceroyalty. The Society met in the library of the University of San Marcos (from which women were barred; but previously, when it had existed as the 'Filarmónica', women were listed among its members) (Clément 1997: 21–23; 81). According to Jean-Pierre Clément, who takes his data from *El Mercurio Peruano*, the readers of the Lima press at the time (the *Mercurio Peruano* and the *Diario de Lima*) were the local elite of *letrados* and the women in their social circle.

The population of Lima in 1790 was 52,000, among whom 19,000 were 'active' (employed) (64 per cent of the population were 'inactive'). One-third of the Lima subscribers to the *Mercurio Peruano* also subscribed to the *Diario de Perú* (Clément 1997: 69). The *Mercurio Peruano* had some 517 registered subscribers and about 4,000 readers (Clément 1997: 65, 67), over half of whom resided in Lima. One of every two white Lima men read the newspaper.[6] The vast majority of readers were employees in public or financial administration, the professional middle classes (lawyers, journalists, doctors and so on), army officers, industrialists and ecclesiastics (Clément 1997: 73, 77). Most of the subscribers would have known each other and, as noted above, newspapers were passed around from hand to hand. The *Mercurio Peruano* was not cheap: each issue cost 2 reales, equivalent to 8 kilos of bread (Clément 1997: 47). The preferred subjects covered by the newspaper were geography (of Peru, mainly), history, medicine and practical information (Clément 1997: 95, 98), followed by sciences, economics, literature and education. Politics and religion did not feature large. The *Mercurio Peruano* published 655 items, 75 per cent written by known authors, though this decreased to just below 50 per cent towards the end of its life. After initial successes, the paper did not sell well towards the middle of the 1790s, hence its demise.

There were seven women subscribers or *mujeres ilustradas* belonging to the group classified by Clément as 'intellectuals' (1997: 77; Rosas Lauro 1999a:

408), that is, one in ten of this group. The famous *tertulias* of elite Lima women Isabel de Orbea, Josefa Portocarrero and Mariana de Queréjazu Concha, and the fact that San Martín awarded the Orden del Sol to more than 200 women patriots (see Chapter 6), indicates the importance of the intervention of Lima women in the social and political sphere (Clément 1997: 81). Indeed, two elite women, Isabel Orbea and the Condesa de Fuente González, were accused in 1790 of reading books proscribed by the Church (Rosas Lauro 1999a: 409).

Most likely, this public read the newspaper articles written by and about women, including the satirical writings, for entertainment and moral instruction. Some women readers may have taken offence, but reading the satire attentively shows that its purpose was not primarily to poke fun at women. This was political discourse with more subversive intentions. The satirical articles construct a reader who, if knowing and astute, can assume a double vision and a double reading. Such a reader will participate in the collective joke, while perceiving a subtext critical of the late colonial regime. Satire flourishes in conservative societies such as that of 1790s Peru, where there was a strong consensus regarding appropriate ethical and rational norms. It is taken for granted by the editors that the readers of the dominant creole elite will share this humorous view of the experiences of everyday life, or they might cancel their subscription. But although satire requires a homogeneous reading public that identifies with the author's point of view, in order for there to be laughter and a certain frisson, the consensus should not be so overwhelming as to result in absolute conformity. There must be an element of doubt, a space for contestation, the possibility of a counter-hegemonic discourse. The author of satire belongs to a particular society and often subscribes to its mores, yet to ridicule its failings he or she needs to be distanced from it. With respect to the articles studied below, there are at least two possible interpretations of each, depending on the reading strategy adopted. The targets of criticism are twofold: simple-minded women and the colonial administration. Both need to be controlled, dominated and governed, and neither deserves respect.

The theme of women's usefulness to society and their moral reform was important in the *Mercurio Peruano*, as Clément amply demonstrates (1997, 1: 167–75). Lima women, particularly those of the elite and emerging bourgeoisie, were criticised, as in earlier satire, for their excesses, their independence (many were legally separated from their husbands and lived apart;[7] adultery was common), their abandonment of their infants to nursemaids and slaves; and their lack of useful skills such as sewing and spinning. They were blamed above all for the bankruptcy of their husbands and fathers. The enlightened model woman should be a good wife, mother and housekeeper and confined to the home. Indigent women who relied on charity should find employment. Uncontrolled women (along with the poor and the young) undermined enlightened order and stability (Clément 1997, 1: 167). Items published on this topic include a reader's satirical account of his wife's coquettishness (*MP*, 1: 112) in which he notes her '25 modos de reír y más de 40 de mirar' (Clément 1997, 1: 169); José Rossi y Rubí's poem 'Descripción del faldellín de las *limeñas*' (*MP*

March 6 1791, I: 173–75; Clément 1997, II, 73–74), which apparently condones this costume as quintessentially Peruvian but laments its exorbitant cost; a 'Carta ... sobre los gastos de una tapada' (*MP*, I: 111–14), in which a concerned husband outlines his household accounts to demonstrate his wife's profligacy; and a 'Sueño alegórico' by J.R. Hiponóbates, in which a powdered woman represents social and moral decay (*MP* April 10 1791, I: 271–72). The economics of the problem were not to be taken lightly. The price of a *faldellín*, according to Rossi y Rubí, was 350 pesos, the equivalent of almost half the annual salary of a doctor, or the cost of 350 kilos of meat; each flower in a corsage could cost 25 pesos (Clément 1997, I: 169, 170, n. 16, n. 17). In the accounts outlined in the 'Carta', an annual income of 2,000 pesos was spent as follows: 450 pesos on house rental; 1,000 pesos on food and shoes (women needed to buy a pair, made out of sheepskin, every other day); 600 pesos on the wife's personal purchases (*'gastos menores'*); total 2,050 pesos, discounting doctors' fees (for the wife), fashion (four *faldellines* in summer, two in winter), furniture, crockery, household linen, carriages and coaches (Clément 1997, I: 171).

The article '*Amas de Leche*. Segunda carta de Filómates sobre la educación', (*MP* January 27 1791, I: 59–64), written by Eustaqio Filómates (possibly Demetrio Guasque), is a letter to the editor of the *Mercurio Peruano* allegedly sent in by a henpecked husband. He complains that his household has been taken over by the black nursemaid, María, who wields total power over his servants, young daughter (who calls her 'mi mamá'), wife and tyrannical mother-in-law, to the extent that he is required to intercede on behalf of a relative of María's friend, who is arrested for thieving. A coda written by the editor points out that this problem is not confined to Lima, but is endemic across the Americas (Clément 1997, II: 43–46). The situation of a distinguished paterfamilias dominated by a black female slave is presented as humorously absurd, yet perceived as a serious social problem, and recalls Terralla's lines: 'que los negros son los amos / y los blancos son los negros / y que habrá de llegar día / que sean esclavos aquéllos' (Terralla y Landa 1798: 42).

'Sueño alegórico', modelled on Quevedo's *Sueños*, typical of colonial Menippean satire, recounts the reader's opium-induced dream after having perused the significantly entitled *Mercurio Peruano* article 'Apólogo histórico sobre la corrupción de las colonias romanas de Africa'. In the dream-parable the shipwrecked reader is washed up on a utopian desert island that resembles Peru, and is told by an old man named 'Verdadero Mérito', who resembles the 'viejos Godos' (Spanish) of former times that this is the land of the Astrea, goddess of justice and virtue, who has made it her home after fleeing from the wicked world of lies. A beautiful nymph descends from the skies. It is Eugenia (the well-born) who wants her fame as the friendliest of women to be confirmed by the stranger. The nymph, with dark hair, dark eyes and the whitest skin, resembles a human female, a Peruvian woman. Her arms and hands are beautiful, but the rest of her body is kept under wraps. The dreamer is smitten, but the old man tells him to pay attention to her skin. It is covered by a coat of white lead, a fashion among Eugenia's 'compatriotas', which ruins their natural beauty and gives them bad teeth and stinking breath. Her hands might be aesthetically fine, but they are morally defective as they show no sign of honourable work. Eugenia is too proud to stitch a sock and has no idea how to hem a collar. The stains on her fingertips show that she uses her fingers to eat, instead of a fork. Where is this awful creature from? asks the dreamer. She hails from a place 2,000 leagues from Peking and 10 'millas itinerarias' from Madrid, that is, Lima (Clément 1997, II: 90–92) (for further discussion of women's contribution to the *Mercurio Peruano* see Chapter 6).

The *Diario de Lima*

Several satirical pieces of this type were also published in the *Diario de Lima* (1790–93), the other important periodical of the 1790s. Created by *peninsular* Francisco Antonio Cabello y Mesa (known as Jaime Bausate y Mesa), who took as his model the *Diario de Madrid*, it lasted for just over two years, but its circulation was widespread, reaching not only Lima but also Cuzco and the outlying provinces. The *Diario de Lima*, strong on local news rather than intellectual debate, published several poems, letters and short pieces signed, apparently, by anonymous women: for example, an extract of a letter written by 'una señorita' to 'una amiga suya' (May 21, 22, 23 1792), published in the *Diario de Madrid* (November 16 1791), six months earlier; a long article and two poems entitled 'Miscelánea joco-seria', by 'La Costurera' (March 17, 27 1791); a poem that 'prueba que es más reprehensible el afeite en los hombres que en las mujeres', signed by 'La limeña ofendida' (July 15 1791) and a poem by 'Una Madama de Cuzco' (April 23 1792), which will be discussed in more detail later.

The articles on women might be didactic or satirical. The former advise men and women on the correct behaviour prescribed for women from childhood to maturity. An article published on December 9 1790, 'Definición de lujo', deplores footmen who wear gold buckles and two pocket watches, cooks dressed in silk stockings and artesans in velvet and gold braid, although it recognises that 'muchas personas especialmente mujeres se ven precisadas a sostener este enemigo común [lujo] aunque sea contra su voluntad y fuerza'; if appearance no longer denotes status, then fashion is a useless luxury (quoted in Clément, 1997, I: 171). Another of many possible examples is the two-part article 'Cuanto importa la buena educación de las Doncellas' and 'Advertencias o notas sobre muchos defectos de las Doncellas, aun cuando sean muy niñas' (December 17, 24 1791), 'piezas' taken from the *Tratado de la Educación de las Doncellas* of the 'Grande y siempre Ilustre' Fénelon (1651–1715), Archbishop and Duke of Cambrai.[8] This article complains of the lack of education opportunities for women, not so that they will become scholars, because 'Es cierto, que se debe temer formar sabias ridículas', but in order to fortify them against their own natural weaknesses (December 17 1791: 2). In this way women will be able to properly fulfil 'sus deberes y obligaciones', that is, care for third parties – their husbands and children. According to the Archbishop, one of the most important lessons women should learn is to hold their tongue:

> Conviene así mismo habituarlas a que hagan estudio de hablar poco, y lo más preciso. El buen talento consiste en cercenar todo discurso inútil y en decir mucho en pocas palabras: sucediendo al contrario en casi todas las mujeres, que dicen poco, y hablan mucho. Seducidas por su amor propio toman la facilidad de hablar, y la vivacidad de la imaginación por el ingenio, y de aquí proviene que no saben elegir de sus pensamientos los mejores, ni menos colocar con orden y exactitud lo que quieren explicar.... no obstante cualquiera [sic] buen cultivo, no se puede esperar nada exquisito de mujer que habla mucho, y si no se la reduce a reflexionar las consecuencias, a examinar sus pensamientos, a manifestarlos de un modo exacto, y preciso, y saber callar cuando lo exige la ocasión ... Las mujeres no reflexionan o es muy poco, en el examen de si es o no es conveniente desear esta o aquella cosa, pero son industriosísimas para lograrla. (*Diario de Lima* December 24 1791: 2–3)

The imposition of censorship on women's speech was a recurrent topic and is used for more subversive political purposes elsewhere in the *Diario de Lima*. Evidently, European Catholic gender *doxa* were imported to Peru through the Spanish press, and the articles, which are signed, apparently, by women, usually ratify such ideas, confirming women's real or alleged complicity in their own subordination. A typical contribution is the following didactic poem, entitled 'Décimas hechas por una Madama de Cuzco', reproduced here in its entirety. 'Décimas' being the traditional mode of complaint, its anonymous author is not only well educated but also skilled at composing an ingenious gloss in the classical Spanish tradition:

> *Aprended flores de mí,*
> *Lo que va de ayer a hoy,*
> *Ayer, ni mi sombra fui,*
> *Hoy si maravilla soy.*
>
> Ayer con suma crueldad,
> Solo por jazmín del Campo,
> Todos tiraron al blanco,
> Contra toda inmunidad:
> O engañosa vanidad
> Del mundo, y su frenesí,
> Ya yo el desengaño vi,
> Tomen ejemplo las flores,
> Y sin jactar de primores,
> *Aprended flores de mí.*
>
> Hoy encendido Clavel,
> En el jardín de mi esposo,
> Retoñaré con reposo,
> Disciplinado por él:
> En tan diverso plantel,
> Sola yo la estéril soy,

Los deseos con que voy
Anegándome en mis llanto
Harán me arrepienta cuanto
Lo que va de ayer a hoy.

Emulada flor del día
Espiré ayer en su ocaso
Hoy en los rayos me abraso,
De quien solo es mi alegría:
Tú señor eres mi guía,
Y tan sólo sé de mí
Que fui un pálido alelí,
Una marchitada flor,
Por que conozco Señor
Ayer ni mi sombra fui.

Ya no Catarina errante
En este Centro prolijo
Acercará a punto fijo
A dar muestras tan constantes
Que mi corazón amante
Te promete desde hoy
No estar en mí, pues estoy
Tan toda entregada a vos
Que sólo para mi Dios
Hoy si maravilla soy.

(*Diario de Lima* April 23 1792: 1–3)

Here a woman rejects human eros, which has brought her only sadness and disappointment, for agape, divine love. The poem reaffirms woman's resignation and conformity. The woman, like flowers, passes from a state of pure innocence (the white jasmine) to a sexual subject within the bounds of marriage (the flaming carnation), but she cannot fulfil her purpose in life because she is 'estéril' and fails to reproduce, the only role conceded to her. Like a gillyflower that has lost its bloom, she fades in maturity until finally she encounters peace in religion. Accosted by men when a virgin, rejected as a wife, she represents herself as a victim who takes refuge in the constancy of God's love.

Quite different are the humorous and satirical texts that focus on women. Of these there are many. Satire and burlesque predominate to such an extent that the mere mention of women in the public sphere seems intended to create laughter. The world of women, their everyday lives, as they are (not as they should be) cannot be taken seriously. Women are objects of constant fun and ridicule. For example, the title page of the issue published on December 16 1791 features two poems by the Spanish sixteenth-century poet Francisco de la Torre, whose preferred theme was, paradoxically, platonic love. The poems, 'piezas exquisitas' according to the editor, were taken from the second volume of de la Torre's *Agudezas*, published in Madrid. The first is 'Paralelo entre mujeres y niños':

> Lea de la Escritura tu cuidado
> El profundo volumen más sagrado,
> Y en él advertirá tu vista atenta,
> Que de Niño y Mujer no se hace cuenta
> Quedan Niño y Mujer nunca admitidos
> De los civiles cargos excluidos,
> Para las armas, es aun más llano,
> Que ni esta tiene aliento, ni aquél mano
> Suelen Niño y Mujer, unos en todo,
> Largas faldas vestir de un mismo modo,
> Y en aspecto lampiño
> Son semejantes la Mujer y Niño.
> Fácil el niño llora, y otro tanto
> Fácil, y pronta es la Mujer al llanto,
> Y suelen engañarles sin malicias
> A la Mujer y al Niño las caricias …
>
> (*Diario de Lima* December 16 1791)

The second, 'Semejanzas y diferencias entre las mujeres y los niños', continues in the same style: 'Las Mujeres y los Niños / Tienen una condición, / Pues se acallan con un don, / Más que con treinta cariños …' (December 16 1791: 1–3). To infantalise women and subordinate them to the authority of the paterfamilias as if they were minors (especially married women, whose legal status largely subjected them to the authority of their husbands), was a discursive strategy that legitimated a patriarchal economic and political order. So as not to offend his women readers, however, the editor adds a note in which he refers to de la Torre as a man 'bien complexionado', whose verses should not be taken amiss by 'las señoras mujeres que atentas a su obligación y asidas celosamente a la constitución y leyes de su sexo y estado cumplen con sus deberes'. Satirical literature, 'todos los fragmentos o pequeños poemas satíricos que haya escritos contra la mujer' should only be understood as criticism of 'la mujer mala', that is, women who 'en aquel o aquellos vicios reprehendidos adolecen contaminadas' (December 16 1791: 3). This commentary is of interest in that it identifies a hypothetical woman reader and, more importantly, inscribes women's duties and obligations in terms usually associated with political discourse (constitution, laws, state), but which here, in the context of women's 'sexo', align women (defined as their bodies) not with the government of the state but with the laws of nature and biology.

Women readers are confronted with this satirical, often misogynistic, onslaught at every turn of the page. Were they sufficiently magnanimous to laugh at themselves? Were they complicit in their own degradation? The response of women readers to such newspaper items may be gauged by their purported letters, poems or comments to the editor. Even if the replies were not written by women readers but by the editors themselves or other men, in order to encourage contention and thus circulation, the point is that a critical reaction to the consensus of burlesque (in which the editors are implicated and to which they actively contribute) was deemed not only acceptable but also anticipated. The aim was to goad women (or men mimicking women) to respond, to create a witty ongoing dialogue in the press. An example of a satirical reply signed by a woman (of which there are few) is the poem, again a series of 'décimas', signed by 'La limeña ofendida' in which she (or he?) mocks men who primp themselves as if they were women. While 'este afeite' might be 'propio de mi sexo', it is certainly not appropriate for men. Three strophes, in which a 'petimetre' who uses cosmetics is referred to as a 'mono sin talento', 'mono afeminado', and 'fingido narciso / de maricones modelo', are quoted below:

Aquel que al estilo nuevo
Con el afeite prolijo
Es su cabeza amasijo
De manteca, harina, y sebo:
Aquel infeliz mancebo
Del espejo y el cepillo
De continuo en el bolsillo,
A aquel mono sin talento,
Que sin verse en Regimiento
Sentó plaza de Blanquillo.

A aquel Mono afeminado
Que discurriendo que brilla
Anda siempre de puntilla
Con el pañuelo sahumado:
A aquel que en cualquier Estrado
Muestra femenino ser
Y por mejor parecer,
El vulgo lo desestima
Por querer tener encima
Más cintas que un mercader.

A aquel fingido Narciso
De maricones modelo
Que en redecilla de Velo
Encierra el pelo postizo;
A aquel a quien le es preciso
Seguir modas extranjeras
Y porque son las primeras
E imitar a otras naciones
Vestirse de unos calzones
Que parecen pistoleras
¿Si esto ya se llega a ver

En un mono afeminado
Llevando el cuerpo ambareado
Qué le queda a la mujer?
(*Diario de Lima* 15 July 1791: 2–3)

The poem continues in this vein, punning on the words 'mono' / 'mona' (monkey/pretty) and citing, ironically, women's 'fragilidad' as justification for such censure. To ridicule men is to attribute to them what were considered to be women's concerns (fashion, adornment, artifice) and to thus question men's masculinity 'a lo natural'. Educated society (men and women) sets the norms for acceptable masculinities. Effeminate men look like monkeys and fashion divests them of culture and civilisation, whereas fashion makes women pretty and lends them social status. Again, the blurring of the visible markers of social difference, this time of gender rather than race, is perceived as a social threat. In order to be recognised as men, *limeños* must avoid exposing themselves to the negative attributes associated with femininity; such negative feminine attributes must be contained and ascribed only to the female sex.

Women, however, were not always the prime target of satire in these articles. Writers might use this convention to disguise anti-colonial political discourse. This will be demonstrated with reference to two unsigned articles published in the *Diario de Lima*: 'El pedimento presentado por los maridos al tribunal de la moda los habitantes del Cantón de la miseria conyugal' (December 5 1790) and its second part, 'Sigue el pedimento presentado por los maridos al Tribunal de la moda' (December 16 1790) and 'A las mujeres habladoras. Del filósofo a la moda' (December 3 1792). They are the lead articles of their corresponding issues. The anonymous satirical writer employs wit and humour to ridicule the object of his attack: the women of his class, the educated elite. He criticises the conduct and customs of elite women, above all the way they speak and dress in public. They are ridiculed because they break the precepts of rational and virtuous social behaviour. The desired norm is that women should be barred from speaking in public and from dressing fashionably (according to foreign values), as such conduct is an irrational and imprudent aberration. Ultimately, women should not be allowed to take part in the symbolic economy of the public sphere by performing or speaking. It is clear that the articles interpellate readers (men and women) who share similar values and beliefs and therefore are able to laugh at the women of their class and/or themselves. The interlocutors specifically identified are heads of family (husbands, fathers), who have been impoverished by the excesses of spendthrift women (wives, sisters, daughters), and men who are exasperated by women's incessant nonsensical chatter.

'El pedimento presentado por los maridos al tribunal de la moda'

The remonstration against fashion is conceived in this article as a 'pedimento' or petition, and is inscribed in the language of litigation. It is couched in terms of bringing a lawsuit to court, with resonances of religious entreaty. The first paragraph is as follows:

> Alta y Poderosa Señora
>
> Por alta que sea tu dignidad y naturaleza, nos atrevemos a suplicarte con la mayor humildad te dignes mirar con compasión a este desgraciado país en que gimen los pobres maridos bajo del yugo más riguroso de un dominio que no conocemos, pero que sin duda es cosa de alta consideración, y que no sin alguna razón suponemos será alguna divinidad tan oculta como poderosa, pues no podemos persuadirnos de que este mundo tan refinado, tan culto, y tan ilustrado, se deje gobernar por un ente imaginario o por el simple móvil de la mera imitación.
>
> No, tu eres, cruel soberana la que por una influencia muda, pero irresistible gobiernas las cabezas de aquí abajo, y uno de aquellos entes superiores al que nuestros poetas sujetan el destino de los hombres. (*Diario de Lima* December 5 1790: 1–2)

The implied author/litigant/supplicant's address to fashion, 'alta y poderosa señora', mimics hegemonic viceregal discourses: those of the state and the Church. The author represents himself as a victim who dares to ask 'con la mayor humildad' a 'cruel soberana' who 'irresistible gobiernas las cabezas de aquí abajo', referring both to her subjects' heads and the ladies' hats. The country is 'desgraciado' and the 'maridos', the citizens, 'gimen' under the 'yugo más riguroso'. As is obvious, the text denounces the despotism of the Spanish Crown as much as the tyranny of fashion. It was published a year after the French Revolution, and no doubt would have been censored if it were not for the fact that a 'soberano', Carlos IV, reigned at the time. Floridablanca did not obtain the royal decree that censored all non-official newspapers until February 1791 (Clément 1979: 12). Godoy did not replace the Conde de Aranda as Prime Minister until 1792, although by that time his alleged intimate relationship with Queen María Luisa was well known and respect for the monarchy at a low ebb. An intelligent reader, trained in the skills of reading between the lines, would immediately recognise the double discourse identifying the oppression of fashion with that of the Crown. Fashion functions as a rhetorical figure, a euphemistic substitute for the monarchy: both are an expensive, superfluous luxury. The comparison that equates fashion (a frivolity) and the Crown (which should demand respect) devalues the latter and elevates the former; the monarchy is ridiculed while fashion, women's self-representation in public, acquires social and economic significance.

The author goes on to compare the 'señora' (fashion) with the 'Parcas' (Fates Parcae), fate, death (and, by analogy, absolutism), in that 'tus voluntades son tan despóticas e ilimitadas' (December 5 1790: 2). But he then corrects himself. The good lady cannot belong to the family of fates because her conduct is not constant and 'invariable', but rather undergoes 'continuas y eternas transformaciones con que diviertas al Universo', an allusion perhaps to the famous Bourbon reforms introduced by Carlos III, much resented by the creole elite. He reserves his most biting comment for the last lines of the article: the 'señora' cannot belong to the family of 'Parcas' because these at least cut thread and spin whereas the good lady is 'enemiga jurada de todo trabajo de su sexo' (December 5 1790: 2). Women, fashion and the monarchy are equally lazy and unproductive.

The second part of this article, entitled, 'Sigue el pedimento ...', published eleven days later, continues similarly. As a result of the señora's regime, the good families of the country are ruined and face 'bancarrotas todos los días' (December 16 1790: 1). If there are no reforms, 'tus Estados serán otros tantos desiertos y tus vasallos serán inválidos', since everyone is in debt. What the author/litigant demands is some kind of order or system imposed on rules and regulations that are not only 'variables' but also 'contradictorias'. A jurist, another 'Triboniano'[9], should be appointed to implement these reforms: 'recurrimos a tu tribunal a fin de que moderes tus leyes, y disminuyas el número de reglamentos que inundan nuestra provincia' (December 16 1790: 2). Of course, the author is not referring directly to the code of laws governing the Viceroyalty but to the 'Código de modas', nevertheless, the astute reader would have no problem interpreting the subtext here: the demand for nothing less than a new colonial code of laws. Alluding perhaps to the famous codification of Alfonso X, the author appeals to the glorious history of such reforms recorded in the 'Anales de tu reino' and compares the situation in Peru unfavourably with that of the Turks, Tartars and Lapps; if he and other 'maridos' are worth less than such barbarians, in that they are not governed by good and stable laws, at least some effort should be made not to introduce any new rules for at least three years. This way, each 'trienio' would be celebrated in the same way that the Olympics were celebrated every five years in Greece. He asks that a 'gabinete' be created, filled 'de sombreros, de pelucas, de vestidos' so that order will be brought to fashion (December 16 1790: 2–3). The subtext refers not only to cabinet-furniture but to cabinet-ministries of government, which should control the proliferation of edicts. If this were to happen, writes the author, it would not be necessary to 'ceder' to the 'antiguos Mexicanos que cuentan los siglos y los años por medio de nudos llenos de sutileza y de misterio'. Reform is thus inscribed in terms of the civilisation of classical antiquity (Greece not Mexico). Fashion, rapid and constant innovation, here associated with thread, signifies the failure to control time (chronology), knowledge (cf. the 'misterio de los nudos'), or order. Reform and the codification of laws make for rational, regulated society; the contrary leads to chaos. The text makes clear that fashion is above all an economic issue. If there were no fashion, what would become of the artisans, shopkeepers and wigmakers who prosper from the husbands? The solution proposed by the author favours commercial expansion; the artesans should emigrate to Japan, China, or any other place where 'abrirán un campo inmenso a su industria y destreza' (December 16 1790: 3). In the name of civilisation, therefore, the economy, society and change must be controlled; reform should be introduced calmly and rationally, and the sign of this control is men's effective government of women.

The article attacks fashion because, according to the author, it damages the country's economy. He criticises the expenditure (by women) of valuable economic resources (produced and administered by men) on commodities (cloth, shoes, wigs) that are often imported; these purchases are considered unnecessary by men and bring them to bankruptcy. Women are thus made responsible for the indebtedness of their husbands and fathers, in short, of the country (see Earle 2001). The author presents fashion as a 'código', and so it is. Fashion is a complex of rules and regulations regarding good taste and public appearance. It was precisely for this reason that elite women considered it so important, as their appearance indicated their social status. Women performed and represented their social rank with their bodies and were accordingly judged by others. In this sense, fashion was used as a code indicating a woman's wealth, and therefore that of her husband and family, and also demonstrated her knowledge of the latest novelties, which usually came from abroad. The target of criticism is women's special knowledge, behaviour and power, especially their economic clout, which threaten patriarchal authority and control. The defensive response of the men of the hegemonic elite is to ridicule matters of which they have little knowledge or understanding. Women are disparaged and fashion is presented as an effeminate and frivolous concern.

But, as has been stated, the prime objective is not to lampoon women. In fact, such criticism merely disguises a much more dangerous and subversive attack. The aim of the text is to raise questions about the 'tiranía' and bad government of the Crown. In this sense, woman functions as a rhetorical figure symbolising what women never possessed: absolute power; while uncontrolled fashion represents the outcome of what was not introduced: deep-seated, lasting reforms that favoured the local economy. The 'querella de las mujeres' is employed as a rhetorical strategy for purposes that were more radically political than the trivial issue of women's social role.

'A las mujeres habladoras. Del filósofo a la moda'

Without entering into as much detail, it soon becomes apparent that 'A las mujeres habladoras. Del filósofo a la moda' employs a similar discursive strategy. This article satirises talkative women and at the same time attacks the oratory and power of the colonial judiciary. It begins with a Latin quotation: *Nunquam gratiose loqui permittunt* (they never permit gracious speaking), which women readers, untrained in Latin, were not likely to understand. It continues:

> Algunos escritores, antiguos, nos refieren, que una mujer llamada (si no me engaño) Aspacia, enseñó la elocuencia a Sócrates. Confieso, ingenuamente, que yo he mirado siempre este arte, como el más propio para las mujeres y me parece que las Universidades deberían admitirlas a las Cátedras de la Retórica con exclusión de los hombres. (*Diario de Lima*, December 3 1792: 1)

Despite the reference to Aspasia de Miteo, the woman companion of Pericles who was recognised for her intelligence, the author devalues women and oratory by juxtaposing them with the absurd proposition in the second sentence. As is well known, oratory was considered a privileged art in classical antiquity, to the extent that higher education consisted almost entirely of lessons in rhetoric. The exaggerated reductio ad absurdum, that only women should be allowed into universities, to conceive of women in terms of formal higher education, puts paid to the very idea of women's higher education. There are 'grandes varones', the article continues, who are able to speak for several hours on a particular subject but the 'damas' deserve greater honour, as they know how to 'perorar días enteros, sobre nada' (December 3 1790: 2). An example is given of a woman who spoke for hours on the subject of a shirt seam. This type of exaggerated, ironic eulogy devalues not only women's public speaking but also their skills and knowledge, and condemns them to passive silence. But, as in the previous article, the target of satire is not primarily women. By comparing women with court clerks, notaries public and solicitors, and suggesting that women would resolve court cases more rapidly and effectively because they know how to always win an argument, the author ridicules the judiciary. Women, with the skill to move the hardened hearts of judges, would improve the eloquence of the forum; women would immediately notice the 'estudiados descuidos' of clerks who deliberately prejudice the poor (December 3 1790: 2). From this it is easy to infer the lack of debate in the courtroom, the unprofessional behaviour of judges, and the corruption and bribery of clerks and solicitors. The association of women and oratory raises the status of the former and discredits that of the latter.

The text then changes tack, perhaps because the subject of corruption in the courtroom was considered to be too risky to pursue. But it does not end without a few jibes against the Church. The author refers to a woman who bored her 'contertulianos' with her lengthy criticism of the Easter liturgy and the '"abuso" del rezo en idioma latino' and laments that her husband did not arrive until ten o'clock to take her home. He adds, however, 'Cuánto me hubiera alegrado oír sus razones, y lo que aducían contra un uso que la Iglesia instituyó cuando ni había más lengua vulgar que la latina' (December 3 1790: 3). The pun on the word 'vulgar' associates women, Latin, the Vulgate and the Church with the vulgar tongues (the Romance languages), common vulgarity and its offence on good taste, the inanities of women's speech and the coarse language and vulgarisms of the uneducated. Both women and the Church are debased.

The article presents a typology of women 'que entienden la oratoria', who are divided into four groups: 'las declamadoras', who manipulate the emotions; 'las murmuradoras', who employ imaginative and violent invective; 'las parleras', who slip from the sublime to the ridiculous; and 'las presumidas', who talk non-stop with a profusion of exaggerated gestures, thus demonstrating their 'particular afición a aquella parte de la oratoria que se llama acción' (December 3 1790: 2–3). Satire such as this mocks everything it apparently praises and ridicules the values and opinions attributed to women. In his description of the 'parleras', the author is indignant that such women should annoy 'una tertulia de sujetos distinguidos' (that is, men) with their chatter about the delights of a baby son who cannot even speak yet or, it is inferred, reason like an adult. He gives a fictitious example of a 'murmuradora', a sixty-year-old woman who spoke for six months on the subject of a wedding that was delayed for a week; the lady spoke in favour and against the bride and groom and, after having criticised them, visited them to offer her congratulations (December 3 1790: 2). The result is not to present her as skilled in oratory, that is, the art of persuasion irrespective of the truth; she is presented as a frivolous woman without principles or an opinion of her own: 'la censura y aprobación de semejantes mujeres no sirve más que para llenar el vació de la conversaciones' (December 3 1790: 3). Women's speech is inscribed as noise that fills the gaps of serious conversation between men. According to these articles, the world to which women were confined, their experiences, knowledge and skills – weddings, children, love relationships, dress codes, sewing – is valueless. Oratory is the art of speaking in public, whereas these feminine topics of conversation should be restricted to the private domestic world. Oratory is also a practical skill, a performance that relies for its effectiveness on theatricality. As can be seen in the satire against the 'parleras', women's gestures during a speech performance are belittled and ridiculed. And yet, as mentioned above, women indicated their social status by the theatrical performance of their bodies draped in the latest fashion. These articles discredit the behaviour and comportment of women, which women were nevertheless obliged to assume, and poke fun at any indication of women's attempted agency or subjectivity.

Derision is, however, a symptom of fear. As Claudia Rosas Lauro argues, the press represents woman as 'un ser peligroso en esencia, que era necesario contener' (Rosas Lauro 1999b: 144). Colonial patricentric society is afraid of women's power in the economic sphere and their capacity as consumers, and of women's knowledge, not only with respect to the bearing and raising of children, but also in connection with their privileged position of the bearers of secrets. Women knew all about the intimate lives of their husbands, fathers, brothers – an intimate familiarity that on no account should transcend the private sphere. Public indiscretions, accidental or deliberate, could have serious consequences. For this reason, the recourse of the dominant sex is to discredit women's oral communication in the public sphere in its entirety, especially with men who are not members of the family: because women 'no ignoran lo que pasa en el barrio, saben los chismes de la vecindad, rabian por tener noticias; y todo con el solo fin de hablar' (December 3 1790: 3). The press, in this sense, acts as an instrument of hegemonic control.

These two articles establish equivalences between woman as trope and the colonial regime. The implied reader is the educated male creole, who feels threatened by the power of the colonial judiciary and by a consumer economy. His objective is liberation from the domination of the Crown, to which he is subjected, and at the same time to subject the rest of society, including the women of his social sector, to his power. The satirical author again employs the subgenre of the 'querella de las mujeres', an innocuous debate when all is said and done, for the more dangerous purposes of subverting colonial government.[10] Women do not enter this debate other than metaphorically, as symbols of the target of scorn.

Woman continues to figure as social corruption in the less scathing and injurious modes of satire that continued through the nineteenth century in the light-hearted articles of manners, which are often called *costumbrismo* and include Ricardo Palma's *tradiciones.* This was a continental phenomenon. The tastefully entertaining pieces written by one of Venezuela's most popular creole *costumbristas,* Daniel Mendoza (1823–67) and published from the mid-1840s ('Los muchachos a la moda', 'Las niñas', 'Gran Sarao o las niñas de la moda') are a case in point. In 'Gran Sarao', the frivolous young girl, Pepita[11], symbolises weak republican government in Venezuela. She dances with a succession of partners for no apparent reason, tires immediately of them all, and breaks her promises to the (wiser, mature) male narrator. She is lazy, useless (cannot sew or spin), badly educated (in singing, dancing, drawing, a smattering of French) and without a purpose in life. Dressed up to impress, she is the personification of fickleness and inconsequentiality, 'Venía toda recargada de lazos, de bouquets, de ...¡Qué aglomeración de cosas! ¡Qué de superposiciones! Era una viva metáfora' (Mendoza 1964: 126). The political allusions are explicit:

> en materia de amores Pepita era enteramente democrática ... aborrecía de muerte a cuanto oliese a monarquía o gobierno de uno solo ... Entusiasta por las repúblicas de amores, le sentaban todos los apodos de nuestro gobierno: su tierno corazón era popular, representativo y alternativo ¡Lástima no fuera responsable!

Mendoza compares a complicated 'contradanza', which causes chaos on the dance floor, to the lack of direction and strong government in Venezuela:

> Una contradanza es la fiel expresión de nuestra república. Cada cual aspira a dirigirla ... el desorden cundió de arriba abajo; opresiones a un lado, tirones a otro, anárquicas tendencias por todas partes. (Mendoza 1964: 129)

Finally, in 'Los muchachos a la moda' he writes specifically, 'Escribir contra Páez es lo mismo que escribir contra las mujeres. Todos las pintan con los colores del infierno y, llegada la ocasión, todos les rinden homenaje' (Mendoza 1964: 114), a fitting summary of this particular technique.

Fact not fiction: Flora Tristan

In order to gauge the gender bias of the Peruvian press, the above representations may be compared to accounts attempting to demonstrate the worth of Peruvian women. Flora Tristan (1803–44) wrote a sympathetic documentary description of 1830s Lima women, which could not contrast more strongly with the fictional misrepresentations of the male-authored satire studied so far. If in colonial satire Lima women represent enfeeblement and retrogression, in Tristan's study, the women of newly independent Peru stand for strength, independence and modernity. Tristan's travel journal, *Peregrinations of a Pariah (Mémoires et pérégrinations d'une paria),* published in Paris in 1838, recounted her fifteen-month stay in Peru in 1833–34. Her father, a Peruvian general, had married a French woman in Spain, but the marriage was not legally recognised. At the age of 30, Flora travelled to Peru to reclaim her inheritance. In this she was unsuccessful, but her keenly observed account of Peruvian urban society, in particular the habits and customs of its elite women, are an invaluable historical source. The picture she paints is of a social group of elegant, strong-minded, self-confident, intelligent and, above all, autonomous women, whose freedom of movement, ensured by their unique costume or disguise (the *saya* and the *manto*, described in great detail), is unrivalled in Europe. Tristan writes that all the Lima women, including her aunt, Manuela Tristán, discuss politics at length; she herself attended debates in Congress on several occasions, where she met a number of women listening to the speeches, reading, or conversing on politics. These women go out on their own (to bullfights, political meetings, balls, church), accompanied perhaps only by a maid; they like parties, smoke cigars, gamble, ride horses – not side-saddle, but wearing baggy trousers – swim in the sea, sing and dance (Tristan 1979: 340).[12] They have a 'penchant décidé' for intrigue and seek out posts and employment for their husbands, sons and acquaintances; no obstacle will stand in their way. In short, 'les femmes de Lima gouvernent les hommes'. They are superior in intelligence and willpower ('force morale') and enjoy 'la grande liberté et l'influence dominatrice' (Tristan 1979: 335). Tristan was particularly impressed by Francisca Zubiaga, 'La Mariscala', the warfaring wife of the Peruvian president, Agustín Gamarra (1829–33) and by the intrepid but filthy *rabonas,* or women camp followers (see Chapter 6).

According to Tristan, although Peru is underdeveloped in comparison with Europe, Lima women have a much more progressive mindset ('tout autre ordre d'idées') than European women who, from their earliest infancy are slaves to laws, habits, customs, prejudice and fashion (Tristan 1979: 338). For Tristan, development, or 'civilisation', is not so for women. In fact, it is precisely because of this underdevelopment, this time lag, and the lack of educational institutions available in Peru for either sex, that women have been able to fulfil themselves independently and to use to their advantage their naturally superior minds, a superiority 'que Dieu leur a départie' (Tristan 1979: 335). Formal education, it is implied, the social and cultural institutions emerging in European modernity, function only to women's disadvantage. Instead, women must look to the Americas for what Mary Louise Pratt terms their 'feminotopias', 'idealised worlds of female autonomy, empowerment and pleasure' (Pratt 1992: 167). Ironically, this is a Eurocentric perspective. Tristan, despite her parentage, was a Frenchwoman, who wrote an autobiographical travelogue to make money and take revenge on her husband. But it is also a gendered perspective, and Tristan's admiration for Lima women leads her to query any easy identification of Europe with modernity and Peru with backwardness. For her, Lima women are naturally strong and their resistance to containment by man-made bourgeois morality is (from the point of view of gender politics) revolutionary. On her return to France, partly due to these experiences, Tristan became a revolutionary socialist feminist. Her book *L'emancipation de la femme ou le testament de la paria,* was published posthumously in Paris in 1846.

The woman satirist: María Leoncia Pérez Rojo (Montevideo)

Satire, however, does not need to be misogynistic to be effective. A satirical poem written by a woman in Montevideo shortly after independence makes its political point without targeting women. Political satire written by a woman was a rare occurrence, and pro-royalist satire by a woman almost unknown. María Leoncia Pérez Rojo's lengthy annotated ballad, 'Crítica de las fiestas mayas montevideanas', written in 1816, was brought to public attention in 1954 by Uruguayan historian Flavio A. Garcia, who found it in the Archivo Histórico Nacional, Madrid (García 1954; 1956).[13] The poem, though not as biting as the texts discussed above, is laden with the irony and wit characteristic of Menippean spectacle. Cast in mock-heroic style, the poem deflates republican and independence rhetoric by describing commonplace events in elevated language peppered with colloquialisms. The 'Crítica' exposes the foibles not of the colonial regime but of the newly independent province of Oriente or, as García puts it, of 'nuestros humildes orígenes democráticos' (García 1956: 84). Pérez Rojo, who was probably born in Spain, was a fervent royalist. Little is known of her life; in the poem she refers to herself as an old woman, suggesting perhaps sixty years old, giving a birth date of c. 1760 (García 1956: 83). She was married to José María Aldana y Malpica, a captain in the Spanish navy who had served away from home for some fifteen years. Her son was also a distinguished naval officer, based at Callao, who had defended the River Plate during the English invasion of 1806. After the Declaration of Independence in the Banda Oriental (a province of the Viceroyalty of the Río de la Plata) in 1811 under José Gervasio Artigas, and the end of Spanish rule in 1814, Pérez Rojo awaited her husband's return in Montevideo, working with her niece, María del Rosario Bozique, for the royalist cause. Her house was converted to a refuge and hospital for royalists and she herself was imprisoned for a short time (García 1954: 380; Knaster 1977: 506).[14]

The poem is an ironic description of the first May fiestas held in Oriente Province after the Declaration of Independence of May 25 1810 in Buenos Aires. This was a three-day festival organised by the Montevideo town council *(Cabildo)*, which took place in the Plaza Mayor and the church and involved all the local populace, notably the parish priest, the town dignitaries, the pupils at the public school and their teacher, and the gauchos who worked on the surrounding cattle ranches (García 1954: 383). The festivities included market stalls, fireworks, speeches, patriotic songs composed by Bartolomé Hidalgo and Francisco de Araucho, sung by the schoolchildren, street performances (by the children dressed as Indians and by the black population, who sang their own songs), theatrical productions, buffets, dances and banquets. The third day was marked by the inauguration of the National Library and the opening speech of its director, Dámaso Larrañaga. Fortunately, the programme of events is described in detail, including the words of songs and speeches, in the official record of the *fiestas cívicas* (Biblioteca de impresos raros 1951). In what follows, this favourable official account of the festivities will be compared with Pérez

Rojo's soured view to show how satire is achieved primarily by mobilising differences of race, caste and class rather than gender difference. The targets of the satire are creoles, especially the men (a white woman narrator ridicules how these upstarts assume the power and authority of government), and the mixed-race population of men and women. The poem thus foregrounds the relational complexities of sexual difference. It is an example of colonial discourse ridiculing the colonised other, the *americanos*, its female author/narrator having adopted a royalist, colonialist point of view. The implied readers are the formerly hegemonic colonial and metropolitan elite. In this respect, differences of race, caste and class override those of gender. Caricature is effective, but women are lampooned no more than men. Similarities may be traced between this poem and Terralla y Landa's in that both are racist and Eurocentric, but Pérez Rojo's poem is not misogynistic. Woman does not function as a trope of social degradation.

The target of the poem's criticism is primarily creole men, the dignitaries on the town council, the sergeant major, the gauchos and hacendados from the local estates, the priest, the market men and shopkeepers, who are all portrayed as arrogant, ignorant, puffed-up fools representing their parts in a tragicomedy, a farce in the poorest taste. They are ridiculed in that their ambitious self-importance belies their scarce resources and trivial achievements. Colloquialisms are employed to undermine inflated official rhetoric. So, for example, what is described in the official memoir as 'una alta y majestuosa pirámide, circulada de gradería, y primorosos balaustres' erected in the main square, adorned with the symbols of independence, including 'en la cúspide el gran gorro de la *Libertad*' (the Phrygian cap) (Biblioteca 1951: 8) is deflated in Pérez Rojo's version as 'un pirámide de trapo / que a todo el mundo asombró / En la coronilla tiene un birrete colorado / tutelar de a Nación' (García 1956: 79); the official 'suntuosa mesa de cien cubiertos' (Biblioteca 1951: 14), is for her a table covered with 'la limosna recogida' (García 1956: 82); the 'himnos patrióticos y relaciones' (Biblioteca 1951: 13) performed by the schoolchildren dressed up as Indians are described in the poem thus: 'acabada ya la danza / la mojiganga empezó / a representar la farsa / que el fraile les enseñó' (García 1956: 80). Similarly, the 'señoras y ciudadanos' (Biblioteca 1951: 17) (not 'cuidadanas', note) and the 'treinta y cuatro parejas' who took to the dance floor, according to the official version, leaving the 'estrados ocupados por señores – estos se esmeraron en la delicadeza de sus atavíos que daban un grado de poder a los alhagueños [sic] dones de la naturaleza' (Biblioteca 1951: 14), are dismissed by the narrator as 'gentuza de la Campaña / metidos a caballeros' (García 1956: 82), 'mulatas' and 'chatas' (Chinese), 'ostentando sus narices', and 'fregatrices'. The authentic ladies for Pérez Rojo are the 'señoras / con el corazón Patricio / y la apariencia de Godos' (García 1956: 82). The sergeant major's official 'proclama' to the troops, to the 'soldados orientales: cuidadanos armados' 'ilustres defensores de la patria' and so on (Biblioteca 1951: 11) is so annoying to the narrator that 'por no oir tal mentecato / ni tanta majadería' (García 1956: 81) she enters the church to pray. In short, the poem trivialises and delegitimises republican discourse intent on cementing the authority and status of new civic institutions. The official rhetoric of acclaim is substituted for an alternative vocabulary connoting censorious disrespect. This is most apparent in the poem's deconstruction of key republican words. The text glosses a song, which, according to the narrator was sung by the children to welcome the sun (though it is not quoted in the official record): 'América por deidad / tutelar en este día / que ahuyentó la tiranía / y fijó la libertad' (García 1956: 84):

De cuando en cuando salía
De la danza un Indiecillo,
Y al Pirámide apuntando
Con vocecilla de Grillo
De esta manera gritaba:
América por deidad.
¡Esta será la pereza
Que es la deidad que los pilla
De los pies a la Cabeza!
El segundo que salió
Apuntó y con alegría
Dijo tutelar en este día.
De malos americanos
Pues se le quedaron libres
Para robar las dos manos.
El tercero que salió
También demuestra alegría
Y dice apuntando al Sol
Que ahuyentó la Tiranía.
Así llaman a las Leyes
La Justicia y Religión
Que para todo rebelde
Era mucha sujeción.
El cuarto salió querida
Muy lleno de vanidad
Diciendo a grito Pelado
Y fijó la libertad.
De vicios y asesinatos
De mala fe y malos tratos,
Y de ninguna verdad.

(García 1956: 80, my emphases)

The *americanos* are thieving, lazy and ignorant. Their fund-raising is represented as begging and robbery and their republican pettiness ridiculed: aubergines are not served as food because they are (royal) purple, and the figure of Saint Balthasar in the church is left unadorned, because he is one of the Three Kings. The narrator asks the saint:

¿Por qué a oscuras aún estás
El Santo me respondió
Por que soy Rey, no más.
Yo repetí mi pregunta
¿por qué no te encienden luces?
Si no me cuidan Gallegos
No me visten Andaluces.
¿Por qué no las dijo amigo
Que has venido del Oriente?
Por que no hay razón que baste
A convencer a esta gente (García 1956: 81)

The poem's political agenda is resistance to anti-colonialism. In the official version, the sermon of the priest, Dr Tomás Xavier de Gomensoro, demonstrated 'hasta la evidencia los sólidos fundamentos de nuestra causa y tributando toda la admiración y encomios de que son dignas las victorias y la grandeza de los guerreros orientales' (Biblioteca 1951: 12). In the poem, Gomensoro is described as insane: 'estaba de frenesí / Al legítimo gobierno le llamaba tirano / y con muy poco respeto / trató la soberanía' (García 1956: 81). The concept of equality is similarly deflated in the poem's reference to the democratic mix of people in the banquet: 'Lució muy bien la igualdad / Pues te digo con verdad / Que todo era miscelánea. / Gentuza de la Campaña / Metido a Caballeros ...' (García 1956: 82). The wives, or first ladies, of the dignitaries are 'las primeras actrices / de la farsa del estado' (García 1956: 83). The pompous ignorance of social etiquette is similarly mocked:

Uno llegó a una señora
Y le dijo muy ufano
Echeme de esos fideos
Que están cerca de su mano.
Ella dijo, no ve amigo
Que estos son huevos hilados.
Pues fuese lo que fuese
Echeme de esos gusanos. (García 1956: 83)

Finally, the 'señores carniceros' are shown learning how to drink coffee and tea, but willingly succumb to the delights of Spanish 'aguardiente':

Estuvieron en su trono
Los Señores Aguardientes
Pero la España triunfó
A pesar de las inconvenientes.
Pues con su fuerza y denuedo,
A toditos los dejó
Tendiditos en el suelo. (García 1956: 83)

With wit and humour, the narrator represents herself as a marginalised subject belonging to a persecuted minority. She identifies with the 'Godos cabizbajos' (García 1956: 81), but refuses to give in; hers is a discourse of resistance. Pérez Rojo writes as a formerly privileged woman, empowered by differences of race and class, and by the historical status of the metropolitan elite. As Hernández Sánchez-Barba writes,

> Hay que considerar la superioridad que supone la posición de la raza conquistadora sobre la conquistada. Los testiminios abundan ... hay uno del 4 de agosto de 1790 del Fiscal del Consejo de Indias en el que dice: 'Es indubitable que se reputa en aquellos reinos por noble a cualquier español que pasa a ellos siempre que no se dedica a ningún oficio indecoroso y adquiere algunos fondos.' Humboldt es mucho más tajante: 'un blanco, aunque monte descalzo a caballo, se imagina ser la nobleza del país'. (Hernández Sánchez-Barba 1972: 337–38)

What makes the poem so effective is its double ploy: its mockery of the colonised subject's mimicry of the metropolitan elite. There is no menace in this mimicry (Bhabha 1994). The attempted emulation is doomed to failure because the copy falls so short of original, authentic distinction. Whatever their status, race or gender, these are colonial subjects in need of government. Put another way, order needs to be imposed on racially inferior subjects, irrespective of gender.

In the 1790s press articles studied earlier, woman represents all that is reprehensible in absolutist colonial rule. In this poem, the colonial subject represents all that is censorious in republican self-government: inclusiveness, civic institutions, education, welfare and social levelling. The poem makes no mention of the inauguration of the National Library the next day, the charity events, or the lottery for assisting the poor. It exploits the social relations of difference (race, class and gender) to target primarily white men and mixed-race men and women, the material and symbolic representatives of creole government. But gender is not the only dynamic of imperialism (McClintock 1995: 7); the conventions of the long-established 'querella de las mujeres' are of less significance in this poem than the equally inveterate 'querelle d'Amérique', despite the close interweaving of gender and race in the discourses of colonialism (Leitner 2003).[15] The poem is also an elderly woman's riposte to colonial satire's lampooning of old women (for example, the work of Terralla y Landa and, later, Francisco de Acuña Figeroa (Uruguay, 1791–1862), whose 'La malambrunada' associated old women (as in *La Celestina*) with the devil). Pérez Rojo's poem ends with the narrator poking fun at herself, a deliberately ironic and politicising allusion to this satirical practice:

> Soy anciana y achacosa
> Y muy llena de accidentes
> Y el mayor de todos ellos
> Es vivir entre insurgentes. (García 1956: 84)

Notes

1 Palma's ten series of *Tradiciones* appeared between 1879 and 1902.
2 'Rasgos inéditos de los escritores peruanos' in the *Mercurio Peruano*, 34, 1791: 312–13; 'Es rasgo póstumo de nuestro anti-galeno Cabiedes' in the *Mercurio Peruano*, 157, 1792: 152–55.
3 For example, in the work of Bernal Díaz and Ercilla. See Johnson 1983: 9–59.
4 Menippean satire is indirect prose satire framed as a narrative and employed usually to expound intellectual debate or expose sophistry.
5 For example, Fray Francisco de Paula Castañeda's *porteño* journal, *Doña María Retazos* (1821–23), allegedly written by said Doña María. See Castañeda 2001; MacIntyre 2005.
6 Of the *Mercuario Peruano* subscribers, 75 per cent lived in Peru and 9 per cent in other parts of Spanish America (Clément 1997, 1: 71).
7 It was possible to be legally separated, and this arrangement was referred to at the time as divorce. An example is the separation of the Marquesa de Valdelirios in 1809 (Clément 1997, 1: 146)
8 A note explains that the book was published in Amsterdam and Leipzig (Arkestee and Merku) in 1754 and the author's essays may be found in *Obras del Autor* (Madrid: Imprenta Real, 1754).
9 Tribonianus was a Roman jurist who compiled the *Corpus Juris Civilis*.
10 The 'querelle des femmes' originated in fourteenth-century Europe and is said to have lasted until the end of the French Revolution, although it persisted at least throughout the 1790s in the Americas. See the articles by Rivera Garretas, Zimmermann, and Leitner in Aichinger et al. 2003.
11 'No tener pepita en la lengua', means to be outspoken; the author/narrator is asked by a lady at the dance to produce a humorous 'pepita', a nugget (of his witty writings). A *pepito* is a dandy.
12 The first edition consisted of two volumes, 180,000 words. The 1986 English translation consists of just one-third of the original text and the French edition of 1979 is also much abridged.
13 It is not clear if it was published, but it was presumably meant for publication in the royalist press in Spain or the Americas, for example, the *Gaceta de Gobierno del Perú* (1810–21). Thanks to Iona MacIntyre for bringing this text to my attention.
14 The Banda Oriental came under Portuguese control until 1824 and was then occupied by Brazil until 1827. Full independence was recognised in 1828. The first constitution of the República Oriental del Uruguay dates from 1830.
15 For the 'pugna entre "criollos" y "españoles"' in the work of Caviedes, see Lasarte 1999: 135.

PART II

CHAPTER SIX

Women, War and Spanish American Independence

> Ansí mismo alanceó Hernando Cortés en esta batalla aquel día á otro señor llamado Tochtlahuatzal ... En estos reencuentros se halló aquella señora llamado María de Estrada, donde peleó con la lanza á caballo como si fuera uno de los más valerosos hombres del mundo.
>
> Diego Muñoz Camargo, c. 1576 (Muñoz Camargo, 1892: 227)

María Leoncia Pérez Rojo's poetry of resistance appropriately introduces the second part of this book, which focuses on women's literary culture. How did women inscribe gender, and how did they conceptualise sexual difference in their writings? What kind of dialogue did they initiate with the canonical texts and gender *doxa* studied so far? These questions can only be answered with reference to historical context. Before analysing in detail a selection of women's published and unpublished writings, therefore, this chapter will provide an overview of the impact of the Spanish American Wars of Independence on women and on gender.

Women have long been associated with warfare in South America. In his *History of Tlaxcala*, Diego Muñoz Camargo described María de Estrada's part in the conquest of Mexico, even though he had not personally witnessed her action and would have been repeating prevalent tales and accounts. It is interesting, although not surprising, that Hernán Cortés did not mention María de Estrada's efforts in his letters to Carlos V of Spain. Indeed, Cortés barely acknowledged the part played by his translator and guide, Doña Marina ('La Malinche'), without whom the conquest would have been much more difficult (Cortés 1963: 269).[1] Although he specifically praised the role of several women in his eyewitness account of the conquest, Bernal Díaz del Castillo did not refer to María de Estrada's fighting prowess either. He merely stated that she was the only Spanish woman in Mexico and that she escaped from the Aztec capital, Tenochtitlán, with the help of their Tlaxcalan allies (Díaz del Castillo 1963: 302; 1955: 399).[2] Muñoz Camargo was, perhaps, applying poetic licence in portraying María de Estrada as strong, warlike and rebellious. The tendency can be traced at least as far back as Christopher Columbus. An avid reader of *Travels of Sir John Mandeville*, Columbus was fascinated by his revival of the myth of the Amazons. Columbus became obsessed with finding the tribe of women, and 'twice during his explorations in the New World he thought he had encountered, or narrowly missed such beings' (Fernández-Armesto 1992: 34). The myth was rooted in Asia, and at the time Columbus was unshaken in his belief that he had encountered a new route to the Spice Islands. This mistaken belief did not prevent subsequent explorers from drawing on the Amazons. In his fourth letter to Carlos V, Cortés repeated a reported sighting of a community of women:

> Me trajo relación de los señores de la provincia de Ciguatán, que se afirman mucho haber una isla toda poblada de mujeres, sin varón ninguno, y que en ciertos tiempos van de la tierra firme hombres, con los cuales han acceso, y las que preñadas se paren mujeres las guardan, y si hombres los echan de su compañía. (Cortés 1963: 213)

Cortés was careful not to admit a personal sighting of the Amazons, yet his words indicate that he expected to encounter these Amazons. He did so with details borrowed from the novels of chivalry, citing the adventures of Sergas de Esplandían, no doubt to engage the interest and to encourage further sponsorship from his patron, Carlos V, who was himself an avid reader of these stories (Leonard 1949: 20–21).[3] Indeed, so keen had been the interest in these legendary beings that the original orders to Cortés from the governor of Cuba, Diego Velázquez, were to locate the mythical tribe (Leonard 1949: 46).[4] The desire to see women in Spanish America as warriors was based on fiction, not fact: Sir John Mandeville was 'a first class liar who related a lot of tall tales about countries he had never visited' (Janes 1960: xx). Whatever his intentions,[5] Mandeville's stories of monsters and unknown lands were generally accepted as the truth and continued to be believed for over 300 years (Adams 1983: 73). The myth was fuelled by Columbus's misconception that he had reached the Far East.

Later accounts also drew on the Amazons of Spanish America. In his 'Defensa de las mujeres' (1726), Feijóo claimed that although the legend of the Amazons had been distorted by fable, the early Spanish explorers had actually encountered such beings:

> In America, they were seen ... marching, armed along the greatest river in the World, the Marañón; and, on account of that singular phenomenon, they gave it the name, which it retains to this day: The River of the Amazons. (Feijóo 1774: 73)

Furthermore, Feijóo referred to Diego Muñoz Camargo's account of the part played by María de Estrada in the conquest of Mexico, embellishing it to prove his point that women could be as brave as men: 'In this battle, María de Estrada ... was] charging on horseback, with a courage not inferior to any in the whole army' (Feijóo 1774: 71). The legacy of the hope and expectancy of finding women warriors in the American continent has endured, leading to a tendency to exaggerate the efforts of Spanish American women. Some 300 years after Muñoz Camargo, Julie Greer Johnson claimed that María de Estrada 'accompanied

Cortés and fought with his troops against the Indians' (Johnson 1983: 19, 48).[6] While no doubt intended to praise their contribution, such hyperbole has placed unsolicited attributes on women who have taken part in battles and it undermines the important tasks they have undertaken in following their beliefs.

As Elizabeth Leonard points out, women have taken part in battles since at least the fourteenth century (Leonard 1999: 100). At the outbreak of the Spanish American Wars of Independence in 1808, the memoirs of Catalina de Erauso, 'La Monja Alférez' (1595–1650) had already passed into folklore and were well known in Latin America, fuelling the view that Spanish America was fertile soil for Amazon-like exploits. Erauso had escaped from a Spanish convent in 1600, dressed as a boy, and sailed to Chile. She joined the army there and was promoted to lieutenant. She kept her true identity hidden for several years before confessing her origins to the Bishop of Huamanga, Peru. Remarkably, the Spanish Crown and the Pope gave Erauso permission to dress as a man and to use the name Monja Alférez. She then settled in Mexico and worked as a muleteer until her death (Merrim 1994: 177–205; Erauso, 1996). Indeed, Spanish American women had much more recent role models: as discussed below, women played a prominent role in the Túpac Amaru rebellion. William Taylor demonstrates that women featured prominently in eighteenth-century rural rebellions in central Mexico, since many men worked away from their villages. He finds that around twenty-five per cent of revolts were led by 'aggressive, insulting and rebellious' women (Taylor 1979: 116, 155).

Yet although women's participation in rebellions and their consequent punishment were already well established by the end of the colonial period, the Spanish American Wars of Independence and the political and social instability that followed brought unprecedented opportunities for individual advancement. This chapter attempts to investigate the relations between the hyperbole and the actuality and explores the ways in which women from a range of social classes participated in the independence cause. It also examines the attitudes towards women of some of the leading male protagonists of independence. The focus is on women's participation in distinct areas of South America to reveal to what extent royalist and patriot authorities vilified or praised the women who took part. The women's motives for actively supporting the independence cause are likely to be as individual as the women themselves: many did so from family loyalty; others sought to escape family duties and ties; others followed their husbands; some aimed to break free from unhappy marriages; whereas others simply looked for adventure.

Women in late colonial rebellions

Before centring on the struggles for independence, it is worth considering some of the immediate precedents that shaped the minds of men and women during the late colonial period. Women played a significant part in the 1780–81 Túpac Amaru rebellion, in the 1781–82 Comuneros rebellion, and in the Gual España revolt of 1797.

Surviving records of the subsequent trials of the instigators and letters written at the time pay testimony to the roles women played in the Túpac Amaru rebellion. In 1780, mestizo José Gabriel Condorcanqui drew on his Inca heritage and rose up against the colonial authorities under the name Túpac Amaru II. Indigenous and mestizo men and women rallied to a cause that at its height threatened Spanish control of Peru and Upper Peru (Bolivia). Túpac Amaru appointed his wife, Micaela Bastidas, as commander in his absence. As Leon Campbell argues, this was in keeping with indigenous society, in which family and clan ties afforded women an elevated position and, when circumstances demanded, the wives and sisters of the rebel chiefs were accepted as legitimate leaders. Indigenous soldiers respected Bastidas as the wife of Túpac Amaru (Campbell 1985: 190–91). Tomasa Titu Condemayta, the *cacica* of Arcos, was an officer in the insurgent army, whose brigade of women soldiers successfully defended the Arcos Bridge (Silverblatt 1987: 123). Marcela Castro, wife of Marcos Túpac Amaru, also participated in the fighting (García y García 1924: 169–70). Bartolina Sisa took part in the siege of La Paz alongside her husband, Julián Apaza (Túpac Kapari), and her sister-in-law, Gregoria Apaza, went into battle beside Andrés Túpac Amaru (Pallis 1980: 23; Querejazu 1987: 406–14; Guardia 1985: 45).

Were these women subject to the hyperbole that has characterised allegedly bellicose Spanish American women? Meri Knaster states that Cecilia Túpac Amaru (sister of José Gabriel Túpac Amaru) 'instigated and abetted' the revolt (Knaster 1977: 468). Others claim that rather than follow him, Bastidas was the driving force behind her husband. Probably writing in 1854, José de Austria described the Túpac Amaru rebellion as led by Bastidas, her sons Hipólito and Fernando and her brother-in-law, Antonio Bastidas (de Austria 1960: 55). The following extract from a letter said to have been written by Bastidas to Túpac Amaru reveals an intense dedication to the cause that in this instant at least, seems to surpass that of Túpac Amaru himself:

> Tú me has acabado de pesadumbres, pues andas muy despacio paseándote en los pueblos, y más en Yauri, tardándote dos días con grande descuido, pues los soldados tienen razón de aburrirse e irse cada uno a sus pueblos.
>
> Yo ya no tengo paciencia para aguantar todo esto, pues yo misma soy capaz de entregarme a los enemigos para que me quiten la vida, porque veo el poco anhelo con que ves este asunto tan grave que corre con detrimento de la vida de todos, y estamos en medio de los enemigos que no tenemos ahora segura la vida; y por tu causa están a pique de peligrar todos mis hijos, y los demás de nuestra parte. Harto te he encargado que no te demores en esos pueblos donde no hay que hacer cosa ninguna; ... y entonces se retirarán todos, dejándonos desamparados, para que paguemos con nuestras vidas; ... y se perderá todo la gente que tengo prevenida para la bajada al Cuzco.
>
> ...
> Bastante advertencias te di para que inmediatamente fueses al Cuzco, pero

has dado tanto a la barata dándoles tiempo para que se prevengan, como lo han hecho, poniendo cañones en el cerro de Piccho y otras tramoyas tan peligrosas, que ya no eres sujeto de darles avance.

. . .

También te hago presente como los indios de Quispicanchi, ya se hallan rendidos y aburridos con tanto tiempo de servir de guardias; en fin Dios querría que padezca por mis pecados –

Es tu esposa.

Después de concluida ésta he tenido propio, que me da noticia cierta que los de Paruro están en Acos; y así voy a caminar aunque sepa perder la vida.

Tungasuca, December 6 1780 (Cornejo Bournoncle 1949: 53–54)

The letter shows Bastidas's frustration at her husband's lack of energy and nerve and her exasperation is evident. From this letter, at least, Bastidas is in command of a reluctant Túpac Amaru and fears her preparations will be wasted because he is not following her advice. Her postscript reveals that she was aware of the enemy's movements and that she was willing and able to use her own instincts to react to changing circumstances. However, Túpac Amaru ignored her advice and did not return to Cuzco until late December, after government forces had reached the former Inca capital, a decision that may have cost the rebels control of the highlands (Campbell 1985: 177–78).

The assault on Cuzco having failed, Bastidas, Túpac Amaru and their sons were captured. During her trial, Bastidas cleverly tried to defend herself by drawing on popular perceptions that women were illiterate and incapable of strategic planning: 'Mariano Banda wrote out my orders and I did not examine them, since I could neither read nor write' (O'Phelan 1985: 236). Others adopted similar tactics when attempting to defend the women. Diego Túpac Amaru insisted they should be pardoned 'since [women] are incapable of having an opinion and cannot disobey their husbands'. Campbell argues that it was a considerable anomaly that these women came before the courts at all, since Spanish law dictated that, as the property of their husbands, women could not be tried. An exception had to be made for the women to be charged with treason against the Crown (Campbell 1985: 187–88).

Campbell concludes that 'women played crucially important roles in the conflict' (Campbell 1985: 190). Certainly their punishments were sufficiently severe to support this finding. Bastidas, Marcela Castro and Titu Condemayta were condemned to death. Cecilia Túpac Amaru was given 200 lashes and sentenced to ten years' exile in Mexico (she died in prison before leaving Peru). Several other women were exiled, including Túpac Amaru's mother, who died during the voyage (Querejazu 1987: 401–04; Guardia 1985: 45–46).[7] On May 18 1781, Bastidas and Titu Condemayta were among a group of nine people who were executed in the main plaza, Cuzco. Bastidas's tongue was cut out before her death. The victims' bodies were dismembered and their heads and limbs displayed in several towns that had participated in the rebellion (Cornejo

Bournoncle 1949: 105–106; de Austria 1960: 55). Gregoria Apaza and Bartolina Sisa were hanged in 1782; their bodies quartered and exhibited (Guardia 1985: 45; O'Phelan 1985: 270–71, 307–09). The following year, Marcela Castro was arrested; she was stuffed into a sack and dragged to the plaza. Her tongue was cut out and she was hanged and quartered (García y García 1924: 169–70; Cornejo Bournoncle 1949: 152–72). The violence of these women's horrific fates pays testimony to the leading roles they played in this rebellion and their experiences would surely have had some bearing on popular perceptions of women's capabilities. The impact on the crowd was stronger, as these were the first public executions of this kind in the region.[8]

The Comuneros rebellion began in Socorro, (present-day Colombia) as wide sectors of society took to the streets to object to tax increases imposed by the authorities. Among the leaders was Jorge Lozano y Peralta, the Marqués de San Jorge. Manuela Beltrán, a shopkeeper from Socorro, took up the call. José Donoso Monsalve describes how, on March 16 1781, watched by a delighted crowd, she tore down the edict bearing the royal seal and cried, 'Viva el Rey y muera el mal Gobierno' (Monsalve 1926: 5–7).[9] The call was taken up by mestizo and indigenous campesinos, who marched to Bogotá, gathering supporters on the way. In this instance, Beltrán appears to have been more radical than the upper-class creole male leaders of the rebellion. Benjamin Keen describes the organisers as 'hesitant or unwilling' to lead a group composed of members of the lower classes. A face-saving compromise was reached: an agreement was drafted in which the colonial authorities accepted all the rebel demands, but the viceroy then simply ignored it. The creole rebel leaders feared a widespread class or race rebellion that ran the risk of damaging their assets, and they joined forces with the authorities (Keen 1992: 143).

Similarly, the Gual-España revolt of 1797 in the port La Guaira (present-day Venezuela) proved to be, in John Lynch's words, 'too radical for creole property owners'. The rebellion was heavily influenced by the French Revolution. The rebels, led by Manuel Gual and José María España, sought a republican government, freedom of trade, racial equality, and an end to slavery and indigenous tribute (Lynch 1973: 193). Several women took part in the conspiracy, including España's wife, Josefa Sánchez, and his sister, Joaquina España. According to Monsalve, Sánchez persuaded one of her slaves to incite a slave rebellion, and then to launch an attack on Caracas. Sánchez's servant, Josefa Rufina Acosta, delivered messages to the rebels. The movement was discovered days before the planned rebellion and the conspirators were arrested. Sánchez hid España in their home in La Guaira before he was eventually arrested and executed (Díaz 2004: 55; Cherpak 1978: 220). Two slaves belonging to Sánchez, named only as Margarita and Isidora, were sentenced to four years each in jail in 1799 for their part in the conspiracy. In February 1800, Sánchez was sentenced to eight years in prison for hiding her husband from the authorities; Acosta was imprisoned for six months. Just how willing were the servant and slaves of Sánchez to take part in the conspiracy has not been explored (Monsalve 1926: 18–20).

Women and Belgrano

Moving on to the independence period, the attitude of Manuel Belgrano towards women is of particular interest, as it represents a progressive, liberal current of thought. Born in Buenos Aires, Belgrano was educated at the University of Salamanca, Spain, where he was influenced by the work of Rousseau, Montesquieu and Adam Smith (Aguirre 1999: 11, 13, 25). His *Educación popular* advocated schools for both sexes in Buenos Aires and he claimed that the well-being and virtue of an educated woman was the basis of sociability:

> Se deben poner escuelas gratuitas para las niñas, donde se les enseñará la doctrina cristiana, a leer, escribir, coser, bordar etcétera, y principalmente inspirarlas amor al trabajo, para separarlas de la ociosidad, tan perjudicial, o más en la mujeres que en los hombres. (Mitre 1927: 74)

Belgrano became a leading figure in the independence movement, commanding a patriot army that conducted campaigns in Paraguay and Upper Peru (Bolivia). Schooling for girls was just one part of Belgrano's vision of the future; he was also concerned with the indigenous population. Ricardo Piccirilli comments that in 1816 the indigenous people were 'como electrizado' by Belgrano's 'nuevo proyecto' to establish 'un gran imperio en la América meridional, gobernado por los descendientes de la familia imperial de los Incas'. Several groups of indigenous soldiers were formed and united under the 'bandera del sol', provoking concerns of a race war: 'Están armándose y se cree que pronto se formará un ejército en el Alto Perú de Quito a Potosí, Lima y Cuzco'.[10]

Among the many indigenous soldiers who fought under Belgrano's banner, the figure of Juana Azurduy (c. 1781–1862) is outstanding. She was born in the 1780s, a mestiza from Chuquisaca (Sucre, Bolivia) and received a basic convent education. This, José Urquidi writes, awoke her 'alma varonil'. Rather than read stories of piety, he claims that she preferred to learn about the exploits of chivalric heroes and the Crusaders. She left the convent; married Manuel Padilla in 1805, and they had several children (Urquidi 1918: 32–33, 35–38). Padilla and Azurduy were strong supporters of the independence movement, collecting money and arms for the cause. Padilla enlisted in Belgrano's troops, which lost the battle of Chuquisaca in January 1811. Padilla escaped and took his family to the town of La Laguna. When, in 1813, Belgrano returned to Potosí to regroup after further defeats, Padilla raised an army of 10,000 men to assist him. The mainly indigenous soldiers were poorly equipped and armed. Urquidi claims that Azurduy was tired of watching Padilla's sacrifices and of the suffering of their prolonged absences and resolved to become his *compañera* in danger and in glory. From then on Azurduy took an active part in the campaigns, and eventually led her own legion of male soldiers, 'Los Leales'. She wore a distinctive red jacket and had a personal guard of some twenty-five 'Amazonas', specially trained women, who fought alongside her. The reference to the Amazons showed respect for these women soldiers. Azurduy seems to have been a charismatic leader, whose enthusiasm and bravery earned her the respect of her troops. Urquidi maintains that she led them like a commander and loved them as a mother. She was the first on to the battlefield and the last to leave it, and she cured and comforted the wounded (Urquidi 1918: 45–48). Juan Pablo Echaque states that her 'varonil' power and feminine grace enabled her both to inspire the troops and to comfort and console them; otherwise she was just another local caudillo who understood her soldiers' concerns and knew the land and climate (Echaque 1947: 72–79).

'Los Leales' took part in sixteen battles under Azurduy. Belgrano presented her with a sword in recognition of her efforts and recommended her for an order of merit for her part in the taking of the Cerro de la Plata (Urquidi 1918: 47–48).[11] On September 5 1814, she personally captured a royalist standard and on March 3 1816, she led a counter-attack against General Santos la Hera, in which she killed fifteen men and is said to have pursued others on horseback who were trying to escape (Pérez Godoy 1948: 33–37). On August 13 1816, Antonio Berrutti wrote to Belgrano praising the 'varonil esfuerzo y bizarría de la amazona doña Juana Azurduy' and he recommended that 'esta virtuosa americana' be awarded the rank of lieutenant colonel (Urquidi 1918: 106). In recalling the myth of the Amazons, Berrutti was underlining the importance of Azurduy to the independence cause. Moreover he was not making a retrospective claim on her merits and fighting prowess, but stating it in a document at the time. He based his assessment on what she had done and the contribution she was continuing to make.

Taking part in combat brought Azurduy accolades, but did not prevent personal tragedy. In September 1816 patriot troops suffered a serious defeat at the battle of La Laguna. Some 600 bodies were left on the battlefield and the royalists went in search of Azurduy and Padilla. Padilla was found and shot twice at close range, which killed him instantly. The royalists then captured and killed a woman dressed in a red jacket, assuming her to be Azurduy; the bodies of both were dismembered and their heads displayed at the entrance of La Laguna (Urquidi 1918: 121–24). Such treatment is a grotesque testimony of the esteem in which Azurduy was held by the royalists. This punishment was by then standard practice, but it shows that she was considered worthy of a man's punishment. The woman they had caught and killed was not Azurduy, however, but one of her guards. Azurduy had been seriously injured, but continued to fight to avenge Padilla's death. She never again wore her red jacket, but dressed in black, partly as a semi-disguise, but also as an outward sign of her mourning (Echaque 1947: 78).

Azurduy's story offers several lines of enquiry for further research: it could be said that she followed her husband into battle, but this does not explain why she took such a leading part in the physical fighting. She must have realised the likely consequences of such action: Chuquisaca had seen much bloodshed in the Túpac Amaru rebellion and, although it had ended before her birth, Azurduy would have heard stories about the grisly deaths of its protagonists, including the execution and dismembering of Micaela Bastidas, a fate that would have been her own, but for mistaken identity. What compelled Azurduy to become a soldier? Was she inspired by Belgrano's project to create an independent empire governed by the descendants of the Incas? Did her comparatively humble background make it easier for her to take up arms? Why, in a patriarchal and class-conscious society, did men accept her authority? What Azurduy's story undoubtedly demonstrates is that the role played by some women in the independence struggles was more than passive. In these uncertain times, warfare offered opportunities for women to seize the initiative, and in this case, albeit temporarily, Azurduy was accepted on merit by men and women alike.

Azurduy was a remarkable woman, but she was not unique; nor was she the only woman commended by Belgrano. The case of Juana de la Patria, a slave woman from Potosí, seems to confirm a pattern of mobilisation of women from the lower sectors of society. In 1813 she worked as a spy for the patriot troops and informed Belgrano that a group of royalists in Potosí were monitoring the patriots' movements. As a reward, Belgrano ordered her release from slavery. In this case, Juana de la Patria's motives are not difficult to ascertain, since her owner was among those she denounced (Blanchard 2004: 3).

Other evidence, however, contradicts any neat conclusions about the social and economic reasons for women's participation. Women from a variety of regions and from diverse social backgrounds took part in the independence cause. María Remedios del Valle from Buenos Aires, for example, also fought in Belgrano's army. She joined the troops in the northern provinces with her husband and two sons, and took part in several battles. Her husband and sons were all killed in battle, and she was wounded at Ayohúma. She was taken prisoner by the royalists and whipped in a public place on nine consecutive days. She managed to escape and rejoined the army, where she continued to fight and to work as a nurse (Sosa de Newton 1986: 653). Gertrudis Medeiros de Fernández, from one of the leading families in Salta, gave her wealth to the independence cause. Her husband was killed fighting for the patriots in 1811 (Carranza 1910: 148–49). She was imprisoned in Salta but was able to work as a spy, smuggling out news of the royalists' movements, before escaping and fleeing to Tucumán. On March 18 1818 Belgrano described her as a 'distinguida y benemérita hija de la patria' (Sosa de Newton 1986: 401). Martina Silva de Gurruchaga gave Belgrano lodging at her home and contributed uniforms and arms to the independence troops. On the eve of the battle of Salta, she armed the citizens of the town, an act that contributed to the victory. She made a flag and gave it to Belgrano, who is said to have received it with the following words: 'Señora, si en todos los corazones americanos existe la misma decisión que en el vuestro, el triunfo de la causa porque luchamos será fácil'. In 1813 Belgrano gave her the honorary title 'Capitana del ejército' (Carranza 1910: 148–49). Belgrano evidently valued women's financial support for his troops, as well as their direct fighting skills. Gregoria Pérez Larramendi, from one of the leading families in Santa Fe and described by Mitre as of 'mediana fortuna' (Mitre 1940, VI: 350), sent a letter to Belgrano pledging support for the independence cause and putting her wealth, land and servants at his disposal for his Paraguay campaign (Carranza 1910: 155). Belgrano's reply has survived: 'Ha conmovido todos los sentimientos de ternura y gratitud de mi corazón, al manifestarme los suyos tan llenos del más generoso patriotismo. La Junta colocará a Vd. en el catálogo de los beneméritos de la patria, para ejemplo de los poderosos que la miran con frialdad' (Belgrano 1914: 102).

Given the bravery of women from such a range of social backgrounds and the demonstrable gratitude expressed by Belgrano, one might have expected that many women received honour and acclaim after independence was achieved. Yet even the women in these specific cases of activism were largely ignored after they had served their purpose. Juana Azurduy settled in Salta, Argentina until 1825, when she returned to her birthplace. That year, Simón Bolívar awarded her a monthly pension of 60 pesos for two years. She appealed to General Sucre, who agreed that it should be paid to her throughout her life. But internal politics and the economic chaos following independence meant that she never received her pension. Azurduy died in poverty on May 26 1862 and was buried in the Cementerio General; the exact plot is not known (Pérez Godoy 1948: 36–37; Urquidi 1918: 134–43). After independence Gertrudis Medeiros unsuccessfully applied for a pension and, like Azurduy, died in poverty (Sosa de Newton 1986: 401). As Peter Blanchard notes, six years after Belgrano had ordered her manumission, Juana de la Patria had not obtained her freedom (Blanchard 2004: 3). In 1827 María Remedios del Valle was left to beg for food from convents. General Viamonte took up her cause and obtained a salary for her (as an infantry captain), but the political climate prevented her from receiving it. She continued to beg for her survival and died an old, forgotten woman (Knaster 1977: 505).

Yet although early independent society found it hard to give acknowledgment to the women who had fought and assisted in the fight against Spain, later generations showed their gratitude. Sucre's airport is today named Juana Azurduy de Padilla, and Calle Azurduy is one of the capital's main streets. Two streets in Buenos Aires and Santa Fe are named after Gregoria Pérez Larramendi, and another is named after María Remedios del Valle (Sosa de Newton 1986: 65, 490). This posthumous recognition indicates the changing attitudes towards women with the passage of time. What of the attitudes of the male heads of state in the nascent Spanish American republics? Belgrano's untimely death in 1820 prevented him from participating in the formation of independent Argentina, but José de San Martín was able to take the opportunity to enact some of his ideas. It is useful, therefore, to analyse his actions for evidence of the extent to which he esteemed women's participation in the independence cause.

San Martín's Orden del Sol

The complex nature of Spanish American independence was particularly apparent in Peru. Indeed, the colonial capital, Lima, was often at odds with the rest of Peru during the Wars of Independence, where ties between the creole elite and Spain were traditionally strong. San Martín, an Argentine, gave the first call to independence in the northern town of Trujillo. He then set up camp on the outskirts of Lima and stayed there for a year, with the aim of convincing the Lima loyalists that it was in their best interests to join the patriots. According to John Lynch, San Martín was determined not to shed unnecessary American blood in achieving independence (Lynch 1973: 174). By remaining outside rather than storming the city, he saved Lima from needless destruction and was given a warm welcome when he entered the city in triumph on July 28 1821.

In taking this stance of waiting to persuade *limeños* to join him in peace, San Martín revealed that he was as much a builder of nations as he was an opponent of the Spanish. He took the title 'Protector' rather than 'Liberator', and while this may have been to avoid confrontation with Simón Bolívar, it indicates that he intended to assume a more compassionate and less military role in the independent republic. San Martín had ambitions to create a united America that was free from European control (Martínez Riaza 1985: 46, 67). The spirit of hope and change that was present during Lima's first months of independence can be seen in the pages of the government newspaper, the *Gaceta del Gobierno de Lima Independiente*. The sense of optimism and pride is particularly apparent from 1821 to July 1822, and it indicates the creative ambitions of San Martín and fellow Argentine Bernardo Monteagudo, as they built new institutions and rewarded those who had worked for the independence cause. Although neither man was able to oversee the course of Peruvian independence (San Martín retired to civilian life in 1822 and Monteagudo was assassinated in 1825), it is likely that they hoped to extend their plans for Lima into the emerging republics. Certainly, some of their Peruvian organisations resembled those of Argentina. In 1822 Monteagudo founded the all-male Sociedad Patriótica de Lima, which was based on a similar society in Buenos Aires. Their views were expressed in the newspaper *El Sol del Perú*, published from March to June 1822 (Romero de Valle 1966: 214, 302; Martínez Riaza 1985: 50–51).

One of the few tools through which we may analyse San Martín's attitude towards women is his Orden del Sol, established in Lima on October 8 1821 to reward civil and military merit in the struggle for independence. It was modelled on France's Legion of Honour (Lynch 1973: 180).[12] Recipients had to be nominated for three classes of distinction: *fundadores*, *beneméritos*, and *asociados*. Those admitted to the Order were to receive a pension and had to swear to devote their lives and wealth to the defence of Peruvian liberties, to maintain public order and to support the general welfare of America. All received medals (gold for the first two classes and silver for the third). Men and women were eligible for nomination, and the names of 256 men and 112 women were put forward at the first meeting (Sutcliffe 1841: 56). (For a list of all the women who received this award, see *Gaceta del Gobierno de Lima Independiente*, January 23 1822: 3–4.) This is a considerable percentage of women and within a few months the figure had increased to 180. Although no records have been found of how the nomination process worked, it is significant, and not surprising, that several of the first women recipients had directly helped San Martín. Indeed, on July 1 1821, San Martín had specifically addressed the women of Lima, acknowledging their suffering as wives, daughters and sisters, but also noting their love for their country and the part they had played in the fight for independence (Pérez Vila 1983, January 3 1822: 33). In establishing the Order, San Martín again made particular reference to women; on January 11 1822 he proclaimed:

> El sexo más sensible naturalmente debe ser el más patriota: el carácter tierno de sus relaciones en la sociedad, ligándolo más al país en que nace, predispone doblemente en su favor todas sus inclinaciones. Las que tienen los nombres expresivos de madre, esposa, ó hija no pueden menos de interesarse con ardor en la suerte de los que son su objeto. El bello sexo del Perú cuyos delicados sentimientos relevan sus atractivos, no podía dejar de distinguirse por su decidido patriotismo, al contemplar que bajo el régimen de bronce que nos ha precedido, sus caras relaciones en general solo servían para hacerle sufrir mayor número de sinsabores de parte de los agentes de un gobierno, que a todos hacían desgraciados a su turno. Ya que estos días de aflicción universal no volverán jamás para nosotros, el gobierno que desea distinguir el merito de toda persona cuyo corazón ha suspirado sinceramente por la Patria, acaba de expedir el decreto que sigue:
>
> ...
>
> Las patriotas que más se hayan distinguido por su adhesión a la causa de la independencia del Perú usaran el distintivo de una banda de seda bicolor, blanca y encarnada que baje del hombro izquierdo al costado derecho donde se enlazara con una pequeña borla de oro, llevando hacia la mitad de la misma banda una medalla de oro con las armas del estado en el anverso, y esta inscripción en el reverso: Al patriotismo de las más sensibles. (*Gaceta del Gobierno de Lima Independiente*, January 4, 12. 1822: 3)

In stressing women's contribution to independence, San Martín was making a considerable departure from previous conduct towards women. In including them in the first awards given in the new republic, he underlined that their contribution was not achieved by adopting attributes of traditional masculinity such as aggression, but by aligning themselves with the acceptably feminine (sensitivity, tenderness, beauty), motivated by family love. He did not portray these women as social misfits, but as women who had been working for the benefit of their societies. Traditional feminine attributes were therefore marked as being as valuable to the nation-building process as masculinity.

He certainly had good reason to praise the women of Lima. As is well documented, several women of that city had contributed to the patriot cause, delivering messages, working as spies and spreading propaganda (Balta 1998; Basadre 1981; Cúneo Vidal 1978; García y García 1924; Guardia 1985; Knaster 1977; Neuhaus 1997; Parra de Riego 1935). Several of the recipients of the Orden del Sol belonged to leading Lima families who had welcomed San Martín's troops into the capital, indicating the importance San Martín placed on achieving a peaceful transition to independence. Women who received the

Orden del Sol had to be nominated, which would automatically exclude those who were less well connected, those who had acted anonymously or in disguise, and, since it was given to living persons, those who had died in the course of their work.

Yet this award was by no means restricted to members of the elite who fêted the victorious army: outlining the lives of some of the women who received it reveals the many ways in which women from a range of backgrounds were drawn into the fight against the royalists. Brígida Silva de Ochoa, for example, delivered messages for San Martín from 1819 to 1820. She had become politicised after two of her brothers were imprisoned by the royalists (Balta Campbell 1998: 28). Her eldest son, Manuel, joined the Spanish artillery, which was based in Santa Catalina barracks where one of her brothers, Remedio, was detained. On the pretext of visiting him, Silva de Ochoa passed correspondence to and from Remedio and the other prisoners, keeping them informed of events outside, and although she was not a wealthy woman, she provided them with food and clothing (García y García 1924: 211–14; Balta Campbell 1998: 28). It is not known if Silva de Ochoa's son, Manuel, was an accomplice, but this case shows that ordinary families were divided and that often such divided loyalties were accepted as the norm: she was evidently able to visit both her royalist son and her patriot brother without attracting suspicion.

Other recipients of the Orden del Sol were Ecuadorians Rosa Campusano (c. 1798–c. 1860) from Guayaquil, and Quito-born Manuela Sáenz. Campusano moved to Lima in 1817 and Sáenz two years later with her husband, James Thorne (Carvajal 1949: 41–43). The two women attended rebel meetings and distributed propaganda. Campusano hosted pro-independence *tertulias* for Lima's youth in Calle San Marcelo (Estrada 1984: 48–50). Like Silva de Ochoa, Campusano also socialised with the royalists and held political and literary *tertulias* that were attended by Viceroy La Serna. Campusano would then send political news gained at these events to San Martín (Neuhaus 1997: 117, 121, 122, 125). She also persuaded royalists to join the patriot cause; notably Tomás Heres of the 900-strong Numancia Batallón (Estrada 1984: 48–50).

Women supported the independence cause both openly and covertly. Manuela Estacio was involved in several conspiracy projects. Like Campusano, she persuaded royalist officials to join the patriots, and she also worked to obtain freedom for those who had been imprisoned for their liberal beliefs. This action led Viceroy Pezuela to imprison her. It seems that she obtained her release, possibly after the absolutist Pezuela was deposed by royalist liberals in January 1821; she then worked as a spy, informing San Martín camped on the outskirts of Lima (García y García 1924: 215–16). The upper-class Josefa Carrillo, the Marquesa de Castellón, is said to have openly conspired against the Viceroy by sending and receiving messages and information to the rebels. She used her influence to persuade other upper-class members of Lima to support San Martín. When San Martín entered Lima, he nominated her 'prócera de la Independencia'. Carrillo, celebrated for her beauty and talent, was instrumental in the post-independence celebrations in Lima and worked as an unofficial diplomat to gain foreign support (Parra de Riego 1935: 249; García y García 1924: 231–32). Andrea de Mendoza, the Marquesa de Casa Dávila, hosted aristocratic salons in Lima and invited San Martín to a reception after he entered the city. Her action is said to have broken the coldness of many of the nobility towards San Martín and his troops (García y García 1924: 290). Narcisa Arias de Saavedra y Lavalle was also among those who welcomed San Martín's troops. During the Wars of Independence she had established a hospital at her Lima home and kept food for the patriots there (Parra de Riego 1935: 250; García y García 1924: 280–81). Camila Arnao wrote to San Martín in the name of 'Las Patriotas,' a group of Lima women who offered their services as soldiers in the independence cause. The women pledged to take over from any man who became tired of fighting. This letter was intercepted and given to the Viceroy. Arnao and several of the other women who signed it were imprisoned and then transferred to work in a hospital (García y García 1924: 248, 292).

Not all women who received the award were directly or indirectly connected to San Martín. Manuela Carbajal from Ica, Peru, gave most of her fortune to the independence cause and during the royalist occupation of Ica she smuggled information to the patriots. The royalists issued a warrant for her arrest, but Carbajal went into hiding and continued to work as a spy (García y García 1924: 246–47). Petronila Carrillo de Albornoz of Lima (possibly related to Josefa Carrillo, the Marquesa de Castellón), wrote poems inciting mothers to unite and fight for independence together with their husbands and children. She hosted *tertulias* at which elite women discussed revolutionary themes and donated money and jewels to the cause. She also mingled in Spanish circles, working as a spy, apparently using her beauty and guiles to obtain information for the insurgents (Balta Campbell 1998: 23–27). Not all recipients were young and pretty: seventy year-old María Hermenegilda de Guisla, assisted by her niece, María Simona de Guisla y Vergara, encouraged young revolutionaries to gather at her Lima house. She used her age to divert suspicion, meeting upper-class Spaniards during the daytime, and related their news to the insurgents at night (Balta Campbell 1998: 24). These are just a few from many examples of literate, educated and well-connected women who worked for the independence cause. Many of them did so from within their homes, using them as covers to dupe the Spanish authorities. Yet in doing so they extended beyond their traditional sphere of influence to become actors in the public world of politics.

Andrea de Mendoza was a staunch supporter of San Martín and was later loyal to Bolívar (García y García 1924: 290). But what happened to these women when the royalists retook Lima in 1822; and what of those who had been closely affiliated to San Martín, yet did not support Bolívar when he finally defeated the royalists at the battle of Ayacucho? Elvira García y García offers a possible explanation of how some may have survived. Mercedes Nogareda was one of the first women imprisoned for her work smuggling messages for the patriots and she, like Camila Arnao, was transferred from prison and made to work in a hospital. She managed to escape from the hospital and, according to García y García, continued to smuggle correspondence in Lima under cover of darkness, since it was difficult to distinguish one woman from another (García y García 1924: 250). Here, García y García refers to *tapadas*: the traditional Lima dress of the *saya* and *manto,* behind which women could hide their identities. Basil Hall, an English traveller to Peru in the 1820s, offers a vivid image:

> To us, who took all things as we found them, the saya and manto afforded much amusement and sometimes not a little vexation. It happened occasionally, that we were spoken to in the streets by ladies, who appeared to know us well, but whom we could not discover, till some apparently trivial remark in company long afterwards betrayed the Tapadas, as they call themselves. Ladies of the first rank indulge in this amusement, and will wear the meanest saya, or stoop to any contrivance to effect a thorough disguise. I myself knew two young ladies who completely deceived their brother and me, although we were aware of their fondness for such pranks, and I had even some suspicions of them at the very moment. Their superior dexterity, however, was more than a match for his discernment, or my suspicions; and so completely did they deceive our eyes, and mislead our thoughts, that we could scarcely believe our senses, when they at length chose to discover themselves. (Hall 1840: 23)

Women who had a higher profile had to go into more secure hiding and convents were commonly used as havens or prisons, depending on the leaning of each institution. Numbers could be vast. In one extreme example, some 1,400 people took refuge in the San Francisco convent, Barcelona, Venezuela, which was then defended by the patriot troops (N.A. 1964: 19–21; Knaster 1977: 479–80). Other women simply fled: Rosa Campusano decided to leave Lima in 1822. Her position was perhaps less secure than that of those who had been born in the city; it could have been that as a relative newcomer she felt freer to go; or she perhaps felt that she was too closely linked to San Martín to risk remaining after he left for Guayaquil (Guardia 1985: 48).[13] This attachment did not bring her any lasting harm: Campusano is one of a rare group of women who was given a modest pension by the Peruvian government (Estrada 1984: 48–50) and her name is included on a monument to independence in Quito. She is the only woman mentioned on this plaque; the name of Quito-born Manuela Sáenz is a notable omission.

Sáenz (1793–1856) also left Lima during the royalist reoccupation and assumed a more active role in the fight against Spain. She became Bolívar's mistress in 1822 and took part in the battles of Junín and Ayacucho (see Chapter 2). She was promoted to captain following the battle of Junín. Writing to her in an official capacity from his Junín headquarters on August 6 1824, Bolívar stated:

> En consideración a la Resolución de la junta de Generales de División, y habiendo obtenido de ellos su consentimiento y alegada su ambición personal de usted de participar en la contienda; visto su coraje y valentía de usted de su valiosa humanidad en ayudar a planificar desde su columna las acciones

> que culminaron en el glorioso éxito de este memorable día; me apresuro, siendo las 16:00 horas en punto, en otorgarle el Grado de Capitán de Húzares. (Alvarez 1995: 80)

Bolívar was at pains to stress that the decision to make her a captain was not his alone. Indeed, on December 10 1824, after the battle of Ayacucho, Marshal Antonio José de Sucre wrote to Bolívar recommending Sáenz for further promotion:

> Se ha destacado particularmente Doña Manuela Sáenz por su valentía; incorporándose desde el primer momento a la división de Húzares y luego a la de Vencedores, organizando y proporcionando el avituallamiento de las tropas, atendiendo a los soldados heridos, batiéndose a tiro limpio bajo los fuegos enemigos; rescatando a los heridos. La Providencia nos ha favorecido demasiadamente estos combates. Doña Manuela merece un homenaje particular por su conducta; por lo que ruego a S.E. le otorgue el Grado de Coronel del Ejército Colombiano. (Alvarez 1995: 85)

Some women were, of course, unable to escape punishment and, as the case of Mariana Echevarría de Santiago y Ulloa shows, economic status did not always provide protection. Echevarría married the aristocrat, the Marqués de Torre Tagle, Governor of La Paz province, Bolivia, a brigadier in the royalist army and later governor of Trujillo, Peru. In a move described by Lynch as 'politically devious' (Lynch 1973: xxi), the Marqués de Torre Tagle changed sides after meeting San Martín in 1820 in Trujillo. The Marqués and Echevarría became good friends with San Martín and they moved with him to Lima. Echevarría had a high profile at the fiesta to celebrate the independence of Peru in 1821. According to García y García, she took San Martín's arm and 'con la magestad de una reina' acted as hostess (García y García 1924: 262). Both she and the Marqués were awarded the Orden del Sol, and when San Martín left for Guayaquil to meet Bolívar, he left the Marqués de Torre Tagle holding executive power in his absence, with Monteagudo as Minister of Foreign Affairs. But San Martín's control of Lima was tentative. In his absence, the Lima elite turned against him: Monteagudo was overthrown, and Torre Tagle was attacked. San Martín resigned in September 1822 and left for Europe. Torre Tagle remained in Lima and in January 1824, with Lima in chaos and Bolívar seriously ill, Torre Tagle, further described by Lynch as a 'weak and confused opportunist', again changed sides, along with the leading officials in Lima and over 300 army officers (Lynch 1973: 268). But Bolívar recovered his health and his troops regrouped north of Lima.

The Torre Tagle family hid for a time in the Convento de las Descalzas, before trying to leave Peru from the port of Callao. They were detained by royalist forces, who offered them asylum in Spain provided they recognise the Viceroy as the legitimate ruler of Peru. The Marqués refused, however, and the family was imprisoned (García y García 1924: 262–63). Echevarría died soon afterwards, followed by the Marqués and all but two of their children (Clément

1979: 129; García y García 1924: 263–64). Carlos Parra de Riego claims that Echevarría was persecuted by the spitefulness of Bolívar, who could not forgive her support of San Martín (Parra de Riego 1935: 250). There is also perhaps another reason: in her youth, Echevarría had been married to Demetrio O'Higgins, the Marqués de Osorno, a relative of Bernardo O'Higgins. Bernardo O'Higgins was also closely linked to San Martín and had been forced to abdicate as governor of Chile in 1823. In this case, at least, links with high society proved to be a liability rather than an asset.

The Torre Tagles seem to have been an exception, however; most of the women who were rewarded by San Martín remained in their homes in Lima during the royalist reoccupation and witnessed Bolívar's eventual victory at the end of 1824. The fact that they were women may have afforded them sufficient protection during the royalists' brief return to power; there were simply too many opponents for the royalists to deal with and these women would not have been a priority. Yet, as their names had been printed in official newspapers, it is logical to suppose that, had the royalists succeeded in defeating the patriots, the women may have been punished and exiled in the same way suffered by the women of Bogotá in 1816.

It is, of course, impossible to ascertain San Martín's motives in specifically rewarding so many women, but his attitude suggests that, had he been given the opportunity, he may have encouraged more participation by women in the organisation of the new republics. Looking at San Martín's strategy towards the abolition of slavery may provide an insight into his approach to fundamental changes to the structure of society. Blanchard notes that in August 1821, San Martín embarked on a mission to end Peruvian slavery and the slave trade, but that in doing so he took pains to avoid specifying a date for abolition. San Martín gave the slave owners time to adjust to the new circumstances in much the same way as he had done when he and his soldiers camped on the outskirts of Lima to achieve a peaceful transition to independence. In the case of the abolition of slavery, San Martín's tactics also allowed time to institute laws to protect and to assist former slaves, especially their children, who were to be educated and cared for by their mothers' masters. As Blanchard points out, San Martín's motives were questionable, since he had shown little evidence of pro-abolitionist sympathies in the past, and it may have been that his aim was to secure slave support for independence (Blanchard 1992: 6–10). For the purpose of ascertaining his attitude towards women, however, San Martín's rationale matters less than his action. Not only did he legislate to ensure the abolition of slavery but he also did so in such a way that it could not be reversed. Significantly, part of that law was that freed slaves, *libertos*, of both sexes would gain full citizenship rights at the age of twenty-one (Blanchard 1992: 8). Women, then, were in this case treated equally. While this may have been more of an anti-slavery issue than an indication of his stance towards women in general, that San Martín promised to give former slave women full citizenship indicates that he was offering them more than freedom from a life of subservience beyond emancipation. Broadening the analysis beyond the slavery issue, San Martín's inclusion of so many women in his Orden del Sol suggests that he endorsed at least a degree of recognition for women, if not political equality. He was perhaps preparing the stage for women to take more prominent roles.

The fate of the Orden del Sol helps to clarify why the role of women in the independence struggles took so long to receive national recognition: it was suspended on March 9 1825 because those who received it were said to be using it as a privilege.[14] This seems to substantiate the notion that it was San Martín's initiative, rather an award that Bolívar endorsed, and may indicate Bolívar's determination not to create a new oligarchy that was more in tune with San Martín than with him.

Women patriots of Nueva Granada

The contribution of women to the independence cause was particularly strong in Venezuela and Colombia; moreover, their efforts were praised and welcomed by male patriots. On October 18 1811, for example, twenty-one women from the province of Barinas, Venezuela, signed a 'Representación que hace el bello sexo al gobierno de Barinas, en nombre de las demás de su sexo', offering to enlist in the republican army:

> No ignoran que V.E., atendida la debilidad de su sexo, acaso ha procurado eximirnos de las fatigas militares: pero sabe muy bien V.E. que el amor a la patria vivifica a entes más desnaturalizados y no hay obstáculos por insuperables que no venza. Nosotras, revestidas de un carácter firme y apartando a un lado de flaqueza que se nos atribuye, conocemos en el día los peligros a que está expuesto el país; él nos llama a su socorro y sería una ingratitud negarle unas vidas que sostiene. El sexo femenino, Señor, no teme los horrores de la guerra: el estallido del cañón no hará más que alentarle: su fuego encenderá el deseo de su libertad, que sostendrá a toda costa en obsequio del suelo Patrio. En esa virtud y deseando alistarse en el servicio para suplir el defecto de los Militares que han partido a S. Fernando, suplican a V.E. se sirva tenerlas presente y destinarlas a donde parezca conveniente, baxo el supuesto de que no omitirán sacrificios que conciernan a la seguridad y defensa. (Pérez Vila 1983. November 5 1811: 3–4)

Although their offer was rejected, the republican government forwarded this letter to the *Gazeta de Caracas* to be printed as an example to others. It was duly published with an acknowledgment, expressing the government's appreciation at this display of 'sentimientos nacidos de un verdadero amor a la Patria'. In presenting themselves as patriots, the women stress that neither their perceived physical weakness nor the horrors of war should be seen as barriers to their fighting. Indeed, they could be pointing out that the love of the patria had given strength to certain 'entes desnaturalizados', such as effeminate men: why should not women, too, join them? Vigilio Tosta regards the women's stance as evidence of the patriotic enthusiasm that was sweeping Barinas at that time, due to the presence of Coronel Pedro Briceño Pumar (who was married to Bolívar's niece). Certainly, three of the women who signed this letter were named Briceño. Although Tosta does not raise the issue, his brief details reveal that at least seven of these women were members of the Briceño family, and that the first name to appear was Nicolasa Briceño, the colonel's daughter (Tosta 1987: 73). Evelyn Cherpak states that the women's offer to fight was rejected by the secretary of the provincial government, Nicolás Pumar (Cherpak 1978: 223). Two of the women were named Pumar. The majority of these women who signed the letter were, therefore, upper-class, well-connected women. At this time, independence had been declared in Caracas, but it had not been secured. Were these women genuinely offering to fight, or was their letter a tactic to shame or to inspire more men into recruiting? Whatever the women's motives, or, indeed, if the letter had been instigated by leading male patriots, the fact remains that in 1811 the topic of women's participation was deliberately raised in the Caracas press with a clear statement that their offer of physical participation was welcomed as an example for others. Certainly, in 1813, at least one of the women who signed the letter, Josefa Camejo Venancia (who was married to Coronel Juan Nepomuceno Briceño Méndez) was part of the Patriotic Army in Barinas, and it is said that on May 3 1821 she read out the manifesto declaring the Province of Falcón to be free (N.A. 1964: 40–41).

Women also played important roles in the battles for independence in the southern part of Nueva Granada (present-day Colombia) and several of those who took part were linked to the Comuneros rebellion. Petronila Lozano y Manrique, the daughter of the Comuneros leader, Jorge Lozano y Peralta, was among a group of women who marched to the Viceroy's palace, Bogotá, on July 20 1810, when independence from Spain was first announced (Monsalve 1926: 84–85). On September 28 1817, Gertrudis Vanegas and her mother hid a group of patriots at their home in Machetá, Colombia. The men had escaped from their royalist captors and included the leading rebels, Vicente and Ambrosio Ameyda. Vanegas's husband, Vicente Vásquez, was then fighting for the independence cause and had also been involved in the Comuneros rebellion.[15] A tradition of independent action can also be traced through the descendents of Petronila Prieto y Ricaurte. She was from one of the richest and most influential families in Bogotá and both she and her husband, Francisco Sanz de Santamaría, supported the Comuneros rebellion (Monsalve 1926: 10). Prieto believed in the importance of education for girls, and her daughter, Manuela Sanz de Santamaría de González Manrique, was taught Latin, Italian and French. Manuela Sanz de Santamaría, in turn, wrote an article discussing public education, which was published in the *Papel periódico de Santafé de Bogotá* (Socolow 2000: 170–71). She also hosted *tertulias* of the literary circle *El Buen Gusto* in Bogotá, at which politics and notions of independence from Spain were discussed (Cherpak 1978: 220).[16] Her children, José Angel and Josefa Manrique Sanz de Santamaría, attended. That many of the men known to have frequented these *tertulias* were executed in 1816 during the royalist reoccupation of Bogotá indicates both the radical nature of the discussions and the difficult times in which they were living; other members of the circle were exiled, including Josefa Manrique Sanz de Santamaría, who was sent to Tena (Ecuador).[17]

The many women who were punished for their participation in the independence of Nueva Granada give testimony to the roles they played and to the threat they were deemed to present. At least fifty-four women were executed by the royalists in Colombia alone.[18] Perhaps the best known of these is Policarpa Salavarrieta Ríos 'La Pola'.[19] She was born in Guaduas, Socorro province, around 1795. As Germán Arciniegas points out, she was from the same area as Manuela Beltrán, and although she had been born after the Comuneros rebellion she might have been inspired by those who had taken part (Arciniegas 1961: 80). According to Monsalve, Salavarrieta became active in the independence cause during the Spanish reconquest of Nueva Granada under General Pablo Morillo. Morillo laid siege to Cartagena in 1815, occupied it and then marched south. Bartolomé Mitre describes Salavarrieta as possessing 'alma varonil', and states that her love of her country was equal to that she had for her young *novio,* Alejo Sarabaín, who fought for the patriots (Mitre 1939, IV: 279).

Salavarrieta was persecuted by the royalists for her activities and moved to Bogotá (Monsalve 1926: 190). This was far from a safe haven: Morillo soon reached Bogotá and by May 1816 it was 'besieged, overwhelmed, and immediately subjected to an unprecedented reign of terror' (Lynch 1973: 241). During this time, civilians of all classes suffered; several hundred women were imprisoned and exiled.[20] Salavarrieta became part of a women's spy network based in the home of Andrea Ricaurte de Lozano, where Salavarrieta was lodging. Ricaurte de Lozano had a revolutionary pedigree: she was related to the Comuneros leader, Jorge Lozano, Marqués de San Jorge, and to Petronila Prieto y Ricaurte and Manuela Sanz de Santamaría (mentioned above); and she had been among the group of women who marched on the Viceroy's palace on July 20 1810 (Monsalve 1926: 85). Salavarrieta visited the prisoners' cells, taking food and passing on strategic news heard in the streets; the women kept lists of those who had donated money and jewels to the patriots and the names of those enlisted in the independence army (Arciniegas 1961: 77–89). Sarabaín was detained by the royalists and found to be carrying documents bearing Salavarrieta's name, and a warrant was issued for her arrest. Before she was captured, Salavarrieta managed to warn her *compañeras* to destroy incriminating evidence, and thus saved further prosecutions (Zabala 1948: 40–42).

General Juan Sámano found Salavarrieta guilty of conspiring against the Crown and ordered her execution, along with eight accomplices, including Sarabaín. On November 14 1817, in Bogotá's main plaza, Salavarrieta was shot in the back. She is said to have addressed the crowd before she died: '¡Pueblo indolente! ¡Cuán diversa sería vuestra suerte si conocieses el precio de la libertad! Pero no es tarde. Ved que aunque mujer y joven, me sobra valor para sufrir la muerte y mil muertes más, y no olvidéis este ejemplo' (Monsalve 1926: 195). She would not take water from the Spaniards and refused to have her eyes covered, crying '¡Viva la Patria!' before being shot (Zabala 1948: 42–43).[21]

Salavarrieta quickly passed into folklore; since her death, poems, verses and plays have been written about her, there have been commemorative postage stamps and even beers and a wine label use her image. Alicia Hincapie Borda believes that, although many women were executed in Colombia in the independence cause, Salavarrieta's extreme youth, the execution of her *novio*, her attitude, her defiant speech and the conduct with which she faced her executioners moved the nation, producing great indignation and sorrow and raising patriotic feeling (Hincapie Borda 2000: 155). It is said that General Francisco de Paula Santander commissioned the Colombian playwright José María Domínguez Roche (1788–1858) to write a dramatic piece about Salavarrieta. It was performed for the first time in a Bogotá theatre on July 23 1820 and the audience intervened to prevent her 'execution' (Ardila 1984: 464, 469–70).[22] Eggs, tomatoes, tamales and stones were thrown at the stage to 'save' Salavarrieta, endangering the actors' lives. Order was restored when the management persuaded the audience to shout, as Salavarrieta is alleged to have done, 'Viva la Patria!', thus transforming the riot into an ovation. It was, perhaps, with this in mind that Mitre decided not to have Salavarrieta shot in his play about her story. Instead, it ends with her glorification as she enters the immortality of history (Arciniegas 1961: 77–89).[23]

What inspired women such as Salavarrieta and Ricaurte to support independence from Spain? In a testimony recorded in Bogotá on April 20 1875, Ricaurte explained that her husband, brothers and father-in-law were among the many middle-class creoles who were in favour of independence. On hearing of General Morillo's advance, those who were able fled Bogotá for the mountains, other patriots hid in the city, among them members of Ricaurte's family and social network. When Morillo reached Bogotá, he began to seek out these people, many of whom were executed. In Ricaurte's words:

> Los fusilamientos habían empezado y las persecuciones eran diarios, y el terror tenía sumergidos a los habitantes de la ciudad en luto y lágrimas. Los patriotas, ocultos en los montes, resueltos a trabajar por la libertad de la Patria, se pusieron en comunicación con los que estaban escondidos en la ciudad para formar guerrilleras...
> Se necesitaba un centro de operaciones que se entendiera con las juntas que se reunían en la ciudad y poderse comunicar con las guerrillas; eligieron mi casa, que quedaba en la quinta cuadra de la Carrera de Antioquia; de allí se mandaban las comunicaciones, noticias, recursos y gente para las guerrillas, lo mismo que para Casanare, en donde los Generales Bolívar y Santander estaban formando el ejército libertador. (Monsalve 1926: 191–95)[24]

Ricaurte explained that in 1817, her compadres Ambrosio Almeyda and José Ignacio Rodríguez asked her to give shelter to Salavarrieta, who was escaping the royalists in Guaduas (Monsalve 1926: 193).[25]

Salavarrieta was able to continue to work as a spy in Bogotá, since she was not known in the city and was thus able to move freely and to talk to the prisoners without attracting suspicion. Other members of the spy network were apprehended, however, and soldiers came to Ricaurte's home to arrest Salavarrieta. Seeing the soldiers arrive, Ricaurte continued, Salavarrieta threw papers containing details of patriot movements into the oven, burning them before the soldiers entered. When the royalists had asked about Salavarrieta, Ricaurte had answered 'no sé qué es insurgente'. Ricaurte confirmed in her testimony,

> los papeles quemados contenían cartas de muchos patriotas, la lista de los que daban recursos para auxiliar a los que se iban a las guerrillas, comunicaciones de los jefes de éstas y borrador del estado de las fuerzas de los españoles. (Monsalve 1926: 194)

Although Salavarrieta was apprehended in the kitchen of Ricaurte's home, the traditional women's sphere, the setting saved Ricaurte and the other patriots, whose names were written in the papers: the fire in the oven did not attract suspicion, nor did Ricaurte's professed ignorance of any intrigue.

Were Salavarrieta and Ricaurte merely following their families when supporting the patriots? Was Ricaurte forced into housing Salavarrieta by her patriot relatives? If this were the case, she surely need not have gone to the great lengths that she did to fulfil these duties, and it does not explain the parts played by Salavarrieta and many other women who worked as spies in Spanish American cities during their occupation by the royalists. Indeed, Salavarrieta had moved from Guaduas to continue her work in Bogotá, where she was not known and, presumably, knew few people. Was she manipulated into acting as a spy in return for lodging in a safe house? Again, this seems unlikely: it would have been a high price to pay and Salavarrieta could have simply reported Ricaurte and her circle to the authorities. Did these women and others want independence from Spain for its own sake, or did they hope to use it to achieve more freedom for themselves? In 1875, Ricaurte gave no insight into her motives, merely stating that several members of her family were involved in the independence struggles and that 'en esa época la idea de la emancipación germinaba en muchos de los habitantes de esta ciudad' (Monsalve 1926: 191). Ricaurte may have been diminishing her own role in the light of Salavarrieta's greater sacrifice; she may have been reflecting that men and women were simply caught up in a tide of unrest and were unable to remain neutral in such a political and social climate. Is it significant that she used the term 'emancipation' rather than 'independence'? Is it reading too much into her testimony to suggest that her use of 'en esa época' indicates that she believed times had changed and that the hope and expectations generated by the independence struggles had brought disappointment?

Women and *ciudadanía*

As Arlene Díaz points out, although Venezuela's constitution of 1811 included 'ideas of equality, liberty, individuality, and citizenship'; these initiatives were designed for 'propertied men' (Díaz 2004: 3). Yet Díaz's study of gender relations in Caracas shows that women were influenced by liberal ideas and used the courts to claim their civil liberties. Díaz quotes María Antonia Pérez, who in February 1812 stated, 'the law makes us all equals as citizens, and if my husband is by this right authorised to behave in a free manner, I am, by the same right, entitled to resolve my needs on my own' (Díaz 2004: 1). What is interesting about this case is that Pérez was not citing the law to obtain her status as a citizen, but using it as a starting point for her petition in her divorce case. Díaz states that Pérez '*expected* the laws of the new republic to protect her individual liberties as well as they protected those of men' (Díaz 2004: 2 (my emphasis); see also Whigham 1997).

Women of all classes in Nueva Granada had been using the courts to claim their legal rights before the Wars of Independence (Díaz 2004: 1–65). They continued to see themselves as active participants in the new social order: in Gran Colombia at least, the term 'ciudadana' was regularly used by men and women as early as 1811 during the patriots' control, as can be seen from the pages of the *Gazeta de Caracas*. Remarkably, this newspaper continued to be published almost uninterruptedly during the twelve years of war, and was the official organ of royalists and patriots in turn, according to the leading faction of the day. In addition, Simón Bolívar used 'ciudadana' in official correspondence concerning women who had directly or indirectly supported the independence cause. As the following examples reveal, the term was widely accepted and applied. In November 1811 thirteen 'ciudadanas' were each awarded monthly pensions of 8 pesos after their husbands and/or only sons were killed in the independence struggles (Pérez Vila 1983, November 22 1811: 4). In March the following year, twenty-six 'ciudadanas' from San Luis de Cura, Venezuela, were listed as having donated between 2 reales and 5 pesos each to the Treasury (Pérez Vila 1983, March 17 1812: 4). In 1814 four women from Caracas donated clothing to the independence soldiers and another, Manuela Suarez Urbina, gave cacao to the troops, all are listed as 'ciudadanas' (Pérez Vila 1983, February 7 1814: 156). In October 1821, 'ciudadanas' from Guanare, Venezuela, donated between 2 and 50 pesos to the patriot troops for their fight against Puerto Cabello (Pérez Vila 1983, November 15 1821: 4).

What do these statistics indicate? If one follows the assumption that these women were making donations according to their ability to pay, then 'ciudadana' was designated regardless of class and economic status. Even if this were not the case, this evidence seems to suggest that it was not simply a case of being able to buy one's way into 'ciudadanía'. If it were, at a minimum of 2 reales, it could come comparatively cheaply. In short, the term 'ciudadana' appears to have been used as a conventional description for any woman who was deemed to deserve it. In these cases, at least, this meant women who, to a greater or lesser extent, supported the independence cause directly through economic support to the armies, or those whose husbands and/or sons had been killed in the battles.

General Bernardo O'Higgins employed the term in a decree of December 2 1818, in which he declared María Cornelia Olivares of Chillán, Chile, 'una de las ciudadanas beneméritas del Estado'. Although she was from a royalist family, in 1817 Olivares spoke publicly against the Spaniards in Chillán, Chile, about her hatred of foreigners, the oppressors of the patria. She urged people to fight: 'Hombres y mujeres deben tomar las armas contra los tiranos ... la libertad a todos benefica, todos deben amarla y defenderla.' She was arrested by the royalists, her head was shaved and she was exhibited in the public plaza. She won public admiration because she is said to have remained silent throughout her ordeal, apart from having answered some soldiers who shouted at her: 'La afrente que se recibe por la patria en vez de humillar engrandece' (Miranda 1948: 56–7).

The case of Francisca Prieto y Ricaurte from Bogotá reveals the high cost of gaining citizenship. Prieto y Ricaurte was a member of the upper-class clan that united many of the leading Bogotá families: she was the cousin of Manuela Sanz de Santamaría de González Manrique and was also related to Andrea Ricaurte Lozano. On November 6 1821 Bolívar awarded her an annual pension of 1,000 pesos, explaining in a letter:

> la viuda del más respetable ciudadano de la antigua República de Nueva Granada, se halla reducida a una espantosa miseria, mientras yo gozo de treinta mil pesos de sueldo. Así he venido en ceder a la ciudadana Francisca Prieto mil pesos anuales de los que a mí me corresponden. (Monsalve 1926: 167)

Her husband, 'el respetable ciudadano' Camilo Torres, was the radical politician and the first President of the United Provinces of Gran Colombia. Together, Torres and Prieto y Ricaurte had begun hosting pro-independence meetings in 1810 (Monsalve 1926: 36). In August 1816, Torres, Prieto y Ricaurte and their children were imprisoned by General Morillo, and their wealth was confiscated. As Monsalve notes, the family was left with nothing: items taken included all their household utensils. Prieto y Ricaurte and her children were then forced to walk into exile to the town of Espinal. Torres was executed in Bogotá and his head displayed in the city (Monsalve 1926: 94, 159, 161, 165). Although there is no evidence that Prieto y Ricaurte actually received the pension, Bolívar at least officially acknowledged her sacrifice.

Bolívar's use of 'ciudadana' extended to his sister (see Chapter 2). On March 31 1824 he issued a document authorising María Antonia Bolívar to take over the running of his mines in the Aroa Valley:

> Por la presente autorizo competentemente a mí hermana María Antonia Bolívar para los fines que aquí se expresan.
> 1° — Para tomar posesión en mi nombre del Valle de Aroa y minas de Cocorote.
> 2° — Para reclamar jurídicamente todos los derechos que me corresponden como propietario de estas posesiones, contra todos aquellos arrendatarios intrusos que han disfrutado de mi propiedad injustamente por muchos años.
> 3° — Para que pueda entrar en un contrato expreso y particular con cualquier

> individuo que ofrezca las mayores ventajas por el arrendamiento de dichas mina Valle de Aroa.
> 4º — Ultimamente autorizo a la citada María Antonia Bolívar para que arriende por un tiempo señalado el Valle de Aroa y sus minas, pero con la precisa condición de que de ningún modo seré responsable al pagamiento de las mejoras y bienhechurías que se encuentren en dicho Valle de Aroa, luego que llegue el término del arrendamiento, y sea devuelto a mi inmediato dominio y uso propio. También entrará como cláusula expresa del contrato su no validez mientras que no sea aprobado por mí, y mandado a ejecutar según mi dictamen y decisión posterior.
> En virtud de este poder que doy en la mejor forma posible, la ciudadana María Antonia Bolívar se encuentra ampliamente autorizada para llenar los fines que aquí se expresan, para lo que le otorgo el competente instrumento, conforme a derecho, y lo más que conviniere conforme a las cláusulas de estilo que añadirá el escribano por ante quien se ha de otorgar este poder. (Lecuna 1929: 423–24)

In designating his sister trustee of the mines, Bolívar revealed his confidence in her and his faith in her judgement as a competent businesswoman. Bolívar described her as a 'ciudadana' to underline her legal rights as a citizen in the republic. Indeed, in each of the cases illustrated here he used 'la ciudadana' to designate that each of these women had legal rights within republican legislation. He employed the term deliberately, as a matter of course, indicating that he considered that all women who contributed to the patriot cause merited the designation 'ciudadana'.

Bolívar did not only designate upper class women 'ciudadanas'. On November 19 1817 he ordered that María de Jesús Correa and María de Jesús Silva and their families be given daily rations:

> Disponga Vuestra Señoría que a las familias del ciudadano Mayor Pedro Correa y de su hermana María de Jesús, se le pasen seis raciones diariamente y una a la ciudadana María del Jesús Silva; previniendo al Comandante del Batallón de esta plaza que no reclute al joven Miguel Orta, hijo de la expresada ciudadana María del Jesús Correa, pues es el único apoyo de esa familia para solicitar los demás medios de subsistencia. (Monsalve 1926: 255)

On the death of her husband, José de Orta, María de Jesús Correa had offered her sons to the independence cause. Bolívar had insisted that her youngest son, Miguel, stay with her. María del Jesús Silva's brother, General Leurecio Silva, had served in the campaigns of 1817 (Monsalve 1926: 79–80). In these cases, the contribution of husbands, brothers and sons directly reflected on their female relatives.

The term 'ciudadana' was publicly used by a variety of people in different circumstances. What did it mean? Jay Kinsbruner, among others (see Chapter 1), makes the distinction 'active' citizens, namely, those who had a vote and could hold office (Kinsbruner 1973: 52). Literacy and property restrictions ensured that the majority of Spanish Americans, men and women alike, were not eligible to vote in the early nineteenth century. As Lynch notes, 'the new rulers were careful to guard their inheritance' (Lynch 1973: 226) and these 'new rulers' were overwhelmingly white, educated, wealthy men. These women, then, were among the majority 'passive' 'ciudadanos'. Yet there seems to be little doubt that women's participation, both overt and covert, was welcomed by the patriots during the independence struggles and it is probable that their contribution was actively sought at specific times. Women soldiers, for example, were more able to accomplish certain tasks than men: Juana Azurduy's combination of 'varonil' power and feminine grace was an inspiration to her troops and a source of comfort and consolation. Both María Remedios del Valle and Manuela Sáenz fulfilled the roles of soldier and nurse during their time in combat. In designating women 'el sexo más sensible', San Martín appears to have deemed women to be worthy patriots in their own right. Indeed, he drew on the basis of their supposed natural sensitivity: the feelings and emotions that made them instrumental in binding society together.

Women may have been valued during the struggles for independence, but once independence from Spain was finally achieved, they were expected to return to their embroidery. San Martín and Belgrano may have intended to set the foundations for the social advancement of women, but neither of them had the opportunity to put these ideas into long-term practice. Bolívar was better placed to do so, but by 1830 he, too, was on his way to exile and death. Although he had rewarded his mistress for her prowess as a soldier, and freely used the term 'ciudadana', he made no concrete concessions in his legislation to give women a greater voice in the independent Spanish America than they had possessed during the colonial period (see Chapter 2). The aftermath of independence saw a patriarchal, hierarchical regime perpetuated by the creole elite; yet in taking the initiative at a time of political and social crisis, women had clearly revealed their physical and mental strength as valuable participants in the development of their societies.

Notes

1 As Johnson notes, Cortés scarcely mentions women at all. She is among those who underline the great importance of Doña Marina (Johnson 1983: 48, 51). See also Díaz del Castillo 1963: 85–87.

2 Díaz later recalled that there were six women from Castile who were killed in Tustepeque (Díaz del Castillo 1968: 74).

3 Charles V is said to have personally requested a sequel to the adventures of Belianis de Grecia and to have ordered the translation into Spanish of a French chivalric novel.

4 Velázquez's orders dated October 23 1518 were heavily influenced by Mandeville. They specified that Cortés should find out about the people and the land, 'because it is said that there are people with large, broad ears and others with faces like dogs, and also where and in what direction are the Amazons, who are nearby according to the Indians whom you are taking with you' (Leonard 1949: 46).

5 Although Stephen Greenblatt introduces Mandeville as a 'steady liar', he traces the name Mandeville to the fourteenth-century satirical story *Le Roman de Mandevie* and suggests that the travels were never intended to be taken seriously (Greenblatt 1991: 7, 32).

6 Her source, however, is Bernal Díaz, who does not mention María de Estrada's contribution as a soldier.

7 For a list of the men and women convicted and sentenced see O'Phelan 1985: 299–309.

8 An anonymous chronicler commented on the inhumane and ungodly attitude of the Spaniards. See Cornejo Bournoncle 1949: 105–106, 152–72; de Austria 1960: 55.

9 Monsalve conducted an archival search to ascertain more information about Beltrán and what happened to her afterwards. He was unable to find any details other than that she had a shop on Socorro's main plaza and had the title doña, which was then reserved for distinguished people. He adds that one *cronista* described her as elderly, but Monsalve found nothing to substantiate this and claims her enthusiasm and behaviour were not those usually attributed to the elderly. M. Pallis and Mary Louise Pratt describe Beltrán as a former cigarette seller from Socorro (Pallis 1980: 24; Pratt 1990: 48).

10 Jean Adam Graaner, *Las Provincias del Río de la Plata en 1816*, Buenos Aires 1949, pp. 65–116, quoted by Piccirilli 1957: 249.

11 She took part in the assault of Chuquisaca on February 10 and 11 1816 and battles at Tarabuco and La Laguna. On June 11 1816 she led one of six columns in another attack on Chuquisaca.

12 Women were also eligible for inclusion in France's legion, although there is no evidence that women were among the early recipients.

13 Campusano may have become San Martín's mistress. Jenny Estrada claims that he was deeply in love with her and gave her the title 'La Protectora'; Rumazo González states that she possibly became his mistress in 1821, whereas Carlos Neuhaus doubts that she had a relationship with San Martín and maintains that the title 'La Protectora' came from the Peruvian author Ricardo Palma, who met Campusano in 1846 and was taken by her beauty (Estrada 1984: 48–50; Rumazo González 1945: 112; Neuhaus 1997: 117, 121, 122, 125).

14 Ministerio de Relaciones Exteriores del Perú website, http://www.rree.gob.pe/portal/dcanciller.

15 Díaz y Díaz 1962: 74–75; Monsalve 1926: 190. Vanegas saved the Almeyda brothers, but her husband was captured at the battle of Tibirita and taken to Bogotá, where he was executed six months later.

16 Among those who attended were Camilo Torres and Alexander Von Humboldt.

17 For more details of those who attended and their fates, see the database created from the research from this book http://genderlatam.org.uk/.

18 The names and brief details of the lives of these women can be seen on http://genderlatam.org.uk/.

19 Her name also appears as Salavatierra and Salvatierra. This is probably due to the rush to prove that her name was an anagram of 'Nace por salvar la tierra'. She was named in Bello's poem 'Alocución a la poesía'.

20 For details of these women and others see http://genderlatam.org.uk/.

21 It is not possible to verify the authenticity of these secondary sources, but that so many exist reveals the power of her image.

22 The date of the first performance of this play is provided by Hincapie Borda 2000: 47–48.

23 He adds that the play was performed in Montevideo and that Mitre's intention was to inflame Argentine patriotism and to denounce the then dictator of Argentina, Juan Manuel Rosas.

24 In reproducing her testimony, Monsalve notes that there are many historical inaccuracies, and that this should be expected, as it was made a considerable number of years after the event.

25 Ricaurte's network may have been connected to that of Gertrudis Vanegas, as both were linked to the Almeydas.

CHAPTER SEVEN

Women, Letter-Writing and the Wars of Independence in Chile

Nosotras solo sabíamos
ir a oír misa y rezar
Adornar nuestros vestidos
Y zurcir y remendar
(Mariquita Sánchez de Thompson in Gómez Paz 1976: 45–46)[1]

As will have become apparent, despite efforts to restrict their education many Spanish American women were literate during the colonial period and were writing letters in the public and private spheres. The quality of education of women varied throughout Spanish America: in Peru, for example, the education of selected elite girls in convent schools had been formalised by the end of the sixteenth century (Martín 1983: 75); whereas Mexican laws in 1810 stated that women could be taught to read, but not to write. This was said to prevent women from composing love letters (Arrom 1985: 296). But such legal anomalies did not deter women. The social and political turbulence during the Wars of Independence, however, gave women reason to embark on a frenzy of letter-writing as families were separated and women were actively and passively drawn into the civil wars by accident or their own design. As mentioned in Chapter 6, letters from women offering to fight for the independence cause were printed in the national press, but the political situation meant that the majority of letters written by women at that time were distributed in the private sphere. This chapter gives an overview of the development of women's education in the late colonial period. It discusses the growth of women's literacy through the *tertulias* they hosted in their homes and how the public sphere increasingly encroached on these meetings as political events dominated social gatherings. It then looks at letters written and sent to Santiago de Chile, especially those of the Carrera family, and how women voiced their personal and political aspirations through this medium.

Women, education and the late colonial press

During the colonial period, liberal ideas had spread to Latin America from Europe and North America. Scientific discoveries and experiments in physiology led to new debates about the capabilities of men and women and the intellectual differences between them. In Spain, as mentioned previously, Feijóo challenged so-called female inferiority. In his 'Defensa de las mujeres' (1726) he referred to the current debate about whether women's brains were softer than those of men. While acknowledging this might well be the case, he decided that this did not imply that women were inferior. He agreed that women were less physically strong, but claimed that the intellectual capacities of men and women were equal. He added that in the interests of order and harmony women should be subservient to men: 'Though both be equal in talents and understanding, the decorum and tranquillity of the house and family require subordination, as otherwise it would have frequently been a scene of clamour and confusion' (Feijóo 1774: 213–14). Feijóo's work was widely distributed in Spanish America: at the beginning of the nineteenth century, Alexander Von Humboldt found a copy of Feijóo's *Teatro Crítico* among a collection of books at the isolated Convent of Caripe, New Andalusia (Venezuela). He commented, 'it seemed as if the progress of knowledge advanced even in the forests of America' (Humboldt 1852: 252).

Education for girls became an important issue of discussion. In 1790, Josefa Amar y Borbón of Bogotá wrote *Discurso sobre la educación física y moral de las mujeres,* in which she objected to the idea that girls should be attractive and obedient.[2] She took Feijóo's idea that with proper instruction women could be equal in capabilities to men, and expanded it to insist on their education (Arrom 1985: 16). Josefina Zoraida Vásquez points out that Amar y Borbón was 'less of an innovator than Feijóo', because she claimed that a lack of education prevented women from becoming 'true human beings' and that this was 'to the detriment of their husbands and children' (Zoraida Vásquez 1994: 20). While this may have been the case, it could also have been a ruse: she perhaps deliberately tailored her ideas to make them more acceptable to male-dominated society. Possibly using the same tactic, in 1802 an article in the Buenos Aires publication *El Telégrafo Mercantil,* translated from French by a Buenos Aires woman, stated that women should be educated to enable them to become useful wives (Mendelson 1978: 203). In December 1805, the *Diario de México* pointed out that women were denied learning opportunities and underlined that an intelligent wife was an asset. Four years later, the question 'should women be enlightened' was asked in the *Semanario Económica de México.* It maintained that women had the right to schooling so they could be respected as wives and mothers (Mendelson 1978: 201–03).

The Lima newspaper *El Mercurio Peruano* was established in January 1791 as the spokespiece for the literary group the Amantes del País (see Chapter 5).[3] The following month, it issued a direct appeal for letters from women: 'De todos modos deseámos, que alguna Señorita de las muchas ilustradas y filósofas, de que abunda esta Capital, nos honrase con alguna carta ó disertacion justificativa de los supuestos defectos de su amable sexo, y descubridora de los verdaderos del nuestro' (*Mercurio Peruano* 12, February 10 1791: 114). In February 1791, a contributor identified by the initials MYCYV reviewed the first five editions and voiced regret about the lack of female contributors; there had been only two women's names, one of which was an anagram, the other hidden behind a family name. She or he challenged women to write openly to the paper:

> ¿Es posible que en una Capital como esa, adonde la viveza, la penetracion, y el buen gusto parecen prendas vinculadas á la hermosura del sexo amable, no haya habido siquiera doce ó veinte Señoritas capaces de hacer parecer su nombre en el frontispicio de una obra periódica? (*Mercurio Peruano* 17, February 27 1791: 152–56)

Female literacy, it continues, is nothing to be ashamed of: 'No es defecto en una muger el deseo de ilustrarse, ó á lo menos pasar el tiempo en la lectura'.

When women responded to the challenge, however, they did not necessarily discuss topics that were deemed to be safe or suitable. Three months later, 'Acignio Sartoc' reported on a debate surrounding the case of Doña N., a Cuzco woman who had torn up a legal document, describing her as the 'muger legítima' of her husband. Instead, Doña N. insisted that 'señora legítima y conjunta persona de Don –' be used. She explained, 'mugeres son infinitas que andan por este mundo. Yo soy Señora y jamas admito otro título' (*Mercurio Peruano* 40, May 19 1791: 45). Luis Martín claims that 'Doña N.' became the heroine of women who desired freedom and equality and shocked many men by her 'incredible' behaviour (Martín 1983: 307–08). In her eyes, at least, 'muger' was a category and not a term of respect, whereas 'Señora' indicated increased status. Doña Lucinda del Cuzco then replied 'en defensa del Señorio de las mugeres' stating that women should be treated with respect regardless of birth. Doña Lucinda's letter was dated June 30 1791, but did not appear in the paper until the following January. A note from the editors explained they had not published it earlier due to the vast amount of correspondence received on a variety of subjects (*Mercurio Peruano* 111, January 26 1792: 62–67). Yet a six-month delay seems to contradict the paper's earlier messages of encouragement to women contributors and suggests that if women were offered a voice it would be limited and controlled. By broadening the issue to include other social classes, Doña Lucinda had perhaps overstepped the newspaper editors' bounds of social acceptability: in their opinion women, whether 'mugers' or 'señoras', came from the upper reaches of society. Her letter was published, but at a time when interest in the affair had receded.

A major theme of the *Semanario crítico* (Lima, 1791) was to provide advice to elite women as to how they might be good mothers and suggested the best ways to educate their children (Rosas Lauro 1999b: 145) (see Chapter 5). While the emphasis of the paper was didactic and educational, it included many polemics with *El Mercurio Peruano*.[4] The *Semanario crítico,* a weekly, published a serialised sketch entitled 'Rasgo pintoresco de una Madama Limeña', a Romantic, first-person narration of a man leaving his homeland by sea and caught in a storm.[5] Ella Dunbar Temple describes the pieces, rather unfairly, as mediocre literary fantasy and adds that the anonymous author was likely to have been a man, as were many of the allegedly 'female' contributors to other newspapers of that time.[6] Why would men do this: to encourage women to write, to give the appearance of being liberal, or to shirk responsibility for their work? The series ends in the penultimate edition of the newspaper with the note 'Por indisposicion actual de la Madama Autora no ha podido verificarse en este discurso la conclusion del presente rasgo'.[7] *Semanario Crítico* lasted for just sixteen editions; Dunbar Temple concludes that it folded because its moral tone was out of tune with the times. It did not fulfil the pledges of its prospectus, among them to discuss literary salons, café culture and other social events: subjects that would have interested female readers (Dunbar Temple 1943: 29–30).

Women used their traditional ties with the Church and charitable institutions to expand into the sphere of education. As the well-documented case of Sor Juana Inés de la Cruz illustrates, convents provided sanctuaries for Latin American women, giving them the space and freedom to follow their intellectual ambitions. In the seventeenth century, it was common practice for upper-class women to enter convents, with as many as 20 per cent of Lima women in such institutions (Keen 1992: 118). In late colonial Mexico City, an elderly widow, a former Countess of Cortina, María Ana Gómez, founded the community of Las Hermanas de San Vicente de Paul with ten Spanish sisters and a mother superior. A house was set up in the Colegio de las Bonitas to protect illegitimate daughters from prostitution. She extended this community to include four hospitals.[8] Gómez then requested that Sisters of Charity staff Mexico City's hospitals and establish schools for artisans' daughters (Arrom 1985: 48).[9]

At the end of the colonial period, the emphasis on women's education was strongly domestic, although some women did object to the courses of study. In Buenos Aires, for example, Josefa de Carballo set up a *Colegio* for female enlightenment that specialised in 'decency'. The 1802 curriculum for her school for girls aged eight years and over was music, embroidery and physical education (Mendelson 1978: 203–04). In 1808, Mexican María Francisca de Nava issued a pamphlet that condemned women's relegation to 'the sewing cushion and the stove' as 'an abuse' (Arrom 1985: 48, 50). Nine years later, Dalmira Regurviasa petitioned the Mexican courts for better education for women (Zoraida Vásquez 1994: 21).

Women's literary activity in colonial Chile

Women, then, particularly those living in the colonial cities, were receiving some form of education at the end of the colonial era. Pupils were mainly, but not exclusively, from wealthier backgrounds: the lower class mestiza, Juana Azurduy, for example, whose military career is discussed in Chapter 6, was taught basic literacy in a convent. Education for girls was largely conducted in the private sphere, in nunneries and in the home, but towards the end of the colonial period, women's literacy was expanding. Women read newspapers and may have contributed to them; a café culture was developing and literary salons, *tertulias* and *veladas,* enabled women to write and to present their work in public. *Tertulias* were centres of serious discussion and circles of intellectual exchange, at which poems and manuscripts were read and criticised. During the colonial period, Manuela de Orantia hosted *tertulias* in Lima, at which she recited poems in French and Italian (Denegri 1996: 120, n. 32).[10]

Colonial society in Chile was concentrated in and around the capital Santiago de Chile. A province of the Viceroyalty of Peru until 1778, it was politically and economically subservient to Lima until 1798. Nonetheless, there was a strong creole elite and during the late colonial period, Santiago was developing a thriving culture. The Carmelite nun, Sor Tadea de San Joaquín, (c. 1750–1827) wrote what is considered to be the first poem by a Chilean woman (Knaster 1977: 75). Her graphic account of the flooding of the Monasterio del Carmen de San Rafael in 1770, when the Mapocho River burst its banks, and the nuns' miraculous escape by wading through water that was waist high, was published in Lima in 1784 (Urzua and Adriasola: 13–14).

Several upper-class women hosted literary *tertulias.* Among them was Louisa Recabarren (b. 1777) who, with her husband Gaspar Marín (b. 1772), held meetings that were attended by leading literary figures who would later become involved in the struggle for independence.[11] In the build-up to independence, the social, historical and religious discussions became increasingly political. Recabarren recognised the value of education and taught her children at home: Ventura Marín became a writer and philosopher, Francisco an orator and statesman, and Mercedes Marín de Solar a renowned poet (Grez 1966: 63–65; Weeks 1940: 176–77) (see Chapter 8).

Literary activity had its dangers during the independence period. In October 1814 Gaspar Marín went into hiding and later into exile in Mendoza. Recabarren remained in Santiago, where patriots continued to meet at her home (see Chapter 8). In an exchange of letters, Marín sent news from Mendoza and Recabarren kept Marín informed of political developments in Santiago. A letter from Recabarren to Manuel Rodríguez was discovered when Rodríguez was captured by the royalists in Melipilla. Recabarren was arrested and detained in the Monasterio de las Agustinas on January 4 1817. Her imprisonment ended six weeks later, after the patriots defeated the royalists at Chacabuco (Grez 1966: 65–66; Weeks 1940: 176–77).

Manuela Rozas likewise held *tertulias* in her Santiago home, at which independence was discussed (Arambel Guiñazú and Martin 2001: 37). Although from an influential royalist family, she openly conspired with the patriots and pledged her fortune to the independence cause. Rozas was followed on suspicion of amassing a cache of arms and was apprehended while reading a letter from an exiled patriot. According to Vicente Grez, she managed to destroy the letter by swallowing it; she is then alleged to have smiled at the royalist solider and suggested he should conduct an autopsy (Grez 1966: 89–91).

Not all well-connected Chilean women fared so well. Agueda Monasterio (c. 1776–1817), from a very old colonial family, became a supporter of the independence cause following her marriage to Juan Lattapiat, a French official who had served in Buenos Aires under Liniers. She hosted *tertulias* that were modest in comparison to others, and those who attended were less wealthy than those of 'el mundo elegante'. Grez describes Monasterio as 'una figura noble, llena de altivez y de energía', who dominated these meetings with her talent, character, virtues and enthusiasm. Together with her daughter, Juana Lattapiat Monasterio (born around 1797), she wrote letters to patriots in exile with news of political developments. In early 1817 a letter addressed to San Martín was intercepted and the two were arrested. Juana was found guilty of writing letters dictated by her mother, and her right hand was cut off; Monasterio was sentenced to be executed. The execution was suspended, however, possibly for fear of public outcry, and the two were released. Her imprisonment and Juana's mutilation had taken their toll on Monasterio, who died a few days after her release and just six days before the patriot's victory at Chacabuco (Grez 1966: 67–70). This case is important, as it shows that *tertulias* were not exclusively the domain of the upper classes; indeed, Grez portrays them as the democratic force of the revolution for independence. It also reveals the seriousness with which the writing of subversive texts was perceived by the authorities. Although Monasterio was not executed, the royalists apparently had no qualms about severing the hand of a young girl, the instrument of her 'sins'. It seems they believed that by removing her hand, her physical means of writing, she would no longer be a threat to their control.

Letters continued to be written, of course, and increasingly so as families were torn apart by war and exile. Many of those written were political in nature, but many more belonged to the private sphere, which was extended by the political circumstances to stretch across the American continent. As well as providing invaluable snapshots of everyday life during these turbulent times, letters show how women were acting despite efforts to restrict their education to domestic roles. The letters of the Carrera family from 1814 to 1821, many of which are still only available as manuscripts, offer a personalised story of the course of Chilean independence and provide a representative case study of the historical significance of women's personal correspondence. They reveal the multiples roles of women: as wives, sisters and mothers; their growing roles as informants to those in exile, their work to support political prisoners; their means of personal and political expression; and their dealings with those in political power. The letters also expose the fluctuating fortunes of war, the fickle nature of being a Chilean patriot, and the anguish of separation, disgrace and death.

The Carrera correspondence

The Carreras were from a privileged background in colonial Santiago. A monarchist and moderate, Ignacio de la Carrera (c. 1747–1818) was a military man who became a member of the *cabildo abierto* of September 18 1810, and he was elected to the junta of 1811. His three sons played active parts in the Wars of Independence: Juan José Carrera Verdugo (1782–1819) became a brigadier; General José Miguel Carrera Verdugo (1785–1821) led Chile's junta from 1811 to 1814, and was the first president of Chile; and Luis Florentino Carrera Verdugo (1791–1819) was a colonel. His daughter, Francisca Javiera Carrera Verdugo (1781–1862), hosted *tertulias* in Santiago with Mercedes Fuentecilla (b. 1799) the wife of José Miguel and Ana Cotapos (1794–c. 1832), who was married to Juan José. Grez describes these meetings as 'el verdadero hogar de la revolución'. Politics dominated the discussions and at one of them a blue, white and yellow flag was designed. Grez maintains that it was 'confeccionada por manos femeninas y según todas probabilidades la idea fue exclusiva de doña Javiera Carrera' (Grez 1966: 55–56). As a leading figure in Santiago with a tragic story, with which Chileans remain uncomfortable, Javiera Carrera has been given much attention in secondary sources. As pointed out in Chapter 6, the roles of women in Latin America have long been subject to exaggeration, making it difficult to tease out the facts; those of Javiera Carrera, Ana Cotapos and Mercedes Fuentecilla are no exceptions. Grez maintains that Fuentecilla gave birth to her son in the Argentine desert (Grez 1966: 75–78); yet according to her letters, José Miguel Carrera was born in the town of Rosario (Vergara Quiroz 1987: 106). Both Grez and Elsa Chaney claim that Javiera Carrera accompanied her brothers into battle (Grez 1966: 60–62; Chaney 1979: 51, 56), although there seems to be nothing in the primary sources to substantiate this. Sergio Vergara Quiroz states that Javiera Carrera proposed education for women in 1812 (Vergara Quiroz 1987: xxv, xxx), but the degree to which she was directly involved is unclear. Certainly, education was one of José Miguel Carrera's priorities during his rule of the junta. In 1813, he decreed that there should be two schools for each settlement of over fifty families (one for boys and one for girls). He also ordered that every convent should create a school for girls. Education at all of these institutions was to be free of charge (Galdames. 1941: 134). It is likely that Javiera Carrera fully supported these measures and it is feasible that she persuaded her brother to enact the necessary legislation to ensure that education for girls was considerably expanded in the early Chilean republic. By examining the written evidence left by these women, it is hoped to gain a more accurate idea of how they acted and reacted to their changing circumstances. In doing so this chapter offers an insight into their characters and emotions.

The fortunes of the Carrera family fluctuated more than most during the Wars of Independence. In 1811 José Miguel Carrera, with substantial military support, became leader of the new junta with Gaspar Marín and Juan Martínez de Rozas (Bernardo O'Higgins was the temporary representative of Rozas). It was an uneasy alliance: Lynch describes Carrera as a 'military caudillo' who was 'fired with ambition for personal power'. Furthermore, he adds that for a man who claimed to have popular support and to represent 'the people', 'Carrera was singularly reticent in voicing their needs' (Lynch 1973: 134). Shortly after taking control of the junta, Carrera assumed dictatorial powers, widening the rift between him and the other members. Rozas refused to recognise Carrera, but was exiled to Mendoza, where he died in 1813 (Galdames 1941: 172). This move would have important repercussions, in that it made an enemy of O'Higgins. The Carreras had military support, but their attitude in power created much resentment. Grez describes a fiesta held at the Palacio de la Moneda on September 18 1811 to celebrate the first anniversary of the junta, at which the Carrera family played a leading role. Javiera Carrera wore 'una guirnalda de perlas y diamantes, de la cual pendía una corona trastornada'. Josefa Aldunate (a cousin of the Carreras) was dressed as Libertad and Mercedes Fuentecilla as Aurora ('La aurora de la nueva patria'). Luis and José Miguel Carrera 'llevaban una corona de oro bordada en sus sombreros, sobre lo cual caía con violencia una espalda que debía partirla'. Without giving his sources,[12] Grez maintains that royalists began rumours that the Carreras were giving themselves royal airs. He states that a banner proclaimed: '1810 – Ultimo año del despotismo', to which was added 'Y el principio de lo mismo' (Grez 1966: 60–62). Whether accurate or not, the impression created is one of a rich and powerful family and it is not difficult to imagine that royalists and republicans alike would have viewed the exchange of a distant king for this new creole 'royal' family with dismay.

There may have been murmurs against the Carreras, but factions within the patriot ranks could be temporarily forgotten while there was a bigger common enemy. In early 1813, royalist forces from Lima were sent to pacify the patriots and Chileans united under the Carreras and O'Higgins. The patriots suffered heavy strategic losses in Concepción in the south, and José Miguel and Luis Carrera were captured and imprisoned. O'Higgins managed to retain control of Santiago, and Francisco de la Lastra became director of Chile. In May 1814 Lastra signed a treaty with the royalists, into which a secret clause was inserted that the Carreras should remain in prison; Luis Galdames maintains that the royalists then allowed the Carreras to escape, in the hope of weakening their opponents. The Carreras went to Santiago, where they staged a coup against Lastra, set up a junta, and sent any possible Chilean opponents to exile in Argentina. This group included Juan Mackenna, a close associate of O'Higgins. O'Higgins then marched on Santiago, where he clashed with Luis Carrera's troops. Taking advantage of the disruption, the Viceroy of Lima sent more royalist troops to retake Chile. Again, the prospect of losing the gains of the past four years brought a temporary reconciliation, and O'Higgins recognised Carrera's junta. Patriots under O'Higgins and Carrera were defeated at the battle of Rancagua on October 2 1814, and those who were able fled to Mendoza, among them O'Higgins and the Carrera brothers (Galdames 1941: 177–85). Javiera Carrera, Mercedes Fuentecilla and Ana Cotapos also made their way across the Andes.

According to Thomas Sutcliffe, many of those who crossed the Andes travelled on foot; he emphasises, 'the hardships and sufferings they had to undergo are not to be described' (Sutcliffe 1841: 110). Javiera Carrera had left her Spanish-born husband, Pedro Díaz de Valdez, and their children in Santiago. On November 15 1814 she wrote to Díaz de Valdés from Mendoza, explaining her situation:

> Valdés: Nunca creí sería tanta tu indolencia en los graves apuros que sufrimos desde la Aconcagua. Te escribí haciéndote ver emprendía el paso de la cordillera a mi pesar, por sólo el temor del Ejército Real que se aproximaba aquel punto en donde creí hay tormento que no sufra. Creo que los más emigrados que hay aquí han tenido cartas de su casa, sólo tú no has podido hacer un propio mil sujetos habrán para este fin. ¿Qué se han hecho las protestas que me hacías contando con que una mujer no se mezcla en gobierno, y si tuve influjo? Todo fue a favor de ustedes, ¿no me asegurabas que verías a señor Osorio y en mi casa no habría novedad? (Vergara Quiroz 1987: 86)

Her greeting is abrupt: she begins other letters to him with the more affable 'Mi amado Valdés'; 'Mi Valdés'.[13] She is clearly very annoyed with him because he has neither helped her nor appeared to have taken her problems seriously. She refers to an earlier letter in which she had explained that she had gone into exile only because she was afraid of the royalist army pursuing them. She had not intended to leave Chile, but to go into hiding for a while, and voices her regret that she felt she had to flee. She also reveals the importance of letters to those in exile: this was their only means of contact, and that Valdés had not answered hers only serves to increase her irritation. Letters were clearly getting through, since she states that most of the others have received news from home. Javiera Carrera and Valdés evidently did not part on good terms: she refers to previous arguments in which he had expressed the view that women should not interfere in politics. Far from conceding to this view from her position of forced exile, Carrera feels vindicated: Valdés had left her to safeguard her own interests; he neither protected her nor used his influence as a Spaniard by putting their case to General Mariano Osorio (the commander of the invading royalist forces from Peru).

In the same letter, Carrera underlines the importance of news from home: in its absence rumours abound:

> Dios quiera sean falsas todas las que corren aquí, la que más me atormenta es la prisión de mi amado padre, no puedo figurarme hayan hombres tan desconocidos e injustos que a un señor tan separado de toda idea contra las sarasas, más bien, siempre de una opinión con ustedes, lo reduzcan a la miseria, esto sería una crueldad. Tú creo puedes evitarlo, así como por ti el propio mi padre y yo mil veces los hemos servido, en fin sin pérdida de momento dime todo lo que hay, así para regresarme allá como mi padre y nuestros bienes. Si entiende para volver había con pasaporte de señor Osorio y que tú u otro amigo viniese hasta el pie de la Cordillera, sí se trata de escoltarme no alguno que sabes soy de poca paciencia. (Vergara Quiroz 1987: 86–87)

The rumours were correct. Ignacio Carrera had been arrested and would be imprisoned for over two years on Juan Fernández island. The way in which the former monarchist and member of the junta was treated perhaps justified Javiera

Carrera's decision to go into exile, but she nonetheless feels guilty and uneasy about leaving him behind. She entreats Díaz de Valdés to use his influence to help her father, reminding him of all she and her family have done for him in the past. In doing so she shows herself to be dominant in their relationship: despite her position and her distance from Santiago, she is telling Valdés what he should be doing. Above all, she needs to know what is happening in Santiago. She is a practical woman and spells out to Valdés that she must have a passport to return to Chile and that he, or someone else, must take it to the foot of the Andes. Finally, she underlines that she is a woman of little patience: he must act, and he must act quickly.

It is intriguing that Javiera Carrera did not mention the difficulties of her journey across the Andes, as described by Thomas Sutcliffe. Sutcliffe arrived in Chile in 1822 and presumably heard about the crossing from the people who had undertaken it eight years earlier. It is feasible that Carrera had written of this in the earlier letter to Valdés to which she refers, but the prospect of returning so soon did not seem to present a problem to her. Fear of the royalist army had driven her across the Andes and caused her to leave the rest of her family behind (or at least this is what she told her husband). This leads one to deduce that she was in good physical condition and easily withstood the crossing; that the fear of the royalists was so strong she did not notice the exertion of the journey; that it was only later, when the danger had passed, that the former exiles spoke of the difficulties they had endured; or that Sutcliffe exaggerated their plight.

She also had news of events in Mendoza: 'Aquí nos han hecho un recibimiento terrible, sin saber por qué tuvieron a J.M y J.J. cuatro días in cuartel con Uribe y Diego Benavente, y después los mandan escoltados a Buenos Aires' (Vergara Quiroz 1987: 87). The privileges enjoyed by José Miguel and Juan José Carrera in Chile, due to their wealth and considerable military following, no longer applied in Mendoza. The Carreras were no longer in command, but subject to others; moreover, they had been escorted to Buenos Aires to ensure that they followed their orders. They were in San Martín's territory and he soon became more favourably disposed towards the O'Higgins/Mackenna faction. Galdames maintains that the arrogance of the Carreras 'obliged San Martín to take energetic measures against them' (Galdames 1941: 193). Anticipating that there might be problems in Mendoza, José Miguel Carrera had already sent Luis Carrera to Buenos Aires to put their case before the governor of Buenos Aires, Gervasio Antonio Posadas. According to Benjamin Vicuña Mackenna, Posadas gave Carrera 'vagas promesas' during talks on November 6 1814. Tensions increased on November 15, when Luis Carrera killed Juan Mackenna in a duel. Three days later José Miguel Carrera arrived in Buenos Aires (Vicuña Mackenna 1938: 409).[14] Again, while there was a common enemy in Spain and the royalists, the Carreras were not treated too severely: in May 1815 San Martín refused to sanction José Miguel's plan to invade Chile via Coquimbo, but in November 1815 he was allowed to travel to the United States to try to obtain support for the independence of Chile. Mercedes Fuentecilla remained in

Buenos Aires with their young children; Javiera Carrera had also moved there in 1814.

In the meantime, O'Higgins worked closely with San Martín planning to retake Chile from the royalists. In February 1817, the patriots won the battle of Chacabuco and entered Santiago. The prisoners on Juan Fernández island were released, among them Ignacio Carrera, who wrote to Javiera Carrera voicing his appreciation of her letters to him: 'Las memorias que me dices a mi madre, mujer y hermana, tu tía Damianita que ha sido todo mi consuelo y alivio en el horrible presidio que he sufrido'.[15] Evidently, Javiera's letters were a means of bringing him this comfort, as she seems to have suggested evoking the memories of his mother, wife and sister to bring solace during his imprisonment. She also told him that José Miguel had gone to the United States; Ignacio Carrera voices his approval: 'La noticia que me comunicas de haber dado la vela para Norte América mis dos hijos es el mayor consuelo como lo tendré cuando marche Juan José de quien no he tenido carta'.[16] In a climate where rumours were rife, it was only through the medium of letters that Ignacio Carrera could trust news of the whereabouts of his family.

In February 1817, José Miguel Carrera returned to Buenos Aires with three ships equipped and armed in the United States. He prepared to return to Chile, but was detained. Meanwhile, Juan José and Luis Carrera tried to cross the Andes to raise a rebellion against O'Higgins. According to Stephen Clissold, Javiera Carrera was one of the instigators of this plan. He describes her as:

> of imperious character, even more fanatically attached to the cult of the family than her brothers. She had done her utmost to arouse José Miguel's ambitions as a means of saving him from the consequences of his youthful escapades, and her domineering, vengeful nature found satisfaction into goading him on to ever wilder pretensions. (Clissold 1968: 93)

She was, Clissold continues, 'as intelligent and restless as her brother, but also more fanatical and vindictive'. He claims that plans were made at her Buenos Aires house to capture San Martín and O'Higgins and to make them resign. If they refused, or this failed, they would instigate a guerrilla war in Chile. A Chilean army would then take Peru, and José Miguel would become commander-in-chief of the region. Clissold also maintains that when José Miguel heard of this plot he was horrified and warned her that Juan José and Luis would not be able to complete their assigned roles (Clissold 1968: 123, 165–72). However, there is no indication of any friction between members of the Carrera family about this matter in the letters that have survived.

Luis was captured in Mendoza on August 5 1817 and on August 26 Javiera Carrera wrote to José Miguel from Buenos Aires to give him the bad news: 'Quisiera con mi vida ahorrarte la noticia que te voy a participar. Nuestro infeliz Luis dicen que está preso en Mendoza con dos barras de grillos' (Vicuña Mackenna 1938: 139). Luis was in chains in Mendoza, the humiliation and pain of which was of bitter concern to Javiera. Six weeks later, Ana Cotapos was anxiously waiting in Santiago for news from her husband, Juan José. She had returned there when Juan José and Luis Carrera were planning their rebellion. Evidently there were no obstacles to women returning to Chile; even those directly related to enemies of the government. She wrote of her anguish in a letter to Javiera Carrera:

> Mi inseparable Xaviera: ha llegado el correo y no he tenido una letra de mi J.J , ni tuya. La última que tuve de mi amado Juan, fue el 14 de Julio, y antes de esta hacían 6 semanas que no recibía ninguna, y desde el 14 que estamos, han llegado 4 correos y me ha sucedido lo propio, la última tuya fue del 19 de Junio, pero ayer tarde tuve el consuelo de saber de ti, por lo que escribo a mi pobre taita y por ella también he aliviado un poco de la terrible congoja que sufría mi abatida Alma, con las supuestas noticias que en estos días han servido, luego que en esta se supo la prisión de nuestro desgraciado Luis, que siento en mi corazón como es natural, se empezó a esparcir que a mi Juan lo habían preso, en la Punta de San Luis.[17]

Cotapos is clearly desperate for news and has been counting the days and weeks between letters that are few and far between. The news she has received brings little comfort, particularly that of the imprisonment of Luis, although she is relieved to hear of Javiera's safety. Her suffering is apparent and she continues, 'es imposible que en el mundo haya mujer más desgraciada que tu Ana, no sé como vivo con tantos pesares'. Her only comfort has been in writing, but now this is denied her: 'A mi J.J. no escribo porque ignoro su paradero, solo en este correo me he privado de mi único consuelo'. She tells Javiera that if she is in contact with Juan José she should warn him not to try to return to Santiago: 'Te estimaré en mi corazón mi Xaviera que le adviertas a que no dirija su marcha a esta, porque es muy peligrosa en el día y están muy vigilantes en los caminos'. In doing so she reveals her knowledge about security on the roads and that their enemies are guarding them. As for herself, she is living shut up in her room: 'Mi vida es la más retirada que cabe, encerrada en mi cuarto'.[18] She is lonely and afraid; it is almost as if she is as much a prisoner as Luis Carrera.

Cotapos's anguish was protracted: and when news came it did not bring relief:

> Y tu mi Xaviera, es posible que no me des ningún consuelo acerca de mi Juan, pues no sabes que en la distancia corren las noticias tan funestas y abultadas que te aseguro que no sé como he resistido estos días con los que me han venido a decir, de que a mi J. J lo habían preso en la Punta y que de allí lo trajeran a Mendoza, después de esta noticia he tenido carta de Tomacita [Tomasa Alonso Gomero] y no me dice nada que era muy natural me la participara, para auxiliarle, por lo que tu le dices a mi suegro, en al que le escribes de fecha de 1 de septiembre, de que J. J. después de que supo la desgraciada prisión de nuestro Luis no había vuelto a tu casa, esto es lo que me hace dudar la voz que aquí corre por que no me cabe en la cabeza que se viniese el mismo a entregar por un camino en que debía saber que estaban con la mayor vigilancia y que de los tres es el más conocido en todas estas partes. Te aseguro mi Xaviera que con esta incertidumbre paso ansias de

muerte ... Yo espero que tu me has de hablar con toda la sinceridad de tu alma.[19]

The letters reaching Cotapos were giving her news that she hopes is wrong. She tells Javiera that she has heard of Juan José's capture, though she does not want to believe it. She is receiving contradictory rumours from intermittent letters, and those that do arrive take time to reach her. Cotapos employs logic based on the only reliable news she has: letters from trusted friends and family. Her cousin, Tomasa Alonso Gamero, had written to her, but did not mention Juan José's imprisonment: surely, Cotapos reasons, her friend would have told her if he had been arrested.[20] Again, she reveals her knowledge of what is happening: she knows which roads are being watched and believes that Juan José would too. She ends in a plea to Javiera to write to tell her all she knows.

By the following week Cotapos's worst fears had been realised. She voiced her desperation to José Miguel:

> Estoy loca y desesperada. Considera, mi José Miguel, cómo estará tu infeliz y desgraciada hermana, al considerar a mi desventurada Juan en las garras de unos tigres, que todo su empeño es devorarnos, y para ello no vale la inocencia, pues en el día padece el hombre de bien y el que se sostiene con carácter ... Ahora es cuando deseo tener posibles para socorrer a los míos, pues para mi nada quiero, solo vivir con mi Juan aunque fuese en la choza más miserable. (Oct. 17 1817, Vicuña Mackenna 1938: 138)

Cotapos is frantic, realising that Juan José is at the mercy of those who want to kill him. She maintains that he is innocent of any wrongdoing and wishes only to be able to live a simple life with her husband, far from politics and wealth. Indeed, Cotapos may have long held such sentiments: the descriptions of the lavish celebrations of the first anniversary of the Chilean junta at the height of the Carrera family's power do not mention Cotapos and Juan José (Grez 1966: 60–62). Clissold suggests that Juan José, the eldest brother, was led astray by José Miguel. He describes Juan José as 'conscious of his seniority [and] sometimes sullenly resentful of his more brilliant brother's pretensions, but his own manifest inferiority of gifts and personality always compelled his eventual submission' (Clissold 1968: 93). It is possible that Cotapos was referring to previous conversations she had held with her husband.[21] Yet there is no trace of resentment or accusation against José Miguel. She seeks his assistance and knows it will be given.

Javiera Carrera was working in Buenos Aires to gain support for Luis and Juan José and kept José Miguel informed of her progress:

> Después de innumerables pasos, he descubierto la idea del Director. No quiere juzgar a mis hermanos aquí; quiere que los juzgue San Martín o los demás, que todo es lo propio. ¿Cuál será la suerte de estos desgraciados? Trabajo incesantemente por mover a tres individuos del Congreso en mi favor, y haré por mí una enérgica representación, pidiendo, como debo, que se les traiga aquí, se les oiga y castigue si son delincuentes: pero como en

> nada tengo suerte, puede que no lo logre, pero me quedará el consuelo de hacer más de lo posible. Ya mis pies son sangre, y ojalá que la de mis venas fuese la suficiente a salvarlos. Juan José tiene otras dos barras de grillos. Dios te conserve a ti feliz y libre no precipitado. ¡Adiós, adiós! (August/September 1817, Vicuña Mackenna 1938: 139)

In giving José Miguel useful information regarding the brothers' position and the possible attitudes and plans of those detaining them, Javiera reveals the efforts she has been making for her brothers. She was aware of the politics behind the decisions of San Martín and O'Higgins and was working, not to free her brothers, but to ensure their trial was held in Buenos Aires, where she had some hope of influencing members of Congress in their favour. It is clear that she liked to be in a position where she could act and was not afraid to deal directly with those in power. Yet she is aware that her efforts may not succeed. This she attributes to misfortune: it does not occur to her to consider that it could be because of any lack of effort on her part; nor due to the serious nature of her brothers' crimes; nor that she is a woman meddling in politics. As she had stated in her letter to Díaz de Valdés three years earlier, Javiera had long been accustomed to acting in the political sphere.[22] In her rush to send this news to José Miguel, Javiera presents the poignant image that she has worn her feet to the bone in her efforts to petition members of the Congress to stage the trial of her brothers in Buenos Aires; while her brothers have their feet crushed in shackles in their Mendoza prison.

The removal of the manacles was an important issue for Javiera Carrera. As stated above, she drew José Miguel's attention to the use of chains when she informed him of the capture of their brothers. Tomasa Alonso Gamero visited the brothers during their imprisonment and she regularly wrote to Javiera regarding their health, and outlining their needs. Alonso Gamero tries to reassure Javiera that she is doing all she can for the brothers: 'No tenga el menor cuidado por la asistencia por su amable hermano Luis, de mi casa se le manda todo lo necesario, menos dinero ... para que no se le permita ninguno, esto no es culpa mía'. She continues, 'Yo escribiré más con oportunidad cuando haya alguna novedad y avisaré lo que ocurra, descanse vd. Que todos sentimos sus padecimientos, mucho más no poder remediarlos'.[23] Alonso Gamero shows her awareness of Javiera's suffering and shares it; she will endeavour to send good news to ease her concerns. Alonso Gamero's letter of October 8 1817 reveals Javiera's agitation:

> Recibo su apreciada de 24 pasado y en ella veo las agitaciones que le cuestan a usted sus desgraciados hermanos, cuya situación compadezco. Me dice usted le diga el estado de ellos, si están buenos y sin prisiones, a lo que contesto que Luis está aquí, no tiene novedad en la salud aunque me dicen está muy flaco, se mantiene con una barra de grillos en la cárcel, en el cuarto que sirve para poner los reos en capilla e incomunicado estrechamente.
>
> Juan José me aseguran está del mismo modo en la Punta de San Luis; cuyas noticias no había querido comunicar a usted por no aumentar sus

> congojas y lo hago en esta vez en fuerza de suplicármelo usted. (Vergara Quiroz 1987: 91)

Javiera's anxious questions can be discerned from this reply, which would not have brought her any comfort. Alonso Gamero stresses that she did not want to give her this information and only did so because Javiera had insisted. This was perhaps also the case when she wrote to Cotapos: Juan José had been imprisoned in August, and Cotapos referred to a recent letter from Alonso Gamero in October. In seeking to protect the Carrera family from bad news, Alonso Gamero was succeeding in raising false hopes. She perhaps felt culpable in being the messenger, but she must have been a frustrating correspondent for Javiera.

The following month, Alonso Gamero reported to Javiera Carrera that the brothers were being kept under closer surveillance:

> Como vd me tiene suplicada con instancia que cualesquiera noticia sea favorable o adverso acerca de sus hermanos, se las comunique: lo hago en esta ocasión diciéndole que hoy están como siempre con la diferencia de cada dos horas se les registran las prisiones por las centinelas que cuidan de su seguridad.[24]

This detail gives an insight into what life was like for the prisoners; they are frequently disturbed day and night. Alonso Gamero's tone is neutral and she does not explain why they were being checked so regularly. Whatever the reason, this could not have been good for the brothers. Indeed, in December 1817 she admitted that she had been unable to write:

> Tengo a la vista su estimada de 1° del – en la que me encarga de nuevo comunique a vd todo lo que sepa de sus desgraciados hermanos, en verdad mi amiga que siento escribirle a vd por que no puedo con mis cartas proporcionarle la mas [illegible] noticia de consuelo, por este motivo no le he escrito en dos correos, pero no puedo ser indiferente a sus desgracias y así le suplico y ruego como amiga y como interesada en el alivio de vd y de sus infelices presos.... No desprecie vd este consejo por un momento. Ya han concluido con la confesión de Luis y están actual con J. José. Vd no debe ignorar que todos los que han entendido en la causa son sus enemigos capitales y por consiguiente han hecho lo que han querido.[25]

The news was so bad that she could not bring herself to write to Javiera, yet Javiera had obviously been desperate for news. Yet after waiting so long to write, Alonso Gamero was underlining that time was running out for the brothers. She warns Javiera that they have many enemies who have been double-crossing them. Rumours were rife and Alonso Gamero tells Javiera not to listen to them: 'En su anterior me dice que ha visto contar de San Martín escrito a un amigo en que le dice que cuando venga a esta tendrá una entrevista con sus hermanos, desprecie vd esto y no crea tal cosa'.[26] Possibly thanks to these false friends, Javiera may have been hearing reports that the authorities were looking more favourably on the brothers: Alonso Gamero confirms that this is not the case and advises Javiera to do all she can to free them.

Cotapos was at least able to write to Juan José while he was in prison, and he did receive her letters. Three of them were confiscated from him by the Governor of Mendoza, Toribio Luzuriaga, and were thus preserved in San Martín's documents. The letters, dated October 22, and November 14 and 24 1817 show Cotapos's suffering and her anxiety for him. She begins these letters, 'Mi amado y suspirado Juan José'; 'Mi inseparado y eternal compañero'; and 'Amadísimo y caro compañero'. Her greetings, as well as revealing her devotion indicate a sense of partnership and equal status. Perhaps not surprisingly, since she knows that he will read the letter in prison, she emphasises his innocence and that this is a comfort to her. She wishes that she could be in prison with him. One source of consolation is that he is not alone and she tells him that she is writing to all her friends in Mendoza to attend to him. Moreover, 'á Tomasita mando un corto auxilio de doce onzas de oro, para que se empleen en tus alimentos'. Here the traditional role of women as carers is given additional importance, as Juan José is relying on the help of Tomasa Alonso Gamero. He is helpless in prison and depends on women to sustain him.[27]

Letters might have been reaching Juan José, but Cotapos was still receiving little news from him. On November 14 a letter finally arrived and, with some relief, Cotapos immediately answered it: 'La última fué de 24 de julio, y antes de éste pasaron once correos sin tener una letra: yo no te he dejado de escribir más que cuando supe tu desgraciada prisión; en fin, en el día tengo el consuelo de que nos comuniquemos mediante la generosidad del señor intendente' ([N.A.] 1910: 600). The knowledge that her letters would be read by Juan José's captors might have made Cotapos more careful about her content, but her relief at being in contact with him again is evident. On November 24 she added that she wished she were in prison in place of him, and voiced concern for his health, as she had heard he was ill: 'En este propio correo iría orden á ese señor intendente para el alivio de las prisiones de los dos' ([N.A.] 1910: 601). Here, Cotapos was trying to take control of the situation: she will order the prison officers to remove the manacles from Juan José and Luis.

On November 23 Alonso Gamero reported to Javiera Carrera that any efforts to alleviate the prisoners' conditions had been thwarted:

> No se permite a ninguno de mi casa entrar donde ellos están, por cuyo motivo no se podrá dar sus efectos; ellos padecen después de su encarcelamiento y prisiones la ninguna asistencia en el servicio que tienen, y una exacción grande en lo que se les manda para sus alimentos, pero suele ser tanta insolencia que el platito de dulce que se le manda a Luis para desengraso se lo toman los cabos y soldados y me mandan un recado de que mande más por ellos, contémpleme usted si estaré quemada con esto, después de eso, de los siguientes yerba, azúcar, ron etcétera que se les manda de los cuatro partes de cada cosa se roban las tres, y uno no puede repetir contra esto porque ha de ser peor, y así estamos sufriendo todos estos insultos. (Vergara Quiroz 1987: 92)

This detail gives an insight into the efforts taken by the family and friends of the Carreras to send gifts, food and drink to alleviate their position, but above all, it reveals the power of the prison guards. They refuse to allow visitors, they steal most of the goods sent to the brothers, and Alonso Gamero dares not complain for fear of the retribution the brothers might suffer as a consequence. She adds that she has received money for Luis and Juan José from Ignacio Carrera and Cotapos, and that she gave it to the governor in the hope that it might have a better chance of reaching the brothers.

At this time Javiera Carrera was working in the political sphere to help her brothers: she continued her efforts to transfer them from Mendoza. From November 1817 to January 1818 she repeatedly wrote to the Governor of Buenos Aires to ask for asylum for her brothers and/or that their trial should take place there. Her letter of January 24 is typical:

> Exmo. Señor
> Doña Francisca Javiera de Carrera por sus hermanos don Juan José y don Luis de Carrera presos en la ciudad de Mendoza, suponiendo que el Gobierno de Chile ha hecho indicaciones de VE a su translación á la capital de aquel Estado, implora el asilo del territorio de las provincias unidas del sud América, y que se acoge á la suprema protección de VE.[28]

Javiera Carrera introduces herself as her brothers' representative and not merely their sister. She is acting for them, as they are in prison and unable to do so themselves: this seems to be a natural position for her to adopt and, rather than use emotional terms that would be traditionally attributed to her gender, she keeps her language measured and polite. She nonetheless implores the governor to give asylum to her brothers, the force of which petition is greater in this formal context. Her handwritten letter contains one alteration: she originally wrote 'á la capital de Chile', before changing it to 'á la capital de aquel Estado' (Buenos Aires) leaving one to wonder if this was a simple mistake, a change of plan, or wishful thinking. It also perhaps reveals a sign of dislocation: she is in Buenos Aires, but her thoughts are with her distant family in Mendoza and Santiago. That this slip should remain in her formal letter also indicates anxiety and the need to hurry. The letter is little more than one page long, and the error is in the first sentence. It does not seem to have occurred to her to begin the letter again.

Yet even if Javiera Carrera did consider Santiago for a trial, it is unlikely to have been a more benign location for the Carreras. On November 2 1818 *El Duende de Santiago* published an article in which it stated that all three Carrera brothers deserved to die painful deaths. It revealed plans that a coded letter from José Miguel from Montevideo on June 27 had fallen into the hands of the secretary of state and had been passed to the newspaper. The code had been interpreted as follows:

onbsqom o noq pomrtq azs ddsqn 5 o paqrbod2ha
asesinar a san martín o'higgins y a monteagudo (Feliú Cruz 1955: 142)

There was no indication of how the code had been deciphered; only that the attempts of the Carreras to disguise their plans had been in vain. The Carreras certainly used code in their letters,[29] but it should be emphasised that *El Duende* was edited by Antonio José de Irisarri, who was opposed to the Carrera brothers.

Attempts to transfer the brothers to Buenos Aires were to no avail. On February 25 1818, a planned rebellion by Juan José and Luis from their Mendoza prison was discovered and a week later José Miguel issued his 'Manifiesto a los Pueblos de Chile' from Montevideo (Vicuña Mackenna 1938: 411). The patriots in Chile, under San Martín, were defeated at the battle of Cancha Rayada on March 19 1818, and the case against the brothers was accelerated with the arrival of San Martín's close associate, Bernardo de Monteagudo, in Mendoza. Juan José and Luis Carrera were declared guilty and executed on April 8 1818. According to Vicuña Mackenna, this took place three hours after the news reached Mendoza of the patriots' victory at Maipú, which secured the independence of Chile (Vicuña Mackenna 1938: 411).[30] On May 22 1818, the aging Ignacio Carrera was presented with a bill for expenses incurred during the imprisonment of his two sons. He died two months later (Vicuña Mackenna 1938: 140).

On August 9 1818, Cotapos wrote to Mercedes Fuentecilla, voicing her agony:

> Con bastante dolor, mi amada Mercedes, me quedé el correo pasado sin contestar tu apreciable cartita de 24 de Julio, y tú no debes extrañar, hija mía, esta falta en la que ya vive sobre lo natural [sic]. No tengo un momento sereno en mi espíritu y salud. El histérico me repite con fuerza hasta privarme del habla.... A instancias de mis padres me medicino, porque lo que me deseo es [que] concluya una vida que no puedo tolerar. ¡Ay!, mi Mercedes, si Dios me conserva unos días más, sabrás todo lo ocurrido para que mi pesar no tenga consuelo! Cuáles no serían mis martirios sabiendo el modo de liberar a mis mártires y no poderlo. (Vicuña Mackenna 1938: 138)

Again, in her grief, Cotapos reveals that she saw herself as powerful. But what did she mean when she said that she had had the wherewithal for liberating the brothers?

Cotapos seems to have aroused passion and pity in those she met. Mary Graham met her in 1822 and describes her as having 'one of the most beautiful faces I ever beheld' (Mavor 1993: 112). Vicuña Mackenna, born two years after her death, pays tribute to the beauty of Cotapos, which contrasted with 'el porte altivo y bizarro' of Javiera Carrera and the 'airosa gentileza' of Mercedes Fuentecilla (Vicuña Mackenna 1938: 137). He further describes her as 'esta noble chilena, tipo verdaderamente adorable' (Vicuña Mackenna 1938: 139). On learning of the imprisonment of Juan José and Luis, Cotapos perhaps employed her natural charms, since she went to considerable pains to secure their release. According to some sources, her efforts were apparently not in vain. On April 21 1823, the Chilean newspaper *El Tizón Republicano* repeated reports that Cotapos had petitioned the authorities in Chile for leniency against the

Carrera brothers. It quotes a letter from O'Higgins to the Toribio Luzuriaga dated April 11 1818, in which O'Higgins asked for clemency for the brothers. A further note from San Martín (undated) clarifies that San Martín had put pressure on O'Higgins to revoke the death sentence on the brothers. These efforts were too late: the brothers had been executed three days before O'Higgins wrote to Luzuriaga. An editorial note, attributed to Simón Carranza, explains that when San Martín and O'Higgins learned of the executions, they were horrified and upset. Carranza nonetheless strongly condemns O'Higgins: 'No son hombres los que gobiernan, sino una manada de brutos destinados á ser el juguete de la barbaridad de sus pasiones' (*El Tizón Republicano* 8, April 21 1823: 90–92). The timing of the release of these documents is significant: O'Higgins had by then resigned and San Martín had retired to civilian life. To publish them at such a time was perhaps as much an attack on the former regime as it was a defence of the Carreras. The lack of date on San Martín's orders for the release of the Carrera brothers is intriguing; was it an oversight and if so deliberate? Or did the editor of *El Tizón* remove it? This episode is not widely reported in secondary sources: in an otherwise highly detailed account, Vicuña Mackenna maintains that on April 4, the eve of the decisive battle of Maipú, San Martín sent secret orders for the execution of the brothers (Vicuña Mackenna 1938: 123, 411). Clissold reports that San Martín had sent messages to prevent the executions, but that they had arrived four hours too late (Clissold 1968: 169).

It was perhaps to her efforts in petitioning the authorities for leniency that Cotapos was referring when she wrote that she had known what to do to save Juan José and Luis but had been unable to achieve it. Yet if the accounts in *El Tizón* were accurate, Cotapos had done enough to secure the brothers' release. That she had not achieved this end was not from any lack of effort or skill on her part, but due to the slowness of communications and possibly unwillingness on the part of O'Higgins, San Martín, or Monteagudo to ensure the message of clemency was delivered and received in time.

José Miguel Carrera valued the efforts made by women of his family on his behalf. On March 8 1818 he wrote to General Alvear, 'Mi esposa es mi más fiel y sigiloso confidente en todos mis pasos. Valen más nuestras mujeres que nuestros hombres para la revolución' (Vicuña Mackenna 1938: 123). In praising his wife, he then extends her efforts to all women, the contribution of whom to the independence cause he considers to worth more than that of men. He was possibly referring to the rivalry and bitterness of the Chilean patriots that had caused him and his family so much grief. He could not be reconciled to his enemies after the executions of his brothers, and he promised Cotapos and Javiera Carrera that he would do all he could to avenge their deaths. In December 1818 he wrote to Javiera, 'Voy a moverme, a vengarte, a vengar y a vengarme' (Vicuña Mackenna, 1938, 148). The diplomatic efforts of Cotapos and Javiera Carrera had been in vain, leaving him no recourse but to fight back.

José Miguel Carrera left Montevideo in July 1819, taking advantage of the rebellion against Buenos Aires in Entre Ríos and Santa Fe. Vicuña Mackenna claims that he had the assistance of the Governor of Montevideo, General Carlos Federico Lecor (Vicuña Mackenna 1938: 411). On November 26 1820 he wrote to his wife, Mercedes Fuentecilla, asking her to look after his affairs:

> Todos mis papeles manuscritos guárdalos bien; esconde el vestuario si puedes; ten mucha política; ... saluda a mi nombre a todos mis amigos y conocidos; ajusta una cuentecita pendiente con don Juan Antonio; cuida tus bueyes que están gordos y deben servirte.
>
> Consérvate; no te agites; que mande el compadre a colocar este ganado; caricias a mis chiquitas y recibe el corazón de tu eterno amante. (Vicuña Mackenna 1938: 255–56)

Carrera shows his trust in his wife in all aspects of his life: his military plans; his personal papers; his financial affairs; his social and political contacts; as well as their children.

Carrera began to foment the support of Chileans in Buenos Aires for his Ejército Restaurador, described as 'a terrifying mob composed of the Chileans who were living in that country and who wished to follow him, and later of the barbarous Indians of the pampas' (Galdames 1941: 206). A letter to his wife, dated December 4 1820, provides an insight into the action of the indigenous soldiers:

> Ayer, mi Mercedes, tomé el Salto sin querer: mi objeto era sacar ganado y el de los indios saquear e incendiar el pueblo. Avanzamos, y mandé la primera compañía con orden de tirar al aire y huir de las primeras calles como aterrados para que los indios desistiesen de su empresa. Así se habría logrado, pero los soldados animados por el pillaje se apoderaron de la plaza con intrepidez, y los indios, contra sus promesas, hicieron tolerías en la iglesia, en las casas y en las familias. Me vi obligado a contenerlos en parte, y aun estuve resuelto a batirlos si no cedían. Por la fuerza, por robo y por intriga les quité casi todas las prisioneras, y esto me costó hasta el echar mano de una pistola para quitar a una tierna joven que en comitiva con doce más volví anoche con la oscuridad acompañadas de una escolta. He comprado por veinte vacas la hija de un honrado, y al instante la mandé. (Vicuña Mackenna 1938: 264)

One should question Carrera's motives: he is excusing his action; yet he does not emerge as a hero. He addresses Fuentecilla as his confessor, friend and military confidant. Yet he is also aware that she is a woman left alone with four young daughters to care for, and he is sufficiently concerned to tell her that he has managed to secure help for her. He had reason to be preoccupied with the welfare of his family. On February 6 1821, Fuentecilla wrote to Javiera Carrera to announce the birth of her son: 'Ya se cumplieron los deseos de tener un varoncito a JM y tú tienes un nuevo sobrino' (Vergara Quiroz 1987: 106).[31] Fuentecilla's tone is subdued and almost formal: she uses the passive tense to describe the safe arrival of her fifth child, José Miguel, a much-desired brother for her four daughters. This news is reduced to one sentence in a letter that is otherwise dominated by political events; such is her personal and political situation that motherhood has had to take secondary status.

The attack on Salta caused Javiera Carrera to flee Buenos Aires to Montevideo (Vicuña Mackenna 1938: 264). Thomas Sutcliffe explains José Miguel's situation, 'the execution of his two brothers, Don Louis and Juan Jose, in Mendoza, and other political affairs, had made him vow eternal enmity to the government of Buenos Aires; particularly to San Martin, whom he much disliked. In his vengeance, he had raised the Indians to assist him. This act lost him many friends' (Sutcliffe 1841: 317–19). There were renewed efforts to prevent Carrera from entering the country. San Martín and O'Higgins may have regretted the executions of Juan José and Luis in 1819, but the fact that José Miguel threatened to stir up a caste war was sufficient to condemn him. José Miguel was arrested and taken to Mendoza, where he was executed on September 4 1821.

José Miguel Carrera's last thoughts were with his wife and children. He wrote a note to Fuentecilla two hours before he was shot:

> Mi adorada, pero muy desgraciada Mercedes; un accidente inesperado y un conjunto de desgraciadas circunstancias me han traído esta situación triste. Ten resignación para escuchar que moriré a las once. Sí, mi querida, moriré con el solo pesar de dejarte abandonada con nuestros tiernos cinco hijos en país extraño, sin amigos, sin relaciones, sin recursos. Mas puede la Providencia que los hombres. (Vicuña Mackenna 1938: 350–51)

A scrap of paper was also found on which he had written: 'Miro con indiferencia la vida. Sólo la idea de separarme para siempre de mi adorada Mercedes y tiernos hijos, despedaza mi corazón. ¡Adiós! ¡Adiós!' (Vicuña Mackenna 1938: 354). José Miguel Carrera was buried 'in the same grave with the brothers he so dearly loved' (Sutcliffe 1841: 319).

The exoneration of the Carreras

The O'Higgins faction may have been victorious against the Carrera brothers, but it did not bring O'Higgins lasting benefits. His support for liberalism and egalitarian policies alienated the oligarchy, which emerged from the Wars of Independence strong and determined not to lose its economic and political power. Lynch explains, 'certain caudillos, first Carrera and then O'Higgins, might be tolerated for specific objectives, the first to provide military organisation, the second a stable administration, but they would be destroyed as soon as they threatened to become an independent power' (Lynch 1973: 142, 152). When San Martín retired to civilian life in 1822, O'Higgins was left with no power base. He abdicated on February 28 1823 and went into exile in Peru. Monteagudo fared worse: he was murdered in Lima in 1825. Meri Knaster maintains that the Carrera family was accused of his assassination (Knaster 1977: 504).

Mary Graham offers an insight into what life was like for members of the

Carrera family who remained in Chile while they were out of political favour. In August 1822 she visited the Cotapos family at their Maipo Valley hacienda. During her time there another visitor appeared, who was introduced as a 'tonto'. Graham notes his 'extraordinary beauty' and that it made her 'quite melancholy'. Eventually the youth admitted he was in disguise:

> [I am] the son of Xabiera, the nephew of José Miguel Carrera ... that unhappy exile Lastra, reduced to fly from desert to desert, to hide in caves, and to feed with the fowls of the air, till my limbs are palsied and my youth is wasted; and my crime has been to love Chile. (Mavor 1993: 112–13)

The Cotapos family, and presumably the Carreras, had retained their wealth and property, yet were clearly living in fear. Graham, who had been 'startled' at the prospect of visiting anyone connected to the still out-of-favour Carreras, was nonetheless sympathetic to the Cotapos family and particularly towards Manuel Joaquín de la Lastra Carrera (the eldest son of Javiera Carrera from her first marriage), whom she invited to her Santiago home on her return to the capital (Mavor 1993: 103, 133).

The exile of O'Higgins enabled Javiera Carrera to return to Chile in 1823 (Vergara Quiroz 1987: xxv). On March 24 1828, Manuel Magellanes awarded a Premio Póstumo to the three Carrera brothers. It was decreed that their remains should be returned to Chile. They were interred in Santiago Cathedral with the pomp and ceremony that had instigated much of the resentment towards the family. An inscription was agreed: 'La Patria a los Carrera, agradecida a sus servicios, compadecida de sus desgracias' (Vicuña Mackenna 1938: 376). This has remained, and the name of Javiera Carrera was added after her death in 1862. Thomas Sutcliffe met the Carrera family around 1832 and revealed that although the Carrera brothers had been exonerated, there had been a high cost:

> This lady [Javiera Carrera] may be classed amongst the heroines of South America; having played a conspicuous part; she has consequently suffered much from the persecutions of her enemies, and the untimely end of her unfortunate brothers, Don Jose Miguel, Don Juan Jose, and Don Luis Carrera. (Sutcliffe 1841: 317)

Javiera Carrera's role in the successes and failures of her family is open to interpretation: in keeping with the tradition of disregarding the contribution of women, she is ignored by many commentators. In his 1863 biography of José Miguel Carrera, however, Tomás Iriarte introduces Javiera Carrera as 'Eve' and blames her for her brothers' downfall. Iriarte describes her as a:

> mujer fuerte y varonil y de un alma templada á un grado tal vez demasiado alta para su sexo, bien que una dama cumplida y de un corazón noble y generoso, fueron sin duda las causas eficientes de los desaciertos y estravios de Carrera y sus hermanos. (Iriarte 1863: 13)

Using Grez as her source, Elsie Weeks claims that the brothers, although brave, were romantic and gentle characters, who were often pushed into action by Javiera (Weeks 1940: 177). Yet although her letters reveal her to be a woman of forceful character, the overwhelming tone is one of frustration and desperation. There is no evidence that José Miguel or her sisters-in-law resented Javiera; indeed, Cotapos addresses her in terms almost as affectionate as those she uses to her husband. Indeed, through their letters it is apparent that all these women were directly engaged in political events and that in the absence of other reliable means of transmitting and receiving news, their letters were a crucial means of contact and of countering the spurious rumours that were such a hindrance and caused increased concern. Above all, these letters reveal the human suffering behind the story of the Carreras and the precarious nature of being a patriot in the independence of Chile.

Notes

1 Thanks to Iona MacIntyre for finding this quotation.
2 Zoraida Vásquez 1994: 20. See also, Lavrin 1978: 28. Lavrin claims that Amar y Borbón influenced Lizardi.
3 The Lima group, originally known as the Academia Filarmónica, was founded in 1787 by José Rossi y Rubí with Dr. Juan Egaña, Demetrio Guasque and Hipólito Unanue (Romero de Valle 1966: 10).
4 See for example, *Semanario Crítico*, 3, 5: 13, 41–56; 'Discurso crítico sobre fomentar, protexer, y autorizar el matrimonio para evitar en parte los desordenes de los celibatarios deducido de una obra periodica', *Semanario Crítico* 10: 94–96. For its part, *El Mercurio Peruano* warned that the Spaniard Olavarrieta was trying to reform Lima customs and society within weeks of arriving in the city. Olavarrieta denied having this objective (Dunbar Temple 1943: 15, 17).
5 See, *Semanario Crítico*, 11: 103–04; 12: 111–12; 13: 115–17; 15: 132–33.
6 Temple specifies *El Mercurio Peruano* and *El Diario de Lima* (Dunbar Temple 1943: 28, 35).
7 *Semanario Crítico*, 15: 133. The newspaper ended with similar words, 'Por actual indisposicion del editor, no puede verificarse la continuacion de este Periódico en algunos dias…'. One can only speculate as to whether Olavarrieta was the author of both. See *Semanario Crítico*, 16: 144.
8 The institution survived until 1874, when it was abolished by President Lerdo de Tejada (Domenella and Pasternac 1997: 364–65).
9 There are several important studies of the lives and writings of religious women and nuns in colonial and early nineteenth-century Latin America. See Lavrin and Loreto 2002.
10 There is no clarification as to whether she wrote these poems.
11 Among them were Fray Camilo Henríquez, Juan Mackenna, Antonio José de Irisarri, Bernardo Vera y Pintado and Manuel Rodríguez (Grez 1966: 63–65).
12 *Las mujeres de la independencia* was first published in 1878; it includes many salient details, but has few sources. Grez (1843–1907) was also a novelist.
13 See, for example, Archivo Nacional de Chile (hereafter ANC), Fondo Varios (hereafter FV), Vol. 238, piaza (hereafter p.) 4194; ANC, FV, Vol. 238, p. 4196; Javiera Carrera to Pedro Díaz de Valdés, dated January 3 1822, September 12 1823. Thanks to Alicia Pololla for her considerable efforts in transcribing these letters.
14 Vicuña Mackenna, the grandson of Juan Mackenna, does not provide an insight

into the cause of the duel.

15 Ignacio Carrera to Javiera Carrera, June 4 1817, ANC, FV, vol. 237, p. 4667.

16 Ignacio Carrera to Javiera Carrera, San Miguel, 4 de Junio 1817, ANC, FV, vol. 237 p. 4777.

17 Ana María Cotapos to Javiera Carrera, Santiago, September 19 1817, ANC, FV, Vol. 237, p. 4671.

18 Ana María Cotapos to Javiera Carrera, Santiago, September 19 1817, ANC, FV, Vol. 237, p. 4671.

19 Ana María Cotapos to Javiera Carrera, dated October 10 1817, ANC, FV, Vol. 237, p. 4680.

20 Sergio Vergara Quiroz states that Tomasa Alonso Gamero, a cousin of the Carreras, was possibly in love with Luis Carrera (Vergara Quiroz 1987: 91 n.1).

21 Clissold quotes a letter from Juan José Carrera to Cotapos, written during his imprisonment: 'Only let them send me back to my country as free as when I left it. Only let me stay quietly on my estates and they can be sure that they will not so much as know I am still alive. If I break my word, I myself will propose the penalty; they can shoot me' (Clissold 1968: 167–68).

22 See Javiera Carrera to Pedro Díaz de Valdés, Mendoza, November 15 1814, ANC, FV, vol. 238, p. 4237.

23 Tomasa Alonso Gamero, Mendoza, September 19 1817, ANC, FV, Vol. 237, p. 4674.

24 Tomasa Alonso Gamero, Mendoza, November 17 1817, ANC, FV, Vol. 237, p. 4677.

25 Tomasa Alonso Gamero, Mendoza December 18 1817, ANC, FV, Vol. 237, p. 4679.

26 Tomasa Alonso Gamero, Mendoza December 18 1817, ANC, FV, Vol. 237, p. 4679.

27 Ana María Cotapos to Juan José Carrera dated October 22, November 14 and 24 1817, reproduced in [N.A.] 1910: 599–602.

28 Javiera Carrera to the Governor of Buenos Aires, dated January 24 1818, ANC, FV, Vol. 237, p. 4514. For other letters written at this time see [N.A.] 1910: 614–26.

29 See, for example, Ana Cotapos to Juan José Carrera, June 1 1817, ANC, FV, Vol. 237, p. 4662. It is difficult to ascertain if this is the same code as that printed in *El Duende*.

30 Galdames, however, claims that news of the patriot victory had not yet reached Mendoza (Galdames 1941: 206).

31 She wrote from Rosario and did not mention anything to suggest that she gave birth in the desert.

CHAPTER EIGHT

Gender, Patriotism and Social Capital: Josefa Acevedo and Mercedes Marín

En Alemania, Francia, e Inglaterra, las mugeres son amigas del hombre, cooperadoras de sus trabajos, partícipes de su suerte, y reguladoras y como magistrados de la familia
('Una señora americana', 1824: 7)

So far, this book has considered the physical political intervention of women and the political significance of their family networks, everyday lives and private correspondence. This chapter will study selected works of two of the earliest published women writers in post-independence Spanish America, Josefa Acevedo (b. 1803) and Mercedes Marín (b. 1804). The focus shifts to the literary cultural sphere of the *letrados*. Both writers are neglected and are thus poorly recognised. As women, they were hindered by negative symbolic capital, a direct consequence of the gendering of the socially female (Moi 1999: 291) (see Chapter 1). However, both were able to compensate by amassing social capital, which they used as leverage to enable them to position themselves as spokespersons for the political options supported by their clan. That they were able to achieve this and win recognition for it (although they were subsequently largely forgotten) could only have been made possible by toeing the line, that is, by tacitly obeying the rules and keeping to form with respect to gender. Otherwise, as women, they risked outright dismissal as ignorant or naïve. Their apparent complicity with the implicit gender assumptions of their times – their symbolic investment in the family – allowed them to be taken seriously and to publish work that was publicly acknowledged. At this time of social and political crisis, no one set of assumptions and values predominated; rather, several options vied for control. As we shall see, both women used their extensive family contacts as social capital, while advocating specific political programmes, one conservative, the other liberal. That they were respected, despite their forays into literature and public life, was due to their gender conservatism and to the fact that the political option they supported became identified (to some extent as a result of their work) with national progress. Nineteenth-century Chilean nationalism was concomitant with post-Portales conservatism, and Colombian liberalism with post-Bolivarian nationalism.

The fortunes of Marín and Acevedo (and, as we shall see in Chapter 9, of

Cunha and Barandas) might be contrasted with those of Juana Manso (see Chapter 10). Manso, who was sixteen years younger than Acevedo, did not play the game correctly and rebelled against prevalent gender and religious *doxa*. As a consequence, she was publicly derided in Argentina (though not in Brazil) and her work was dismissed as silly, or remained unpublished; and she found no support for the publication of her women's journal in Argentina. Although in later life Manso attempted to build up her ravaged social capital with important Argentine political contacts (Sarmiento, the Alsinas, the Avellanedas), the damage had been done. She had lost social respect and reputation. All three women were keenly interested in women's education, not merely to ensure that women were literate, but also to contest the ideological effects of education (Catholic or republican, depending on their political allegiances), the symbolic violence, in Bourdieu's terms, which reproduces the power elite by means of indoctrination and the recognition of competency according to its own established social rules. Women writers were well aware of the risks they took and the potential consequences for themselves and their families. Josefa Acevedo, who had already published several works, wrote in her *Ensayo sobre los deberes de los casados* (which, by 1857 had reached its fifth edition) the following warning:

> Y ¿a qué otra cosa puede aspirar una mujer si no cifra su gloria en obtener la estimación y respeto del público, el amor y obediencia de su familia y la calma interior de su espíritu? ... ¿Ambicionará, pues, la gloria literaria? ¡O mujeres! No os dejéis arrebatar por el brillo de esta aureola divina, que jamás rodeará vuestra frente de un modo satisfactorio. Luciréis como un meteoro y probablemente a costa de vuestra reputación. *Los hombres miran como su patrimonio el templo de Minerva y si entráis en él, os castigarán cruelmente esta usurpación. Os quieren ilustradas, pero no literatas*. La mujer que se ocupa en escribir libros, dicen ellos, deja presumir que descuida sus diarios, minuciosos y sagrados deberes, y se le censura con rigor porque intentó salir de su esfera. Si sus obras son esencialmente útiles y bellas, se insinúa con arte que no hizo sino el oficio de amanuense, y se nombra públicamente el hombre que con razón o sin ella, se supone que trabajó en la redacción de estas obras queriendo darlas alguna singularidad con el nombre femenino ... ¿Y es esto lo que pretendéis? ¡Qué locura! (Acevedo 1857: 64–65, my emphasis)

Women are punished for ignoring or contesting the implicit rules of the literary field. It would be assumed that, as was often the case, their women's names and identities were appropriated by men, the only legitimate players of the literary game, for novelty value or as a sales ploy.

One way to beat the system was to help to further the social and political aspirations of groups of important men, political parties or allegiances, many of which were already family- and clan-based. That these political options later became identified with nationalist programmes was another factor in a woman's favour. How many royalist writers, men or women, are recorded in Spanish American literary history? It was possible for women to write about politics and, indeed, this was encouraged as long as the political option was condoned by a strong and publicly respected family network, and as long as women conformed to a conservative Catholic gender ideology. It was perfectly acceptable for women to write patriotic texts.

What we understand by patriotic poetry largely depends on how we define 'patria'. This term was not coterminous with 'nation', 'state' or 'nation state' in nineteenth-century Spain or in Spanish America. A working definition of patriotism, suggested by John Schaar, is 'love of one's homeplace' or, 'to have a patrimony ... the gift of land, people, language, gods, memories, customs' which we inherit, defines who we are and which we aim to pass on (Schaar 1981: 287, 288). Schaar differentiates between patriotism and nationalism: patriotism belongs to the language of classical republicanism, is critical and invokes republican principles such as liberty and self-sacrifice for the common good; whereas nationalism is uncritical, supremacist and bellicose. Patriotism is the defence of universal principles; nationalism is xenophobic loyalty to kin (Schaar 1981: 296–300). Viroli takes a similar view in his historical study of the legacy of classical republican patriotism through to the nationalisation of patriotism in the mid-nineteenth century. For Viroli, the patriot's core value is the republic – the res publica – and the free way of life it makes possible; patriotic love is charity, respect and generosity, and patriotic discourse the language of common liberty. The principle value for the nationalist is the cultural and spiritual unity of a particular people; nationalist love is loyalty and exclusive attachment, and nationalist dicourse the language of oneness and uniqueness (Viroli 1995: 2–3). But, as Margaret Canovan argues, 'Patriotism that demands loyalty to a particular community ... is bound at some point to conflict with the demands of universalist [liberal] principles' (Canovan 1996: 188).

The first part of this chapter discusses the patriotic poems of Mercedes Marín and Josefa Acevedo. Although their concepts of patria differ and they employ the conventions of patriotic poetry for dissimilar political ends, their poetry points up the tensions between post-independence liberal discourse and grass-roots identifications. I will trace how the polity is shaped discursively and poetically in the interest of groups competing for power and, especially, the ways in which gender is used to construct particular versions of the patria to suit these political agendas. As we know, the making of patrias is a fluid process, dependent on historical circumstance. Marín's concept of patria extends to Chile but not to Peru, Bolivia or the Peruvian-Bolivian Confederation, which was viewed as a threat to Chile. Acevedo's patria is Nueva Granada rather than Colombia and certainly not Bolívar's confederate Gran Colombia. Which myths of belonging, inclusion, and solidarity are mobilised by these women to form and consolidate a sense of shared cultures, values, mutual rights and duties, and for whose benefit?

To be effective, these texts needed to be published, that is, to reach the public domain and to circulate. This was achieved by the publication of the poems in the press or, occasionally, as pamphlets, sometimes anonymously, or by their recital in public and semi-public events. But the most common means of dissemination was through the institution and network that was by far the most significant and empowering for elite creole women at the time: the extended family, friends and relations, kith and kin. The family had always been important to patrician women; the home was the space where they were educated as children, where, once married, they exercised some authority, and where they socialised. The public rooms of the family homes, often semi-clandestine centres of political conspiracy, as well as *tertulias,* provided a liminal space between the public and private spheres in which women might exercise political power informally. Moreover, as in classical Rome, political allegiances were forged in families: family circles were replicated at all levels of government, public service and the professions (the law, the military, the Church, letters). The material and symbolic significance of the family cannot be overstated. As argued earlier, in political discourse, both 'patria' (deriving from 'father') and 'nation' (deriving from 'born' – organic nationalism) rely on the figurative work of family tropes to reinforce bonds, to naturalise otherwise contingent relationships and to authorise competing political communities: 'the rhetoric of nationhood ... is concerned to assimilate national solidarity to kinship and to make loyalties and obligations seem natural and inevitable' (Canovan 1996: 178). The family, then, serves as a template for the polity.

Closely associated with the family tropes that were deeply embedded in the political discourse of the time (republican, nationalist, patriotic, colonial and anti-colonial) is memory. Historicism was thought to explain the past and, therefore, the present; memory performed important ideological work in the construction and transmission of cultural history by tying the individual, the self, to the collective. Rhetoric strengthened these ties 'by using poignant images that refer to shared memories and by telling meaningful stories' (Viroli 1995: 9). Who controlled memory was crucial. In chaotic post-independence Spanish America, when republican states were successively raised and then decommissioned, when 'patria' was not mapped on to 'nation' or 'state' for any length of time, clashing historical memories were constantly employed to legitimise favoured political options. Some elite women, well placed as members of patrician or *letradas* families (Rama 1996), thought it their duty and obligation to speak on behalf of their clan, patria or political community. They positioned themselves as the repositories of shared values, the voices of their family and its collective political will, which to some extent, as family members and *letradas,* they controlled. As we shall see, the work of Marín and Acevedo shapes the patria to fit the image of the extended family to which they belonged. But as the institutions of the nation states solidified, women found themselves victims of their own success, sidelined by the very constructions of historical memory that privileged 'man's truth' and 'man's community', which they had themselves created (Kucich 2000: 17). Nevertheless, these two women writers were not entirely forgotten. In their day they were, in fact, much celebrated as the inaugurators of a national literary tradition which, in as much as it was liberal, republican and modern, could claim to be superior to colonial Spanish literature in its inclusion of women authors. Once this tradition was established, however, and an impressive list of men's names mustered to the cause, the women were conveniently relegated to the sidelines. To date, there are no modern editions or in-depth critical studies of these two women's works.

Mercedes Marín (1804–66), born in Santiago de Chile, was the daughter of José Gaspar Marín, Secretary of the first Chilean Junta Nacional de Gobierno established in response to the French invasion of Spain. Her family was respected, wealthy and deeply Catholic. She was educated by her mother, Luisa Recabbaren (see Chapter 7) and by her cousin, Ventura Blanco Encalada. She married her first cousin, José María del Solar. Her brother, journalist and congressman Ventura Marín (1806–77), published important books on philosophy and religious doctrine; her children, Amelia de Claro (1836–1915) and Enrique del Solar (1844–93), and her grandson, (Javier Vial del Solar (1854–1935)), all published literary works (Amunátegui 1867).

Mercedes Marín was the first recognised woman writer of independent Chile. According to her son, hers was the first volume of poetry published by a Chilean woman (del Solar 1874: xvii). According to her biographer, writing in 1867, she was 'la primera mujer que supo manejar la pluma en Chile' (Amunátegui 1867: 14); while José Domingo Cortés considered her 'una de los fundadores de la poesía chilena; ella y [Salvador] Sanfuentes [1817–60] son, no hay duda, los primeros poetas que en Chile merecieron el nombre de tales después de la independencia' (Cortés 1875: 55). More recently, Máximo Fernández Fraile commended her as 'la primera poetisa, y la única perdurable, de su siglo' (Fernández Fraile 1994: 231).

Marín's first two sonnets were published anonymously:[1] one lamenting the death of M. la Chenaye, the French Consul in Santiago (*Mercurio* August 1835); the other, 'A Don Juan Egaña', the author of the 1823 Chilean Constitution, who had died in 1836 (*Mercurio* May 1836) (reproduced in Amunátegui 1867: 41–42).[2] It was published with a poem written by her brother, 'Elogio del señor don Juan Egaña', and both were recited in the Instituto Nacional in 1836. Marín became a celebrity, however, after publishing the 'Canto fúnebre a la muerte de don Diego Portales' in 1837. An early version, 'Homenaje de gratitud a la memoria del benemérito ministro Don Diego Portales' was published anonymously two months before hearing of the death of Portales in *El Araucano*, July 28 1837 (Medina 1923: 22), and then, after Andrés Bello had corrected the poem, as a pamphlet.[3] She included in the pamphlet her sonnet dedicated to General Manuel Blanco Encalada (her cousin), who had defeated Colonel Vidaurre, the officer responsible for the assassination of Portales. She also published biographies, including one of her father (in *El Araucano*, April 12 1839), which was later included in the *Galería de Hombres Célebres de Chile* (1856) (Amunátegui 1867: 16); and, in 1847, a biography of the Archdeacon of Santiago, José Miguel del Solar.

All in all, Mercedes Marín wrote some one hundred poems, including fifty sonnets, virtually all *poemas de ocasión,* to mark an event (a birthday, a funeral, an anniversary) in the lives of her family and their often politically powerful friends. This is formal public poetry, often religious, and much influenced by Bello, a close family friend. Bello, who had settled in Chile in 1829 and was

Senator of the Chilean Republic (1837–55) at the time, also edited *El Araucano* (1830–53). He provided Marín with strong social and cultural capital and was instrumental in the publication of her work. Her collected poems, dating from 1837 to 1866, were published in the 300-page *Poesías de la señora Da. Mercedes Marín de Solar, dadas a luz por su hijo Enrique del Solar* (Santiago: Imprenta Andrés Bello, 1874)[4]. Ricardo Palma, writing about Marín in 1874, stressed the correctness of her versification 'que casi podríamos llamar académica', and praised her for resisting the kind of Romantic sentimentalism displayed by the Spanish poets Zorrilla, 'el Verdi de la musa castellana', and Espronceda, or 'demás apóstoles de la falange innovadora' (Medina 1923: 24–25). In the elegy 'A la muerte del ilustre sabio don Andrés Bello' (1865), written on Bello's death, Marín publicly acknowledged his guiding influence on her early poetry: 'Yo sentí su poder; a su influencia / se alzó mi voz i resonó mi canto, / Eco de un gran dolor, voz de quebranto / que escuchó con benévola induljencia! ¡Ai!, cuántas horas de apacible calma / I de grato solaz pasé a su lado, / amable sabio, amigo venerado ...' (del Solar 1874: 260–27, 264). Like Bello, she tended to privilege the conventions of neoclassical allegory.

Josefa Acevedo de Gómez (1803–61), born in Bogotá, was the daughter of José Acevedo y Gómez, 'El Tribuno del Pueblo', who played a key role in the first Junta de Gobierno of Nueva Granada of July 1810, which deposed the Viceroy. He died seven years later, during the Spanish 'reconquest' of the region (Lynch 1986: 243). Josefa was the eldest of eight: among her brothers were General José, Coronel Pedro and Lieutenant Colonel Alfonso Acevedo Tejada, all liberals who fought in the Wars of Independence with Francisco de Paula Santander. In 1828, José and Alfonso refused to sign the resolution to make Bolívar dictator of Colombia. Alfonso was taken out of active service and José was imprisoned. Josefa married the magistrate Dr. Diego Fernando Gómez, her father's cousin, who was seventeen years her senior and one of the three civilians who governed Nueva Granada in the constitutional period immediately preceding Santander's presidency of Colombia (1832). Following the 1828 attempt to assassinate Bolívar, Diego Gómez was accused of complicity and exiled to Tibacui (Cartagena) for three years. When he returned (in 1831), the couple separated and lived apart for twenty years, until his death in 1853. Josefa's son-in-law, Anselmo León, her literary executor, published her collection of poems: *Poesías de una Granadina* (Bogotá 1854). The poems date from 1823.

Unlike Marín's poetry, Acevedo's is personal, lyrical, and subjective, voicing her inmost thoughts and anxieties. The collection is a diary of her life; every poem is dated and many are dedicated to members of her family (including her daughters and grandchildren) or commissioned by friends. Acevedo also published, among other works, short biographies of her father, brothers and husband (all published as pamphlets in the 1850s)[5]. Of particular interest (though outside the scope of this book) are the sketches or short stories, *Cuadros de la vida privada de algunos granadinos* (1861), semi-fictional accounts of local events recounted to her or that she experienced, the publication of which was financed by her brother, José. Her best-selling works were the two manuals:

Tratado sobre economía doméstica (1848), in which she quotes Benjamin Franklin (1706–90) in French, and the popular *Ensayo sobre los deberes de los casados*, which first circulated in Bogotá in 1845 and went into five editions in the 1850s, three in Bogotá, one in New York and one in Paris, commissioned by the Peruvian Dirección General de Instrucción Pública.[6] Acevedo is generally acknowledged as the first woman writer of the Colombian republic.

Marín's patriotic poetry

Passing from the significance of the material family to the family as trope, Mercedes Marín's most celebrated poem, the 'Canto fúnebre a la muerte de Don Diego Portales', will now be considered. The poem laments the assassination of Chilean Minister Diego Portales by a faction of the Chilean army, led by Vidaurre, which was opposed to Chile's declaration of war against the newly created Bolivian-Peruvian Confederation. This elegy, apparently written in one night (Amunátegui 1867: 44), was timely: published less than two months after the death of Portales, it was the first of its kind, hence its public resonance (Medina 1923: 22). Portales (Minister of Interior in the Prieto government) was largely responsible for ending the anarchy of the 1820s with the introduction of the 1833 Chilean Constitution (which lasted until 1924). But he was a conservative, who restricted the franchise and increased the power of the Church and the army.[7] Some Chileans hold that he ruled as a virtual dictator between 1830 and 1831.[8] During his second term (after 1835), he orchestrated the Pacific War against Andrés de Santa Cruz, President of the Bolivian-Peruvian Confederation, which lasted until 1839. It was at the outset of this war that he was assassinated by his political enemies.

One of the more striking features of Marín's sentimental, religious poem is the way she employs the conventions of patriotic poetry (the *silva* form and classical motifs and vocabulary) to present Portales not as the leader of the conservatives but as a national hero; she constructs a Chilean patria that is naturally coterminous with the Portales agenda. One strategy involves appropriating independence discourse for these ends: thus, the 'Canto' is a defence of liberty against the machinations of a 'tirano', no longer the Spanish King, but Santa Cruz. A more sustained strategy is the use of the family trope, the natural bonds of family love: Chile is the personified motherland, the patria 'adorada', 'doliente', 'afligida': the poet speaks on behalf of the collective 'nosotros', the patria family to which she and her readers belong. Portales was the 'genio' who gave 'nuestra patria amada vida'; 'nuestros bravos' will revenge his death, and so on. The patria is gendered feminine, not only grammatically but figuratively as a mythical female figure (cf. Bello) and, more importantly, as the 'familia chilena' (del Solar 1874: 9), consisting of women and children governed by the republican hero, 'El', who brought order and peace. The disruption of order is marked by these women being out of place, showing themselves in public, rather than remaining in their homes: 'La fiel matrona / sorprendida, aterrada / su morada, sus hijos abandona / I se muestra también', and 'en medio de las calles, las doncellas / están de sí olvidadas' (del Solar 1874: 8). Portales was not a military hero, but demonstrated exemplary 'civismo heroico' ('Elegía'). He represents the republican manly ideal: 'el alma firme, impávida, serena / la mirada sagaz i penetrante, / la voluntad resuelta y decidida' (del Solar 1874: 10), that is, uprightness, decision and confidence. The republican statesman thus subjects and orders the collective feminine patria, as might the paterfamilias bring order to his household.

In 'Elegía', a shorter version of the 'Canto', the men who executed Portales are also sons of the patria, but traitors: they are 'impuros'. The allegorical Patria, represented as a mother clutching the dead body of Portales with 'maternos brazos', will have to wash away the stain of their names ('Lave la Patria con amargo llanto / de impuros hijos el baldón funesto / borre sus nombres, i el olvido cubre / su tumba solitaria' (del Solar 1874: 14)). To be forgotten, uncommemorated, is a fate worse than death. The poem achieves remembrance of Portales by naming only him (the final line reads 'el nombre de Portales') and the officers (Necochea, Cavada) who defended him. It silences the names of his opponents who are, instead, compared collectively to poisonous snakes, bloodthirsty wolves and furies from hell. This strategy does not quite work, because the reference to the death of Portales inevitably recalls to contemporary readers the identities of his executioners.

The 'Elegía' and 'Canto' are encomiums and memorials to Portales in which Marín takes up the role of voice or spokeswoman of the patria, authorised and empowered as the transmitter of her family's version of common collective values. It could be said that she assumes the role of a bard or poet laureate for which she was well placed, given her family connections (social capital) and poetic competency (symbolic capital); the verses are certainly accomplished, as noted by Bello (del Solar 1874: 264), but poet laureate of the conservative version of the Chilean national epic, of which this is the latest episode. This is not so much patriotic poetry as political propaganda. In a note added to the later 1846 edition of the 'Canto' in *América poética,* Marín explains that she had not wished to republish the poem because Portales was still a controversial figure with as many enemies as admirers. She portrays herself as apolitical: 'ajena a toda cuestión política, yo no quiero pertenecer ni a unos ni a otros' (Amunátegui 1867: 42). But she justifies her intervention: as 'hija de ilustres patriotas' who cannot be indifferent to the public's view on her opinion of Portales. She regarded Portales as an energetic and talented man who ruled decisively at a time of crisis; his aims were for the benefit of the patria and not motivated by self-interest, and he respected men's lives, including those of his enemies. Employing the woman writer's familiar 'mask of improvisatrice' (Mellor 1993: 69), Marín thus represents herself as the representative voice of the community:

> i con todo, no he creído ser otra cosa en aquellos días, que *intérprete fiel del sentimiento general.* Mi canto hallo eco en todas partes i para mi tiene algo de mui estraordinario que una simple mujer, poetisa improvisada al parecer solo

para aquel momento, sin relaciones de ninguna clase con Portales, se alzase entonando su elojio. (Amunátegui 1867: 43–44, my emphasis)

The poem was favourably reviewed (see the review published in *Mercurio* August 4 1837 in Amunátegui 1867: 45): 'se descubrió con no poca sorpresa' that the poet was Marín; 'no se creía deber al bello sexo un homenaje tan digno del hombre ilustre'. The reviewer hoped that she would continue to publish 'porque anuncia los frutos más preciosos a la literatura nacional' (Amunátegui 1867: 45–46).[9]

In 'Marcha a la salida de la Espedición libertadora del Perú' (1837), a series of octavas, Marín incorporates the Pacific War into the continental epic; this is the Chilean struggle for liberty against the 'indigno opresor' (del Solar 1874: 16), no longer Spain, but Santa Cruz. In this poem the oppressed 'patria querida' is 'América hermosa', implicitly conflated with a mythical precolonial Chile, whose 'faz angustiada' is 'de los Incas'. The poem presents inter-state conflict (rather than, as Bolívar, anti-colonial conflict) as allegory, a family story: the mother patria (America), 'llorosa' and 'enlutada', calls her sons (including Chile) to defend her from an intruder (Santa Cruz). The Peruvians, Bolivians and Argentines ('pueblos hermanos') who come to her defence are, in reality of course, only those who oppose the Bolivian-Peruvian Confederation. Thus, political strategies are occluded and naturalised in the family trope. The Chileans and their allies are represented as the true, enlightened American patriots, whose imminent victory is witnessed by the ghost of Portales, 'coronada de eternos laureles', who (opportunely remembered) looks down and smiles at them from on high.

The 'Himno Patriótico a la Victoria de Yungai' (1839) written, as might be inferred, on the Chilean victory over the Confederation, is yet another example of independence discourse employed for factional purposes. The struggle for liberty of the 'patria querida' entails the elimination of the 'feroz tirano' (Santa Cruz) and his 'cadena opresora' and the resurrection of the 'sombras augustas / de los Incas peruanos' (del Solar 1874: 24), Peru now being, after the break-up of the Confederation, an acceptable 'pueblo hermano'. In her sonnet 'A Bolívar', it was the 'Capitán del siglo', as Marín calls him, who broke 'la cadena' 'de América / y el hispánico orgullo sepultado'. In 'Himno Patriótico', Bolívar and Portales fly down from the heavens and place a laurel wreath on the head of the 'Héroe de Yungai' (Manuel Bulnes, later president of Chile through the 1840s and the first half of the 1850s). Bulnes is not named, suggesting that the poem assumes that all readers recognise his identity. He, like Portales, is celebrated for his 'heroico civismo' (del Solar 1874: 23, 19, 25), although arguably, his victory was due to his military acumen rather than his public spiritedness. In 'Brindis' (1839), written to commemorate the victory of the Battle of Chacabuco (February 12 1817), a gynomorphic Chile breaks the chains of the tyranny 'de la España'.[10] Once free, Chile resembles a beautiful young mother who, 'con voz melodiosa / arrulla al tierno infante / i lo adormece sobre el seno amante' (del Solar 1874: 20); the Chilean mother-patria protects her children, among whom the poet includes herself. In the second stanza of the poem, however, which recounts the fortunes of the post-independence republic, the country's gender switches (as prompted by grammar) to the masculine: Chile is 'ufano' and 'sabio'. The poet desires peace and happiness in the new era, 'no más sangre vertida / no más odio i furor' and she hopes that 'el pueblo peruano / se torne nuestro hermano' (del Solar 1874: 21). The independent Chilean republic (the polity) is gendered masculine, while the plight of its inhabitants (society) is represented by the effects of war on dependants, children and women (mothers, wives, widows) defined according to their relation with men.

A significant shift of emphasis is noted in the twenty-page *silva*, 'Canto a la Patria' (1857), written some twenty years later, dedicated and recited to the Sociedad de Instrucción Primaria de Santiago. 'Canto a la Patria', which retells and recollects the history of the Americas from the earliest days to the present, represents the feminine no longer exclusively as trope (allegory, symbol) as in the above poems, but now identified with women in historical time, real women who, as historical subjects, experienced the Wars of Independence. One such woman was Marín's own mother, Luisa Recabarren.[11] The poem describes in detail women's sufferings and resistance during the wars, with special emphasis on female friendship and sorority, the republican comradeship of family and friends:

¿I aun vivís i alentáis, hijas de Chile?
La vida soportáis con entereza
I el dolor, la pobreza,
Las frentes sin mancilla
No envilece ni humilla?
!Ah! Que sois virtuosas
Tenéis en Dios la fe, puras las almas,
I aquel amor ardiente
Que torna el sacrificio
En placer delicioso.
De padre, del amigo, del esposo
La memoria querida
Animan y sostienen vuestra vida:
No hai penoso trabajo
Que rehuséis por humillantes i bajos,
Si con él dais holgura
Al que oculto tal vez i en amargura
Pasa tristes los días
I os es prenda de amor i de ternura.

(del Solar 1874: 42)

Women are thus inscribed as the heroines of the epic Wars of Independence, the embodiment of Christian and republican virtue. These 'hijas de Chile' are both 'patriotas varoniles / y modelos de madres i de esposas' (del Solar 1874: 41, 42); they are family members and 'patriotas', that is, citizens and, insofar as citizenship is predicated on masculinity, they are endowed with masculine attributes. These republican patriots are implictly elevated to the rank of queen, since the poem includes encomiums to powerful women, the Spanish monarchs Isabel I ('si, que del pecho heróico / de una mujer virtuosa a par que bella / súbito surje vívida centella / I en el réjio palacio de Castilla / un foco de luz brilla / que dirije la marcha al nuevo Atlante / por los remotos i anchurosos mares' and the 'augusta soberana' (del Solar 1874: 33, 36), Isabel II. Paradoxically, it was possible to mobilise historical precedence of all-powerful women in dicourses on monarchy (a supreme family), but as yet none were available in republicanism (see Chapter 11).

Although the vast majority of Marín's poems were written in homage to eminent male public personages, historical and contemporary (military officers, government ministers, ecclesiastics and so on), not all her poems belong to the patriotic genre. Her collected poems written between 1818 and 1866 (most of which are included in the *Poesías* (1874) or in Amunátegui) provide insight into the networks (familial, social and cultural) established by well-connected, educated women like her. Several poems (the majority dated) are commemorative and also personal; some are dedicated to female family members ('A mi hija Luisa en sus días'; 'A mi hija Carolina en su partida'; 'A mi hija Elena en su partida a Norte-América', 1858; 'En el album de mi hija Amelia, 1855'; 'A mi hija Matilde'; 'A la memoria de la joven i virtuosa señora Adela Solar de Aldunante', 1853); others are dedicated to female friends and acquaintances ('Epitafio', 1839; 'A una amiga en la ausencia de su marido'; 'A la misma'; 'Remitido a la viuda del coronel Devic Tupper en el día en que se colocaron en el cementerio de Santiago las cenizas de éste'; 'A la señorita Anjela Caamaño, joven poetisa guayaquileña', 1856; 'A mi amiga Mercedes Recasens de Zegers', 1860; 'A la señora doña María Henríquez de Toledo en la muerte de su hija Lucila i de su yerno don Eliseo Cox, ahogados en el Río Claro', 1860); and others to notable female public figures ('A la distinguida cantatriz doña Teresa Rossi', and 'La Caridad' (1855), dedicated to Antonia Salas, President of the Santiago Sociedad de Beneficencia).[12] Notable too is Marín's sonnet written for 'la poetisa cubana' Getrudis Gómez de Avellaneda, 1857, which, according to Amunátegui (1867: 59) she was too shy to send her.[13]

A few poems inform us about the fragility of women's everyday lives, often cut short by childbirth: the following titles are particularly poignant: 'A un niño que nació antes del término a los nueve meses i murió inmediatamente', and 'Epitafio de una señora que deseando tener sucesión en su matrimonio fue víctima del cumplimiento de sus deseos', 1839. The feminine is thus conflated with figures of real women living in real time. However, it was Marín's patriotic rather than her personal poetry that gained her a place in the Parnassus of independent Chile. As mentioned, several poems were included in the important 1846 anthology *América Poética*; the 1864 anthology *Poetas chilenos* (edited by José Domingo Cortés) (Fernández Fraile 1994: 166), and the 1875 edition of *América poética* (edited by Cortés, which also included personal poems: 'A un niño', 'Al sueño', 'En la muerte de mi yerno' and 'En la sepultura', as well as 'A Manuel Rodríguez'). By the end of the century, however, Marín's name was all but forgotten. She was omitted from Menéndez y Pelayo's seminal *Antología de poetas hispano-americanos* (1895).[14]

Undoubtedly, Amunátegui's biography and critical study of 1867 consolidated Marín's standing as a worthy early addition to Chilean symbolic capital. The biography's post-colonial national agenda is explicit. The development of women's literary capabilities is presented as a sign of modernity and progress. Amunátegui represents Chile as a close-knit community to which he, his readers and Marín belonged: she was 'entre nosotros la primera persona de su sexo que haya sabido escribir con lucimiento en prosa i verso'. He knows of only one earlier Chilean woman writer, the nun Ursula Suárez (1668–1749), and she was mad, 'enferma de alucinaciones' (Amunátegui 1867: 1). He blames the Moorish influence of Spain for the scarcity of literary women writing in Spanish (he mentions only four: Santa Teresa, Sor Juana, Fernán Caballero and Gómez de Avellaneda). Spanish culture, he argues, unlike that of France and the USA, is synonymous with oriental degeneracy, the sign of which is the repression of women, 'la estremada sujección en que las mantenían estaba manifestando que la influencia del harem de los árabes había sido demasiado durable en la sociedad de la Península' (Amunátegui 1867: 7).[15] The Spanish colonial heritage (he refers to García Hurtado de Mendoza's views that women should be silenced and locked up) was pernicious for women, 'puede atacarse o defenderse como se quiera semejante orden de cosas, pero creo que nadie sostendrá que estaba bien calculada para formar literatas' (Amunátegui 1867: 14). This further justifies the American break with the colonial order. Marín, he claims, learned to think for herself and express herself as few men could. Her existence neatly fitted the republican bill.

Amunátegui's information on Marín's education and reading preferences is instructive. She was, like all women of her generation, deeply influenced by Fleury's catechism, which was staple reading at the time. She was a religious young woman and even considered entering a convent; she became immersed in the work of San Francisco de Salas. She had learned French and had read *Cartas de la educación* by Mme de Genlis, as well as the Spanish and European classics (Byron, the Italian patriotic poet Vittorio Alfieri, Quintana, Arriaza, Meléndez) with her cousin, Ventura Blanco. Keen to promote girls' education, in the 1840s she drew up a 'plan de estudios', which included reading *el Nuevo Robinson*, Poujet's catechism, and the historical works of Rollin. The subjects to be taught in her studies programme were: religion, reading, writing, geography, history, composition, French, sewing and music, but not mathematics or Latin (which would exclude women from public service employment). She had read and discussed Cervantes, Chateaubriand, Fénelon, and Mme. de Staël in the mixed-sex *tertulias*, which had disappeared by the 1860s and which she wanted to reintroduce on European models (Amunátegui 1867: 32–35).

However, although Amunátegui implicitly credits women such as Marín with the potential for highly developed intellectual capabilities in a modern, independent America, so that her literary acumen is a sign of social progress, his argument is undermined by deeply entrenched, unacknowledged gender *doxa* that embedded women in the realm of the instinctive rather than the rational. Hers was a natural, not a learned or acquired ability: 'compuso poesías como las plantas producen flores, como los árboles dan frutos, por la sola fuerza de su naturaleza, sin conocer siquiera las reglas de la métrica' (Amunátegui 1867: 38). The comment was evidently untrue, since Bello had advised her in metrical composition. But this way, women poets (naturally suited to express feeling, patriotic or otherwise) posed no threat to men. Almunátegui ends his book by calling for an edition of her poetry which, as we know, her family (her son, Enrique del Solar) provided in 1874. In order to match literary practice and publication with respectability, even at this late date, del Solar found it necessary to emphasise his mother's piety, modesty and domestic virtues (del Solar 1874: xvi), yet, in urging historians to consult her 'Canto a la patria' (del Solar 1874: xii), he does not hesitate to present her as a major contributor to Chilean historiography.

Acevedo's family poetry

Josefa Acevedo, like Marín, mobilised the family as trope, more often inscribed in her work as historical reality. Each poem in her *Poesías de una Granadina* (1854) is dated in chronological sequence from 1823 to 1853. The collection is a poetic diary written mainly in the first person. The lyrical 'yo' is not always the poet, but sometimes a family member or friend whose voice she assumes. Acevedo was most productive as a poet between 1829 and 1833 (especially 1831), years which mark an unhappy crisis in her life, and in the late 1830s and in the early 1850s, when she took up residence with her daughter, Rosa, and son-in-law, Anselmo León, her literary executor. Her prime motivation for publishing her work was to earn money to help repay them for their kindness ('Un pensamiento a Anselmo', 1852, in *Poesías*: 1854b: 105).

Considering the important roles the men of her family played in Nueva Granada politics in the early 1830s, the poetry collection is an irreplaceable historical document. It complements Acevedo's insightful *Cuadros de la vida privada* (sketches or short stories published posthumously in 1861) and the several biographies she wrote; by means of these publications family events are represented as public events. Equally, the writings confer public recognition and respect on the family in question, and show how public and political events impact on and derive from family life, at the centre of which are women. Here I will mention just two of the *Cuadros:* one recounts the flight of Acevedo's father from Spanish troops with his young son, Pedro, and his illness and death (as told by Pedro and recorded by Josefa). This was published separately as a biography, aptly entitled *Recuerdos nacionales. José Acevedo i Gómez* (1860). Another 'Cuadro', a deftly written psychological study, tells the story of a husband's infidelity and his wife's offer to take in his illegitimate child (Josefa brought up Diego Fernando Gómez's son, Joaquín, born possibly to his first wife). In her writings, poetry and prose, Acevedo provides a first-hand account of woman's experiences of the post-independence political conflicts. Generally, she represents the public side of life in prose and the private in poetry, but in her most effective writings (such as the biography of her father) the one is integrally enmeshed in the other. Josefa was the eldest daughter (and second oldest child after Pedro) of the family and felt it her duty to contribute to the collective patriotic efforts with her writing. Her father and husband were civilian patriots, and her younger brothers all served in Santander's army. As a woman, the pen (rather than the sword or the forum) was her only viable option.

The Acevedo family was well connected politically. Progressive liberals and fervent patriots (that is, Granadinos), they supported Santander, who had been imprisoned following the famously frustrated attempt on Bolívar's life in Bogotá in 1828. Until his death, Bolívar attempted to govern the northern republics of Gran Colombia (1819–29). But in 1829 Venezuela seceded, Ecuador seceded in 1830, and Nueva Granada, today's Colombia, in 1831. Santander was declared President of Nueva Granada and drew up the 1832 Constitution. From then on, Colombian politics consisted of violent clashes between the conservative/Unitarians (former bolivarianos) and the liberal/federalists (Santanderistas). The years 1828–31 were difficult for liberal granadino families such as the Acevedos, who considered Venezuelan Bolívar an intruder. Unlike Marín, Acevedo wrote no encomiums to Bolívar. Evidently, one woman's liberator was another woman's dictator. The patria here is liberal Nueva Granada, not Gran Colombia.

Reading Acevedo's poetry provides a rare insight into the affective everyday impact of the Wars of Independence and their aftermath on one family from the subjective point of view of a key participant and witness. The collection is a year-by-year diary charting the emotional response to these public and private events and constitutes a life history of one woman. It is, in effect, autobiography in poetry. It also discloses a woman's motivations for writing and publishing, the procedures by which publication is achieved and the process whereby the author and her work contribute to, indeed initiate, post-independence national literary history. The poetry maps the close connections between family members and their friends, the dynamic of family life and related social networks and the links between these networks, the nation and the state, not merely in historical and factual terms but also with respect to psychology, morality, values and a shared culture. It constitutes reflexive memory, a personal record of an individual's private life and of the private lives of other, more public figures. In this it is the textual representation of concepts of self and self-identity in relation to others, changing over time. As far as form is concerned, the poetry is lyrical and subjective, rather than narrative or descriptive. Its aim is certainly not entertainment, though at times it verges on the didactic; its purpose is self-expression and in this sense it is Romantic. Although the poet writes according to classic Spanish convention, strictly adhering to identifiable meters and strophic forms, the poetry is not overtly neoclassical or Romantic in style, but rather plain and understated; rhetorical and figurative language, gendered or otherwise, is scarce. Neither is it overtly sentimental or religious, but rather direct and conversational. The poet usually addresses and engages with an interlocutor, often the reader, sometimes the dedicatee, with a sense of urgency. The aim is to communicate a reflexive, subjective response. In this respect the poetry is modern in tone. The persona projected is that of a sensitive woman who is adversely affected by life's misfortunes; the overall tone shifts from one of sadness and disappointment in the early poems to resistance and fulfilment through writing and through the family in the later ones.

Like Marín, Acevedo wrote formal patriotic poetry, though infrequently. One such poem of 1831 (in octavas) is entitled 'A petición de las señoras Sabogales i Padillas se escribió esta canción en honor de los generales Obando, López i Moreno'. The title suggests some shifting of responsibility for a political hymn of this importance and is also an indication of Acevedo's social capital.[16] Like Marín, she employs independence discourse to legitimate a particular political option. The poet addresses the victorious 'granadinos' thus: the 'patria querida' is grateful because the 'yugo más duro y fatal' has been removed by the three generals in question. On this occasion the 'astuto tirano', the 'déspota' who wished to turn free men into slaves, is ironically none other than the Liberator himself, Simón Bolívar, and the generals are those responsible for ending his dictatorship (though Bolívar had died in 1830, the year before the poem was written). Other such poems are the 1838 sonnet, 'Santa Elena', written 'para poner al pie de un paisaje representando la tumba i la sombra de Napoleon', who had been dead since 1821. Acevedo does not hesitate to refer to Napoleón as the 'héroe de Francia' brought down by 'tiranos'and 'verdugos humanos'. She had met Baron Gros, who was famous for his stylised portraits of Napoleon, as proved by her poem dedicated to him in October 1843.[17]

More effective and affective than the formal commemorations are Acevedo's lyrical poems, in which personal loss and pain (redolent of Romantic sensibilities) feature strongly. In 'Todo lo he perdido' (1829), written in informal 'romance', the poet laments the loss not only of her baby daughter (Amalia Julia) but also of her father, brother (Pedro) and husband, all dead or exiled on account of wars. Her style is understated; the tone intimate. Particularly emotive yet unsentimental is the poem 'Amalia Julia', commemorating the death of her first-born: 'Vacía i helada encuentrase tu cuna / I mustia i silenciosa esta mansion; / Nada quiero pedirle a la fortuna / Que está vacío también mi corazón' (Acevedo 1854b: 3). This technique is employed in poems where the 'yo' is not Josefa but a member of her family. In 'Un recuerdo del Capitán José Acevedo a su hermano el coronel Pedro Acevedo' (1830), the younger brother laments the death of he who was 'mi amigo, mi Mentor i mi hermano' (Acevedo 1854b: 12), a surrogate 'padre benéfico', who protected him from political intrigue. The poem ascribes to military men feelings and emotions, while real fraternal ties are presented as exemplary for republican fraternity. 'La Proscripción del Dr D.F.G a nombre de su hijo Joaquín' (1830) (a series of octavas) is a child's lament for the imprisonment and exile of the 'buen ciudadano' his father, Josefa's husband: 'Con rigor implacable el tirano [i.e. Bolívar] / lo arrancó de su dulce morada' (Acevedo 1854b: 17). In 'El coronel

José Acevedo desde su prisión en los últimos días de febrero de 1831' (signed March 22 1831), the colonel laments that although he has fought in the army since the age of 14 to 'libertar la patria', he has been imprisoned on the orders of the same 'déspota inhumano': 'Aun no había abandonado de la infancia / Los juegos bulliciosos i pueriles; / Contaba apenas ¡ah! catorce abriles / Cuando fui por mi madre presentado / Para aprender en los valientes filas / El oficio penoso del soldado' (Acevedo 1854b: 19). These are soldiers' confessions and memoirs.

One of the most poignant poems is the earliest in the collection, dated 1823, an elegy to the poet's father. 'Una tumba en los Andaquíes' opens with a personal memory 'Hubo un tiempo mui grato a mi memoria / Cuando a mi tierno padre acompañaba / y que él con sus caricias me llenaba / de gratitud, de complacencia y gloria' and ends lamenting that only an abandoned wooden cross in the jungle marks his burial place, 'no hay monumento, ni inscripción, ni loza' (Acevedo 1854b: 1); he is not publicly commemorated. Yet he is remembered, by his daughter, whose published poem is his memorial. Personal loss extends to close women friends, as in 'Elegía. Sobre la muerte de la señora Teresa Villa de Montoya' (1831), who died in childbirth. These poems are a forceful reminder of the ephemerality of life in which men die young in war and women in childbirth. 'La vida' (1829) and 'El pesar' (1829), written while the poet watches her sleeping daughter, mourn the passing of childhood, peace and happiness. The year 1830, when Acevedo's husband was exiled, was one of her bleakest. In 'Mis desahogos en los días del infortunio' (1830) the poet turns to God for comfort, though generally hers is not religious poetry. 'Al Leteo' (1831), written in remembrance of her estranged husband and deceased daughter, pleads for relief in oblivion. The poet writes simply, in 'tono' and 'arte menor', of the painful (and apparently permanent) separation from Gómez: 'Yo fui feliz un tiempo / Cuando a su lado estaba / Cuando él me acariciaba / Cuando vivía para él'; '¡Para siempre ha pasado / La época venturosa! / Ya el título de esposa / No volveré a escuchar' (Acevedo 1854b: 25).

Several poems are letters in verse to her brothers. In one addressed to Alfonso (1835), she asks him to confide in her about the troubles he experienced in 'la opulenta Quito' (Acevedo 1854b: 48). In 'La ausencia eterna', an elegy written after his death in Rome in 1851, the poet recounts Alfonso's travels in Europe and his views on the widespead social misery he saw there, especially in England. Her poem-letter to Juan Miguel. 'A mi hermano Juan Miguel Acevedo' (1839), written in octavillas, portrays the poet as a victim rescued by her brother in a series of simple but effective analogies: his encouragement is like dew on a flower; his friendship, a port to a mariner returning from a perilous voyage; his consolation, that of a mother for her baby; his face lights up her darkness like the sun and, significantly, the poetry she writes for him is like the song of a caged bird:

El ave aprisionada
En su jaula de hierro

Cantando allá en su encierro
Distrae su soledad
I yo, infeliz cautiva,
Calmo mis inquietudes
Cantando tus virtudes
Tu afecto i tu amistad

(Acevedo 1854b: 54)

Although in this poetry there is little direct vindication of women's rights, it is possible to identify, as in the above poem, an acute awareness of and resistance to women's subordination. As with Marín, there are several poems of female friendship, such as 'A las señoritas Parises Santamarías' (1837).[18] The poem 'Al señor Aristides Calcaño' (1848) rehearses the social roles the poet feels obliged to discharge as a republican woman, but that bring her little joy: 'Esposa, madre, amiga, ciudadana / En cada estado i situación buscaba / Esta felicidad que se escapaba / Dejándome una huella de pesar' (Acevedo 1854b: 92). In 'Tequendama' (1847), she wonders as she contemplates the great waterfall if, in past civilisations, 'en estas ignoradas tierras, / se conocía gobiernos i tiranos, / si los pueblos se amaban como hermanos, / si siempre esclava ha sido la mujer' (Acevedo 1854b: 81). One of the light-hearted early poems, dated 1825, 'A pedimento de una amiga para dirigirlo a un joven de 19 años' is delightfully risqué. As the title indicates, the poem is written for a girlfriend who has taken a fancy to a young man. He remains oblivious to her feelings which, because she is a respectable woman, she cannot express. The letter in verse, addressed to him in the first person by the girl, is the only way of communicating her unrequited love. She complains that she cannot sleep at night thinking of him, while he sleeps on unaware of her passion. When they meet he is friendly but ultimately indifferent. He has no inkling that she loves him. She wants to shout out her love: 'Pero, ¿qué es lo que digo? !Soi mujer! / I a hablar así de mi pasión me atrevo? / Mas, la decencia prohibe ... Sí, amor mío / Yo no hablaré a los hombres de mi afecto' (Acevedo 1854b: 4).[19] In 'Qué será esto' (1848), voiced by a young 'coqueta', the poet gives advice to young women on how to appear respectable and attract a husband, a theme she was concurrently developing in prose in her *Tratado sobre economía doméstica* (1848) and *Ensayo sobre los deberes de los casados* (1845). Acevedo writes as sister, mother, mother-in-law, grandmother ('El primer nieto' (1846), 'A Ernesto' (1847), 'Un sueño dichoso realizado' (1853)), and daughter, as a sentient, rational individual embedded in and defined by family relationships. Strangely, there are no poems written for her mother, though her mother features large in the prose works, as we shall see.

Acevedo's poetry internalises public events and publicises a woman's inner feelings; the private is made public and the public private. In so doing, woman is represented as historical subject, a real person with thoughts and feelings, and, as poet, sister, daughter, wife and mother, an active contributor to and shaper of the cultural memory of her patria. In Angela Keane's words referring to English women writers at the time, this strategy gave women 'invisible visibility in print' (Keane 2000: 12). Women took on the indispensable role as chroniclers of men's heroic feats, which without commemoration could not be heroic. They were the makers of heroes; honour depended on public recognition and to be forgotten was worse than death. They also provided, as no others could, insight into these men's private lives, their thoughts, feelings, strengths and weakness. The men were heroes but also good family men and, in as much as the family was social and public, they were good citizens and human beings. However, as in other countries, 'the links to forgetting backfired as cultural amnesia eventually obscured the very women whose writing was cited as ensuring cultural continuance' (Kucich 2000: 9). Ultimately, while the memory of the heroes lives on (some, at least), the women who were complicit in their remembrance are forgotten.

Acevedo's family biographies

In her prose work Acevedo creates social capital by representing her family as distinguished by its noble ancestry (which she does not fail to point out, despite republican beliefs)[20] and more importantly for its patriotic contribution to Colombian (Nueva Granadan) nationhood. The Acevedo family, identified metonymically with the patria family, is both representative and exemplary. The family, widely accepted as the natural sphere for women, is thus shown to be the kernel, the nucleus of the republican polity. It is here that the bonds of affect, belonging and origins are born and nurtured, naturally and organically. The nation is constituted by the everyday of family life; biography is history. Women are thus positioned at the centre of national history, and the domestic domain at the centre of public life. Similarly the boundaries between public and private are represented as porous.

Written after the General's death in 1850, the co-authored *Biografía del General José Acevedo Tejada* focuses on the socialisation of children, who were raised and educated to be patriots by their parents, especially by their mothers in view of the high mortality rate among men.[21] Acevedo claims that social (that is, republican) values and ideals are inculcated in children from the earliest age and passed on genetically through the generations: 'esta enseñanza doméstica que casi jamás se borra, i que así como las facciones i rasgos de una raza, conserva hasta generaciones muy remotas lo que podríamos llamar la fisonomía moral de una familia' (Acevedo and Acevedo 1850: 5). This is the work of the republican mother. The sketch also shows how decisions are made concerning the patriot-children's future careers, dramatising the intimate discussions between husband and wife, parents and children, that lead ultimately to political action. Women are inscribed at the centre of this life-changing decision-making; their advice and vital support is sought and given, and often their judgement is proved to be sounder than that of men. One such example is Josefa Acevedo's heroic mother who, widowed and impoverished by 'la causa de la Independencia y la Libertad de su Patria' (Acevedo and Acevedo 1850: 4), brought up nine children to follow their father's example. Catalina Sánchez de Tejada was 'dotada de un talento despejado, de un juicio sano, i de un espíritu superior a sus sexo i a su época'; this makes her 'una madre patriota y previsa' (Acevedo and Acevedo 1850: 5). Time and time again the family and the patria are textually represented as one. The death of General José Acevedo was 'un golpe doloroso para los que le amaban, i una calamidad para la Patria' (Acevedo and Acevedo 1850: 4).

Josefa's biography of her husband, *Biografía del Doctor Diego Fernández Gómez* (1854), was completed by 1853. The circumstances of its writing and publication provide further insight into the significance of social capital for women writers. Josefa originally wrote a short piece to give to her eldest daughter, who she thought would appreciate an account of 'la vida pública de su padre', as a birthday gift (Acevedo 1854a: Preface). However, when her estranged husband saw it, he complained it was too short and asked her to write a more substantial version after his death, for which he sent her a number of documents. After Gómez died, several mutual friends asked her to finish the biography, including Colonel Pineda. Sr. Vergara promised her space in his newspaper. Josefa is concerned that public opinion might accuse her of writing in praise of her own family, but she cites Mme. de Staël, who focused on her own father rather than the French Revolution, as an estimable precedent. She presents herself humbly, unworthy of serious comparison with de Staël but, nevertheless, charged with the public duty of bringing to knowledge the life of an exemplary citizen and patriot, and ends with the observation that she has documentary proof of the historical accuracy of all the facts. So it is that Josefa Acevedo is positioned as family biographer and, concurrently, national historian.

Acevedo represents Gómez (1786–1853) as the ideal republican servant: a deputy in all congresses since 1810; provincial governor; magistrate; judge; state counsellor; secretary in Hacienda; and member of prestigious literary societies. His exemplary republican character was that of the 'juez íntegro e incorruptible, del firme republicano, del legislador prudente e filántropo, y del hombre ilustrado' (Acevedo 1854a: 2). He refused to 'doblar la rodilla delante del opresor [Bolívar] que intentaba esclavizar la Patria' and suffered as a consequence 'injustas proscripciones' (Acevedo 1854a: 3). However, this is the public life and public persona of Gómez. It is interesting to speculate that it may be a quite different, apparently fictitious, version of his life as father of an illegitimate child, written from the point of view of the wronged wife who agrees to raise the child, that provides the plot of a 'Cuadro' in the *Cuadros de la vida privada*.

The *Biografía del Teniente Coronel Alfonso Acevedo y Tejada* (1855) was written to compensate for the failure of the 'hijos de esta ciudad' (Santa Fe de Bogotá) to publish an obituary or memorial to Josefa's younger brother Alfonso (1809–51), despite his four-year governorship of the city and his services to the 'capital de la República, a la nación, i a toda la humanidad' (Acevedo 1855: 1). The style of this biography is more personal and colourful than that of *Diego Fernández Gómez*. It is full of intriguing anecdotes. Josefa is more concerned to represent the character, values, habits and personality of her younger brother than merely list his achievements in the public sphere. Having joined the army aged 15 he refused, in 1828, aged 19, to sign the Act that gave Bolívar absolute power in Nueva Granada. As a consequence he was separated, with his brother, from the army with 'licencia indefinida'. His final public posting was as Colombian representative to the Vatican, where he died and was buried. Josefa describes him as a young man:

> siempre festivo, chancero, i alegre, era el primer contribuyente para los bailes, el más acrito promovedor de paseos, el asiduo cortejo de las damas, i el apasionado constante de las lecturas sentimentales que tanto agradan a la juventud. Pero, por un contraste que es bastante común en las personas dotadas de una grande sensibilidad, Alfonso era inclinado a las meditaciones melancólicas, amaba la soledad, buscaba las fuertes conmociones del alma en la contemplación de la desgracia ajena que siempre procuraba aliviar. (Acevedo 1955: 3)

She achieves a rounder, more attractive, personality than the dry account of public merit reserved for her husband. Alfonso is romantic, warm and personable, and the reader can identify and empathise with him on a human level. These are the ties of understanding and affection that binds the patria, the family of citizens, to their res publica.

Acevedo's biographies of her father, brothers and husband provide the means by which these men are established in the collective memory as important figures in modern Colombian history. Her first-hand accounts of their individual contributions to national independence, as civilians, soldiers and magistrates, constitute the initial chapters of post-independence history. Yet the fact that the biographies are written by their sister, daughter or wife, that is, from an intimate and personal point of view, ensures that the men come across first and foremost as human beings. They are represented and subsequently recognised as national heroes, but within a republican morality. Like ordinary human beings they have their faults and make the wrong decisions, but in times of crisis they act bravely and resolutely as citizens for the collective good. The heroes are demythified; they are represented as good republican family men, making their achievements even more remarkable. They were not born heroes, but acquired heroism through their efforts on behalf of the patria/family. Once the family members have been incorporated into the collective memory as celebrated public figures, largely due to the success of these biographies, the same texts provide for readers the personal details of these public men's private lives, thus allowing insight into their very human thoughts, feelings, and dilemmas. The biographies are the essence of postcolonial national history; they conflate national and family history and personal and collective memory. The author makes this possible by integrating two distinctive narrative voices: one that objectively recounts historical events; and another that intersperses personal anecdotes, colourful scenes, and carefully selected funny or dramatic details from a more subjective point of view. The emphasis is on these men's early formation, their childhood and adolescence, told from an insider's perspective; their upbringing by an exemplary republican mother at the centre of an exemplary middle-class republican family. Above all, these biographies could only have been written by a family member. The author therefore has full, indeed exclusive authority to write and publish to the benefit of the nation.

Acevedo's essays on domesticity

Acevedo's most popular and lucrative writings, however, were her essays on domestic economy, household management and family values for young married women. They gave her the means to earn money and repay her son-in-law. Like the biographies, their purpose was to disseminate advice and instruction on how to achieve exemplary republican morality, especially republican motherhood. These self-help conduct books attest to the importance of secular middle-class values and lifestyles, as is to be expected in states that by the mid-century had begun to establish national consolidation. The books are invaluable to social and cultural historians, as they are replete with information about the everyday lives, daily routines, education, habits, conduct, norms, values and expectations of ordinary men and women in middle-sector, mid-century Colombian households, recounted from a woman's perspective. This provides, furthermore, a window onto the material culture, consumer trends, and class relations of post-independence society at the time.

Not surprisingly, the books focus on women's lives at the heart of the family and are particularly informative with regard to the dynamics of power and authority in the middle-class family. Overall, the books strongly encourage women to conform to contemporary *doxa* and social hierarchies of sexual difference. However, at the same time they make a strong case for positioning familial social relations and the domestic economy at the centre of national society and the political economy of the state, so that the smooth-running of the one is essential to the success of the other. National progress is concomitant with women's skilful management of the home. Women's future role in the modern republic is indispensable to progress, because the microeconomics of the household (the Greek *oikonomia* or economy) is the linchpin of the political economy of the state. In the *Ensayo sobre los deberes de los casados* (1845) and the *Tratado sobre economía doméstica* (1848), the author/narrator addresses the reader, as in the biographies, with authority. Hers is the voice of experience, as wife, mother and household manager in her own right. She is firm, didactic, yet kind and conciliatory. She realises that she is asking women, mainly the newly wed, to put to one side their individual inclinations, personal desires and any sense of fulfilment outside the family home. This is a major sacrifice they have to make for the good of their family, their nation and their own happiness. Within these limits, once they have conformed to the *doxa* of their times, they can exert authority and take charge of their lives and those of others in the ways the author suggests. Her books have replaced the religious conduct books that abounded in colonial society. In Acevedo's work, religion is not a major issue for women;

in fact, the family is harmed if too much time is spent on religious devotion. Instead, the aim is to build a morally sound, useful, productive and thrifty family on the Anglo model.

The *Ensayo sobre los deberes de los casados*, dedicated to the 'juventud granadina', is divided in two parts: the first explains a husband's duties to his wife; and the second, a wife's duties to her husband. The qualities expected of a good husband are, briefly: respect for his wife, tolerance, good example, generosity, trust, friendship and instruction. A wife, in her turn, should show her husband loyalty, kindness, trust, obedience, patience, order and cleanliness. Evidently this is a conservative agenda. However, Acevedo's motives were patriotic: to persuade reluctant young men to marry, 'he notado que en esta tierra los hombres temen al matrimonio, ya porque aman demasiado la vida libre i disipada ... ya porque les asusta el pensar en la coquetería y despilfarro de las mujeres' (Acevedo 1857: 2), and to help make the 'yugo del matrimonio' (Acevedo 1857: 105) more bearable, indeed pleasurable, for women. This programme spells out the rights and duties of the citizen in the social institution that is the family, 'Acordaos que de una i otra parte hai derechos que es justo respetar i deberes que es preciso cumplir' (Acevedo 1857: 106), rights and duties which are equally important but gendered according to sexual difference. Acevedo asks young people to follow her sound advice for the common good, 'la sociedad se pervierte i corrompe i la República se perjudica porque los casados no son lo que deberían ser' (Acevedo 1857: 106). By the mid-1850s, the sign of patriotism was no longer military conquest but the building of a good marriage and prosperous family. This was the right and duty of both men and women, who needed to work togther to succeed.

The *Tratado sobre economía doméstica*, which Josefa attempted to publish in 1844, is dedicated to her niece, Dolores Neira, who financed its publication with savings put to one side for recreation and adornments. Josefa was also supported by León, her son-in-law. In the *advertencia* she states that she had no desire to gain a literary reputation, but published the book to earn money and to communicate useful advice. Her target public is middle-class women: 'escribo para mujeres, i especialmente para aquellas que no tienen una inmensa fortuna, pero sí una casa que gobernar y una familia que educar' (Acevedo 1848: 7). Epigraphs by Benjamin Franklin head each chapter. The first, which sets the tone for the volume, is ' le temps perdu ne se retrouve jamais' (Acevedo 1848: 5) and the chapter in question, 'De la economía del tiempo', imparts advice on how to use time wisely, for time is money. In order to sweeten the pill and to illustrate her points more persuasively, the author includes anecdotes and short stories.

With respect to daily routine and time management, Acevedo advises married women to rise early, spend an hour tidying their room and home, an hour on personal hygiene, half an hour on breakfast, and then the rest of the morning sewing, drawing, teaching, making flowers and generally caring for their children and keeping order. A married woman should take exercise to prolong her life expectancy, which at the time was no more than 40 to 50 years, cut social visits to a minimum and refrain from gossip. Evening visits are preferable and topics for discussion should be useful and informative: for example, recipes, horticulture, crafts, books, news of misfortunes that require assistance, and so on. Music, dancing, singing, painting and novels are acceptable pursuits as long as they do not interfere with the duties of mothering, 'una madre, por lo común, no puede ser artista' (Acevedo 1848: 11). Fashion (for men and women) is a waste of time and money; so is excessive piety. A woman who spends her entire day visiting a succession of churches and attending masses 'no es buena para esposa, para madre de familia, para preceptora, para jefe de un establecimiento cualquiera, excepto un beaterío' (Acevedo 1848: 13). Women likewise should avoid parties, fiestas and *tertulias*. Reading is good, as long as the material is constructive. In sum, life is short and time must be spent usefully. This is a sign of human civilisation: 'se emplean bien las horas trabajando, aprendiendo, pensando y diviertiéndose. La inteligencia debe presidir a todo ... no gemiremos como animales de carga, no nos reiremos como estúpidas cotorras' (Acevedo 1848: 14).

Each chapter of advice is followed by an *episodio*, a short story or parable illustrating the previous lesson. The first recounts the tale of Edmundo, who for four years searches for a suitable bride, one who employs her time usefully. One young lady wastes time making embroideries and reading her brother's medical books, which she cannot understand. Three silly sisters disappoint him by constantly mislaying their possessions and forgetting to make even the most necessary arrangements, such as buying food. Isabel is too pious; the country girls, Rosalía and Victorina, too superstitious and credulous; Serafina too vain. Finally he meets two sisters whose common sense, intelligence and sincerity convince him that there are indeed women who know how to make the most of their time. Acevedo comments wryly in a note:

> es más común de lo que se piensa el desprecio con que miran los hombres la inteligencia de las mujeres. ¡Que Dios bendiga a los esposos, padres i hermanos que tratan de sacarlas de la estrecha esfera del fanatismo, los errores i la ignorancia. (Acevedo 1848: 23)

The second chapter discusses money matters, the domestic economy. Money should be spent on necessities, useful items, charity and pleasure, strictly in that order. Luxury needs to be avoided, by men and women, but also false economies: good-quality tools, instruments and clothes last longer. Above all, a family should not get into debt or live beyond its means. Expenditure on education is recommended, but as long as the education fits the needs of the child. An unnecessarily brilliant education is wasteful. Children should be taught morality and religion, the three Rs, national history, love of liberal institutions, civic rights and geometry. Charity, that is, social welfare, on the other hand, is a civic obligation, but should reach the right kind of recipient. This does not include 'las beatas y mogigatas que hormiguean en esta cuidad i que se emplean únicamente en rezar, comer i charlar' (Acevedo 1848:48).

The second *episodio* tells the story of Alejandro, who attempts to correct the tremendously wasteful habits of his family and friends by setting up a charity fund, to which they must contribute if he catches them wasting money. Perpetrators include a couple of *petimetres,* his friend's sons, who spend a fortune on new clothes in the style of Louis Philippe's heirs (that is, the Princes of Joinville and D'Aumale), only to find out that the outfits of the Grand Duke of Russia are far more chic and desirable. Similarly wasteful is money spent on inappropriate education: botany and astronomy taught to an elderly grandmother who cannot take the evening air, algebra taught to a fifteen-year-old girl, and foreign languages to an illiterate doorman; the motto is 'el que mucho abarca poco aprieta' (Acevedo 1848: 46). Interestingly, not only women are targeted as spendthrifts. Young men are also accused of wasting money, on dogs, gambling, dancing and inebriation. A further example is that of a family who buy 25 plant pots, but not the soil or seeds. A pet monkey breaks nine pots and the family gives away the rest before they, too, are broken, to save money. Alejandro demonstrates that twenty-two families waste 200,000 pesos per year, a half per cent of which (1,000 pesos) he takes for charity. Thrift is the key to social progress.

The final chapter of the *Tratado* focuses on economies of jewels, clothes, furniture and provisions. Women should take care of their possessions and keep them clean at all times. They must maintain order in their homes, because an expensive dress 'como una joya de gran precio, representa una capital' (Acevedo 1848: 55). Copious tips follow on how to wash, repair and care for clothes, adornments and household objects. For example, it is best to sew torn clothes after washing but before starching or ironing. Girls should be taught to sew from an early age; a girl who has to mend her torn clothes will refrain from climbing trees, playing with fire or the dog and generally forgetting 'la moderación y compostura que deben acompañar a una mujer' (Acevedo 1848: 59). A man with a poorly sewn shirt, a broken collar, an unhemmed tie, or buttons missing from his waistcoat reflects badly on his wife. Further advice includes not to buy too much furniture and not to sleep on the sofa or spit on the carpet. A good housewife should know exactly how many items she has in her home, especially the kitchen, to guard against theft by the servants. She should treat domestic economy seriously and girls should be taught to 'llevar la cuenta de sus gastos, a calcular, comprar i dirijir por sí mismas todo lo que tiene relación con ellos' (Acevedo 1848: 64), especially in Bogotá, which is known for its uncleanliness and where good servants are rare. She should learn how keep eggs, milk, fruit and tabacco fresh, and how to make chocolate, jam and starch, but not waste time making bread, candles, sausages or soap, which may be easily purchased elsewhere.

The final *episodio*, the longest of the three, is a morality tale illustrating the dire consequences of bad parenting and lax discipline. Three naughty, over-indulged children gradually destroy their wealthy parents's home and eventually lead the family to ruin. Amelia cannot find a match and the boys gamble away the family's fortune. One boy commits suicide and the mother dies. Amelia, her father and brother Adolfo, live in misery until Amelia meets Julia, who teaches her how to run a home and earn a living. Julia had learned from her own mother, who had lived in England:

> había estudiado el orden i la economía en el país del orden, de la economía i del cálculo. En Inglaterra casi no se conoce la holgazanería, i las mujeres de la clase media en aquel país no son una carga para sus esposos sino un consuelo, un auxiliar de su industria i las administradoras prudentes de lo que aquellos laboriosos isleños trabajan i ahorran. (Acevedo 1848: 79)

So it is that Adolfo finds employment as a home tutor to girls, the father as a clerk in a business run by an Englishman, and Amelia gives singing lessons. The boss introduces his son and nephew, 'jóvenes ingleses de bastante mérito' (Acevedo 1848: 85), to the family. Julia marries the nephew and Adolfo travels to London with the son, 'ya estaba en la populosa metrópoli de la más industriosa de las naciones'. Immersed in hard work, he forgets his misfortunes, including his unrequited love for Julia. Work and industry 'debilitan las pasiones tiernas i él que ejercita el comercio en Inglaterra con dificultad tendrá tiempo para pensar en sus amores' (Acevedo 1848: 86).

The final lesson of the book is that Colombian families should learn to make use of what might appear to be 'inservible'. Acevedo states that the English and Dutch, who throw away nothing, have honed this art to perfection:

> por consigiente será de la mayor utilidad un establecimiento donde pudiera cada uno vender lo que ya no quiere, bien fuesen muebles, vestidos, loza etc etc i donde los que tienen pocas comodidades i necesitan cosas baratas aunque no sean de moda, pudieran proveerse de ellas a precios cómodos. (Acevedo 1848: 86–87)

In other words, second-hand shops, useful in that they allow people to dispose of unneccessary objects, are a good business opportunity for aspiring Colombian entrepeneurs (Acevedo 1848: 87).

These writings privilege the significance of the extended family, the household and the socialisation of children in national politics and economic development. The family is presented as the chief agent of cultivation, the means by which moral values and culture are transmitted to children and internalised, so that an individual's life may conform to social norms and expectations. The family is the device by means of which individuals are integrated into society, yet are differentiated as individuals with their personal quirks and foibles. Similarly, socialisation is seen as the bridge between individual psychology and collective sociology. A woman's experience and knowledge is indispensable to social progress, as a repository of collective memory, morality and affect, and as a capable, rational individual in her own right with legitimate aspirations to self-fulfilment, albeit within the protective confines of the home.

Notes

1 Her first poem, a sonnet written to a friend in 1818, is reproduced in Amunátegui 1867: 39.

2 Juan Egaña (1768–1836), Dean of the Royal and Pontifical University of San Felipe and Professor of Rhetoric.

3 'Homenaje de gratitud a la memoria del benemérito Ministro Diego Portales' (1837), reprinted in *América poética. Poesías selectas americanas con noticias biográficas de los autores* (Valparaíso, 1846), according to Amunátegui, but not included in the 1875 edition of this anthology, edited by José Domingo Cortés, in which five of Marín's poems are included.

4 Marín also published *leyendas* in verse. Her first 'La novia y la carta', the story of how a girl resigns herself to marriage with an odious husband, was published in *El Crepúsculo* in 1843 and as a pamphlet in 1874. See Medina 1923: 24.

5 Publication began under José María Obando's presidency (1853–54). The 'Confederación granadina' dates from 1858 and the Estados Unidos de Colombia from1861.

6 *Tratado sobre economía doméstica* preceded *Mrs Beeton's Book of Household Management*, 1861, by more than a decade, although the *Englishwoman's Domestic Magazine*, in which Isabella Beeton's book was first serialised in 1859, dates from 1852. Beeton's book played an important part in the mid-Victorian cult of domesticity in Britain. Her aims, to preserve the family as a social unit, promote self-improvement and enhance women's social standing by crediting their domestic responsibilities with great significance, were similar to Acevedo's. See Nicola Humble's Introduction to the 2000 edition (Humble 2000).

7 Only married men of property aged over 25 (a few thousand) could vote. Portales also reintroduced primogeniture. As Minister of the Interior, he exiled O'Higgins in 1830.

8 He dismissed a number of distinguished generals, including General Freire, who attempted to take Valparaiso in retaliation.

9 Her son wrote as follows: 'se dejó oír el canto de un poeta desconocido ... ¿Quién era ese poeta? Bello i Felipe Pardo no habían escrito estas estrofas; fuera de estos eminentes literatos no había en Chile persona alguna a quien atribuirlas'. Soon the public found out the author's identity 'con mayor sorpresa' and her name 'corrió de boca en boca' ('Dos palabras', del Solar 1874: xi).

10 Although Spain is referred to in the masculine as 'gran coloso' in 'Canto a la Patria', 1857, in the same poem, the 'monstruo execrable' that threatens to devour Chile is not Spain but anarchy (del Solar 1874: 51).

11 ¿I he de hablar yo de ti, madre adorada,
Cuya imagen en lo hondo de mi pecho
Con eterno buril está grabada?
No: porque ya tu nombre han proferido
Tus nobles compatriotas, i en sus fastos
Con honrosa memoria
A la posteridad le han trasmitido. (del Solar 1874: 42)

12 The Sociedad de Beneficencia de Señoras was organised by elite women in the early 1850s, and a branch was established in Valparaíso. It was founded by Juana Ross de Edwards in 1855. The Santiago Society's Board included the following women: President, Antonia Salas de Errázuriz; Vice-President, Josefa Larraín de Aldunante; Secretary, Enriqueta Pinto de Bulnes; Treasurer, Nicolasa Toro de Correa; members: Rosa Carrera de Aldunante, Carmen Velazco de Alcalde, Carmen Gana

de Blanco, Emilia Herrera de Toro, Magdalena Vicuña de Subercaseaux, Rosa Concha de Cerda, Manuela Portales de Morán, Dolores Errázuriz de Salas, and Rita Larraín de Echevarría (Maza Valenzuela 1995: 11).

13 The second edition of Gómez de Avellaneda's *Poesías* (1841) was published in Madrid in 1850, and the third in Mexico in 1852.

14 Nor was she included in *Poesía americana*, edited by Juan María Gutiérrez (1866).

15 Sarmiento held similar views on Spain and the repression of women, see Chapter 10 on Manso. In an article published in *Mercurio* (July 1841), Sarmiento encouraged Marín to continue writing, 'Sentimos que la distinguida señora Marín ... no favorezca el público con nuevas producciones ... ' (Amunátegui 1867: 47).

16 Admiral General José Prudencio Padilla had taken part in the Battle of Trafalgar before joining the Spanish American independence cause. He was accused of conspiring against Bolívar and was executed in 1828. The conspirators met in the house of Luis Vargas Tejada, who was related possibly to Josefa's mother, Catalina Sánchez de Tejada. His brother, General José Antonio Padilla, fought with Obando and died in the federal revolt of 1841. José María Obando was Vice-President of the Colombian Republic 1831–32, and President 1853–54. José Hilario López was President of Colombia 1849–53.

17 'Al señor Baron Gros sobre sus pinturas' (Acevedo 1854b: 74–75).

18 José Ignacio París was acknowledged as a magnanimous benefactor to local schools in *Tratado de economía doméstica* (Acevedo 1848: 35).

19 See also the poem written for a young man who asks forgiveness from his Julia 'El arrepentimiento. Pedido por un joven' (1829) (Acevedo 1854b: 7).

20 'lo que se llamó nobleza de cuna bajo el régimen colonial', *Biografía del General José Acevedo Tejada* (Acevedo and Acevedo 1850: 4).

21 José Acevedo, 1806–50, joined Santander's army at the age of 13.

CHAPTER NINE

Gender and Revolution in Southern Brazil: Restitching the Farroupilha Revolt in the Works of Delfina Benigna da Cunha and Ana de Barandas[1]

Quando os homens vão à guerra, as mulheres vão à luta

A Casa das Sete Mulheres 2003, dir. Jayme Monjardim

The idea that women's political activism is stimulated by men going to war is a recurrent concept in women's history and certainly applicable to Spanish America, as we have seen. This chapter, focusing on Brazil, will argue that it describes the Farroupilha or Ragamuffin Revolt of Rio Grande do Sul (1835–45) particularly well, not only as regards the changes wrought in women's consciousness about their role in society, but also in respect of women's self-perceptions in relation to Brazilian national and regional identities in the wake of formal independence in 1822. The Farroupilha Revolt has long since entered the popular imaginary of the Brazilian south, fuelling the strong sense of a separate, regionalist *gaúcho* identity.[2] For a period of ten years in the first half of the nineteenth century, a liberal revolution, followed by the declaration of an independent republican and federalist state, split Brazil's southernmost province on the Uruguay border off from the rest of the nation, sparking a protracted civil war. In addition to the deep-rooted regional mythology that still attaches to these events in the state of Rio Grande do Sul, the success of the historical television mini-series, *A Casa das Sete Mulheres,* produced by Som Livre/Rede Globo in 2003, tended to reinforce the image of the Farroupilha Revolt as Brazil's nostalgic national emblem of a utopian republican ideal.[3]

In fact, the Farroupilha Revolt crystallised a specific point of crisis in the tension between regional and national identifications in Brazil, which brought a new dimension to the ways in which the women and men of Rio Grande do Sul conceived their patriotic sense of belonging. Closely related to this, and as this chapter will endeavour to show, the war was also a field of gender conflict and transformation. The declaration in 1836 of an independent republic in Rio Grande do Sul predictably did not include citizen rights for women, any more than it made provision for the liberation of slaves (M. Flores 2002: 91). However, the question of women's cultural, social and military participation in Brazil's public, political life did clearly emerge as a contingent, instrumental issue brought about by the crisis of the conflict. In this context, a small but identifiable caucus of women, writing poetry, journalism and prose, sought to intervene politically in the discursive construction of gender and imperial national identity immediately before, during and after the war. This chapter discusses the gender implications of the changing political and cultural circumstances in which these women were writing, before engaging in a close comparative reading of two of them, Delfina Benigna da Cunha (1791–1857) and Ana Eurídice Eufrosina de Barandas (1806 – ?). Both Cunha and Barandas have remained largely neglected by scholarship outside their home state of Rio Grande do Sul; and both were strong, conservative supporters of monarchist, imperial rule, although Barandas was more open to the possibilities that liberal philosophy appeared to offer women.

The conflict between liberal and conservative positions on the type of constitutional monarchy that post-independence Brazil should be was not, of course, new, nor was it only pertinent to Rio Grande do Sul. However, it became particularly relevant to the national unity of Brazil during the early years of the regency, from 1831–40. Pressured by liberal and army opposition, the Emperor Pedro I had abdicated in 1831 in favour of his five-year-old son, later Pedro II, who could not rule until he came of age and was therefore replaced in the short term by a regency. In the absence of an immediate and visible unifying focus in the form of the monarch, the first phase of this regency period (1831–37) was one of intense competition between ruling elites, involving radical changes in the organisation and distribution of Brazil's governing power, which was to pose a long-term threat to national unity. A major turning point was the Ato Adicional (Additional Act) of 1834, which reformed the Brazilian Constitution by providing for the devolution of considerable autonomy and legislative power to the regional level through the establishment of provincial assemblies. This act of decentralisation effectively widened the fault lines between the local loyalties that pertained to the regional province or *pátria,* and those that could realistically be commanded by the central, imperial government in Rio de Janeiro. As Roderick J. Barman remarks, during the first six years of the regency, until September 1837, 'Brazil's rulers sought to equate the nation with the *pátrias.* Thereafter they sought, no matter what the cost, to re-establish the primacy of nation over *pátria*' (Barman 1988: 160–61).

At the same time as the Ato Adicional increased popular participation by shifting the focus of popular politics from the national to the provincial, it also intensified the struggle to defend traditional power structures, vested economic interests and networks of patronage precisely at the localised level of the *pátria.* As Barman claims, where the winners of the newly created provincial assembly elections could 'use the assembly's powers to entrench their supremacy and to damage their traditional foes, no family clan or interest group with any claim to influence could afford to abstain from politics' (Barman 1988: 180). In this unstable climate, the 1830s and 1840s witnessed a countrywide outbreak of republican, federalist and separatist revolts in provinces as diverse as Ceará, Pernambuco, Bahia, Minas Gerais, São Paulo, Grão-Pará and Maranhão. However, none was as long-lasting and threatening to centralised unity as the one that engulfed Rio Grande do Sul and effectively brought down the liberal regent, Padre Diogo Antônio Feijó in 1837. The Farroupilha Revolt was dangerous to the central government and national unity partly because, unlike other regional revolts, which galvanised Indians and the socially oppressed, it was a liberal white landowners' rising, which did not overtly challenge the established social and racial order (Barman 1988: 182).

In the Rio Grande do Sul context, the term *farroupilha* or *farrapo,* meaning 'ragamuffin' or 'ragged', was actually used to designate a broad band of different liberal factions, which took up quite diverse stances on the issues of republicanism and federalism. Thus, at different times the Farroupilha cause embraced moderate liberals or *chimangos* of both monarchist and republican stamp, as well as the more revolutionary, extremist or *exaltado* wings of liberalism. As Moacyr Flores has noted, '*farroupilha*' described the liberal ideologies of a militarised land- and slave-owning *estancieiro* (rancher) elite, not a workers' movement or peasant uprising (2003: 90; 1990: 25). The Farroupilhas' conservative opponents, the *Legalistas* (Legalists) were also known as monarchists or *caramuras* and were, broadly speaking, opposed to political decentralisation supporting the continued integration of Rio Grande do Sul into a Brazilian empire, under the emperor's regency in Rio de Janeiro.

If the Farroupilha power base was the rural, property-owning *estancieiro* sector, the military and members of the National Guard, the Legalist cause found its natural home in the cities, particularly the capital, Porto Alegre, where professional, public service, trading and commercial classes had developed in the early nineteenth century. These were very distinct and distant from the *estancieiros* of the interior and their economic interests (M. Flores 2002: 220). However, the ideological division between the two factions was never absolute and, indeed, there was frequent changing of sides during the war. The cause that ostensibly brought the two groups into conflict and sparked the Farroupilha Revolt centred on liberal moves to install a more autonomous, democratic legislative assembly and the call for greater local control over the levying and use of taxes. The immediate factor motivating the *estancieiros* and *fazendeiros* of the interior to take this stance was the government taxation of land and of the export of dried meat, which hit the cattle trade (Fachel 2002: 65–66, 70–71).

The Republic of Rio Grande do Sul

The first phase of the Farroupilha conflict centred on the deposition of the provincial President Antônio Rodrigues Fernando Braga, a former moderate republican liberal who had come under conservative influence and denounced republican separatism (M. Flores 1990: 33–34; 2003: 91). Motivated by the promise of regional devolution that the Ato Adicional held out, the liberal majority in the Rio Grande do Sul assembly united to overthrow Braga in 1835. Bento Gonçalves da Silva, a former imperial military officer and a moderate monarchist liberal, then led an army of some two hundred Farroupilha followers and rural *estancieiros* to capture the provincial capital, Porto Alegre, in

September that year. However, the revolt was not predominantly separatist at this stage. In a conciliatory move, the liberal-dominated central government in Rio nominated José de Araújo Ribeiro, a cousin of Bento Gonçalves, as the new provincial president, although the Farrapos, unconvinced, repeatedly pre vented him from taking office in the Assembléia Legislativa (M. Flores 2003: 92).

Government forces retook Porto Alegre after a counter-rising in 1836 and the city was to remain subject to repeated Farroupilha sieges and massive population displacement as civilians fled to and fro between city and interior, depending on the scene of the fighting. A year of military encounters following the deposition of Braga culminated in Colonel Neto's Farroupilha victory over the monarchists at the battle of Seival. Spurred by this high tide of confidence, the conflict took a radical, new turn beyond the liberal drive for greater power at the regional assembly level. In September 1836, partly as a result of extreme, separatist dominance in the Farroupilha movement, Rio Grande do Sul was declared a Federal Republic, independent from the Brazilian union, with the slogan *'Igualdade, Fraternidade, Humanidade'* (Barman 1988: 182, 187; M. Flores 1990: 61–67; 2002: 91). Bento Gonçalves was chosen as the president of the new republic, which attempted to bring the neighbouring state of Santa Catarina into the confederacy in 1839. The republic was based in a series of different provisional capitals, Piratini, Caçapava and Alegrete (M. Flores 1990: 79) and had its own press, most notably *O Povo* and *O Mensageiro*. The official religion of the new republic remained Roman Catholicism, although it created its own constitution, Article 6 of which granted rights of citizenship to all free men born in the territory of the republic. It did not extend these rights to women or to slaves, although women born within the republic could transmit citizen rights to their sons (M. Flores 2002: 91).

Despite its original liberal and democratic aims, the republican experiment of Rio Grande do Sul never effectively consolidated a popular democratic state. Indeed, during the whole period of the republic (1836–45), Bento Gonçalves repeatedly delayed calling elections for the Assembléia Legislativa, and emerged as an increasingly dictatorial, discretionary and unrepresentative power (M. Flores 2003: 94). The fighting dragged on for years, nevertheless, as the central government in Rio pursued the rebels with greater or lesser zeal depending on the liberal or conservative tenor of the ruling party at the time. Furthermore, the Farroupilha's geographical proximity to, and support from, the newly created state of Uruguay afforded the rebels a rear base that enabled them to evade capture and also raised the spectre of a hostile Rio Grande do Sul alliance with Uruguay and Argentina on Brazil's southern border (Skidmore 1999: 46). Not until after the end of the regency period, with the accession to the throne of Pedro II and the revocation of the decentralising powers granted by the Ato Adicional in 1840, was the imperial centre finally successful in suppressing the rebels and reintegrating Rio Grande do Sul into the Brazilian empire (Skidmore 1999: 46–47).

Luís Alves de Lima, the Barão de Caxias, took on the official, imperial presidency of Rio Grande do Sul in 1842 and eventually gained control. He won popularity among the people of the now physically devastated province by bringing stability and food supplies to the towns he retook. At the same time, the republican cause fragmented violently (Fachel 2002: 83) and many liberals and republicans became disillusioned by the undemocratic stance of Bento Gonçalves. He was progressively marginalised by his own military officers, who were intent on participating in a negotiated peace settlement with the central government, which granted amnesty to the rebels, effectively bringing the Farroupilha Revolt and the Republic of Rio Grande do Sul to a close in 1845 (M. Flores 1990: 98–100; Barman 1988: 227). This marked a major turning point for the imperial centre in maintaining a politically united Brazil.

For all the compromise of its republican, liberal and federalist ideals, the Farroupilha Revolt arose from, and further stimulated, an important period of intellectual, literary and cultural ferment in the province. It is highly questionable whether the Farroupilha Revolt could have happened without the burgeoning of a free press in the 1830s (Soares 1980: 125), the strong incursion of liberal ideologies from Europe and the existence of O Continentino, the public reading room in Porto Alegre, in which the liberals met. In its immediate context, the war brought about a questioning of the meanings of Brazilian nationhood, patriotism, and loyalty to the provincial *pátria,* which was to have a lasting effect, arguably to the present day, on the way citizens of Rio Grande do Sul perceive themselves in relation to the rest of Brazil.

Restitching the Farroupilhas – women at war

The political and cultural process certainly had an impact on a small number of urban, bourgeois women in the towns, the literate few who read the press, wrote literature and communicated with one another in their tight-knit, oligarchic family circles. The years immediately before the war saw the publication and circulation in Porto Alegre of an important founding text for Brazilian liberal feminist thinking, Nísia Floresta's *Direitos das Mulheres e Injustiça dos Homens,* which was first printed in Recife in 1832. It went into a second edition in Porto Alegre in 1833 and a third in Rio de Janeiro in 1939. Although she was a native of northern Brazil, Floresta lived, wrote and taught in Porto Alegre from 1832 to 1837 (Duarte 2005: 50; Liddell 2005). As Pallares-Burke has now demonstrated, however, the text called *Direitos das Mulheres e Injustiça dos Homens,* which Floresta claimed to be (and quite possibly believed was) a free Portuguese translation of Mary Wollstonecraft's *A Vindication of the Rights of Woman* was, in fact, a very precise Portuguese translation of the earlier 1739 English tract that had influenced Wollstonecraft herself, namely *Woman not Inferior to Man,* by the pseudonymous Sophia. Although the impact of Floresta's text, *Direitos,* is difficult to ascertain, Liddell has remarked on the surprising lack of comment it generated in a contemporary press not otherwise slow to condemn political participation by women (Liddell 2005). I return in the course of this chapter to the influence Nísia Floresta's translation of *Woman not Inferior to Man* almost certainly had on Ana de Barandas.

On the face of it, neither the conservative nor the liberal political programmes embraced by the men in the Farroupilha Revolt offered women a discursive framework for participating in intellectual debate about the construction of national identity or women's rights. One of the most famous measures taken by the Barão de Caxias to secure popular support during his pacification of the province consisted of distributing cloth to the women, including the women of Farroupilha families, which they were required to sew into uniforms for the imperial soldiers (M. Flores 2003: 94). In point of fact, the stitching of 'uniform' masculine identities for military men seems to have exercised a powerful hold over both Legalist and Farroupilha fantasies in terms of its role in controlling errant women. In the correspondence pages of the Farroupilha newspaper *O Povo*, Frigeri and Rüdiger note the following injunctions made by an anonymous author:

> Me limito a pedir às nossas belas que, como as americanas do norte, façam fios para os hospitais da República e queiram coser os fardamentos das tropas, contentando-se para satisfação deste trabalho com o reconhecimento público e os louvores da história. (*O Povo*, Piratini, January 2 1839: 4, cited in Frigeri and Rüdiger 1985: 177; M. Flores 2002: 113–14)

This prescriptive intervention appears to have been a response to the suggestion that educating women would make them better marriage partners (M. Flores 2002: 113–14). The part that women played in the Farroupilha cause, both in the rural interior and in the cities, actually went considerably beyond needlework, encompassing a variety of activities that resisted and extended established gender typologies. The most famous of the women *guerrilheiras* to participate directly in the war on the Farroupilha side was Ana Maria Jesús de Ribeiro (Anita Garibaldi), who left her husband in order to fight alongside her Italian lover and, later, husband, Giuseppe Garibaldi (Ribeiro 1985: 6–12; H. Flores 1989a: 31–36).[4] A far more common war scenario, however, concerned an expansion of the duties already undertaken by the women on the *estancias*. There, women found themselves under greater pressure to maintain their domestic environment and food production on account of the physical devastation of the province and the social instability caused by the uprooting of male *estancieiros* and the absence of manual labour. In addition to this, women provided significant logistical support by transporting and storing ammunition, as well as by spying and transmitting intelligence. Intelligence activities were particularly dangerous, sometimes leading to their arrest (H. Flores 1989a: 37–58; Frigeri and Rüdiger 1985: 167–75).

The provincial capital of Porto Alegre was predominantly Legalist, and was retaken by government forces in 1836. There, women have been credited with effectively keeping the Farroupilha resistance alive inside the city walls by maintaining supplies and information for their men fighting in the interior (Frigeri and Rüdiger 1985: 173–76). Given that official Farroupilha newspapers such as *O Povo* and *O Mensageiro* (Ribeiro 1985: 22; Soares 1980: 130) commented very little on female participation in the war, much of what is known regarding the actions of Farrapa women in Porto Alegre has been drawn from the Legalist press, most notably the satirical anti-Farroupilha publication, *O Artilheiro*. This paper ran a vituperative, moral campaign in the 1830s, seeking to prevent the spread of liberal ideals and correspondingly 'loose' sexual behaviour among the city's women. Evidently the overtly conservative stance of the paper and its tendency to project misogynistic propaganda make it a problematic source from which to assess exactly how extensive the female Farroupilha action actually was in the city during those years. What does emerge from its pages, however, is a sense of how far the urban professional and commercial middle classes that made up the Legalist cause perceived the political participation of the Farrapa women as a threat to their concept of the natural, gendered, order of society. Indeed, the behaviour of women seems to have functioned as a frontier zone of constant sexual panic between the two competing groups of men.

The main Farrapa activities to which *O Artilheiro* refers concern the passing of information and intelligence and the feeding of the liberal troops by *quitandeiras*, or street vendors. Frigeri and Rüdiger have ascribed the formation of a mainly female Farrapo party in Porto Alegre to the fact that some of them had previously been arrested and interrogated by the Legalist authorities and remained under official vigilance after their release, therefore needing networks of solidarity in self-defence (Frigeri and Rüdiger 1985: 173). The picture that emerges from the descriptions in this newspaper reveals women forming intense networks of political organisation and communication with each other. Certainly a principal concern of *O Artilheiro* is to discredit and discourage the Farrapa women by pointing to their stupidity, their vain hopes for victory, their loose morals and, where all else fails, their equal liability before the law. Observing their behaviour for signs of an imminent Farroupilha attack, *O Artilheiro* claims to exercise total vigilance over their movements, frequently referring to the women as *baratas* (cockroaches) swarming across the city (No. 13, October 14 1837: 3–4).

The tone of *O Artilheiro*'s articles on women varies between the satirical, the morally didactic and the covertly threatening. In all cases, the emphasis rests on the control of women's speech, sexual behaviour and social contact (see Chapter 5 for comparisons with Peru). One satirical piece listed the symptoms that will enable a careful observer to diagnose the Farroupilha 'disease' in the female sex:

> Nas fêmeas o mal começa quasi sempre pela perguiça, permanecência na janela, movimento desordenado da lingua, passeios continuos, luxo exorbitante, bailes de especulação; passa depois ao namoro dos machos a torto e a direito, e a final degenera na mais desenvolta libertinagem. (No. 19, November 24 1837: 2–3)

The only proper alternative role for women is predictably marital and familial, as the following list of female duties clearly indicates: 'o de ser boa filha, se vive na companhia de seu Pai; boa Esposa, sendo casada; boa Mai de Familia, se a tem' (*O Artilheiro* No. 11, September 30 1837: 3–4).[5] Where these structures fail to discipline women, as *O Artilheiro* points out, women are equally liable before the law – which does not mean, of course, that the law will protect them. As the end of the following quotation darkly implies, they need not rely on their female fragility to defend them from male violence as a last resort:

> Ora mais cuidado com a língua, senhoras farrapas, porque a cadêa também se fez para suas mercês e o codigo não as exceptua de soffrerem as penas da lei ... Se querem ser respeitadas, sejão mais comedidas, e menos desavergonhadas, e não se fiem no dictado que diz: caxorro não morde cadella. (No. 8, September 9 1837: 2–3)

By the same token, much of the blame for women's potential truancy and spendthrift behaviour is placed at the door of men, since women have very few duties in which to fail, whereas men have by far the greater burden of responsibility to be good social citizens. In an ongoing diatribe against the *'petit maître'* – the dandy or fop – *O Artilheiro* exhorts men not to encourage women's excesses, especially as regards their frivolous and extravagant modes of dress, remarking, 'a maior parte dos homens são a causa da perversidade das mulheres; elles as pervertem com o seu exemplo, fazem-as mudar de proceder, e de resolução com a sua conduta, e mau pensar' (No. 11, September 30 1837: 3–4). As the criticisms of the *petits maîtres* suggest, the climate of sexual panic surrounding women also extended to a growing homophobic fear of 'degenerate feminised' men. Seemingly directed at its male and female readerships, *O Artilheiro* combines apparently innocuous social conditioning on matters of marriage, fashion and familial duty with a more sinister tone of warning and exhortation to police the boundaries of sexual behaviour, identification and spousal loyalty with increased vigilance.

The urban milieus that were the home of the Legalist cause and its press were predominantly middle class, reflecting the accumulation of capital in the new towns and the development of 'civilising' practices in arts, education and public political life. As Frigeri and Rüdiger note, this ambience was more conducive to a rising degree of individualisation among women, and witnessed their induction into reading, consumer purchasing and education, albeit frequently at home. It also saw, as noted above, the entry of modern, liberal and European ideas through the ports, which had been opened in 1808, the growth of the press, the development of reading rooms and the circulation of printed materials (Soares 1980: 125–27; Frigeri and Rüdiger 1985: 159–66; H. Flores 1991: 23–26). The destruction wrought by Farroupilha rebel actions threatened the stable homes, accumulated capital and benefits of civilisation that the largely Portuguese-descended elites enjoyed in and around Porto Alegre. Women experiencing the war in this context inevitably sought to protect their property and to defend an imperial political status quo that was favourable to them and to their family interests.

The rise of the monarchist women writers

That the women writers of Rio Grande do Sul who began to publish before and during the Farroupilha Revolt should have belonged to this conservative, urban and monarchist environment comes as no surprise. What is interesting to observe is the extent to which Liberal ideals and Romantic aesthetics gained a certain intellectual purchase among these women, challenging if not their loyalty to the empire, at least their perception of the proper place of women within the imperial national order they endorsed. The circle of monarchist women writers from Rio Grande do Sul is conventionally taken to comprise: Maria Clemência da Silveira Sampaio (1789–1862); Maria Josefa (Engrácia) Barreto Pereira Pinto (1786/8?–1837); Delfina Benigna da Cunha (1791–1857); and Ana Eurídice Eufrosina de Barandas (1806– ?).[6]

Among these four, only Delfina Benigna da Cunha and Ana de Barandas have left a substantive published legacy. However, Maria Clemência da Silveira Sampaio was an important precursor of their pro-monarchist stance and Maria Josefa Barreto, who is known to have inspired Cunha, engaged in a public excoriation of the Farroupilhas that was to resound through Cunha's three collections of verse. Sampaio's long poem, *Versos Heróicos*, was declaimed aloud by its author at a public ball held in São Pedro do Rio Grande on October 12 1822 to honour the acclamation of Pedro I as constitutional Emperor of the newly independent Brazil (Moreira 2003: 19–21). It subsequently came into print in 1823 with the Imprensa Nacional, making Sampaio the first published woman poet in Rio Grande do Sul. Addressed to the Empress Carolina on behalf of the women of Rio Grande do Sul, the work was also a hymn of praise to the natural riches of Sampaio's native *pátria*. On one level, as Schmidt has suggested, this nativist focus on the glory of the provincial *pátria* offers a foretaste of the more explosively regionalist and separatist allegiances that emerged in the following decade (in Muzart 2000: 113). At the same time, the natural homage Rio Grande do Sul pays to the new nation in *Versos Heróicos* shows the extent to which *império* and *pátria* were still coterminous in people's minds with the euphoria of 1822; as Sampaio writes: 'Eis, ó grande Princesa, os sentimentos, / Que vos tributa uma Província inteira / A que o Rio Grande dá seu nome' (in Moreira 2003: 73).

A similarly pioneering distinction attaches to Maria Josefa Barreto, who remains one of the earliest known women journalists in Brazil. An ardent monarchist, like Sampaio, she expressed her virulently anti-Farroupilha stance in the press during the years before the revolt of 1835. In addition to writing poetry and working as a teacher, she is known to have founded her own anti-Farroupilha newspaper in 1833, *Belona Irada contra os Sectários de Momo*;[7] and in the same year she wrote for *Idade d'Ouro*, owned by Manoel dos Passos Figueroa, which was similarly pro-Legalist.[8] From the only surviving number of *Idade d'Ouro*, something of Barreto's polemical style is evident, in berating the republican cause:

> Ora eis aqui os nossos fazedores de Repúblicas! E que tal! Sem saberem os

primeiros elementos, querem dar-nos regras, e obrigar-nos a seguir suas doutrinas! Não há maior desaforo! Além de perversos, ignorantes, a ponto de não entenderem o que com a maior clareza está escrito! Quanto é desgraçado o Brasil, a quem esta corja de pedantes afeta querer endireitar!! (cited in Muzart 2000: 78)

While Sampaio and Barreto published relatively little in their own lifetimes, they effectively serve to demonstrate that an elite few women writers in the immediate post-independence years were beginning to express their views in public spheres via the oral declamation of poetry on ceremonial occasions and in the press, even if they tended to speak out in obedient defence of the conservative, monarchist positions their families represented. Cunha and Barandas, who wrote later than Sampaio and lived longer than Barreto, found their lives and works far more profoundly affected by the events of the Farroupilha Revolt and the intellectual and pragmatic crises it generated. Both were repeatedly forced by the dangers of the war to leave their home cities and seek refuge in Rio de Janeiro. Both presented problematic cases in relation to patriarchal family convention, and both almost certainly ended their lives unmarried, Cunha as a single woman and Barandas as a divorcee. Their particular circumstances had, in turn, discernible consequences for the personal and political subjectivities they were able to construct in writing in their attempts to intervene discursively in the intellectual climate of the Farroupilha Revolt.

Delfina Benigna da Cunha was born in 1791 in São José do Norte to Maria Francisca Paula da Cunha and Joaquim Francisco da Cunha Sá e Meneses, a military officer of Portuguese descent. Delfina was tragically left blind by an attack of smallpox at the age of twenty months, but went on to achieve an education, which included knowledge of the classics, as is evident in her later Arcadian verse.[9] She is believed to have begun the spontaneous composition of oral verses at the age of twelve. Cunha lost her father in 1826 and her mother in 1833. She was therefore left without financial means as an adult, since she was never married. After the death of her father in 1826, Cunha presented herself to the imperial court in Rio to seek the direct support and protection of the imperial family. Winning over the emperor with the poem she dedicated to him, she received a *pensão vitalícia,* which was also in recognition of her father's military service. She went on to receive royal charity funding from events staged on her behalf, living and writing for the remainder of her life under the patronage of the imperial family and the court.

In 1835 she left the south to go and live in Rio de Janeiro to escape the ravages of the Farroupilha Revolt, returning to the Rio Grande do Sul in 1845. In Porto Alegre she certainly knew the journalist Maria Josefa Barreto, as she dedicated a poem to her, in response to a now lost verse that Barreto had written for Cunha. She published her first volume of poetry, *Poesias oferecidas às senhoras rio-grandenses,* in Porto Alegre in 1834, with second and third editions in Rio de Janeiro in 1838, in which she inserted her famous diatribes against the Faroupilha leader Bento Gonçalves (H. Flores 1990: 15). Following this, she is also known to have travelled in Bahia and other parts of the northeast. Her second volume *Poesias oferecidas às senhoras brasileiras por sua patrícia*, appeared in Rio in 1838. Her final work, *Collecção de várias poesias dedicadas à imperatriz viúva* was published in 1846, after she collected the signatures of financial supporters to bring out the volume. She remained unmarried, although Schmidt has discovered evidence to suggest that Manuel Marques de Sousa, an important Legalist leader in the 1836 reaction against the Farroupilhas in Porto Alegre, was the real-life object of her unrequited love, and was frequently characterised as Elmano in her sonnets (2001: 18). Cunha also maintained close family relationships with her sister and established some significant poetic and intellectual friendships in Rio, most notably with the patriotic Mineira poet Beatriz de Assis Brandão (1779–1868) who dedicated poetry to Cunha.[10] She died in Rio in 1857.[11]

Across her three published volumes of poetry, Cunha's work can be broadly classified in three categories: her overtly political *poesia engajada* in response to the Farroupilha Revolt; her *poesia de ocasião* marking patriotic landmarks, royal baptisms, deaths and birthdays, and expressing gratitude for gifts and benefits; and finally her intimist love lyrics, principally sonnets. Although her financially dependent situation clearly influenced the content and tenor of her poetry to a very high degree, as Becker has noted, Cunha was, in a sense, an early example of a woman being paid and making a meagre living from composing and reciting her poetry (1991: 48). By presenting herself publicly at court as a vulnerable, blind woman who had no male protector to provide for her, Cunha undoubtedly acquired a certain symbolic value as a metonym of the extended imperial family of nationhood. In this respect she was able to translate precisely her lack of living family connections or social capital into substantial symbolic capital as a public national figurehead. Later nicknamed the '*Musa Cega*', Cunha was quite well known in her lifetime and some of her poems were published in the important *Parnaso brasileiro* collection compiled in Rio in 1830 by cônego Januário da Cunha Barbosa (Schmidt in Muzart 2000: 119). She was certainly more widely published and read in her day than her younger *sul-rio-grandense* compatriot, Ana Eurídice Eufrosina de Barandas.

Born in 1806, Ana de Barandas was the daughter of a widow, Anna Felícia do Nascimento, who was remarried to Joaquim da Fonseca Barandas, a Portuguese surgeon resident in Porto Alegre.[12] She was one of five siblings from this couple and, in addition to this, had three half-siblings from her mother's previous marriage. She also probably had at least one mulatto half-sibling, Sophia Maria, the offspring of her father's relations with a black house slave. She came from a propertied and landed family who, besides their town house in Porto Alegre owned a country residence at Belmonte near Viamão, which was attacked and destroyed by Farroupilha rebels in 1837. She was probably educated at home and seems to have been well versed in neoclassical literature. French influence also seems to have been notable in her family, since two of her older sisters, Carlota and Delfina Cândida, married French men. Ana herself married by choice in 1822, at the age of sixteen, to a Portuguese-descended lawyer named José Joaquim Pena Penalta. She is known to have travelled frequently to Rio, living there between 1836 and 1840; this was possibly in connection with her husband's legal work, but also to escape the fighting and disruption in Rio Grande do Sul during the war. Ana had three children: two daughters, Aurora and Eurídice, and a son, José, who died of hepatitis in early infancy.

Ana was later given charge of educating the two daughters of her already married sister, Delfina Cândida, who became the centre of a local scandal when she had an illegitimate child by her lover, a silk and haberdashery merchant and, again, a French man. As a result, on the death of her estranged husband in 1840, Delfina Cândida was not allowed to retain the care of her two legitimate daughters, who were placed under the tutelage of Ana de Barandas's father and later given to Ana to raise and educate alongside her own. Only when Delfina Cândida married the illegitimate child's father in 1843 was she again allowed legal custody of her other two daughters. Ana's own marriage fared little better than her sister's and she divorced in 1843, probably on account of her husband's infidelity.

The legal arrangement that Ana de Barandas and her lawyer husband obtained was a progressive and unusual settlement for the time, which appears to have been a mutual petition. The contract they signed was to all intents and purposes a legal separation, with certain key variations on the norm. It did, however, significantly use the term 'divorce' to refer to the arrangement (H. Flores 1990: 31–32). It effectively entailed the formal, physical separation of the couple and the division of future financial interests and property, without the marriage bond itself actually being dissolved, so neither had the right to remarry. It also differed from legal separations of that period in that Ana was granted the custody of her daughters, including responsibility for their education and financial upkeep, a role that was nearly always conferred on the father (Costa 2000: 248; Silva 1995, II: 446–47). She thus effectively became the legal head of the household, as well as retaining the material goods she had acquired through the marriage.

A significant further benefit that Barandas derived from her divorce was the opportunity to bring into print in 1845 her only known work to date, *Ramalhete ou flores escolhidas do jardim da imaginação*. She would not have been able to publish this previously without her husband's permission. Although she was involved in prolonged battles with her brother over the execution of her father's generous will after his death in 1849, it appears that she was sufficiently well provided for after her divorce to live and care for her daughters. Unlike Delfina Benigna da Cunha, she was not forced to write or recite poetry for a living. Little more is known of Ana de Barandas's life after the death of her father and no record has yet been discovered of the date of her death. Following the two most challenging statements of her life, her unconventional divorce settlement and her one published work, Barandas disappears from the public records of legal arrangements, wills and inventories that enabled the historian Hilda Hübner Flores to track her principal biography to that point. It is thought probable that she returned to the more cosmopolitan setting of Rio in 1850, rather than remain in Porto Alegre, and she may have known Delfina Benigna da Cunha there. It is also very likely that, during her life in Porto Alegre, she knew the influential feminist writer and thinker from Rio Grande do Norte, Nísia Floresta, who lived close to Ana de Barandas in Porto Alegre between 1833 and 1837. In addition to this residential proximity, Nísia Floresta was related by marriage to a close friend of Barandas and her husband, who acted as *padrinho* at their wedding in 1822.

The fate of Ana de Barandas's book *O Ramalhete,* which saw only one (1845) edition in her lifetime, remained obscure for a century and a half; a complete new version, edited and annotated by Hilda Hübner Flores, appeared in Porto Alegre only in 1990.[13] A diverse collection, as its title suggests, Barandas's anthology unites a series of romantic and patriotic poems; a short Cartesian dialogue on the right of women to intervene in politics, 'Diálogos'; a romantic story, 'Eugênia ou a Filósofa Apaixonada'; a nostalgic fragment, 'Lembrança Saudosa'; and an Arcadian allegory on reason and passion, 'A Queda de Safo'. What connects these pieces is her progressive deconstruction of the image of the docile, marriageable, good daughter in the bourgeois family. In this respect, although Barandas repeatedly declares her allegiance to a united Brazilian empire and her support of the Legalist cause in the war, the very discursive position she adopts in order to make this declaration ultimately undermines the fundamental principles of her own monarchist discourse. Her endorsement of women's right to political participation and independent philosophical thinking, and her expression of strong, individual female desire, point towards distinct, agentive and latently emancipated forms of female subjectivity. They point far beyond the circumscription of the patriarchal Catholic family and its social, cultural and political extension into the united family of the Brazilian empire defended by Delfina Benigna da Cunha.

Delfina Benigna da Cunha: the '*Musa Cega*'

Cunha's poetic output is often described as belonging to the *repentista* tradition, which means that it was spontaneously orally composed in *saraus* (evening gatherings) in particular contexts and for certain events, and then presumably transcribed by an amanuensis. As Moacyr Flores points out, the structure of many Cunha poems is effectively that of a *glosa* on a given theme, or a *mote* suggested by someone else as a competitive challenge to the poet (2002: 213–14); the challenger would provide a series of lines, which the poet would then incorporate at the end of each verse. This effectively means that Cunha's poetry constituted a public event, itself a significant statement for women, for whom it was not conventional to adopt an openly and publicly creative stance. This is evident partly in Cunha's need to provide an explanation and apologia for her decision to publish, in the preface to the 1838 edition of *Poesias oferecidas às senhoras rio-grandenses.* Further, as Schmidt indicates, Cunha effectively adopted a common tactic for women attempting to bring their work into the public sphere without contravening the norms of feminine behaviour, and this was in addressing their poetry to other women, so that they remained, in a crucial, rhetorical sense, 'private' (Schmidt 2001: 22–23). All three of Cunha's collected volumes of poetry are addressed to women: the first to her regional compatriots of Rio Grande do Sul; the second to her national compatriots; and the last directly to her great benefactress, Amélia, the widowed Empress of Pedro I. Inside the volumes, many individual poems are, of course, addressed or dedicated to men, and thus she makes an uneasy transition into the public domain of political and historical occurrences.

Her writings in praise of the Emperor Pedro I and the imperial family belong to a strong poetic tradition of euphoric writing produced in the immediate aftermath of 1822 to greet the coming of independence and to celebrate the royal family (Schmidt 2001: 14). Her *poesia de ocasião* is nearly always indexed to specific events. These may be major landmarks in the history of the nation such as Independence Day, or the death of the Emperor; or they may relate to birthdays and family celebrations, either those of the imperial family, or those of her own family and friends. Where the two sit side by side in her *Poesias oferecidas às senhoras rio-grandenses* volume, the dividing line between her own family, such as her sister, Lucinda Benigna da Cunha, and the royal family is blurred and the naturalisation of monarchic power is reinforced by its juxtaposition with this obviously personal, biographical information. The sense of an immutable natural, universal order is further reinforced by her heavy reliance on neoclassical, mythical and Arcadian tropes praising the reign of reason and enlightenment and, by extension, the absolute entitlement of the monarch to rule by nature and divine right.

A classic example of this is her poem 'A Muito Lamentável Morte de S. M. I. O Senhor D. Pedro I. Duque de Bragança. No dia 24 de Setembro de 1845' published in 1846 in her final collection *Collecção de várias poesias dedicadas à imperatriz viúva,* a full twelve years after the monarch's death in Lisbon in 1834. With the passing of the Emperor Pedro I, darkest night has descended on the country. Brazil, personified as the national body, is convulsed to the core with sobs: 'Que noite he esta que ao Brasil arranca / Das entranhas suspiros tão magoados, / Que nos valles resoão tristemente?!' (Cunha 1846: 7). The experience leaves the poetic persona of Cunha herself, as a loyal subject, in a state of deathly grief. The extent of the emperor's greatness is transposed onto the extensive, natural wealth of the country itself in classic *ufanista* fashion, as the poetic voice laments the loss 'Do fundador do Imperio que se arreia / De ricas matas, de soberbos campos, / Peijados de metaes que o mundo préza. / D'esse Heróe que nos deu a Independencia; / Que mais prezou ser Pai que ser Monarcha, / Inthronisando os filhos que adorava' (Cunha 1846: 8). This last reference clearly glosses the crisis of constitutionalism and the influence of the liberals in the government that had forced Pedro I to abdicate in 1831 in favour of his infant son Pedro II, so that the Bragança family would remain in control of a united, monarchic Brazil. By couching this in the language of sentiment, the loyal love of a father abnegating his own needs for the rights of his son,

Cunha exploits the naturalisation of dynastic monarchy inherent in the metaphor of genealogy, as an unbreakable continuity, a family tree (McClintock 1995: 36–39).

As a woman mourner, the speaker then goes on to identify ever more closely with the personal grief of the widowed Empress Amélia, to whom the collection is addressed, speaking to her as 'tu' and implying not an intimate bond but rather a mystical, deifying reverence. Begging the right to shed her tears alongside those of the Empress, she effectively becomes, by metonymic extension, a further member of the family, falling under the 'sombra paternal de Pedro o Grande, / D'esse heróe vencedor de despotismo' (Cunha 1846: 8). At the same time, she clearly represents herself biographically, as she describes the tears wept 'de meus olhos sem luz' (8), a reference to her own sightlessness. In the final stanzas, her voice and her inspiration, weakened by grief and sorrow, are starting to fade, so she seeks strength from the Empress, who has become her 'Numen tutelar' (9) or inspirational spirit, the term previously applied to Pedro I when she had asked 'E pôde ser mortal quem era Numen?! ... ' (8). The implication here is that she has been distanced from the court and brought low by unnamed 'difficulties' or 'precisões', presumably financial and material, for which she is now seeking relief from the Empress, as she writes: 'Mas forçoso he soffrer a ausencia dura, / Por crueis precisões apoquentada' (9). These in turn cause the weakening and fading of her 'estro' or poetic inspiration. Enacting an explicitly 'performative monarchism', the subtext of the request behind Cunha's poem for the Emperor (now twelve years dead) is easily decoded. In essence, she produces a formal, ritualised statement to the effect that a financial contribution of some kind will bring her poetic 'estro' back to life and produce further verses of praise to the imperial family.

The same stance is overtly present, along with a reference to the damage wrought by the Farroupilha Revolt, in the introduction to her first volume, *Poesias oferecidas às senhoras rio-grandenses*, in which she writes, 'Aos Leitores':

> Qual será, pois, o motor da audácia com que ao Público ofereço meus versos? Leitores é a – necessidade! – A necessidade é o meu amor próprio, eu nem posso ter outro. Filha do Rio Grande, aí, nos estragos gerais, eu padeci, e padeci muito: foi-me forçoso recolher ainda uma ao Rio de Janeiro, mas preciso viver! Tenho precisão de recursos, e eu peço recursos, oferecendo em troca o único trabalho de que é capaz quem é cega desde o berço! Este pensamento é o único que devia estampar no frontispício desta obra, assim o fiz. (Schmidt 2001: 27)

Her reference to her origins in Rio Grande do Sul, the 'estragos gerais' she suffered there in the war and her seeking refuge in Rio de Janeiro, indicate that this was added to the later 1838 edition published in the capital, as were the infamous glosses of the ravages of Bento Gonçalves (H. Flores 1990: 15), which were also clearly designed to align their speaker with central government rule.

In her 1838 edition of *Poesias oferecidas às senhoras rio-grandenses*, there are three poems on Bento Gonçalves, two sonnets (Cunha 2001: 216–17) and a

Quadra (2001: 218–19), which cast him as an unnatural, anarchic antithesis to the natural, universal order over which Pedro I presides. The two sonnets adopt the poetic discourse and reference points of Greek tragedy and epic and index specific events in the Farroupilha war. One has a subtitle referring to the Legalist Reaction in 1836 against the Farroupilha Revolution in 'Rio Grande de São Pedro do Sul' (the old name for Rio Grande do Sul). The other is addressed to the 'chefe dos anarquistas' Bento Gonçalves, as a comment on the Farroupilha occupation of the Fortress of Itopoã in 1836 and the prolonged battle that followed. The first of the two sonnets (2001: 216) calls for the triumph of the monarchy and for Gonçalves's death in hell as the 'monstro da feroz democracia'. Gonçalves becomes here the traitor who inspires hatred in all, as the writer declares 'Floresce a causa da Legalidade / E se arroja no abimso o novo Sila', evoking the classical pairing of Scilla and Charybdis, the twin monster guarding the straits in Homer's Odyssey. The final heresy that Cunha denounces is the liberal principle of equality among men, stating: 'Todos sabem, ninguém jamais vacila / Que não há entre os homens igualdade' (2001: 216).

The second sonnet (2001: 217) wishes divine punishment on Bento Gonçalves; Cunha writes: 'Acaba, oh monstro, em sanguinosa guerra, / Debalde buscas empinada serra'. Nature itself will reject Gonçalves, just as it welcomes and exults the emperor, since it will not give him shelter from his rightful fate. Far from being motivated by noble or collective ends, he is 'só de ambição embriagado'. He will not only be sent to Hades but 'A Plutão disputar o horrível mando' (2001: 217) making him the very rival of the god of the underworld and the dead. Since there is no death that fate could bring him that is equal to his crimes, she wishes that Jove himself would inflict the final punishment he deserves. In the very extremity of her statements on behalf of a united Brazil expelling its traitor son, she positions herself as the classical feminine figuration of wrath. Setting aside her usual political mantle as a meek and imploring poet, Cunha declares the defeat of the 'torva fúria' (2001: 216) of Legalism, effectively taking upon herself in both of these sonnets the role of a Greek Fury pursuing the traitor for his wrongs and haunting his conscience with the ever-present threat of retribution on an epic scale.

The Quadra (2001: 218–19) that follows these two sonnets is simply directed 'ao mesmo' and glosses the following theme:

Maldição te seja dada
Bento infeliz, desvairado,
No Brasil, em toda a parte
Será teu nome odiado.

This longer poem treats Gonçalves as a traitor to his *pátria* of Rio Grande do Sul, beginning: 'A ti qu'um punhal violento / Cravaste na pátria aflita' (2001: 218). He is accused of bringing grief to 'mil famílias de bem' (2001: 218) and is figuratively expelled from the natural landscape of his country to suffer endless physical torments. The speaker wishes that Divine Providence and nature would wreak revenge upon him, so that the very land he has soaked in blood will refuse his body in burial. The ultimate dishonour in death is to have no place for burial in his own *pátria,* rejection by his compatriots and obliteration from memory 'No Brasil, e em toda a parte' (2001: 219). The speaker conjures up the image of his own children 'o seu opróbrio chorando' (2001: 219) and cursing their father. Thus, his posthumous name will be defiled in his family, his *pátria* and his nation, Brazil, as the speaker re-establishes the unquestionable, natural continuity that Gonçalves has broken between the patriarchal family, the regional *pátria* and the imperial nation. In this sense, the poem reclaims the putatively separatist concept of the *pátria* for a rightfully national allegiance of which Cunha is the feminine embodiment par excellence. As Becker (1991: 16) has suggested, her very lack of sight afforded her a certain symbolic resonance with the representation of justice as feminine, as the blindfolded woman holding the scales in one hand and the sword in the other.[14]

The alleged object of Cunha's personal, as well as political, affection was Manoel Marques de Souza, the Legalist Major da Praça of Porto Alegre during the siege of 1836. He was the person to whom many of her love poems were dedicated and addressed, and is often represented among her Arcadian cast of figures as Elmano. This is typified in two poems addressed to him on his birthday (Cunha 2001: 52–53). Here, Cunha works within an entirely formulaic, stylised lexicon, and her love is always distant, respectful and eulogistic. In the first of these (2001: 52), the dolphins play in the sea and hymns of love are sung to celebrate the occasion, evoking the image of Venus rising from the waves. The goddesses of Mounts Parnassus and Pindus chant his praises; and in the final stanza, he becomes the envy of all mortals as Jove himself showers blessings upon him. In the second of these poems to Manoel Marques de Souza (2001: 53), marking the closest that Cunha gets to personal passion or contact, her muse is driven to ecstasy by his personal gifts as 'Abrasada por ti na délia chama / Minha musa em teus dotes se extasia'. He is favoured and acclaimed by Minerva, the goddess of wisdom, by love and by Mars the god of war. The language of abstraction begins to slip only slightly in the last stanza, in which the natural sensitivity of his heart is described as divinely matched with his noble soul and his perfect beauty or 'completa formosura' (2001: 53), which could be read as spiritual or, equally, physical beauty.

Not all of Cunha's love poetry, however, fits so squarely within the straightjacket of the Arcadian and neoclassical legacy, with their reliance on the pastoral ideal and the natural order of the universe. In a small number of works, she shows traces of a more clearly individualised, desiring ego, which is far more consonant with Romanticism than with Arcadianism. As Moacyr Flores notes (2002: 214), in this context she becomes able to refer to 'paixão carnal'. However, in order to adopt this position of active, fulfilled desire, she must, as a woman, assume the poetic voice of a masculine lover speaking about the idealised female object of his sentiments (Schmidt 2001: 18–19). A good example of this is the 'Quadra' written on the following 'mote' (Cunha 2001: 76–77):

Gosto de amar, vou amando,
Confesso minha fraqueza,
O crime não é só meu,
É também da natureza.

Aligning her male poetic persona with the active force of nature, she describes love in physical and reproductive terms as 'Uma flor, e outra flor / Num vergel ameno e brando, / Docemente propagando, / Nos dão lições amorosas' (2001: 76). The desired harmony of the pair of lovers is underlined through images of bodily proximity, breathing the same air, as the poetic voice writes of his loved one 'Se a minha amada suspira / Por se ver de mim a par, / Contente vou respirar / O ar que ela respira' (2001: 76). This is subsequently inflamed to a passion as the male lover writes 'Vi, oh bela o rosto teu, / Senti de amor abrasar-me' (2001: 77). The final defence he makes against any crime or impropriety in loving is the power of nature itself, which is here God-given, but also in proto-Romantic mode, uncontrollable and untrammelled so that 'se do mundo a fereza / De amar um crime tem feito, / Não é só meu o defeito, / *É também da natureza*' (2001: 77). If the direct expression of a female desiring subject is excluded from the Arcadian models from which most of her poetry is derived, the expression of friendship and admiration between women as poetic creators also presents her with certain pitfalls, where inherited conventions of literary genius and natural bonding between poets are paradigmatically masculine.

One of Cunha's most interesting works in this respect, not least because it proves that she knew her compatriot, the female writer and journalist Maria Josefa Barreto, is her 'Epístola', written 'em resposta à outra que lhe dirigiu a Ilma. Sra. D. Maria Josefa Barreto Pereira Pinto' (Cunha 2001: 62); the poem referred to in this epigraph has since been lost. Here, Cunha addresses Barreto as 'Safo brasileira' making her a patriotic, Legalist role model, as well as a poetic exemplum. She describes her inspiration, saying 'eu libo o néctar / Nos magos versos teus, que me enviaste!'. She also indicates that Barreto was already well known to her, as 'Há muito o nome teu prezar sabia' and asks to be allowed to pay her homage as an important source. However, it is interesting that she goes on to describe their meeting in print as being a 'prazer fraternal'. This implied crossover of gender roles intensifies as she writes 'O bem de ouvir-te, Armia, irmana, iguala / À ventura de ver o irmão querido / Nos braços da consorte disfrutando / O celeste prazer que vale a vida'. Here, Cunha likens her joy on hearing Barreto to watching a beloved brother enjoying celestial, life-giving pleasure in the arms of his woman consort.

On one level, the image compares her poetry to the natural harmony of perfect heterosexual union at the base of family relations. Yet it also leaves Cunha's own positioning somewhat ambiguous in relation to the other poet. Is she simply claiming poetic sisterhood, evoked in the verb 'irmana', or is she identifying with her representation of Barreto as the male-sexed source of creative energy, recalling her own self-identification as masculine in those poems where she attempts to adopt the Romantic, speaking ego? Alternatively, is Barreto being placed in the position of the brother in an act of love, which metaphorises the meeting in print of the two women? In the following line, she reaffirms Barreto's active and productive role in their partnership, as she writes, 'Os teus versos a glória me ascrescentam / E me julgo por ti levada ao Pindo' with the result that, through their encounter, she scales new poetic heights to Pindus, the Greek home of the muses. If Cunha is now the poetically inspired beneficiary of this act of love, she is also by the same token the 'consorte', the object of the brother's love. The poem concludes with an evocation of the classical rituals of homage to her talent, as Cunha asks only to be allowed to offer 'os cultos meus, puros, manados / Da santa gratidão, que me avassala' (2001: 62).

Pitched between the opening apostrophe to her 'Safo brasileira' as a source of poetic identification and her voyeuristic construction of a brother's heterosexual love to describe the transmission of poetic genius between women, this poem indicates, at the very least, the difficulty of articulating the affective and literary bonds that connected women as patriots and as poets. Ana de Barandas is similarly positioned in literary historical terms between the orderly conservatism of neoclassical Arcadian models and the emergence of Romantic, individualist poetic identities more consonant with liberal and revolutionary political agendas.[15] As a married woman from a family with means, she was, however, better socially and financially placed than Cunha to challenge the established order from this space of ideological and aesthetic transition. The more daring and progressive poetic stance that Barandas adopts moves towards an active expression of politically conscious and desiring subjectivity, in which the ambivalently masculinised feminine voice discernible in Cunha is openly unmasked as being that of a woman.

Ana de Barandas: a liberal feminist for her times

Barandas, like Cunha, was heavily influenced by the events of the Farroupilha Revolt and by the destruction and displacement that it wrought in her personal life. The piece that reflects this most directly is her shortest prose work, a nostalgic fragment entitled 'Lembrança Saudosa', a pastorally influenced autobiographical piece in which she laments the real-life destruction in 1837 of her family's country residence at Belmonte, near Viamão. She begins with an apostrophic address, 'Oh minha querida Pátria!' relating this to her childhood memories of 'Lares nativos, que fostes testemunha dos brincos da minha infância. Campos, bosques, fontes ... ' (Barandas 1990: 91). The space evokes tender memories of her mother's love for her as a child, as she recalls the idyllic space of civilisation, music, arts, literature and thought that her family created at Belmonte, 'o lugar favorito das Musas' now reduced to 'um perfeito esqueleto' (Barandas 1990: 91). This construction of the house and its surroundings as a haven of cultivated familial harmony and idyllic natural beauty is then contrasted with the overgrown battlefield that it has become since the Farroupilha attacks in the area. Its destruction is associated with the antithesis of natural order and civilisation, the treacherous civil war that breaks up families, pitching brother against brother, and illegitimate son against father, with women mourning over their dead husbands. Aware that her happy memories of past family wholeness and maternal closeness are gone, Barandas permits herself to indulge in a single, consciously nostalgic recollection of Belmonte when she was eight years old.

At this time, her family, including her mother, were still alive, and she sat among the vines listening to her mother singing and accompanying herself on the harpsichord while her father played the flute. Yet she claims that even then she had profound intimations of the mortality and transience of the scene she was enjoying, and was reduced to tears at the thought of her future losses, in a moment of prescience which now, writing from the present, she has seen come true. This brief, circular cameo is thus entirely enclosed within the classic pastoral topos of the lost golden age, destroyed by the coming of the iron age of war, which translates, in personal, individual terms, into the loss of childhood with the coming of the adult symbolic order, associated here with the death of family members. As she notes, 'Ao fim de dezenove anos (em 1837) o meu vatocínio estava quase completo, restava-me apenas um pai ...! Tudo o mais a morte colheu' (Barandas 1990: 93). With this reference to only her father remaining, she equates the ruin of Belmonte with the death of her mother in 1826. Thus her loyalty to the *pátria* of her native region is cast entirely, and unconventionally, in terms of a daughter's rather than a son's primary narcissistic love for a lost mother and a maternal space. By the same token, the process of the war and its disrespect for the newly acquired fruits of urban cultivation, music, poetry and philosophy are represented in terms of irrational masculine brutality in direct conflict with the feminised rule of Enlightenment reason. In this respect, Barandas is able to hijack a classic metaphorical figuration of civilisation, wisdom and the arts as feminine, in order to make an entirely personal, autobiographical statement about her experience of the war and her acquisition of cultural interests from her mother, not her father.

The Arcadian mythological stock-in-trade dominates Barandas's poetic output, as it does da Cunha's, although here the metaphorisation of artistic civilisation as feminine, as the Muse, runs more forcefully up against the challenge of Romanticism and the potential held out by the individual ego as a locus of female self-expression. As Regina Zilberman has pointed out, 'marcante é ... o emprego da primeira pessoa; sob este aspecto, Ana Eurídice Eufrosina de Barandas desmente o cânone clássico, deixando vazar uma sensualidade que não conhece limites para o desejo e a realização amorosa' (Zilberman 1991: 44). Unlike Cunha, Barandas frequently adopts a woman's position from which to address the object of her love in direct, explicit and physically passionate terms. In this respect, despite her strong allegiance to the Legalist cause, she begins even in her lyric poetry to toy with more individualist, libertarian concepts of identity, which push at the limits of Arcadian aesthetic formulae and Enlightenment decorum. Two of her sonnets (Barandas 1990: 84, 89), addressed to the figures of Filinto and Jacínio (the latter is usually thought to refer to her husband, José Joaquim Pena Penalta), illustrate this particularly well. In the first, she describes a sudden reawakening from a rational, disillusioned and loveless state, 'despida de ilusões e fantasia', marking a characteristic liberal philosophical battle between passion and reason, with passion here winning the day. Suddenly stirred from her lethargic, wordly wise state by the intrusion of love, 'Aos Elíseos minha alma é transportada!', she is then drawn against her will towards her new lover as 'Magnético poder a ti me prende; / É só fria amizade? Não: eu minto; / Tanto fogo amizade não acende'. The sight of her 'Belo Felinto!' brings a sudden, lightening revelation as she exclaims, 'Que repentina luz me aclara e fende! ... amor ... é amor que por ti sinto!' (Barandas 1990: 84).

Although the poem describes the transport of the soul, the metaphorical effects are primarily physical and the desire for bodily surrender to an inexorable natural force is pursued further in a subsequent sonnet to Jacínio (89). The poetic subject here longs for the moment of the lover's arrival, since she fears she cannot physically wait any more. She calls to Jacínio, 'Vem, Jacínio adorado, torna em gozo / este cruel tormento, esta agonia; Fazendo-me libar doce ambrosia / Nos lábios teus, n'um teu beijo amoroso'. From the erotic charge of this imagined physical contact in the lover's absence, the poem builds up to a climax of single, passionate exclamations, 'Sim! corre, voa, instante desejado!'. This leads into an image of desire fulfilled, no less ecstatic for being possibly only a mirage. Believing she sees her love approaching, she cries, 'Oh céus! ... É já chegado / Jacínio! Que prazer! É isto um sonho?!' (Barandas 1990: 89).

This free expression of romantic love, clearly addressed by a female speaker to a male object of passion, is dealt with more extensively in Barandas's longest prose fiction work, a short story in the style of a newspaper *folhetin,* entitled 'Eugênia ou a Filósofa Apaixonada', which repeats but also to some degree parodies Romantic tropes. Moacyr Flores has remarked that the reference to the 'Filósofa' in the title points to Barandas's awareness of French liberal philosopher Denis Diderot, indicating that she was 'uma mulher que acreditava no impulso erótico do amor e que ele não era pecaminoso como afirmava a Igreja Católica' (M. Flores 2002: 208). This reading of the protagonist Eugénia as a liberal philosopher and defender of free love is certainly supported by her unusual situation in the narrative. A brilliant court beauty and evidently not a courtesan, she lives in Rio with only her nurse or 'aia' for company. Her surname, d'Alencaster, suggests noble Portuguese origins, but she has no parents or older guardians in the narrative and therefore has no visible networks of social connection or control preventing her from making her own decisions about her emotional destiny. She has known her lover, Dolival, for some time, and yet they are not married. Indeed, the traditional authoritarian practice of marriage arranged by the family patriarch, with all its financial and social constraints, is roundly condemned on account of the tragedy it unleashes. At the same time, there is a tension running throughout the narrative between the exercise of reason and that of passion. The very oxymoron of the title, 'Eugênia, ou a Filósofa Apaixonada', poses the dichotomy of reason and feeling. Furthermore, the Portuguese term for a *philosophe* permits an openly challenging feminisation of the term, which is not available in the French. While the paternal authority of family and Church is discarded, the unlimited indulgence of passion is also criticised as potentially dangerous and placed in rational perspective by Eugênia's constant inner debates with herself, and by the third-person narrator, who engages in logical, analytical asides which comment on Eugênia's various dilemmas.[16]

In this rather chaotic, melodramatic tale, the natural love that unites Eugênia and Dolival is not allowed to continue and flourish, since Dolival's bankrupt and greedy father, Leandro, requires that his son salvage the family fortunes by making an advantageous match with a wealthy heiress, Melinda, who wants to marry him. Thus the two women are clearly represented as desiring subjects, while Dolival is the unhappy object of an arranged marriage transaction.

Through various twists and turns of the plot, the authenticity of Dolival's role as a faithful Romantic hero is placed in some doubt when he accepts too readily Eugênia's selfless offer to give him up to save his family's fortunes, saying 'Ah! Cruel! ... Melinda dádiva tua? ... Pois, bem aceito' (Barandas 1990: 61). Furthermore, a letter is found, suggesting that he has also declared his love to Melinda. Eugênia struggles against her natural emotions and tries to obtain a reasoned position, while the interventionist third-person narrator comments on her efforts, saying what she would have done in Eugênia's situation. For example, the narrator remarks, 'Pobre Dolival! Se fosse for me, lhe perdoava ... bem tarde' (67). This strengthens an implied identification between the narrator and Eugênia as voices of reason and knowledge, associating them both with the 'filósofa' of the title. By making her female heroine Eugênia an enlightened subject, Barandas refuses the male monopoly on the life of the mind, at the same time as she shows the lover Dolival to be prone to violent irrationality.

Dolival's extreme and often aggressive responses are made to contrast with Eugênia's greater dominion over judgement and calm. She tells him, 'é preciso que sejamos superiores às nossas paixões. Ceda-se à razão, e triunfe a realidade de uma ilusão passageira' (Barandas 1990: 66). When Leandro appeals to her to release his son definitively, she writes a letter breaking off her engagement. However, the couple are reunited after she falls ill, and Dolival tries to postpone his marriage to Melinda by going missing. Melinda meanwhile appeals to Eugênia to help her find him. The two women reach an agreement as Eugênia accedes to the seemingly inevitable and tries to help Melinda. When she finds Dolival, the story ends tragically as he kills her in defence of his honour, having been told by his father that Eugênia is really in love with Adolfo. Later, realising his error, he also kills himself. Leandro is left to lament his son; and Melinda is also portrayed as mourning the loss of the husband she had wanted.

Both Zilberman (1991: 45) and H. Flores (1991: 32) have identified Shakespearean resonances in the ending of this story, Flores associating it specifically with *Romeo and Juliet*. However, the fact that jealousy and the defence of honour drive Dolival to kill Eugênia and then himself tends to echo

Othello, rather than the mutual suicide of Romeo and Juliet. Certainly, the facial expression of Dolival on deciding to kill Eugênia is more reminiscent of the Moor of Venice, as 'seus olhos faiscaram de raiva, seus lábios contrairam-se, rangem-lhe os dentes e toda a sua fisionomia era espantosa' (Barandas 1990: 78). If the resonance is with Othello, this serves rather to make a victim of Eugênia and to inculpate Dolival for the irrational impulse of jealousy. Eugênia, in contrast, is presented with a prime occasion for envy through the rivalry of Melinda, but significantly opts instead for friendship and compassion. By endorsing the position of Eugênia as the subject of reason and truth, despite her love for Dolival, the story points to the critique of male homosocial violence, which drives men, as in the Farroupilha Revolt, to expend their passions in defence of their ego, honour and social status. The budding asexual and platonic friendship between the two women, Melinda and Eugênia, suggests the need for some form of defence against the dangers of romance. As the narrator notes, when the two women console each other, 'São seguramente um fenômeno incompreensível os corações destas duas mulheres! Como se podem elas amar, sendo ambas o mútuo instrumento da sua desgraça?' (76). Later, in the same vein, she remarks 'a infeliz amiga tomou sobre si a tarefa de o trazer à razão' (77).

The rational stance of the *philosophe* granted here to Eugênia effectively affords a critique of the patriarchy that underpins both the monarchist and Farroupilha positions. In contrast to Cunha, Barandas does not simply blame the Farroupilhas for the war: she blames men. The oligarchic, property-owning interests and defence of the old order that typify the Legalists, drive Leandro to sell his son into an arranged marriage. At the same time, the story criticises the passionately rebellious excess of the Romantic, Dolival, who is all too ready to believe the tales of Eugênia's infidelity and defend his honour in the militarised hyper-masculine mode of the Farroupilhas. In this father/son clash between the old values and the new, there is an ironic foreclosure on any truly independent destiny for women. This fact is underlined by Barandas's comparison of the plights of the 'rival' women, Melinda and Eugênia, bonded by their shared subjection at different levels to fathers, husbands and lovers, who control the codes of honour.

The issue of asexual friendship and the dangers of romantic love are explored in even more succinct and critical mode in the neoclassical allegory, 'A Queda de Safo ou o Cinco de Maio. Alegoria' (Barandas 1990: 116–25). What is interesting in this didactic tale, as in 'Eugênia', is Barandas's rationally articulated belief, in the mode of the *philosophes,* that excessive passion is destructive, unwise and counter to good sense. Nowhere does she endorse any moral, Catholic notion that it is inherently sinful.

This story involves a substantial rewriting of neoclassical sources and shows Safo being warned by her friend, the hermaphrodite counsellor Tiresias, not to go into the forest, where she might be confronted with the monster called Amor. Ignoring his advice, she strays into the forest, where she meets a beautiful, cupid-like child and agrees to drink the liquid he offers her in order to discover love, only to be stupefied and led away into a deadly palace. There, Cupid tears out her heart, spearing it on the point of a lance, and leaves her in a dangerous trance-like state, unable to think for herself. Her friend Tiresias comes to rescue her and revives her, concluding the tale with a warning about the dangers of love and how to offset them in favour of the value of true friendship. The conclusion of the story takes the form of four maxims of advice to be transmitted to the younger generations in an educational or familial context, namely: to follow the wise advice of others; to treat love seriously as the most important moment in one's life; not to be too curious; and, finally, to be wary of seductive language.

Certainly, this short tale seems to reinforce the representation of platonic, non-sexual friendship, which was broached between the two women in 'Eugênia'. Indeed Moacyr Flores has raised the interesting and important possibility of reading it biographically as a veiled reference to a lesbian attraction that Barandas experienced and subsequently repressed (M. Flores 2002: 211). On the other hand, Safo's fear in this allegory concerns the fall from a Sapphic position of intellectual wisdom, power and good sense. Her identity as 'Safo', to which she returns at the end of the tale, is not something she seeks to escape. It is also significant here that Barandas points so obviously and didactically to her decision to transform Tiresias. Her Tiresias, she tells us, is meant to represent the 'milagre da amizade' (Barandas 1990: 123). He is not the 'pedante da fábula' (presumably referring to his traditional role in the Theban plays) with his 'inúteis lamentações' and 'intempestivas repreensões' (122). By making this bisexual figure a positive model of reason, friendship and truth in this allegory, she seems to be indicating that these qualities may be the properties of both sexes, not of one or the other, and not significantly those of a completely unsexed entity either. They are, however, seen to be destroyed by contact between the sexes, namely Cupid.

Barandas, who was married at sixteen to the man of her choice, reaffirms here women's intellectual ability to conquer the physical passions of the body, the gross matter of nature, which she represents in grotesque, abject terms as an abyss in which 'mil plantas venenosas, de cujas os eflúvios infeccionavam o ar, e serpentes terríveis ali silvaram com um pavoroso estrépito' (121). Barandas's Safo is thus a strategic, political Sappho, the necessary positioning outside sexual relations with men that intellectual activity for women requires, since she effectively reinforces the Cartesian dualistic division of mind and body.[17] However, at the same time as Barandas celebrates in this tale the capacity of women to command reason and logic on the same basis as men, she is forced to acknowledge realistically the role of the body, the suppression of human passions that all such logical rationalisation involves.

The rational prowess and expertise of women forms the basis for her most explicitly liberal feminist intervention in 'Diálogos', where she argues for the rights of women to political self-expression. It was probably written in 1837 when Barandas was in Rio. Here, in a more direct manner than in 'Eugênia', Barandas seeks to drive a wedge between two generations of men. The liberal feminist dichotomy of reason and feeling, mind and body, is central to the brief preface that Barandas herself provided to 'Diálogos', called 'Duas Palavras'. Placing this piece clearly within the context of the Legalist recapture of Porto Alegre in 1836, the period she refers to coincides with the intense debates on Farrapa women and their political actions that filled the pages of *O Artilheiro* in 1837–38. 'Diálogos' repeatedly reveals the influence of the Farroupilha liberals and the political intervention of their women supporters on its heroine's otherwise Legalist thinking. Indeed, her constant references to Farroupilha examples enable her to argue by analogy for the same rights of political allegiance for Legalist women. As Barandas herself writes in her preface, the ferment of opinion on gender and public politics that occurred in 1837 has prompted her to have her own say (Barandas 1990: 98):

> Em 1837, depois da memorável reação de Porto Alegre, não se ouvia falar senão em partidos, desordens, planos de ataques, de defesas, intrigas políticas, etc. E de tal maneira grassou a mania, que as mesmas senhoras, e até as crianças, já não sabiam outro assunto para os seus entretenimentos'.

In the conclusion to this statement, Barandas attempts to spike her critics' guns with a pre-emptive and ironic apologia for having temporarily lost her good sense and annoyed the men, who might disapprove of what she is saying. Thus, she comments: 'hoje que estou a sangue frio, peço perdão aos Srs. que ficarem com a testa franzida, quando os lerem' (98). The text that follows maintains this knowing oscillation between an often ironic conformity with the ideal of the sentimental woman (engaged in her banal occupations, alongside the children) and a playful manipulation of the flaws inherent in the 'natural' logic of men. Fashioned as a Cartesian dialogue, Barandas's 'Diálogos' brings three characters together in a debate: a young woman, Mariana; her father, Huberto; and her cousin, Alfredo. Although it is never made explicit, the cousin is a likely future husband in the oligarchic society of Rio Grande do Sul. Certainly, 'Diálogos' sees the two drawing closer together, to the exclusion of the father, Huberto, through the mutual pleasure of their exercise in reason. Read in this light, it is all the more significant that Mariana gradually deploys strategies of elimination, deduction and logic to 'win over' the younger man and to pit him against the elder, who is far less easily convinced.

Hübner Flores has rightly noted some important points of contact between Barandas's 'Diálogos' and Nísia Floresta's *Direitos das Mulheres e Injustiças dos Homens,* believed at the time to be a translation of Mary Wollstonecraft's *A Vindication of the Rights of Woman*, remarking that the more innovative Barandas effectively 'suplantou o feminismo da sua amiga' (H. Flores 1991: 29). As noted above, the text Floresta translated was not Wollstonecraft's *Vindication*; it was Sophia's *Woman not Inferior to Man* (1739). Clarifying this point removes certain difficulties that the influence of the real Wollstonecraft might have posed, namely the unpalatability of her republicanism and her stance on slavery; Barandas, whatever her seduction by liberal feminist ideals of reason, remained a staunch monarchist from a slave-owning family. *Woman not Inferior to Man* incidentally makes considerable play of Queen Elizabeth I of England as a model of women's ability to gain superior learning and to rule a country (Sophia 1975: 47).

The Wollstonecraft fallacy raises a question, of course, as to whether Floresta's alleged translation of *Woman not Inferior to Man* or Barandas's original text, 'Diálogos', has primacy as the first feminist text of Brazil. In one sense this is immaterial, since Floresta remains undoubtedly and by a long way Brazil's most prolific and sustained early nineteenth-century thinker on women's rights. Moreover, her translation of Sophia was both timely and influential, and there is no concrete proof that she sought to practise a deliberate deception on her readers (Liddell 2005; Pallares-Burke 1996). However, the foundational discourse of Brazilian liberal feminism invests heavily in the image of a nativist transformation of Wollstonecraft's English original into something new, creating, as Duarte puts it 'uma resposta brasileira ao texto inglês' (Duarte 1989: 108). If the founding of Brazilian liberal feminism effectively means the transposition of European Enlightenment feminist thinking into a Brazilian political framework, then Barandas does have a stronger claim to be foundational than Floresta's very faithful work of translation, given that her 'Dialógos' reworks the key premises of *Woman not Inferior to Man* to fit the local circumstances of the Farroupilha Revolt.

Throughout 'Diálogos', Mariana's father, the doyen of the ancien régime, defends the unproven, assumed and unquestioned heritage of the past, while the cousin, increasingly on Mariana's side, shows that reason itself, as the neutral instrument of logic, will prevail if properly argued. Mariana begins by posing in her own terms the question 'o que é uma mulher' as something that actually has a logically deducible answer, thereby discrediting the assumption that woman is 'uma coisa indefinida' (1990: 99). Her questioning of proper gender roles in terms of pre-assigned rights and duties for the sexes leads her to denaturalise the power of the *pátria* as an absolute good when she asks: 'foi o bem da Pátria que acendeu o primeiro facho da discórdia nesta Pronvíncia (sic)' (Barandas 1990: 100). She points to 'interesse' and 'vingança' (100) as the motives that have driven men to take up arms, and then reduces these two motivations to the level of brute egotistical passions. Getting to the heart of the current struggle as a contest of elite male interests, she distances its rhetoric from the noble sentiment of 'verdadeiro patriotismo' (101) and accuses men of trapping and manipulating 'os incautos' (101), who follow their banner unthinkingly. If the *pátria* is nothing but a cover story for masculine instincts and desires, so too, she argues, is the Law, which men have made to protect and justify their vested interests and emotional impulses.

Making an ironic implicit contrast between women's lack of real independence from men and the independence of the nation, Mariana points out that women are subject to the same instincts, feelings, impulses and problems as men, a state worsened by their very dependence on men, their physical weakness, their lack of education and their greater impressionability. The issue of women's sameness to men is then viewed from the reverse perspective, men's sameness to women, as she shows men to be equally driven by passion and desire in their party political choices. Women, meanwhile, are equally affected by the sufferings war visits upon them. As a logical corollary of this, and in a context where women's loyalty to their men was a clear concern of the Legalist cause, in its fear of Farroupilha influence, Mariana represents female political participation not as a violation of sanctioned roles, but as a disputed political asset to be claimed in a hypothetical contest of male interests.

Referring to the Farroupilha leader, Bento Gonçalves, Mariana remarks that one could not blame a woman who loves him for taking sides, as she would inevitably be driven to feel concern for his safety. In this dramatic, romantic hyperbole, she imagines in the following scenario, Bento Gonçalves's lover desperate to save his life (Barandas 1990: 105):

> Vítima de amor e do receio, bem semelhante àquele que a força irresistível da tempestuousa borrasca fez naufragar no meio do Oceano, agita-se, braceja, inda mesmo tendo a terrível convicção que são impotentes todos os seus movimentos para salvar-lhe a vida! Ah! E quem não lhe perdoará? Ponha-se todo o mundo no seu lugar; metam as mãos nas suas consciências, e ninguém, ousará incriminar essa mulher.

Won over by the romantic appeal of this image, her cousin Alfredo not only pardons the hypothetical woman but also admits to harbouring a secret envy for Bento Gonçalves as a hero of the liberal cause who attracts such female devotion; he remarks: 'Que seja mil vezes absolvida! Quase desejei agora ser Bento Gonçalves! Ora, essa mulher necessariamente há de ser uma farroupilha exaltada' (Barandas 1990: 105). By appealing to the men's sense of honour, sexual jealousy and self-preservation, Mariana plays on the type of gender panic evident in the pages of *O Artilheiro*, whereby the women act as frontier zone between the two groups of men, heightening the male need to control their womenfolk as tokens of exchange in war. The implication here is that women could equally (perhaps voluntarily) become Farroupilhas if their menfolk do not allow them to give open expression to their natural loyalty to the Legalist cause. Furthermore, in her reference to death by drowning in the natural forces of the ocean tide Mariana carefully draws men into the same discourse of instinct and feeling as women, arguing for the right of women to base their political choices on the 'naturalness' of their familial allegiances, at the same time as she traps her male cousin into admitting the natural emotions that govern his own political investments. Turning to the Legalist property-owning side, Mariana argues that loyalty to their husbands' suffering and a share in the domestic ill effects of war force women to take up sides to survive and defend the family's interests.

This logic of the loyal wife is extended to serve as the proper model of allegiance and loyalty to the *pátria*. Mariana reinforces her point, particularly with her father, by remarking that a woman would not wish to stand by and watch the family property robbed and despoiled by the Farroupilha hordes, an issue which the materialistic Huberto ultimately concedes. However, whereas Alfredo is increasingly converted by his cousin's logic, Huberto frequently resorts to the arguments of divine scriptural purpose, claiming 'a mulher foi feita e formada só para servir os homens, assim como Deus formou os brutos' (Barandas 1990: 107). To this Mariana responds by deconstructing from within the discourses used against her, or, as she puts it, 'tomando eu as vossas próprias armas, já vos mostro que a nós mulheres é que compete esse pomposo título de – Obra principal da Divindade –' (Barandas 1990: 108). This argument takes the form of a reinterpretation of the story of Genesis, strongly echoing a similar point made in Sophia's *Woman not Inferior to Man*[18], whereby Mariana claims that when God gave man dominion over all he saw around him, he had in fact not yet created woman, which means that woman was actually 'excetuada desse fatal domínio' (108).[19] Her final coup de grâce concerns the familiar liberal feminist claim, central to the arguments both of Sophia and her sources in François Poulain de la Barre, that, reproductive faculties excepted, women have the same bodies, physical functions and senses as men, 'os mesmos atributos, os mesmos sentidos ... (o tato, olfato, vista etc.)' (109), but, more importantly, they have a genuinely spiritual soul and free will.[20]

Despite her defiant stance, Mariana concludes 'Diálogos' with renewed declarations of political loyalty to the male protectors of the Legalista cause, the 'Magnânimos Defensores da Legalidade' (Barandas 1990: 110) as she begs the right to share with men the joy of watching the 'Causa Justa da Integridade do Império' (111) flourish without disunity among good men. As for most women in her day, the main paradox Barandas faces in her self-characterisation as Mariana is the need to engage in a performance of extreme conformism to the good daughter and good future wife roles, in order to express her right to hold a political opinion at all. Thus 'Diálogos' is ultimately a reassertion of the unity of empire, whose primary argument for female patriotic allegiance rests on an extension of the duties of a good wife. However, the 'good wife' role itself has undergone a certain transformation in the text, particularly when read alongside her other prose works, with their repeated emphasis on the philosophical dichotomy of reason and passion. Barandas's 'Diálogos' represents the culmination of women's choice to be rational subjects, marking a crucial reinvestment of female identity in the life of the mind and suggesting that women may contribute to the nation beyond a purely reproductive and domestic function.

The survival of the unified empire that Mariana invokes in her conclusion results from a liberal philosophical dialogue between the sexes striving towards new and more equal terms. In this respect, Barandas foresees a somewhat less patriarchal prospect for any future union between Mariana and her cousin Alfredo, who finally praises Mariana for arguing better than Cicero himself. Further supporting this argument is the fact that the word 'império' itself actually marks a point of division and dissension in the text. It is used with a capital 'I' to refer to the Brazilian Empire in the citation above, and with a small 'i' to refer to the empire of male control over women, when Mariana remarks that men are wasting their time subjecting women through the brute physical strength on which their superiority rests, because 'ela é independente de vosso orgulhoso império' (Barandas 1990: 110). Thus, a crucial rhetorical gap is introduced in the discursive continuity that mandates women's natural integration into the Brazilian empire through her natural integration into the empire of male control. The vision of woman's sexual independence from man's 'orgulhoso império' presented in 'Diálogos' effectively leaves open here the question of women's political integration into the united empire of Brazil, if she is no longer subordinated to the will of man. Barandas did not go on to answer this question but she was certainly one of the first woman writers in Brazil to ask it.

Winners, losers and women

Both Cunha and Barandas warrant further study for their discursive interventions in the national consolidation of post-independence Brazil, influenced profoundly by their attempts to maintain an allegiance both to the *pátria* of Rio Grande do Sul and the imperial court in Rio de Janeiro. While Cunha provides an interesting and complex example of the conditions of public expression that a woman faced even in the most overtly patriotic context, she also demonstrates the peculiarly powerful symbolic capital a woman could deploy by consciously inhabiting the role of the national female metaphor or figurehead. This was particularly true where the Farroupilha Revolt heightened the cracks and tensions in the imperial union and Cunha could present herself as the 'good' *sul-rio-grandense,* intrinsically loyal to the emperor. At the same time, her symptomatic lapses into male-voiced desiring subjectivity reveal the manifest limits of the project she engaged in as a vehicle for the expression of a female affective investment outside formulaic, nationalist ventriloquism. Barandas used the Farroupilha Revolt as a contingent opportunity to think outside the bourgeois frame of marriage and domesticity that had served her and her sisters so badly. This enabled her to advance personal, political and sexual agendas on women's behalf that point beyond the limited social roles of breeding and educating children, stitching uniforms and commanding black house slaves, which both the Farroupilha and Legalist causes ordained for women.

For all the male elitism and militarism of the Farroupilha Revolt, its ultimate failure to install a liberal democratic republic, its controversial and tragic betrayal of its black soldiers and its non-liberation of the slaves,[21] it brought with it a period of undeniable gender anxiety and limited intellectual opportunity for women. The unpredictability and immediacy of the Farroupilha crisis, which often enforced changes in the roles of men and women, enabled both Cunha and Barandas to leave different but indelible marks of female identity, protest and dissent on the history of a Brazilian independence process that was finally drawing towards a certain political unity. If the pacification of Rio Grande do Sul constituted, as Barman claims, a major landmark in the final consolidation of Brazil as a nation state in the decade following 1842 (Barman 1988: 217), the Farroupilha Revolt witnessed women as writers and thinkers becoming politically conscious of the social and cultural conditions that shaped their own sense of national belonging. Both Cunha and Barandas played out particular circumscribed roles in the imperialist dramas of the conservative families they came from. However, as their writings reveal, they were increasingly conscious of the fact that they *were* assuming a constructed role as a matter of convenience or necessity. This was a first step towards thinking what it meant for a woman to identify as 'national' and as a 'patriot' and asking, in the longer term, how she might choose to be 'national' independently, in her own right.

Notes

1 I would like to thank Charlotte Liddell for her generous assistance with this chapter and particularly for allowing me access to her archive work on *O Artilheiro*.

2 See Fernando Osório's highly romanticised account of the women's role in the war, published in 1935, the centenary of the Farroupilha Revolt. As Frigeri and Rüdiger note, Osório casts the frontier women of the Farroupilha period as the eternal feminine essence of Rio Grande do Sul (1985: 156–58).

3 *A Casa das Sete Mulheres* (dir. Jayme Monjardim 2003) tells the story of the Farroupilha Revolt and civil war through an amalgam of selected historical events, regional mythology and copious romance, interweaving the stories of the military heroes of the movement with those of the womenfolk of Bento Gonçalves, the Farroupilha leader. An insightful critique of the series as a representation of southern history is to be found in Mário Maestri, 'As Sete Mulheres e as Negras sem Rosto', *Revista. Espaço Acadêmico*, No. 29, October 2003, available at: http://www.espacoacademico.com.br/029/29maestri.htm. Accessed August 23 2005.

4 Juana Manso met Garibaldi in Montevideo in the 1840s.

5 This is very little different in essence from the list of maxims for women's morality, economy and guardianship of their speech, which the Farroupilha *O Povo* published January 11 1840: 2 (cited in M. Flores 2002: 115).

6 For brief biographical and bibliographical accounts of the lives and works of these writers see Zahidé Lupinacci Muzart's 2000 anthology, *Escritoras Brasileiras do Século XIX*. The entries on Sampaio and Cunha are by Rita Terezinha Schmidt, and on Barreto and Barandas by Muzart. See also Moacyr Flores 2002: 207–20; and Hilda Hübner Flores 1990: 16–50. For more detailed biographical information on Sampaio in particular see also H. Flores 1989b and Maria Eunice Moreira 2003.

7 No remaining copies of this newspaper have been discovered to date.

8 According to Muzart, only one issue of this journal, No. 31, remains and part of this is reproduced in *Escritoras Brasileiras do Século XIX* (2000: 81).

9 Her situation may be compared to that of Bolivian poet María Josefa Mujía, who became blind at the age of fourteen (1834) and whose poems mostly lament her blindness (Cortés 1875).

10 See Muzart 2000: 103 for a reproduction of Assis Brandão's poem, *Carta de Leandro a Hero, traduzida do francês e dedicada à Senhora D. Delfina Benigna da Cunha*.

11 My biographical information on Cunha is drawn from Becker 1997 and 1991, Schmidt 2001 and Schmidt's bio-bibliography in Muzart 2000.

12 The authoritative source on the life of Ana de Barandas, from which my account is drawn, is the work of Hilda Hübner Flores (see 1989a, 1990 and 1991). I am also indebted to Muzart 2000.

13 See Soares 1980: 127 for an account of his discovery of the complete manuscript, of which the first ten pages had been missing.

14 According to Becker, 'Conduziu-se como musa da justiça. Embora esta tenha por símbolo uma mulher de olhos vendados, sustentando em uma das mãos a balança e na outra a espada, vence quem está fortalecido pela razão' (1991: 16).

15 As Luciana Stegagno-Picchio explains regarding the mapping of Arcadian and Romantic aesthetics onto Brazil's political and intellectual independence processes: 'Nasce com os árcades, indubitavelmente sob a influência das idéias da França e da América do Norte, mas com uma precisa referência aos problemas locais, aquela consciência pátria que com os românticos irá desaguar na vontade de independência. Um Iluminismo de burgueses coloniais, dos quais sairá, contudo, tanto na direção política quanto na direção estética, o movimento de autonomia do país' (2004: 127).

16 See Gatens 1991 on the importance of the reason and feeling dichotomy and the legacy of Cartesian dualism in liberal feminist philosophy.

17 Sophia's 1739 text, *Woman not Inferior to Man*, refers to Sappho simply as proof from classical antiquity of women's ability to be poets (47).

18 Cf. Sophia's corresponding remark that, 'Men seem to conclude that all other creatures were made for them, because they themselves were not created till all were in readiness for them' (1975: 11). The original text of *Woman not Inferior to Man* was published in 1739.

19 Similarly, in his *Defensa de las mujeres* (1726) Feijóo argued that Eve was not primarily to blame for the fall of mankind since she was tempted by an angel of superior intelligence, while Adam was tempted by a mere human being.

20 Cf. Sophia's comment, 'that we have not been excluded from a share in the power and privileges which lift their sex above ours, for want of natural capacity, or merit, but for want of an equal spirit of violence, shameless injustice and lawless oppression, with theirs' (1975: 36). Similarly Barandas's remarks on the sameness of the male and female body echo the passage in Sophia's *Woman not Inferior to Man*, which claims, 'We hear with ears, see with eyes, and taste with tongue as well as they' (1975: 24). Duarte also notes this point of textual contact between Floresta's *Direitos* and Ana de Barandas's 'Diálogos' (1989: 126–27).

21 See Moacyr Flores, 2002: 91–93, and 1990: 101–102.

CHAPTER TEN

Juana Manso (1819–75): Women in History

> [T]he first object of laudable ambition is to obtain a character as a human being, regardless of the distinction of sex.
>
> Wollstonecraft [1792] 1992: 82

> Una mujer pensadora es un escándalo.
>
> Sarmiento [1867] 1961: 73

The second quotation above is taken from a letter sent by the soon-to-be Argentine President, Domingo Faustino Sarmiento, from New York to his friend Juana Manso on October 15 1867.[1] Sarmiento was consoling Manso, who had had foul-smelling plant gum (asafoetida) smeared on her dress and stones thrown at her by a group of men during a small ceremony marking the opening of the public library in Chivilcoy, in the Pampas. The object of their anger, Sarmiento writes, is not Manso's speech on women's education, nor that she is a writer and a teacher, but that she is a 'mujer inteligente': 'Sabe usted de otra argentina que ahora o antes haya escrito, hablado o publicado, trabajando por una idea, compuesto versos, redactado un diario?' (Sarmiento 1961: 73). She was the first such woman in Argentina and he knows of only three others: one in Spain (possibly Gertrudis Gómez de Avellaneda); and two in Chile, the poets Clara Condarco and la señora (Mercedes Marín) del Solar, who no longer write. In this letter, Sarmiento typically draws a clear dichotomy between backwardness and progress: the former is represented by Muslim women and the Spanish Catholic Church, and the latter by Parisian science and women in the United States. Manso is instrumental in moving Argentina from barbarism (religion, Spain) to civilisation (science, medicine, education, and Europe/United States):

> ¿Se rompe así no mas la tradición del servilismo oriental que legaron a la mujer los árabes, dejándola la mantilla para que se oculte el rostro, el sentarse en el suelo en la mezquita, que solo la española conserva en la iglesia cristiana? ... Si hubiera visto como yo a los sabios franceses, en París, acompañando y honrando a una norteamericana, doctora en medicina, que visitaba hospitales, escuelas públicas y museos osteológicos. (Sarmiento 1961: 73)

Women's entry into the secular world of education and science is the sign of modernity.

The Argentine constitutions of 1819, 1826 and 1853 were influenced by, though not copies of, the constitutions of the United States, France and Spain, all of which attempted to improve the individual's lot 'sin ningún tipo de diferenciación por raza o color' but they failed to consider gender inequalities (González 1993: 128, 148).[2] In Esteban Echeverría's letter to Pedro de Angelis, in which he explains his concept of republic, there is no reference to women. As mentioned in Chapter 4, Echeverría's *Dogma*, published in 1846 (when Manso began work on her first novel, *Los misterios del Plata*), states that belonging to a patria is not a birthright but a right of citizenship (Echeverría 1972: 126) earned by virtue, action and courage. Society is composed of a cofraternity of individuals who collaborate, demonstrating their 'capacidades y virtudes republicanas': their intelligence, goodness and ability (Echeverría 1972: 136). For Echeverría, natural differences (implicitly, between men), such as innate intelligence, may be overcome by effort and 'mérito por obras'. Men may earn the status of 'grandes hombres' by the sword or the pen as a corollary of their virtue in the domestic sphere and honour in the public arena (Echeverría 1972: 136). Women are not excluded, nor are they explicitly included, although close reading suggests strongly that Echeverría's programme is solely addressed to and was expected to apply to men. The protagonist of *Los misterios del Plata* (1852) is an individual woman who achieves virtue and honour in the domestic and public arenas.

If *Los misterios del Plata* enters into dialogue with Echeverría's political programme, *La familia del Comendador* (1854), Manso's second novel, engages with Alberdi's *Bases* (1852).[3] Under 'Declaraciones, derechos y guarantías', Article 14 of the *Bases* states that all inhabitants of the Argentine Confederation have the right to work, trade, petition, move, enter and leave the territory, publish, learn and teach, and the freedom of religion. Article 15 stipulates the abolition of slavery and the freedom of slaves. Article 16 that there are no 'prerogativas de sangre ni de nacimiento', no noble privilege: 'Todos sus habitantes son iguales ante la ley y admisibles en los empleos, sin otra consideración que la idoneidad' (Alberdi 1942: 330). Yet Alberdi's explicit views on women in society, not far removed from those of Acevedo, are conservative and owe much to Rousseau. Women should stay at home and not waste time in 'vanas reuniones', which compromise their honour:

> En cuanto a la mujer [artífice modesto y poderoso, que desde su rincón, hace las costumbres privadas y públicas, organiza la familia, prepara el ciudadano, y echa las bases del Estado] su instrucción no debe ser brillante [showy, ostentatious]. No debe consistir en talentos de ornato y lujo exterior, como la música, el baile, la pintura, según lo que ha sucedido hasta aquí. Necesitamos señoras y no artistas. La mujer debe brillar con el brillo del honor, de la dignidad, de la modestia de su vida. Sus destinos son serios; no ha venido al mundo para ornar el salón, sino para hermosear la soledad fecunda del hogar. Dale apego a su casa, es salvarla.

> ... Mientras la mujer vive en la calle y en medio de las provocaciones, recogiendo aplausos, como actriz, en el salón, rozándose como un diputado entre ese especie de público que se llama la sociedad, educará los hijos a su imagen, servirá a la República como Lola Montes[4], y será útil para sí misma y para su marido como una Mesalina más o menos decente. (Alberdi 1942: 65; the text in brackets was added in the second edition)

For Alberdi, women in the public sphere were public women, virtual streetwalkers. Nevertheless, Alberdi did underscore the importance of the family for the collective good. In his discussion of the California Constitution of 1849, he argued that 'pensar en educación sin proteger la formación de las familias es esperar ricas cosechas de un suelo sin abono ni preparación'; the family is 'semillero del Estado y de la República' (Alberdi 1942: 51). Women needed to be educated solely to fulfil their republican role of virtuous mothers and spouses in the domestic sphere. *La familia del Comendador* argues that while this may be the case, women's activities at home have far-reaching consequences for the political economy of the state.

Juana Paula Manso, who should rightly be included in the Generation of 1837 (by birth, political beliefs, exile and profession), was one of the first pupils to attend the primary schools set up by the Buenos Aires Sociedad de Beneficencia in 1823 to educate girls. The schools were organised by Mariquita Sánchez de Thompson on behalf of President Bernadino Rivadavia, a friend of Manso's father. Manso's father was Spanish but had fought for the Independence of the Vice Royalty of La Plata and, as a civil engineer, had been charged by the 1813 Assembly with the design of the land and property register of the city of Buenos Aires (Deleis, de Titto, Arguindeguy 2001: 207–18).

In 1832, when Manso was thirteen, her father published her translation from French of *El egoismo y la amistad* and, the following year, of *Mambrogenia o la Heroína de Grecia*. She was supported by her parents in her education and was well connected within the governing elite. During the regime of Juan Manuel Rosas (1835–52), her father, like many Unitarian liberals, fled to Montevideo, where he was appointed to the board of the Uruguay printing press office. In 1840, the rest of the family, including Juana, joined him, and she earned a living by teaching French and Spanish.[5] In 1841 she established a school for young ladies, the Ateneo de Señoritas, in her home, where she taught the three Rs, religion, needlework, Spanish grammar and French, with extra classes in English, music and drawing. She also published poems in the Montevideo press, notably *El Nacional* and *El Constitucional*. 'La mujer poeta' (*El Nacional*, August 4 1841) laments the fortunes of the woman poet 'Resuena su lira en mustio desierto / Que Dios sólo escucha su tímido canto ... / ¡¡¡Mujer!!!... la desprecian, el mundo se ríe / Y al mérito rodea la fría irrisión' (Santomauro 1994: 37). One of Manso's acquaintances from this time was the exiled José Mármol, who wrote to her in 1842 to encourage her to publish; they became close friends. In 1843, when Manuel Oribe joined Rosas and besieged Montevideo, the Manso family moved to Brazil for a short while, returning to Montevideo that same year. Slave-holding Brazil, under the rule of Pedro II, made a strong impression on Manso, as is evidenced in *La familia del Comendador*, set in Brazil.[6] Although she had been born in Buenos Aires and raised in Montevideo, she felt a close affinity with Brazil. In *La familia del Comendador* she wrote: 'Siempre que hable de ti, Brasil, lo haré con entusiasmo, porque has sido por muchos años mi patria adoptiva y estás ligada a mi corazón y a mi pensamiento, por un altar y dos tumbas' (Manso 1854: 127).[7] When she was 24, the government of Uruguay appointed Manso director of the Ateneo de Señoritas and published her reading manual for children. In Montevideo she met Giuseppe Garibaldi, who was married to Brazilian Ana Maria Jesús de Ribeiro (see Chapter 9), and Gian-Batista Cuneo, the dedicatee of her long poem 'A Italia', published in a pamphlet in 1844 (Manso 1844), a friendship which explains her favourable portrayal of Italian republicans in *Los misterios del Plata*.

In 1844 Manso married the Portuguese violinist Francisco de Saá Noronha, the couple moved to Philadelphia with their daughter, and she began to write *Los misterios del Plata*. However, Noronha was unsuccessful and, after a year in Cuba, they returned to Brazil, with a second daughter, and co-authored several successful plays (*La familia Morel*, *A Saloia*, *A Esmeralda*, *Rosas*). It was in Brazil that Manso completed her novel. In 1851, to encourage women's education, Manso founded her own Sunday journal, the *Jornal das Senhoras*,[8] in which she published *Misterios del Plata* (1852) in instalments. The novel was later serialised in Argentina in 1867, though incomplete. In 1852 Noronha abandoned Manso and left for Europe with another woman. That same year, Rosas fell from power and in 1853 Manso returned to Buenos Aires.

In 1854, still earning her living as a teacher in Buenos Aires, Manso founded the journal *Album de Señoritas*, in which she published *La familia del Comendador*.[9] The journal folded after just eight issues and, disillusioned, she returned to Brazil to continue work on the *Jornal das senhoras*. In 1859 she moved to Buenos Aires and met Sarmiento, who put her in charge of the Escuela de Ambos Sexos (Mixed School). Both favoured state co-educational schools and they collaborated closely for almost twenty years. Influenced by the theories of Pestalozzi, she directed the *Anales de la Educación Común* (1859–62), promoted by Sarmiento to disseminate new pedagogical practices. This education campaign was fiercely resisted by the ladies of the Sociedad de Beneficencia, whose long-time president, Mariquita Sánchez, refused to admit the new ideas and resolutely ignored Manso. Manso's history text book, *Compendio de la historia de las Provincias Unidas del Río de la Plata* (1862), was adopted by Bartolomé Mitre for the school curriculum. Unfortunately, the influential Juan María Gutiérrez, head of the Schools Department, had just completed his own history and attempted to prevent Manso's from becoming the set text. Due to constant opposition, Manso resigned as director of the Escuela de Ambos Sexos in 1865, and converted to Anglicanism. From then on she attacked the Catholic Church in her writings and lectures, calling for civil marriage and non-religious education. In 1871, during Sarmiento's presidency, she was appointed to the National Schools Commission, the first woman to achieve this position. She died in 1875, aged 55, during Avellaneda's government, and was buried in the English cemetery, a dissident and sworn enemy of the Church (Mizraje 1999: 74).

Album de señoritas, 1854

Juana Manso was the first feminist intellectual of the River Plate Provinces. Her liberal feminism tended to minimise the significance of sexual difference; in her view, women were autonomous individuals and moral agents, as deserving of citizenship as men; citizenship entailed their participation in the polity as social and historical beings, and modernity was predicated on the education and liberation of all women into public life. Her feminist credo is spelled out clearly in her journalism. The first issue of the *Album* appeared in Buenos Aires on January 1 1854 and, apart from two articles, was written entirely by Manso herself.[10] In 'Redacción' she sets out her aim: to emancipate women's minds from trivia and to liberate their intelligence, freedom of thought and conscience, which had hitherto been oppressed by arbitrary authority that disregarded women's natural rights and god-given equality with men: when God created 'el alma humana, no le dio *sexo*' [sic]. To achieve this end, she aimed to convince women that displaying their intelligence is not a crime or a defect, but 'su mejor adorno' (January 1 1854: 1). Intelligence is the source of virtue and domestic contentment. Enlightened women are as important as men for the progress of the family and society. There can be no justification for the condemnation of women to ignorance while men expand their minds freely.[11] Her objectives include a 'plan de estudios' for women, disseminated in articles in the *Album*, which would give women access to the knowledge forbidden to them and appropriated by men for themselves. She asks for collaborators. As for Literature, she will include only (Latin) American works. In short, she offers a new way of thinking for a new society: 'Todos mis esfuerzos serán consagrados a la ilustración de mis compatriotas' (January 1 1854: 1).

Throughout the *Album*, Manso explicitly addresses 'lectoras', or women readers. In her thoughts on New Year's Eve, 1853, in which she hoped the year to come would be favourable, she explains that she has returned to Argentina after twenty years abroad and that if her journal is not successful, she will leave for 'una *Patria* en alguna parte del mundo, donde la inteligencia de la mujer no sea un delito. Donde su pensamiento no se considere un crimen; y donde la carrera literaria no sea clasificada de pretensiones ridículas' (January 1 1854: 2). In 'Emancipación de la mujer', she argues that while the emancipation of women is a new doctrine in Latin America, it is 'un hecho consumado' in Europe and the United States. In England, she explains, ancient laws are being revised to protect women from domestic abuse, and in August 1853 a man was imprisoned for beating his wife and attempting to sell her on the market. The sign that England is at the forefront of modernity is its treatment of women. This is not just a question of customs and behaviour but of legal reform: progress had made old habits untenable but the law needed to be updated to reflect this. England has confronted the problem by acknowledging women's natural rights and intelligence and by guaranteeing women personal dignity:

> Con efecto, una gran nacíon como Inglaterra, la más libre del mundo, que tiene en su seno millares de instituciones filantrópicas, y que ha hecho a la humanidad el relevante servicio de extirpar el comercio de la carne humana suprimiendo el tráfico de exclavatura [sic], no podía abrigar en sí misma una monstruosidad semejante, como la de conservar a la mujer en el estado de la más degradante y torpe esclavitud. (*Album de Señoritas* January 1 1854: 3)

Manso had lived in the United States and was fully aware of the contrast in women's freedom of movement back home. Her 'Crónica Semanal' is brief, she admits, due to the obstacles (physical and social) that confront women who wish to walk in Buenos Aires: from the way the streets are paved to daily customs, 'no permiten a una señora que haga en Buenos Aires lo que hace en Boston, New York y Philadelphia, que toma su sombrero y manteleta y pasa el día entero en la calle si fuese necesario a sus intereses o quehaceres' (January 1 1854: 7). As the above quotation shows, she was also aware of the arguments rehearsed in the United States and Britain in the 1840s, linking women's suffrage to abolitionism. She had probably read Montesquieu: laws are man-made, she writes, and man has usurped power to subordinate women: 'La sociedad es el hombre: él solo ha escrito las leyes de los pueblos, sus códigos: por consiguiente ha reservado toda la supremacia para sí: el círculo que traza en derredor de la mujer es estrecho, inultrapasable [sic] …'. Man has sidelined woman by excluding her from topical political debates ('cuestiones vitales') on the basis of her alleged weakness of body and mind. Women, oppressed by a 'tutor perpetuo', are forbidden to use their intelligence or to develop a sense of self, 'conciencia de su individualismo'. They are denied their dignity as human beings. In this sense woman is treated as an object, 'no te perteneces a ti misma, eres objeto', an 'hembra', whose only function is to reproduce. Woman is excluded from knowledge, science and industry; she has no sense of self, 'no se conoce a sí misma'. Woman's lucidity will come to nothing without true moral teaching, that is, secular knowledge. Manso's main concern is poor women who have no means of education. If emancipation is achieved, Argentine woman 'nada tendrá que envidiar a las americanas del norte' (January 1 1854: 4).

These ideas were, however, apparently too radical for the mid-century Buenos Aires educated classes.[12] The journal, funded by subscriptions and not advertisements, did not attract a readership.[13] In issue No. 5, Manso advises 'nuestras subscriptoras' that she had foreseen this outcome. Her sole ambition had been to 'fundar un periódico dedicado enteramente a las señoras y cuya única misión fue ilustrar' (January 29 1854: 40). She reminds the readers that her Brazilian *Jornal* was in its third year of successful publication, but she had not received such support in her homeland:

> Es el *Album* una planta exótica, que se marchita rápidamente, porque la tierra donde se quiere hacer germinar es dura como la roca y no hay un rayo de sol benéfico y amigo que la abrigue y le dé vida y calor … El *Album* está desti-

> nado a una muerte prematura ... si algún milagro extraordinario no lo salve de la terrible enfermedad de la nostalgia. (*Album de señoritas* No. 5 January 29 1854)

Three weeks later, on the final page of the final issue (No. 8) she wrote bitterly:

> Concluyen con este número mis tareas y con el derecho del amor maternal, labro aquí el epíteto de este mi querido hijo, cuya muerte prematura es para su madre una decepción de más en la vida, una gota más de acíbar en el cáliz, una espina de más en el alma!
> Vivió y murió desconocido como su madre lo *fue siempre* en la región del Plata: no bastaron ni cuidados ni sacrificios a robustecerle una vida minada por la *consunción*. Desde que nació en el desamparo y en el páramo de la indiferencia ahí quedas hijo mío, página de mi alma que encierras más de un misterio de dolor en tu fosa solitaria, quién depondrá una flor? Nadie!
> Adiós pues, lectoras, perdonad si acostumbrada a escribir en otro idioma, no usé un lenguaje puro y castizo, ni mi corta inteligencia nada creó que os fuere útil, y si mi estilo no tiene la fluidez y la frescura de otros. No fue la voluntad que me faltó, pero cada uno *es lo que es y lo que deberá ser*. Redactora. (*Album de señoritas* No. 8 February 1854, Manso's emphasis)

To communicate the full extent of her disappointment, Manso appropriates an analogy often employed by male authors: the literary work as the author's child, a baby boy in this case, the product of procreativity.[14] She thus suggests that this mother's journal was as important to her as her own children, a radical move, out of tune with contemporary ideas on motherhood. Manso had two healthy daughters at the time, though a son had died at birth. For her, the mother symbolises not only the decisive republican mother of citizen-children, as in *Los misterios del Plata*, but also the mother of her own writings. The creative ability of the mind is as important as that of the body, intellect as central to a woman's capabilities as biology. Manso further reshaped dominant assumptions of the mother in her two novels, the second of which, *La familia del Comendador*, was published as a book that same year.

Los misterios del Plata, 1852: rewriting history/fixing the text

> [A]l escribir estas penosas verdades, cumplimos con el más difícil de los deberes: confesar nuestra infamia y la torpeza, la tolerancia, la deshonra de la nación a que pertenecemos.
>
> Manso de Noroña 1924: 170

Misterios del Plata was published in Manso's Brazilian *Jornal das Senhoras* (January 4–July 4 1852). A final 'Nota da autora' states that the novel was started in Philadelphia in 1846 and finished in Fortaleza do Garavatá (1849–50), where she lived for five months. It was the first of a series of historical novels she hoped to publish in the future. But she had been afraid to publish this novel, since

Rosas was still in power and some of the non-fictional characters still alive. The 'Epilogue' could not appear due to 'inconvenientes independentes da nossa vontade' (*Jornal* July 4: 8).[15]

Misterios del Plata is a political thriller based on contemporary political events. Written in the midst of oppression, it is not a historical romance but, like 'El Matadero', approximates *testimonio*, or documentary fiction (Foley 1986) that aims to denounce the horrors of dictatorship. The mysteries it investigates are the political intrigues and crimes of the Rosas regime. Set in 1838, it narrates the dramatic escape of Unitarian Valentín Alsina (1802–69) from the clutches of Rosas, a factual event that occurred on September 5 1837. Manso may have brought the action of the novel forward to 1838 to coincide with the fall of Manuel Oribe, President of Uruguay (1835–38) who collaborated with Rosas. An unsigned note in a later edition clarifies that Alsina's escape was in 1837, not in 1835 as some readers think and, by inference, not in 1838 as the novel suggests (Manso de Noroña, 1924: 213).

The historical events on which the book is based are as follows: Alsina, living in exile in Uruguay and persecuted by Oribe, attempted to relocate upriver with his wife, Antonia Maza, and son, Adolfo Alsina, in Corrientes, but was arrested by Rosas's men. The arrest was unlawful because he was sailing under a Banda Oriental/Uruguayan flag. He escaped, but in reprisal the Mazas, his father-in-law and brother-in-law, were brutally murdered: Vicente Manuel Maza, President of the Chamber of Representatives, was stabbed in the Legislative Chamber in Buenos Aires on June 27 1839; his son was murdered in prison the following day. Manso began to write the story of Alsina's escape seven years after the event, but the difficulties of writing about a living politician soon became apparent.

Rosas was defeated by Justo José de Urquiza at the battle of Caseros in February 1852 during the serialised publication of *Misterios* in Brazil. The resulting Treaty of San Nicolás attempted to reconcile the powers of Buenos Aires and the demands of the Confederation but was opposed by intransigent *porteños* (Shumway 1991: 174), including liberals Mitre and Valentín Alsina. Alsina, as Jefe Civil of Buenos Aires, marched against Urquiza in September 1852 to keep Buenos Aires province and city out of the Confederation.[16] The final instalment of the novel appeared in Rio in June 1852, three months before Alsina's uprising. Manso had sent a copy of the novel to Alsina and he wrote to thank her in May 1852, though she did not receive the letter until October (*Jornal* November 21: 163–64), after the uprising. Manso made her Unitarian sympathies clear to her female readers, but subsequent events rendered her comments on Alsina's retirement heavily ironic:

> Como sabeis, leitoras, depois da quéda do tyranno, Alsina foi chamado ao ministerio. Assim devia de ser: hoje pediu a sua demissão e se retirou á vida privada; é a ultima prova que esperavamos da virtude do nosso heroe, a quem mais ainda uma vez prestamos nossa homenagem de admiração e respeito. Rio de Janeiro, 2 de Junho de 1852. (*Jornal* July 4: 8)

Valentín Alsina's revolt against Urquiza resulted in the new constitution being ratified in all the River Plate provinces except Buenos Aires. Urquiza became the President of the Argentine Confederation, with its capital in Concepción (Rock 1985: 118), and Buenos Aires province was ruled independently under Alsina, who was elected governor in 1857; the two governments coexisted until 1860, the year the Argentine nation state finally started to take shape.

In 1867, two years before Valentín Alsina's death, part of what was to be a second edition of the novel was published in Spanish in Juan María Gutiérrez's short-lived periodical, *El Inválido Argentino* (December 29 1867–February 16 1868) with a more appropriate title, in that it refers to the female protagonist, 'Guerras civiles del Río de la Plata. Primera parte. Una mujer heroica, por Violeta. 1838'. This was during the War of the Triple Alliance with Paraguay (1865–70). By that time, Alsina's son, Adolfo Alsina (1829–77), who was aged nine in 1838, as in the novel, was an important political figure in his own right. He had lived with his father in exile in Montevideo and was later elected deputy and Governor of Buenos Aires province (1866). Adolfo Alsina, who was more radically separatist than his father, was popular and advocated obligatory education. He went on to be Vice-President during Sarmiento's presidency (1868–74), and Minister of War and the Navy under President Nicolás Avellaneda. His public prominence may account for the change of names of Manso's characters: from Valentín Alsina, Antonia Maza and Adolfo (father, mother, son) in the 1852 edition, to the fictitious Dr Arévalo, Celina Arévalo and Alberto (father, mother, son) in the 1867 Argentine edition, and then to Marcos Avellaneda, Adelaida Maza and Adolfo (father, mother, son) in subsequent editions, thus further complicating the historical referencing.[17]

The Alsinas and Avellanedas of the novel, apart from 'Adolfo Avellaneda', were real-life contemporary politicians. The real name of Marcos Avellaneda's son (who, unlike the nine-year-old character would have been only one year old in 1838) was Nicolás Avellaneda (1837–1885), one of Argentina's most important statesmen. He was Minister of the Government of Buenos Aires province during Adolfo Alsina's administration as Minister of Justicia, Culto e Instrucción Pública during Sarmiento's presidency. Nicolás Avellaneda was involved in setting up the first 'escuelas normales' and reorganising primary education and was in close contact with Manso. Under his presidency (1874–80), Buenos Aires became the capital of Argentina. At some point after February 1868, before her death in 1875 (probably before Avellaneda became President) Manso (or some other hand) changed the names of the novel's characters to Avellaneda (see 1899 edition), thus finally attributing the biography of Valentín Alsina and his family to Marcos Avellaneda and his family. President Nicolás Avellaneda's life-history might thus be erroneously confused with that of his distinguished colleague, Adolfo Alsina, as the novel inextricably intertwines their identities and life-stories.

The 1867 unfinished edition of the novel was, as far as we know, the only edition in Spanish published in Manso's lifetime. The third edition (the second in Spanish), which reverted to the original title, *Los misterios del Plata*, was published as a book in 1899, and Manso's executors or daughters are attributed with its completion (Lewkowicz 2000: 218).[18] The most widely available edition of *Los misterios del Plata* is the fourth, of 1924, published in Buenos Aires and 'prologada y corregida' by Ricardo Isidoro López Muñiz.[19] This edition is interspersed with notes, the majority of which are signed 'La Autora' (27 notes, one signed '1855', which suggests that the novel was rewritten in Spanish in the mid-1850s), or are simply unsigned, six of these in the last chapter, apparently not written by Manso.[20] The majority of the notes signed 'La Autora' clarify historical events (primarily the activities of Rosas) between 1829 and 1846, and correspond with the dates of the novel's composition (1846–50).

Misterios del Plata (1852) is lightly fictionalised biography, therefore, whose characters are named as they were in real life: Valentín Alsina, Antonia Maza, and their son Adolfo. Other real-life characters are Antonia's father and her brother Ramón, although their subsequent murder is omitted (but mentioned in notes in later editions). The plot is virtually the same in the 1852 and subsequent editions, but, as stated, the names of the characters are different and the storyline more compressed in the first edition. A note in *Los misterios del Plata* (1924), signed 'La Autora' (added after 1868)[21] explains that the name Avellaneda refers to Marcos Avellaneda (1813–41), governor of Tucumán and leader of the Liga del Norte, who was murdered in 1841 by Oribe (Manso de Noroña 1924: 24).[22] The 'seudónimo' Avellaneda was used in the novel to commemorate his heroism (Manso de Noroña 1924: 24). As stated, by attributing the historically verifiable account of Valentín Alsina's escape to the fictitious Arévalos and then to the Avellanedas, Manso avoids direct reference to Adolfo Alsina, vice-president elect in 1867–68, and later attributes Valentín Alsina's story to the father of the Minister of Education, later President, Nicolás Avellaneda. Manso's purpose may have been simply to draw attention to the concerted Rosas opposition and to represent the eventual triumph of the Unitarian *porteños* as a collective effort. But there is no doubt that she showed some audacity in rewriting national history in this way. The novel fits the tradition of Spanish American historical novels in which the characters, unlike Walter Scott's fictional heroes, are historical figures. A further contemporary example is Gertrudis Gómez de Avellaneda's *Guatimozín* (1846). However, it was not so common to insert historical figures into a fictional or historically mismatched plot. The various editions of *Los misterios del Plata* do precisely this.

The narrative strategy of fictionalising the lives of historical personages was employed by, among others, Vicente Fidel López in *La novia del hereje* (1854) in Argentina. According to Solares-Larrave, this results in counterhistorical discourse, a 'discourse of syncretic nature and parodic fashion', which, following Michelet, draws attention to history as text: 'Once history became the result of an act of writing, its political value and power came to reside in books' (Solares-Larrave 2003: 59). Counterhistorical discourse undermines authorised histories by rewriting 'history from within'; it allows for dissent in that it shows 'the artificiality of the master narrative known as history' (Solares-Larrave 2003: 59). Manso's 1852 novel, which quotes Michelet in epigraphs and was written to countermine the cultural hegemony of Rosas, confirms the historical fact of Unitarian resistance; the 1867 and subsequent editions, written long after Rosas had departed, more radically rewrite the master narrative, deliberately fictionalising or miscasting historical identities, employing misnomers and misaligning facts. This is, in short, misinformation. It is as if by the 1870s Manso is sceptical of all man-made national histories that consistently fail to acknowledge women's political and historical intervention.

Manso rewrites history from a gendered point of view. The argument of *Misterios del Plata* is that Valentín Alsina was saved by his wife, and Adolfo Alsina, distinguished as he might be, owes his life and career to his mother:

> Alsina estava livre! Sua dedicada esposa quebrara seus ferros! Consignando nos annaes immortaes da nossa historia o facto mais estrondoso da coragem de uma esposa e de uma mai! (*Jornal* 4 July: 8)

Although the heroine, Antonia Maza, is still defined in terms of the family, she acts, as we shall see, as an intrepid individual. This is more apparent in the first edition. Although the plots are substantially the same, there are significant storyline variations between the 1852 and later editions, the most important of which have to do with the ending. The details provided in the Brazilian edition strengthen the character of the female protagonist. She is shown planning her husband's escape with the gaucho Miguel, who later meets up with the influential Colonel Rojas, thus providing a crucial link, which is missing in later editions. In a chapter entitled 'La señora Alsina' (*Jornal* 27 June), omitted from later editions, Antonia crosses the city to meet the Italian boatman, Lostardo, who will help with her plan to bribe the American John Anderson, chief guard of the floating ('El Pontón') prison where Alsina is kept. She consults her mother, who fully supports her, asking her not to tell her father.

The dramatic final chapter, 'A fuga', is skillfully written to create maximum suspense, with an unexpected outcome. There is no such suspense in the final chapter of later editions, since the reader is told the outcome at the start, Alsina knows of his wife's plans (in the first edition he is taken by surprise), and the plot is interrupted by numerous digressions on the political circumstances of the times.[23] 'A fuga' opens with the following description of a 'desconhecido' walking through the city at night with a young boy under his cape: 'Un homen de figura delicada, de passo breve ... rebuçado em uma capa militar, se dirige de um bairro afastado da cidade para a margen do rio'. After an hour's walking he meets another dark figure and asks him, in English, for a light. The two embrace and smoke their cigarettes until a third figure arrives and asks them for a light in Italian. The three smokers then take a boat to the prison. When they arrive, the second prison guard, Englishman Mr Dick, receives orders to release the prisoners (Alsina and Colonel Pueyrredón). He carefully observes the 'desconhecido', described for the first time in some detail: 'Era un moço de fórmas delicadas, cujo rostro estava coberto em grande parte por barbas e bigodes pretos e compridos; a pala de seu boné militar cobria-lhe a testa e os olhos', and thinks to himself, 'que voz de maricas tem o tal Capitão'. The young man identifies himself as Captain Manuel Torres, sent by Rosas to take the prisoners to be executed, but of course, as the reader by now suspects, 'o enviado do governador não era outro que a Sra. Alsina!' (*Jornal* July 4: 7–8). Antonia Maza is able to liberate her husband by disguising herself as a soldier, wearing trousers and smoking a cigarette, in other words, by strategically adopting masculine attributes. In the context of militarisation, such gender-switching performance guarantees success to those otherwise identified as women and may be replicated, one infers, on a grander scale. The only gender ambiguity that remains is in the voice, suggesting the limitations of adopting a masculine persona given unalterable physical sexual differences. Mr Dick's reaction indicates a contemporary perception of androgyny as in-between genders, which is usually disparaged but on this occasion it is offset by the military uniform and mandated political authority.

Los misterios del Plata: the woman patriot and the manly political ideal

As mentioned, the title of the 1867 edition of the novel was changed to reflect the protagonism of the central female figure, 'Una mujer heroica', but subsequent editions reverted to *Los misterios del Plata*, an obvious allusion to the widely imitated *Mysteries of Paris* by Eugene Sue (1804–75). Sue's phenomenally successful novel was serialised in 1842–43, three years before Manso started hers. Although, like Sue, Manso wrote a novel of political intrigue, *Los misterios del Plata* only partly focuses on the urban underworld or low life (robbers, assassins, brigands, spies, prisoners) of the great city. In Manso's novel the low life is the pro-Rosas urban mob, their victims, the novel's heroes, the Unitarian middle classes.

The symbol of the nation in *Los misterios del Plata* is not a woman, either semi-naked or dressed, as in revolutionary France (see Landes 2004a) but a man in chains.[24] Avellaneda, persecuted by Rosas and Oribe, sails up the Paraná to escape to Corrientes, a 'país nuevo' (Manso de Noroña 1924: 30), on a ship named *La Constitución,* sailing under the Uruguay flag 'bajo pabellón oriental' (Manso de Noroña 1924: 56), but is unlawfully captured and imprisoned. He is the exemplary citizen, representing free thought and moral conscience stifled by tyranny. This paragon of virtue, the Argentine nation enchained, is rescued by a woman (mother and wife), who cross-dresses to achieve her objective.

The qualities the novel celebrates are the attributes of good masculinity represented by Avellaneda. He, in turn, embodies the law-abiding, non-violent nation (family) in search of a just state. His goodness extends to Christian virtue: in the church ruins while awaiting trial Avellaneda is likened to Jesus Christ: his is a Holy Family (mother, father and child). While Avellaneda symbolises virtue, Rosas represents infamy: a portrait of Rosas placed on the altar in the Cathedral of Buenos Aires, next to the image of Christ on the cross, is a 'sacrílego horrible' (Manso de Noroña 1924: 170). The novel berates the Catholic Church, but not the Jesuits, who resist Rosas. Catholicism is upheld as a legitimate means of instilling morality into the masses; religion should be encouraged until replaced by secular education. Aligned with Christian virtue, Avellaneda is self-controlled when arrested 'se conducía como hombre, sin arrojar un grito o derramar una lágrima' (Manso de Noroña 1924: 164), but he is also compassionate and weeps when he remembers his wife and son. His weapon against tyranny is free thought: '¡contra la que se estrella el despotismo de los hombres! Verdad que se burla de la esclavitud ¡de la tiranía y del odio!... la libertad de la conciencia individual' (Manso de Noroña 1924: 198). For Avellaneda, the rule of law is paramount.[25] This is underscored by his advice, a veritable code of conduct, to his young son, Adolfo. He urges him to fight against oppression, strive for social justice, uphold the principles of fraternity, generosity and solidarity and, above all, to defend the law. He advises him against a career in the judiciary, since he might have to wield the death penalty, and against acting as prosecutor. Adolfo should dedicate himself to the defence of those who have few, if any, rights: slaves and 'menores', 'la más bella colocación posible' (Manso de Noroña 1924: 68, 69).

Other characters who represent good masculinity and the narrator's Unitarian values are the independence veteran, Simón, who provides the legitimate link between 1810 and the modern nation. Like Avellaneda, Simón is characterised by free thought, intelligence and moral conscience; he fought in the Wars of Independence and is a hero of past battles, but the militarised masculinity he once represented belongs to the past. Violence is to be abhorred. As Alberdi wrote in the *Bases* (1852) 'Ha pasado la época de los héroes: entramos hoy en la edad del buen sentido' (Alberdi 1942: 94).[26] It is Simón who makes the striking claim that the Americas were better off under colonial rule, which brought prosperity and order:

> Yo conocí los días de la España, crea que era mejor que hoy. ... Por supuesto, amigo, nosotros es verdad que éramos colonos de la España, pero todo el mundo trabajaba quieto en su casa, no se prendía, no se degollaba a ninguno, el país era rico y todos vivíamos como hermanos. (Manso de Noroña 1924: 85)

Simón confesses that if he had known he was fighting for the benefit of caudillos such as Rosas he would not have joined the patriot cause.

More surprising (given the narrator's Unitarian views, though possibly in favour of the Treaty of San Nicolás) is that Simón's young friend, the gaucho Miguel, also represents good masculinity. Miguel, an orphan abandoned by a 'madre criminal' (Manso de Noroña 1924: 14) is reserved and compassionate. He is brought up in the pampas and knows the language of the pampas Indians. He works for Rosas's Justice of the Peace because he knows no better. He believes, following prevalent thought at the time, that American patriots should identify with the Indians. The novel charts his *crise de conscience* or inner 'revolución' (Manso de Noroña 1924: 79), the long process of learning and consciousness-raising, enabling him to take his place in the polity not as an ignorant gaucho manipulated by force, but as an educated and enlightened freedom fighter. Other good men are the Mazas family: Adelaida's father (wracked with guilt for having obeyed Rosas and signed the death warrant of the innocent Reinafés), her half-brother Ramón, and Colonel Rojas, the father of Ramón's girlfriend, Emisena. None of these characters is virile in appearance (apart from Miguel); many are blond, and all are in touch with their emotions. Colonel Rojas weeps (Manso de Noroña 1924: 150, 156). Ramón Maza is 'un ser superior', 'una de esas figures esencialmente poéticas' (Manso de Noroña 1924: 128), who looks thin and weak but whose limbs are of steel. Ramón's intelligence and noble face and head distinguish him from the gaucho villain, Julián. These representatives of oppressed republican virtue, here predicated on an ideal, progressive masculinity, not necessarily attributed to any particular class, race or sex (although it tends to be associated with white, middle-class men), are marshalled together by a woman to liberate the new nation. Like María in 'La Cautiva', Adelaida is the protagonist and the agent of redemption.

Adelaida's antagonists, headed by Rosas himself, embody retrogressive masculinity, which at the time of the novel's composition was the hegemonic form. Federal masculinity encapsulates the perversion of justice and the law, dishonour, cowardice, stupidity and needless aggression. The 'moral fuerza de la ley' has been replaced by the 'fuerza brutal del acero' (Manso de Noroña 1924: 106). This masculinity is bought into by a range of characters, from the 'tigre' Rosas, Oribe and the Justice of the Peace, 'uno de los más viles esclavos del tirano', to the mob, 'el populacho', 'toda esa masa de hombres ignorantes' (Manso de Noroña 1924: 18, 88). The masses are not overtly feminised, as, for example, in Echeverría's work, though there is an element of class bias, in that they are referred to as 'gentes de la ínfima clase de la socieded, ordinarios y chabacanos' (Manso de Noroña 1924: 137). The May celebration procession is described as headed by a music band, followed by the portrait of Rosas mounted on a throne, on a cart draped in scarlet velvet, pulled by four leading federalist women; [27] Manuela Rosas mounted on the mulatto Biguán; 100 men on horseback; the mulatto slave 'El Gobernador', in the governor's coach; and finally:

> caminaba en desorden, roto, andrajoso y sucio el populacho, la escoria de la sociedad de Buenos Aires. Mujeres, blancas y negras, mulatas y chinas, viejos, muchachos y pampas, todo iba reunido vociferando a la par de la Mazhorca. (Manso de Noroña 1924: 167)

These are the subaltern/dependant 'pueblo', that is, women of all races, old men, children and Indians. The warring men excluded from the crowd, however, are not citizens but criminals. Irrespective of class or race, such men are dehumanised by the narrator as slaves, robots, mummies, puppets and cannibals; Rosas is 'caribe' and Corbalán (his henchman) 'un autómata viviente', 'maniquí de guerra' and 'viviente disecado', who vegetates 'como vegetan tantos insectos y plantas' (Manso de Noroña 1924: 32, 119). They lack humanity, that is, free will and freedom of conscience. They rule not by law but by aggression, hence the analogies drawn with wild animals. Phrenology and physiology are mustered as evidence of regression to animal-like barbarism, to maleness rather than masculinity. Rosas himself is compared to savage beasts and contagion; he is an 'epidemia personificada' (Manso de Noroña 1924: 109). He is shown to exercise power by means of the degradation of the subaltern (those who are considered less than human and irrational, such as women and non-whites) and by attributing effeminacy to the Unitarians (he refers to them as 'cajetillas', or fops), or by treating them as objects ('los unitarios no son hombres, son cosas' (Manso de Noroña 1924: 49, 43)) outside social relations. Although many of the federalist men and women are described by the narrator as brutish, traditionally feminine characteristics may be attributed to them to connote cowardice. Julián, who tries to stab a defenceless child, looks like an ape and is shown foaming at the mouth like a rabid dog, yet his voice has 'un timbre mujeril y falsa' (Manso de Noroña 1924: 113).

In short, the novel inscribes two competing masculinities to represent progress and regression respectively. Such masculinities are not inherent, or dependent on physical build, class or race, or even sexual difference, as we shall see, but are attained by choice. Both incorporate features traditionally considered feminine. What distinguishes them is morality; the good is honourable and law-abiding; the bad is perverse and violent. This partial disengagement of masculinity from sexual and biological difference makes possible a space for the feminine outside the confines of traditional gender categories, a space occupied by 'la valerosa' (Manso de Noroña 1924: 100) Adelaida who, as wife and mother, embodies accepted notions of femininity but at the same time subverts or supplements these with features attributed to masculinity: determination, control, fearlessness, rationality and action. Above all, Adelaida shows that she is an individual with a free will and a free conscience; she is an autonomous, law-abiding person, who takes the initiative to save her husband entirely on her own. Most importantly, she does this despite, indeed because of, her married status. She is not dependent or controlled by her husband; as with 'La Cautiva', his survival depends on her. She is the woman patriot fit for citizenship.

The institution to which Adelaida belongs, which lends her assistance and on whose behalf she acts, is the family. Her associational life consists of family networks and friends. The good family is thus located at the centre of the virtuous republic and is contrasted with the perverse family elsewhere, notably the household of the Rosas. As in *La familia del Comendador,* domestic interiors and private life are emblematic of moral order. The neat interior of the Maza family home is juxtaposed with the sickening scenes in Rosas's house, where Rosas cruelly tyrannises his two black servants. Similarly, another of his henchmen, Salomón, is described as having treated his wife badly and possibly having beaten his former wives to death. The narrator testifies to having witnessed him brutally beating his fifth wife (Manso de Noroña 1924: 135). According to *Los misterios del Plata,* domestic violence, perpetrated by men and women, produces violence throughout society, and vice-versa:

> El mismo desorden que reina en las instituciones reina en la sociedad, y después en el interior de la familia. Rosas es el amo del pueblo, por consigu-

iente es también amo de la familia. La Federación ... reina también en el interior de su casa. (Manso de Noroña 1924: 108)

On the interrelation between militarism in the public sphere and male aggression in the home, Virginia Woolf commented a century later that 'the public and the private worlds are inseparably connected; the tyrannies and servilities of one are the tyrannies and servilities of the other' (Woolf 1984: 266). Rosas's rule is that of the despotic father, predicated on the forceful domination of the subaltern (women, poor and non-white). It represents the antithesis of the republican family, here redeemed by the mother-patriot.[28] Adelaida thus stands in opposition to the effigy of Rosas installed on church altars. Unlike the men, Unitarian and federalist, she has no possibility of networking outside the family. She works virtually alone with the help of an Italian boatman and, significantly, her slave girl, who is individualised and assigned a character, 'la noble esclava' (Manso de Noroña 1924: 204), and name (Marica).

However, as a respectable woman, Adelaida is circumscribed to socially acceptable spheres of activity. She must disguise herself as a man in order to move freely and complete her plan. She dresses as a soldier, donning a moustache and a military uniform, a kepi and a cape, and takes her imprisoned husband into her own custody. This ploy of performing an assumed gender, irrespective of sexual anatomy, in order to maximise agency and act outside prescribed social spheres is a recurrent feature in Manso's novels. In *La familia del Comendador* Ernesto dresses up as an old woman to enter a convent. In *Los misterios del Plata* Manuela Rosas dresses as a gaucho to dominate and cruelly spur not a horse, but her father's jester, 'Iba la amazona vestida con el traje de los gauchos y enormes espuelas teniendo por montura el mulato Biguán enfrenado y ensillado' (Manso de Noroña 1924: 167). Ramón Maza masquerades as an English sailor in order to sail freely out of port. Gendered affects are illusory rather than self-evident. By means of masquerade and performance, social relations are distanced from sexual difference.

It is useful to compare the deconstruction of gender dichotomy in *Los misterios del Plata* with what Doris Sommer sees as a blurring of gender differences, a 'unisex virtue' (Sommer 1991: 95), in José Mármol's novel, *Amalia* (1851; 1855) (set in 1840 Buenos Aires).[29] I would argue that the gender polarisation noted earlier in Echeverría's work (Chapter 4) is replicated in *Amalia,* rather than blurred, but contested in Manso's novels. The plots of both *Amalia* and *Los misterios del Plata* centre on Unitarians fleeing persecution by the federalists. Both chart the violence, fear and injustice of the Rosas regime of the late 1830s and 1840s. Each tells the story of one family persecuted by Rosas, and is based on historical fact. Both novels focus on a couple (Amalia and Eduardo in *Amalia,* and Adelaida and Avellaneda (Antonia and Alsina in the first edition) in *Los misterios del Plata*), although *Amalia* hinges on romance and *Los misterios del Plata* on a mutually supportive marriage.

The roles of the female protagonists in these novels are similar, but different in important ways. Amalia, like Echeverría's Elvira, personifies the quintessential romantic ideal to which the revolutionary male hero aspires. She is a largely passive object of devotion, a symbol of the nation to be rescued by an active, intelligent man.[30] Amalia cares for her loved one, Eduardo, and (in the 1855 edition) marries him shortly before he is killed. She sustains him morally and physically in her home (the warrior's refuge) but otherwise engages in little action outside the private domestic sphere. Although she is not a mother and, as a widow, she is independent, she functions as the domestic goddess, the 'angel del hogar'.[31] By contrast, Adelaida in *Los misterios del Plata* takes on the key role in the action of the novel and saves the family (and by extension Argentina) with her bravery. Not only does she sustain her husband during his captivity (as Amalia helps Eduardo), but she also takes the initiative, hatches a plot to rescue him and brings it to fruition herself. She is never seen inside her home, but shares her husband's misfortunes in the forest, on a boat, or in the church ruins. She acts in the natural and public spheres. She is not a beautiful woman, but a feisty one, who cross-dresses as a soldier, not to kill but to save a life. She embodies the kind of determination, independence and self-sacrifice that are the distinguishing features of republican citizenship; as Harvey Brown argues 'citizens are persons who act publicly as moral agents' (Harvey Brown 1987: 31). Unlike Amalia, who hardly leaves her home, contributing to the anti-Rosas plot as nurse, networker and spy, and has little contact outside the urban elite, Adelaida is aided by gauchos, Italian boatmen and a slave girl.

The gender structure in these two novels also differs in that, unlike *Los misterios del Plata*, *Amalia* is structured primarily on competing masculinities. As in 'El Matadero', the issue is about diverse masculinities vying for hegemony (Unitarian v. federalist, human v. animal) against the backdrop of the idealised or abject feminine other. In *Amalia*, good masculinity is equated with good citizenship, that is, revolutionary action on behalf of the public concern, uprightness and intelligence, as represented by the Unitarian hero, Daniel Bello. Bad masculinity is mindless destruction of the res publica, personal ambition and lack of self-determination: mob mentality controlled by self-seeking power (federalism). There are also competing femininities, but these are projected out of historical time. Good femininity is represented by Amalia, the Romantic domestic ideal; bad femininity by the demonised other, the mob. As in Echeverría's texts, race and class inequalities and competing political agendas are mapped on to these gender dichotomies. In *Amalia*, the women of the Rosas family, the only women with political power, are also demonised, satirised and ridiculed.

Los misterios del Plata also presents competing masculinities (for example, good Miguel versus evil Julián) but these are not mapped on to political stereotypes (both are gauchos). The question is one of morality and free choice. Manso's novel not only deconstructs the gender polarities inscribed in *Amalia* but it also configures the feminine within historical time. The space of action is occupied by men and women, but good masculinity is incapacitated (the hero in chains) and substituted by an ideal feminine, here ascribed to the values of citizenship usually reserved for citizen-soldier men. From the point of view of women's agency and subjectivity, *Los misterios del Plata* has much in common with *La Cautiva*. The difference is that the setting of *La Cautiva* is outside civilisation, in nature, where the conflict is between the human and the natural, the domesticated and the wild. In *Los misterios del Plata* the heroine acts in the public world of political intrigue. She is the female version of *Amalia*'s Daniel Bello and, moreover, she was real.

Gender deconstruction in *La familia del Comendador*, 1854

The first nine chapters of Manso's second novel, another 'verídica historia' (Manso 1854: 167) according to the narrator, were published in the *Album de señoritas* between January 1 and February 17 1854. At that point the journal folded, but the novel was published as a book later that year. In relation to Echeverría, it was shown that hegemonic masculinity is constructed in contradistinction to an idealised or abject feminine (Chapter 4). An alternative is suggested by Manso's novels and becomes clearer if we compare representations of black women in 'El Matadero' with those in *La familia del Comendador*, where slavery works as a cultural metaphor. Black women are represented as sub-human in 'El Matadero'; the feminine signifies the irrational other, indistinguishable from slime. The depiction of the black woman in *La familia del Comendador*, set in contemporary slave-holding Brazil, is entirely different. The narrator addresses her 'lectoras' (Manso 1854: 56) and calls for sorority between white women and their female slaves. When Gabriela hugs her slave, Alina, the narrator observes, 'allí no había esclava ni ama, ni blanca ni negra, había dos mujeres afligidas ...' (Manso 1854: 73).

As in *Los misterios del Plata*, in *La familia del Comendador* women take the leading roles. An elite girl, Gabriela, refuses an arranged marriage and takes shelter in a convent. In so doing, she undermines parental authority and the system of patriarchal control. The villains of the novel, those who uphold patriarchy, are women, indeed mothers: Gabriela's mother, Carolina, and her monstrous grandmother, Doña María das Neves. Dona María's victim is her son, Don Juan, but this injustice is redressed by Gabriela and by Alina, who dies to save her mistress; Alina is whipped to death by her owner, Carolina. *La familia del Comendador* ends, extraordinarily, with an elite white woman (Mariquita) marrying a mulatto man (Mauricio), a 'bastardo hijo de [la] esclava' (Manso 1854: 171).[32] Intelligence and decisiveness are characteristics of both men and women, irrespective of gender, class or race. In *La Cautiva,* woman is regarded as having a visceral attachment to her family, on whose behalf she is capable of great sacrifice. This is also the case in *Los misterios del Plata*, but not in *La familia del Comendador* where the unmarried heroines aspire to self-fulfilment and where mothers are depicted as monstrous tyrants.

La familia del Comendador is an anti-slavery novel. Pro-slavery sophistry is ridiculed by an ironic narrator mimicking elitist discourse:

> probaban [las palabras de D. María] con evidencia que las víctimas no son

> los negros, arrancados de su país, a sus afecciones y a su libertad, cargados de cadenas, amontonados a la fuerza en buques noseabundos (sic) y después vendidos como cualquier objeto de mercancía o como animales a señores que los compran para vivir del sudor de su esclavo, como se compra un buey para arar, un caballo para montarlo etc., etc. Pero los insolentes negros, no se someten a la superioridad de los blancos sino a fuerza de castigos horribles, y ahí está el busilis y la lidia del blanco en enseñar al negro ciertos puntos del derecho natural que solo se explican a garrotazos; por consecuencia las víctimas son los blancos que oprimen y verdugos son los oprimidos – es una lógica asaz sencilla! (Manso 1854: 39)

This is also the story of three love matches represented not as sentimental romance, which was prevalent in European literature at the time, but as successful modern partnerships based on mutual respect and emotional restraint. It is a deeply moral novel, the most striking feature of which is its repositioning of the mother as the symbol of colonial decadence and oppression, the monstrous mother noted in Bolívar's writings forty years previously. Manso does not argue for the inclusion of women into the new civil and political order exclusively in their capacity as mothers, but rather as autonomous individuals. She challenges any notion of a redeeming, natural, maternal instinct; the symbolic place of women as the mothers of sons, especially soldier sons, as in revolutionary and republican France, is invalidated (Landes 2004a). The matriarchal grandmother, Doña María das Neves, rules her household with an iron rod, abusing her slaves and subjecting her son, Don Juan, to horrific punishment. She is a caricature of oppression, whose domain is the family and the home. Carolina, her daughter-in-law, perpetuates the system. The domestic interior is shown not to be a place of repose and refuge but a house of horrors. As we saw earlier, this extrapolation of the tyranny of the home into the public sphere is a theme developed in *Los misterios del Plata*. It is in the private space of the domestic interior that the true nature of people is revealed: 'el regimen interior de una casa es el medio infalible a llegar al conocimiento moral de los individuos, porque el hombre imprime su carácter a todos los objetos que lo rodean' (Manso 1854: 57). The domestic interior is more revelatory than physiognomy; conduct and custom is more truthful than appearance. The contrasting de Souza household, unlike that of Doña Maria, is a sign of individual virtue: 'el aseo, el orden, la tranquilidad de aquella casa eran el símbolo de la pureza y de la serenidad del alma de sus moradores' (Manso 1854: 61).

In *La familia del Comendador*, the tyrant is not the patriarch but the (grand) mother who exercises absolute patriarchal power.[33] Motivated by the accumulation and retention of family wealth, Doña María, born in the 1790s, a 'masa de carne sin corazón' (Manso 1854: 26), metonymically embodies the social order of the colonial elite, the perpetuation of the colonial slave-holding economy by means of endogamy.[34] Her grandchildren, born in the 1820s and 1830s, the years of Spanish American independence, symbolise future modernity. Her attempt to impose an arranged marriage on her granddaughter

Gabriela constitutes the drama of the novel. By refusing to obey, Gabriela causes a revolution in the family, with far-reaching social consequences. But the feminine is not idealised in this novel as either romantic or republican. Gabriela, unlike Echeverría's Elvira, does not embody ethereal beauty, the object of men's aspiration, but neither is she a strong 'La Cautiva' or Adelaida. She is a passive heroine, rescued from a convent by the man who loves her. Similarly, masculinity is not portrayed as oppressive. All the male characters are good; at worst they are lazy and ineffective. Only the mother is demonised and, once dead, is replaced by the 'masculine maternalism' (Sluga 2004: 248) of a loving father. On his discovery of his father's identity (Don Juan), Mauricio's interpellation of his father (not his mother) – the very use of the word 'Padre' – brings Don Juan back to his senses: 'Y era nombre tan dulce que despierta en el pecho humano cuanto de noble y bueno puede haber, *esa palabra primer sonido que balbuceamos en la cuna*' (Manso 1854: 95, my emphasis).

The target of criticism in the novel is the colonial order: the plantation economy (racism and human rights abuse) and the Catholic Church (fanaticism and corruption), the old regime perpetuated by families such as that of the Comendador. Colonialism is associated with barbarism, prejudice, and violence. The narrator's scathing satire targets the 'maquiavelismo monacal' (Manso 1854: 152) of the Catholic Church, rather than the Catholic religion. Father Antonio, a Carmelite missionary and 'apostol evangélico' (Manso 1854: 124) is affectionate and honourable. It is he who prompts Doña María to confess her sins and rewrite her will. Don Juan and later Mauricio take comfort from the Gospels, 'ese tesoro de eternal sabiduría, de virtud, de abnegación' (Manso 1854: 99). But when the nuns tell Gabriela that crying is a mortal sin, the narrator ripostes 'y otra porción de sofismas con que la Iglesia Católica pretende hacer los hombre a su antojo' (Manso 1854: 109).

Ranged against this is the new order of the younger generation of men and women who, irrespective of sexual difference, collectively embody freedom of conscience, virtue and disinterested love. The strongest representatives of this new order are the two male characters, the elite Ernesto de Souza and the mulatto Mauricio, each personifying the new masculinities most appropriate to a recently independent Brazil. Through each it is possible to trace the relational complexities of gender, though as suggested, in this novel gender differences are less determining, more fluid, than differences of race and class. Both men embody moral uprightness, generosity and the free will of autonomous individuals to choose according to their conscience. Their determination to attain justice through the rule of law for the good of themselves and others is the mark of modernity. Both have been well educated in Europe. Ernesto's bookcase contains works of history, travel and philosophy. Ernesto and Mauricio restore order and marry the girls of their choice, irrespective of differences of race or class. The father of Ernesto de Souza is a retired Portuguese naval officer of noble lineage and the happy ending is largely due to his energy and good will. Throughout the novel, Portugal is portrayed sympathetically and associated with education and scientific exploration and an illustrious past, suggesting that the issue here is not colonialism as such, but, as the novel's title indicates, the perpetuation of the social relations of the colonial regime in Brazil. Ernesto's marriage to Gabriela endows the materialist decadence of the Brazilian family with the moral and spiritual values of an older, though modernised, European civilisation.

More interesting is the radical role played by Mauricio. Mauricio, a doctor, is the son of the demented Don Juan and his slave, the mulatta Camila, the educated daughter of a 'mulata' and a 'blanco' (Manso 1854: 22). As expected in novels about slavery, his physiognomy is described in minute detail.[35] It is difficult to classify him as a mulatto, states the narrator, 'porque ninguna de sus facciones lo traicionaba': his lips are red and thin, not purple; his hair is fine and 'no tenía ni bozo en la cara'; 'era moreno pero había como un reflejo de bronce dorado en su cutis fina y aterciopelada'. The only mark of African ancestry is a dark circle around his nails, 'un filete indeleble de la raza africana' (Manso 1854: 98), yet his hands have a doctor's healing powers. To ensure that Mauricio will not inherit the family wealth, Doña María registers him as a slave at birth and sends him to Paris to train as a doctor because she needs one (free of charge) on the plantation. Mauricio's status as illegitimate, non-white slave is entirely at odds with his modern status as a French-trained medical professional. He might prosper as a doctor, but 'hasta la raza blanca no podía levantar los ojos! Al fin, ¡era mulato!' (Manso 1854: 98). He represents the incommensurable contradictions posed by slavery in the modern liberal world of individual human rights, the disjunction between tradition and modernity. His anomalous situation is resolved by a radical break with the established order signified by Gabriela's revolutionary refusal to obey her grandmother. The old order collapses as a consequence of the young woman's rebellion. Like Gabriela, Mauricio demonstrates his capacity to emancipate himself by his independence of mind and rational decision. He takes the initiative:

> había llegado el día en que les hablaría de igual a igual, no como esclavo sino como hombre, cuyos derechos no son ilusiones, sino verdades, que aunque desconocidos y atropellados, son siempre argumentos irresistibles del lenguaje de la razón y de la conciencia. (Manso 1854: 99)

The novel ends with Mauricio's imminent marriage to his elite cousin Mariquita, Gabriela's sister and Doña María's granddaughter, although the marriage cannot take place in Brazil and the couple are seen sailing away on a British steamship to Southampton. This was a radical move on the part of Manso. Not only does the mulatto son of a slave marry the daughter of one of the most prestigious families of Brazil but he also sells the plantation he has inherited, frees the slaves, converts his capital to cash and transfers his wealth to Europe. The nation cannot hope to prosper until the social relations of race, class and gender are reconfigured to ensure social justice and equality. The greatest reform needed is the abolition of slavery and the racism and human rights abuse it entails. In the novel, this is brought about in one family, a microcosm of Brazilian society, by the determination of one girl to end the perpetuation of the endogamic transfer of wealth by refusing to obey the law-of-the-father as exercised by the matriarch, on the one hand, and the Catholic Church on the other; in short, to seek her own personal self-fulfilment as a rational individual. The love choice of a young woman, an otherwise private, domestic affair, has wide-reaching social and economic consequences in the public sphere. While women may actively participate in the nation-building project, their passive resistance to injustice is shown to be equally effective.

All the characters live happily ever after, except for two. One is Don Juan, who dies prematurely but not before recovering his sanity in time to marry Camila and ensure his children's legitimacy. Like his son, Mauricio, Don Juan represents modernity. He was educated in Europe and had hoped to marry Emily Smith, the daughter of an English vicar (who also displays commendable masculinity: duty, reason and affection). He is attracted to Protestantism; he and Emily read the Gospels together and they swap Bibles when he is called back to Brazil. He deplores slavery, 'un abuso cruel y feroz' (Manso 1854: 18). He explains to his mother that he will settle in England and establish business contacts there to increase the family's fortune, but she opposes him resolutely. When he refuses to obey (he is a minor until the age of 25) she has him whipped. He is a victim of the slave system he wished to abolish, yet his anomalous situation in the family and his attachment to Camila enables his children, the second generation, to put into practice his planned reforms. The other victim is Alina, the slave, who is whipped under the instructions of Carolina. The narrator contrasts Alina's suffering and Carolina's callousness: 'a los gemidos de angustia, a los ayes del dolor, respondía [Carolina] con risa de triunfo y con irónicos motejos' (Manso 1854: 90). Alina is left to die naked, tied up and forgotten, but she does not reveal the whereabouts of her mistress; she is the scapegoat of Carolina's fury. That she is killed and Don Juan made insane by violent mothers highlights the abuse perpetrated in the home, irrespective of gender. What matters is not the gender of oppressor or oppressed, but their positions in relations of power, which are conditioned by their class and caste. Class, race and gender are seen to be intricately connected, to the extent that an alteration in the order of one may ricochet and change another.

Gender is deconstructed so that there is no a priori equivalence of sexual difference and social relations or cultural attributes: men may be inscribed as feminine, women as masculine. The Comendador (Don Juan's brother) is perfumed and frivolous with a 'fisonomía infantil' and is dominated by his overbearing mother and wife, 'nunca supo lo que era una voluntad propia' (Manso 1854: 7, 8). The 'ronca y volumosa' voice of his wife, on the other hand, and her strong will, mark her as unfeminine: 'antes que afeminación bastaba verla una vez para comprender la fuerza de su voluntad'. She treats the slave women, the 'canalla de negras' (Manso 1854: 8, 9) brutally. Imperiousness, a sign of masculinity, may be attributed to men and women alike. Men are not generally portrayed as violent but rather as victims, well-intentioned or apathetic. The priest who attempts to imprison Gabriela in the convent is perverse but his 'faldas' (Manso 1854: 118) detract from his masculinity. Good men such as Mauricio and Ernesto have the physical marks of traditional femininity (slight build, smooth skin, elegant, refined); Ernesto's skin is 'arrazada [sic] como la de una mujer'; his room is as tidy 'como la de una virgen' (Manso 1854: 56, 60), and he weeps when he sees Mauricio at his dead father's bedside. Traditional masculine features (heavy build, beard) are attributed to powerful women. Pedro likens Doña María to 'un tigre viejo' (Manso 1854: 38) with resonances of Rosas.

Unlike Mármol's *Amalia*, *La familia del Comendador* includes few descriptions of dress and outward appearance. Manso is not interested in writing fashion pages to attract her female readers. This is taken to the extreme of dressing in drag (or cross-dressing, as noted in *Los misterios del Plata*). In a curious reversal of the archetypal procuress, Ernesto, a mock Celestina, dresses up as an elderly female vendor to liberate Gabriela from the convent. He shaves his face, dons a wig, paints his eyebrows white and wears full peasant dress. The feminine, which is not predicated on (indeed, is positioned contrary to) motherhood, is inscribed positively. The conduct of feminine women and feminine men is endorsed. Commendable masculinity signifies self-determination, virtuous action and resolution to bring about justice for all. Bad masculinity is indifference to the collective good. Commendable femininity ranges from the exercising of free will and moral choice to passive resistance against oppression. Bad femininity is the assumption and abuse of patriarchal power and authority. The moral ideal is rational negotiation, the meeting of minds and freedom of conscience. The oppressed emancipate themselves and make their choices over and above the gender roles to which they have been assigned. In this respect, Manso's novel again points to gender as performance producing the illusory affects of essential sexual differences.

The family arrangement Doña María defends, a head of family (widow) exercising power over subordinates (that is, a mother wielding patriarchal authority) is shown to be anomalous and monstrous. Other families in the novel, headed by reasonable, liberal men (Don Egas and Alejandro) do not act in this way. By establishing legitimate ties with Portugal (Gabriela) and Brazil's mulatto population (Mariquita), the girls of the Comendador's family shape the new nation to incorporate these diverse cultures and identities. The young generation makes its own decisions. However, though Manso bravely creates a social space for the mulatto in her novel (vis-à-vis Mauricio and Camila), there is none for the black population: Alina, the black slave, is erased from the story. It is also significant that Mauricio and his wife, though wealthy, have to leave Brazil to marry in Europe. Brazil, stymied by racism, has yet to reach European standards of civilisation. Yet Mauricio's actions, selling the plantation, freeing the slaves and marrying a white woman who loves him, spell the end of the colonial regime. Family politics is as important as the politics of the state for ending social injustice and achieving modernity. When Mariquita declares that she will marry of her own choice, Pedro, who believes that 'en nuestra familia el género femenino es el más fuerte', exclaims jovially 'viva la libertad, viva la constitución!' (Manso 1854: 32). These young women will be the mothers of the future, mothers who integrate political values (civic virtue) into their domestic life (private female virtue). According to Kerber, this was the case in the United

States, where Republican women 'began to invent an ideology of citizenship that merged the domestic domain of the pre-industrial woman with the new public ideology of individual responsibility and civic virtue' (Kerber 1980: 269). The novel argues that it is equally possible in constitutional Brazil.

In 1877, twenty years after the publication of *La familia del Comendador* and two years after Manso's death, Cora Olivia recognised the political significance of the novel in her review in *La Ondina del Plata* (No. 27, July 8):

> El interés económico de la nación y las leyes fundamentales del Imperio, opusieron su valla al espíritu democrático que infundió la tendencia liberatriz de la señora Manso, inspiradas en las doctrinas humanitarias de sus congéneres. No obstante, una modificación trascendental fijada en leyes abolicionistas preludia para tiempos no remotos la manumisión de los esclavos del Brasil. ... *La familia del Comendador* pasó por nuestro público como *La Choza de Tom*, saboreadas ambas por los inteligentes, y desconocidos del mayor número de lectores que por falta de discernimiento y buen gusto sólo se apasionan de novelas detestables y corruptoras. (quoted in Lewkowicz 2000: 253–54) [36]

La familia del Comendador argues for abolition and the reform of the family and the Church, the two foundational institutions of Latin American society erected on gender inequalities. The challenge to patriarchal power undermines the foundations of all institutionalised injustice. What matters is the free will and agency of individual human beings. Manso's is a liberal and a Christian humanist view.

Unlike Acevedo, Marín, Cunha and Barandas, during her lifetime Juana Manso did not command social respect in her homeland. She was recognised as an educationalist in later life, but her outspoken views contesting gender and religious *doxa* gained her few friends. She was publicly derided in Argentina (though strangely, given her abolitionist views, not in Brazil) and her literary work was largely dismissed as irrelevant. Although she attempted to build up social capital with Argentine political contacts in later life (Sarmiento, the Alsinas, the Avellanedas), the damage had been done. Manso's mistake was not only to advocate women's rights but, at the same time, to criticise the Catholic Church which, for many women, provided their only outlet for social activity.[37] She placed herself outside the boundaries of social Catholicism, beyond the pale. She was well aware of the risks, but took them nonetheless.

Notes

1 Sarmiento was President of the Argentine Republic 1868–74.

2 In particular: in the United States, The Declaration of Virginia, 1776; The US Declaration of Independence, 1776; the US Constitution of 1787; in France, The Declaration of the Rights of Man and Citizen, 1789; The French Constitution of 1789; and the Spanish Constitution of 1812.

3 The *Bases* were published in Valparaíso (Chile) and Buenos Aires in 1852. A second edition appeared in Buenos Aires (July 1852) and Valparaíso (September 1852), after

the publication of *Los misterios del Plata*. A third edition came out in Besançon, France, in 1856 and the definitive in 1858 (in Besançon).

4 Lola Montes was the pseudonym of María Dolores Elisa Rosana Gilbert, a Scottish dancer who became the mistress of Louis I of Bavaria.

5 Manso's residence is as follows: 1819–40 Buenos Aires; 1840–43 Montevideo; 1843 Río de Janeiro, Montevideo, Rio de Janeiro; 1844–46 Philadelphia; 1846–48 Havana; 1848–52 Río de Janeiro; 1853–54 Buenos Aires; 1854–59 Rio de Janeiro; 1859–75 Buenos Aires.

6 Brazil was nominally independent from Portugal from 1831 but was ruled by the King of Portugal's son, Dom Pedro, who took the title of Emperor Pedro II from 1840 until 1889 when, after the abolition of slavery (1888), he was ousted by the military and the Republic was declared (1889). See Chapter 1.

7 The 'altar' refers to her marriage, and the 'tumbas' to the deaths of her father and first-born child.

8 The *Journal des Dames* (1759–78) was the first French women's monthly to last for some time (Hufton 1997: 455).

9 Previous women's journals published by women in Buenos Aires were: *La Aljaba* (1830–31), written by Montevidean Petrona Rosende de Sierra; *La Camelia* (April–June 1852), on which Manso collaborated, and *La Educación* (June–September 1852), written by Rosa Guerra. None lasted more than a few months. After Manso's *Album* there were no further women's journals until *La Flor del Aire* (1864), on which Manso collaborated with Eduarda Mansilla. See Auza 1988. *La Moda*, 'gacetita semanaria de música, de poesía, de literatura, de costumbres, de modas' dedicated to the 'bello mundo federal', was set up by Alberdi in 1837 and edited by Rafael Jorge Corvalán, the son of Rosas's henchman, for the propagation of liberal ideas. Its apparent frivolity (associated with women) was a mere cover for a progressive political-cultural agenda (Weinberg 1977: 98–99).

10 It consisted of a 'Redacción' (1) [in lieu of a Prospectus]; 'Último día del año nuevo' (2); the essay 'Emancipación moral de la mujer' (2–4); 'Viajes del Conde de Castelneau por el interior de América', an account by the French ambassador in Bahia, presumably translated by Manso (4–5); 'Correspondencia. Modas', written by 'Anarda', the sole contributor (5); 'La familia del Comendador', the first instalment cf Manso's novel (6–7); 'Crónica Semanal' (7–8); the poem 'Una flor sobre la tumba de mi compatriota la Sra Da. María Alvarez de la Pena', dated Río de Janeiro 1850 (8), and 'Anécdotas' (9). For an in-depth study of the journal see Area 2005.

11 This was the view of Montesquieu, Condorcet and Feijóo.

12 Manso was extremely critical of the Church and the government's policy towards the Indians. In 'Las Misiones' (January 29 1854) she writes of the Indians: 'Esta patria es de ellos como nuestra. La conquista los esclavizó, los arrojó de sus lares, los despedazó, y nosotros ... no hemos hecho más que continuar la obra'. See Area 1997, 2005.

13 The only item in the first issue not written or translated by Manso is the article on fashion (December 28 1853) by 'la señorita' 'Anarda', who demands that her anonymity be strictly preserved (as was standard practice across the Americas and elsewhere, see Kelley 1984: 111–37). 'Anarda' wittily laments her incapacity to write about matters of importance, such as freedom of the press, and must restrict herself to the subject of fashion. If she were more competent she might have written about the Crimean War (1854–56), the English expedition, the Russian campaigns, the Argelian war, or Luis Napoleon and Eugenia Montijo, demonstrating her familiarity with current events, but 'qué me importa a mi todo eso?', '¡Qué pena!'. The

substance of her article is the absurdity of Argentine women's penchant for the latest tastes in Paris fashion, so that they wear woollen dresses and velvet capes in sunny December, and when 'algún importuno' shows some surprise, they must reply 'caballero, es la última moda de París'. Evidently these ideas were not well received in fashion-conscious Buenos Aires. See Area 2005: 21–27.

14 Sarmiento wrote in 1853, 'Un libro debe saber a algo y ser el hijo y la imagen de su padre' (Sarmiento 1961: 24).

15 *La Camelia* (1852) (whose motto was '¡libertad!, no licencia; ¡igualdad entre los sexos!'), was a journal for women founded in Buenos Aires by anonymous 'redactoras', probably Rosa Guerra. It ran to 31 issues and among its articles were translations of Rousseau. *La Camelia* ceased publication when the presses were closed down during Urquiza's drafting of the Treaty of San Nicolás. A boom in the Buenos Aires periodical press followed the fall of Rosas (February 1852), with some thirty new periodical publications appearing that year (Auza 1988: 163). After the closure of *La Camelia*, Guerra set up *La Educación* (July–September 1852) to educate the 'bello sexo argentino'. Only six issues were published, despite assistance from Alsina, Mitre and others (Auza 1988: 91).

16 Less radical Unitarians such as Juan María Gutiérrez and the historical novelist Vicente Fidel López accepted the treaty.

17 Liliana Patricia Zuccotti (1995) notes the anachronism of this anti-Rosas novel published fifteen years after the downfall of Rosas, which might explain the title change and the novel's lack of success.

18 *Los misterios del Plata. Novela histórica original escrita en 1846 por Juana P. Manso de Noroña.* Buenos Aires: Imprenta los Mellizos, 1899. At the foot of the title page is the name N. Tommasi. I thank Iona MacIntyre for consulting this edition.

19 To recap: the editions are as follows: 1st 1852; 2nd 1867–68; 3rd 1899; 4th 1924; 5th 1933. A 1936 edition is on the Cervantes Virtual web page. An annotated edition (2005) is available from stockcero.com. None of these are rigorous scholarly editions.

20 There are also notes 'del recopilador' (1) and 'El corrector' (2).

21 The note refers to the fall of Rosas (which occurred as the Brazilian edition of the novel appeared in instalments). Yet 'La Autora' adds, 'como se publicase antes de la caída de Rosas, se hizo uso del seudónimo de Avellaneda para perpetuar el mártir de Tucumán', which is not true; in the 1852 edition he is named Alsina.

22 Marco[s] María Avellaneda organised the provinces to fight against Rosas but was defeated and executed in 1841, and his head was displayed in Tucumán. This is the subject of Echeverría's stirring poem 'Avellaneda'.

23 Other differences are the names of Lostardo's boats: the *Francesa di Rimini* and *Gioven Italia* (1852), and the *Constitución* (1867/1899/1924). A note inserted in the 1924 edition, two-thirds through the penultimate chapter 'El Pontón', states that an 'Editor' completed the novel from this point on: that is, finished the penultimate chapter and added a final chapter, 'La Fuga', and a 'Conclusión'; the editor followed the indications of 'una persona conocedora de nuestra historia nacional' to ensure the historical veracity of the account (1924: 199). The 'Editor' apparently did not consult the Brazilian edition, which was complete.

24 The critical reading that follows is based on the expanded edition of 1924.

25 In 1834, Valentín Alsina was Profesor of 'derecho natural y de gentes' in the University of Buenos Aires and gave night classes to working men. There was much protest when he was forced to resign under Rosas (Weinberg 1977: 11–12).

26 He added, 'Reducir en dos horas una gran masa de hombres a su octava parte por la acción del canon: he aquí el heroísmo antiguo y pasado. Por el contrario, multi-

plicar en pocos días una población pequeña, es el heroísmo del estadista moderno: la grandeza de creación en lugar de la grandeza del exterminio' (Alberdi 1942: 95).

27 Pascuala Belaústegui de Arana, María Josefa Ezcurra, la señora de General Alvear and doña Pilar de Guido (Manso de Noroña 1924: 168).

28 This may be compared with the tragic consequences of the disorder sown in Colonel Rojas's house (according to the narrator) by his adulterous wife, 'el peor de todos los errores e infortunios de una mujer: la infidelidad a su marido y la guerra doméstica' (Manso de Noroña 1924: 153). This is a true case. As a note explains, Rojas's wife was found dead and he was accused of her murder, but later he was pardoned thanks to Valentín Alsina's brilliant defence.

29 *Amalia* was published in *La Semana* (Montevideo) in 1851, months before Rosas's defeat in 1852 and, like *Los misterios del Plata* is a novel about ongoing events of the time. After Rosas was removed it was considered an obstacle to reconciliation and was not published in a complete version, as a book, until 1855 (Zuccotti 2004: 113).

30 According to Beatriz Curia (1989: 20–21), Mármol altered the first, incomplete edition of the novel (1851) to further idealise Amalia as the exemplary Unitarian woman. In the 1855 edition, her husband had died two years earlier (rather than one year, as in the 1851 edition) – the longer her mourning period the greater her honour – and the paragraph in which she is described in 1851 as 'ángel de tentación que se llama mujer' was omitted.

31 See Pierini (2002) for a structural comparison of the novels of Manso and Mármol.

32 All references are to *La familia del Comendador* (Buenos Aires: Librería la Victoria, 1854). A first edition is held in the British Library.

33 Large estates ruled by strong, politically powerful women were by no means anomalous. In late colonial Brazil (Bahia), Maria Joaquina Pereira de Andrade was the largest single slave owner in the region, with four sugar mills and 600 slaves (Schwartz 1997: 112). Chasteen (1997: 27–35) recounts the life of Maria Antônia Muniz who, with thirteen children, indirectly managed the family estate on the Uruguay frontier after her husband's death during the Farroupilha Revolt; in her account of the life of Carlota Lucia de Brito, who ordered the assassination of a conservative enemy in northeast Brazil, Meznar explains that 'patron-client networks protected women and allowed them to act independently' (Meznar 1997: 41).

34 The inheritance laws are explained in detail (Manso 1854: 42). Juan is insane and his wealth is administered by his mother. When he dies, it is passed to her. When she dies, the administration of Juan's share is passed to her other son, Gabriel. However, if Gabriel's daughter, Gabriela, marries her uncle Juan, Gabriel (as the wife's father, in view of the husband's insanity) will also be in full control of Juan's fortune and this cannot be passed on to Juan's (illegitimate, mixed-race) children, Emilia and Mauricio, whose mother is the slave Camila.

35 Compare with a similar description of the mulatto slave Sab in Cuban Gertrudis Gómez de Avellaneda's novel, *Sab* (Madrid 1841) (Gómez de Avellaneda 2001: 40).

36 Manso had collaborated on *La Ondina* (which ran from February 1876 until December 1879), as did Juana Manuela Gorriti. See Auza 1988: 235. Harriet Beecher Stowe's *Uncle Tom's Cabin* was published in 1852. Slavery was not abolished in Brazil until 1888, though the slave trade was meant to end in 1851.

37 As in post-Revolutionary France, where, after 1808 civil authorities encouraged women's activities in the Church, especially new women's orders (Hufton 1992: 143–53; Maza Valenzuela 1998).

CHAPTER ELEVEN

Conclusions: South America, Gender, Politics, Text

The nations who succeed are not the feminine nations, but the masculine.

H. Fielding Hall[1]

La domination masculine est assez assurée pour ce passer de justification.

Bourdieu 1990: 5

During and after independence, political rights continued to be denied to over half the population of Latin America on the basis of sexual difference, a predominant criterion for exclusion after the abolition of slavery and the ending of legal discrimination against indigenous and mixed-race groups. Gender polarity and power asymmetry persisted. Nevertheless, gender parameters shifted notably in the first half of the nineteenth century. In the dominant culture of the late colonial period, the feminine was perceived as a powerful threat to the rational order and authority of the paterfamilias and the colonial state; conversely, threats to the established order (inflation, poor administration, obstacles to progress) were often represented as feminine or effeminate. Derision of the effeminate man (dandy or *petimetre)* was symptomatic of this disquiet; the danger was that masculinity might be feminised (feminine attributes applied to those sexually differentiated as men) and dominant masculinity displaced. Similarly, ridicule of the virago or manly woman indicated fear of feminine encroachment and gender fluidity. As society became increasingly militarised during the 1810s and 1820s, dominant masculinity, more firmly associated with virility, courage and physical strength, recovered ground to the extent that it threatened to engulf the feminine; the manly woman was no longer ridiculed to the same extent, but rather encouraged for the collective good. Virility was not assumed to be a natural, feminine attribute, but a higher value that women might buy into in anomalous circumstances. The term 'viril' (from Latin *vir* or 'man') naturalised the identification of strength and courage with hegemonic masculinity; exceptional women might aspire to these heights. This positive representation of the feisty, combative woman signalled a major shift in gender *doxa* and was reinforced by analogies with the Spanish American tradition of the warrior women, the Amazons, which were usefully mobilised for the patriot cause. Masculinisation of the feminine persisted in literary discourse at least until the 1850s, as is evidenced in Echeverría's 'La Cautiva' (1837) and Manso's soldier-heroine, Antonia Maza (1852).

But as the independence wars came to an end and the new political orders took shape, the interrelation of gender and sexual difference shifted again. Violence and aggression were censured in men and women alike. New political frameworks needed to be erected and social and cultural institutions consolidated. Dominant masculinity came to be identified with the public world of political reconstruction and the feminine with what remained outside; in classical republicanism, the 'rhetorically invoked negative other who defined and centred the male republican subject' (Smith-Rosenberg 2000: 275). Both men and women might subscribe to liberal and republican citizenship, but in separately engendered spheres: the men in public governance (politics), the women as reproducers and as managers (though not the ultimate authority) of private life (the domestic economy). Good masculinity entailed public virtue; good femininity, private morality.

From the 1830s on, generic woman was increasingly identified as mother or prospective mother of the patria, and the feminine with family values, order and nurturance. Women could play their part in building new societies from within the family, the pillar of the state; they are defined in relation to men, not as free-standing individuals. For this reason, all the textual representations studied here of actual women in real time (that is, not as trope or in myth) locate women firmly within the family as wives, mothers and sisters. As we have seen, the social networks in which women are protagonists are family relations. This family might extend to family friends and distant relations, to the family of the Church, with its associated functions promoting child-raising and care (education, charity), to the families of patrons and benefactors (such as the aristocratic elite) and, above all, to the patria family. Patriotism, allegiance to one's patrimony, is closely allied to family bonds and loyalties. Natural patriotism, as defined by John Schaar, signifies:

> territoriality, along with the family, has always been a primary associative bond. We become devoted to the people, places and ways that nurture us, and what is familiar and nurturing seems also natural and right. (Schaar 1981: 287)[2]

San Martín recognised this when he commended women for their courage; they acted not as virile women but as feminine women, that is, as women whose sexual difference (mothering potential) was instrumental in creating and strengthening the affective family bonds necessary for social cohesion. Republican motherhood symbolised social order and stability. Men, on the other hand, played their parts in the new societies as individuals, irrespective of family ties. They might act according to their conscience and in their own interests whether or not they were fathers and husbands. Few women dared to act in this way. Manso attempted to intervene culturally, socially and politically as an individual (though assisted by her two daughters) by cultivating a network of potentially powerful friends. Ultimately, she was unsuccessful, except in the socially acceptable field of education, and largely due to Sarmiento's support.

Nevertheless, the social role mapped out for women in the bourgeois polity and civil society gave women prestige and they commanded respect. In certain political circumstances, notably civil conflict, the family domain might extend to political groups or parties that were largely organised according to local ties and family loyalties. Women could be incorporated into regional power struggles as the authorised voice, scribe or memory of that political/patriotic community (for example, those who supported Portales, Santander, or the Legalistas, or opposed Rosas). In this respect, women's cultural intervention was political, legitimated by their status as family members. The space allotted to them, the family institution (like the Church) was not considered public or political. Post-independence educated men, meanwhile, had better things to do. Thoroughly immersed in politics, legislation, the economy and public culture as never before, the creole elite shaped their new nation states to suit themselves. Any suggestion that women might actively contribute to in the public world of politics was met with incredulity, resistance and even vilification. The solidification of the fledgling republics into bourgeois nation states ossified this gender order. However, secularisation and state appropriation of the Church's social responsibilities, especially in education and welfare, enabled women to enter the state machinery in their capacity as carers and educators (as, for example, in the River Plate region, from Mariquita Sánchez de Thompson to Manso and beyond).

Caudillos and mother-queens

In Spanish America, in attempting to symbolise a new political entity – a postcolonial continent of emerging republican nation states – the creole imaginary shows a predilection bordering on obsession with the restitution of the father figure or patriarch as symbol of authority and continental liberation (Earle 2002a). The space was partially filled by the ubiquitous figure of the military-uniformed soldier-statesman, famously celebrated in iconography and literature, and individually named.[3] As Hernán Vidal points out in his study of the 'mitificación del padre' in José Joaquín Olmedo's canonical ode 'La Victoria de Junín. Canto a Bolívar' (1825), 'el padre de la familia americana, surgido de la burocracia tecnocrática, se transforma en padre militar' (Vidal 2004: 220). Post-independence Spanish America became 'the primeval home of the *golpe* and the caudillo' (Lynch 1986: 353), the military leader wielding maximum power. The caudillo, entirely a product of the Wars of Independence (Lynch 1986: 353), stood for dominant masculinity, force and, at times, the restoration of civil and political society. Yet, as in France, feminine images also filled the symbolic space once occupied by the absolutist king to signify liberty, the republic and so on (Wenke 2000: 69). These were female personifications, not actual women in real time. In the writings of the Spanish American *letrados* studied here, the feminine, including the mother-trope, is historically and politically incapacitated: idealised perhaps, as in Bello's young America, wife of the sun, but also demonised, as in Bolívar's monster-mother (Spain) and the pueblo-slime of 'El Matadero'.

In other countries, however, the mother-nation, symbol of the point of origin and social cohesion, was figured by a flesh and blood woman and put to good political use. Examples are Victorian Britain and also Isabeline Spain, which, though devastated by war, was relatively unaffected by republicanism. Post-Empire Spain identified not with patriarchal absolutism (Fernando) but with liberal constitutionalism. The liberal order was gendered female, not primarily in allegory and myth, but in the real figure of a mother upholding the rule of law with historical precedent and full political authority: the Queen Mother, María Cristina, who granted amnesty to the liberal political exiles even as Fernando (her husband and uncle) lay in his deathbed, and who, after his death, governed Spain for almost a decade (1833–40). The accession of her daughter, Isabel II, to the throne in 1843 further confirmed the maternal line as symbolic of progress and modernity. Isabel II was titled, like her illustrious forebear, the Catholic Queen, suggesting both imperial closure and continuity. The supreme ruler was 'Reina de las Españas',[4] and her accession was a deliberate political choice involving the revocation of the Salic Law forbidding women to inherit the crown.[5] Mother and daughter were kept on the throne by the liberal army, opposed by absolutists who supported Carlos, Fernando's brother (resulting in the Carlist Wars). The risk paid off. Isabel (a contemporary of Queen Victoria) reigned until she was deposed in 1868 and the constitutional monarchy has survived until today, despite two republican interludes and two military dictatorships.

In Spanish America, where early moves to replace the deposed Fernando by his sister Carlota (who had fled to Rio with her husband, the Prince Regent of Portugal) came to nothing, there was to be no such woman head of state. Nor did Portuguese America fare any better. In Brazil, Emperor Pedro I's daughter, born in Rio in 1819, returned to Portugal, where she became Queen Maria II, leaving Brazil to her younger brother, Pedro II. In a situation mirroring that of Spain, her accession in Portugal was only possible because her father, Pedro I, was willing to engage in a civil war against his usurping brother in defence of the liberal constitution and of his own branch of the Bragança family. Indeed, Brazil's eventual transition to a republic in 1889 occurred partly because the male national elites, most notably the military, would not accept as monarch a female heir to the throne: Pedro II's daughter, Isabella.

How might a Mother-Head of State affect the conditions making possible women's inclusion in the public cultural sphere and their access to social and symbolic capital? As explained in Chapter 9, Cunha benefited from protection in the imperial court in Brazil and wrote eulogies to Empress Carolina, though arguably, her blindness made her a special case. This book draws to an end with one further observation. It is that, ironically, the most celebrated Spanish American woman writer of the mid-nineteenth century was born and raised in a part of Spanish American that was not independent from Spain and published her work without restrictions in the metropolitan capital, Madrid.

The success of Cuban poet, dramatist and novelist Gertrudis Gómez de Avellaneda offers a curious contrast to the women writers studied so far. Avellaneda left Cuba with her family in 1836 at the age of 22 and, in 1841, published her writings, begun in Cuba, in Madrid. These were: *Poesías* (forty-five poems dated 1836–41); and the abolitionist novel, *Sab*. She was encouraged by the Spanish liberals, Nicomedes Pastor Díaz and Juan Nicasio Gallego. Pastor Díaz published lengthy, favourable reviews of her work in the press. Avellaneda's writings privileged themes that fitted the progressive liberal agenda: abolitionism, liberty, individualism and love of country. The first edition included translations of the contemporary French poets Alphonse de Lamartine (1790–1869) and Victor Hugo (1802–85), both fervent republicans. Avellaneda was soon incorporated into the Spanish American cultural sphere. She and Mercedes Marín were the only two women poets included in the popular anthology *America poética* (1846–47), published in Chile by Santos Tornero, Juan María Gutiérrez and others (Auza 1992: 149).[6] Yet it was the second (1850) edition of her *Poesías* that catapulted her to fame. This edition comprised a further fifty-two poems written through the 1840s and was reprinted two years later in Mexico as part of the collection 'Biblioteca de la Semana de las Señoritas'. It circulated widely in the Americas and was largely responsible for Avellaneda's international recognition. As is mentioned in Chapter 7, Marín dedicated a sonnet to Avellaneda, written in 1857, though not published until 1874, in which she compared Avellaneda to Sappho and de Staël's Corinne.[7]

The phenomenal success of Avellaneda's second edition was due, in part at least, to royal patronage. The most important event to take place in Spain in the 1840s was Isabel's accession to the throne in 1843 at the age of thirteen. The young woman embodied in her royal person the liberty and hope of the new constitutional Spain. As Fernando Soldevila writes, 'por ella había luchado el país; había hecho de ella el símbolo de la inocencia perseguida, de la libertad amenazada' (Soldevila 1959: 169). The 1850 edition of *Poesías* is dedicated to the Queen. Avellaneda considered it a duty to offer the book 'a los Reales Pies de V.M., puesto que muchas de las composiciones contenidas en él habían sido dedicadas a ensalzar rasgos generosos del magnánimo corazón de V.M. a faustos sucesos de su reinado.' In the Preface to the book she refers to the fact that 'la augusta señora ... se ha dignado acogerlo bajo sus auspicios' as an 'honorífica distinción'. The edition now included four long political compositions celebrating Isabel's rule. The four poems: 'A S.M. La Reina Doña Isabel II. Con motivo de la declaración de su mayoría' (Noviembre 1843); 'Oda en loor de la magnánima piedad de S.M. La Reina Doña Isabel Segunda' (June 1845); 'La Clemencia' (June 1845); and 'A.S.M. La Reina Doña Isabel II, en sus días' (November 1845) each reiterates the concept of the just monarch dispensing liberty, charity and beneficence. They involved Avellaneda in public recitals and performances, usually in the presence of the royal family. 'La Clemencia' and 'Oda en loor' were written for a poetry competition at the Liceo Artístico y Literario in Madrid to celebrate the mercy of the Queen, who had lifted the death penalty for several political prisoners. Avellaneda entered both poems, one signed with her own name and one with her brother's, winning first and second prize. She was publicly acclaimed and crowned with laurel by the Crown Prince, Francisco de Paula. The poem celebrating the Queen's fifteenth birthday (November 1845) was requested by the editor of the newspaper *El Heraldo*, and the poem written for the Queen's majority of age (November 1843) was written for the *Album,* prepared by the Liceo and presented and read to the Queen at a public ceremony. These public activities consolidated Avellaneda's reputation. There is no doubt that the Queen contributed to her social capital in a very real sense. As a corollary, there is no trace in these poems of desire for Cuban independence, quite the contrary. The final strophe of 'A S.M. La Reina Doña Isabel Segunda. Con motivo de la declaración de su mayoría' reads as follows:

> ¡Salud regia beldad! ¡Virgen divina!
> Su magnánima frente
> A tu planta inocente
> La nación fiera de Pelayo inclina:
> *Y allá en el Occidente*
> *La perla de los mares mejicanos,*
> *Al escuchar de nuestros aplausos el grito*
> *Entre el hervor de sus inquietas olas*
> *En las alas del viento*
> *Con eco fiel devolverá el acento*
> *Que atruena ya las playas españolas*
> (Gómez de Avellaneda 1850: 196, my emphasis)

By the time the third and much revised final edition of these poems was published in the *Obras completas* of 1869, Isabel had been deposed and Avellaneda largely forgotten. But adherence to a liberal constitutionalism embodied in the real figure of a powerful woman, and complicity in colonial politics, was apparently a more empowering strategy for literary women and more conducive to gender equality than writing on behalf of national liberation in the patriarchal republics of independent Spanish America. However, the institutions of liberalism also had their limitations: in 1853, despite substantial support from several eminent academicians, Avellaneda was disqualified from taking a seat in the Spanish Royal Academy. The sole criterion for her exclusion was gender.

Letradas

Women were permitted partial entry into the literary cliques of *letrados* as upholders of a generally conservative social order, which might be of republican or liberal persuasion. From a gender perspective, with some exceptions, their writing tended not to be radical. Yet the very fact that they published at all, and in increasing numbers, thus contributing to public culture in their own right and in their own name, was significant in itself. Their literary discourse was markedly different from that of men. With few exceptions, classical, neoclassical and Romantic feminine stereotypes persisted throughout the period in dominant literary discourse that encapsulated revolutionary change in the figure of the inspired young man (Vidal 2004: 203). In these works, the Romantic feminine symbolised the unreachable ideal, the other defining the self, instrumental in male specularisation. The feminine, especially the mother, was also often ridiculed or demonised as in the satirical tradition. The neoclassical feminine represented abstractions or Arcadian ideals in allegories and myth (liberty, truth, justice, etc.). But little space was given to the realistic portrayal of women in real time (see Vogeley 1996 for Mexico).

Women writers, however, seldom idealised or demonised the feminine in this way; in the writers studied here, the feminine hardly figures as trope. Even Mercedes Marín, who modelled her poetry on Bello's, avoided the feminine allegories he was so fond of. Women's poetry was either patriotic poetry (eulogies of the extended family) or grounded in the real, in the everyday life of the home; sometimes it might be love poetry. Women are represented in their letters, journalism, diaries, poetry, narrative fiction and conduct manuals as actual women in real time, circumscribed by the family, perhaps, but acting as individuals with a moral conscience and a sense of purpose. They are attributed with agency and subjectivity. They are identified singly with real or fictitious proper names; the apparently insignificant routines and dramas of the domestic world are represented as politically and patriotically important; and the domestic economy is inscribed as the centre of the political economy of the state. Literary women not only cemented the conventional patria-family trope but turned it to their advantage; if the patria was thought of as a family, so the family might be thought of as a *patria chica,* in which women played a major part. Women's writings reshaped the patria to fit the family model. Purposefully or not, their imaginative literature resisted and undermined the dominant gender order.

At issue was the fundamental question of women's self-representation. Throughout this period, discussion continued as to the meanings of the words 'mujer', 'madama', 'señora', 'dama', 'matrona', 'doña' and 'ciudadana' and their Portuguese equivalents. Slave women were not always considered female human beings, much less part of wider sorority, as indicated by the famous abolitionist motto 'Am I not a sister and a woman?' (Midgley 1995: 99). This subject was raised by Manso in *La familia del Comendador*. However, there were limitations to what South American women writers could do. Although they and their heroines are seen to act as individuals, they nevertheless do so on behalf of (and are supported by) their families. This is the case of all the authors studied here, with the exception of Manso, including Manso's (semi)-fictional heroines, Antonia Maza and Gabriela das Neves. How different are these family-heroines from their lonely, unattached contemporaries: Jane Eyre (1847), Mary Barton (1848) and Lucy Snowe (1853), who have to work for a living and try to forge their own futures as independent women.[8]

The greatest problem confronted by South American women writers throughout the century was the reluctance of certain influential *letrados* to take their work seriously, to concede them symbolic power. Examples abound of strategies to exclude women from the sacred inner circles of public culture, status and prestige. In the introduction to his *Ojeada histórico crítica sobre la poesía ecuatoriana desde su época más remota hasta nuestros días* (1868), Juan León Mera refers to women poets in passing, but refuses to publicly divulge their names because they are 'damas' of the 'sexo delicado'. As Beatriz González-Stephan notes, the effect is threefold: they are silenced, erased from the canon and imputed with immorality for writing in public (González-Stephan 2002: 271). Another example is the following paragraph taken from Juan María Gutiérrez's introduction to his famous anthology *Poesía Americana: composiciones selectas escritas por poetas sud-americanos de fama, tanto modernos como antiguos* (1866), first published in the *Correo del Domingo*, October 1865:

> Hay pobres de espíritu que en servicio de lo que entienden por moral, levantan como a manera de un cordón sanitario de libros indijestos, en torno a las mariposas de su cariño que constituyen la ventura de sus hogares. Pero que, no se aperciben que con esa táctica paraguaya, las echan a volar por los desiertos, expuestos al pico voraz de mil aves de pésima ralea. Dénles por el contrario un rumbo salvador en las correrías de la imaginación. Su mejor piloto será un poeta, y la más segura barquilla de su aerostático un libro de versos selectos. La mujer nacida en el Paraíso en medio de fantasías, seducciones y deseos, fraguará a su modo, entre puntada y puntada de su costura, poemas enmarañados e imposibles que le produzcan vértigo y caídas, si no se los dan hechos de antemano por algunos de esos maestros de corazón, diestros en educarle y en conducirle con riendas de seda. (Gutiérrez 1866: 4)

In this passage, balloon baskets and poetry books are figured as tethering devices to control women, who are prone to flights of fancy and transports of desire. Books of selected verse, like balloon baskets, keep women properly restrained. Women are to be protected above all from writing their own poems, usually stitched together while they sew; their imaginations, if set loose, will make them dizzy. Gutiérrez was a distinguished intellectual, the editor and compiler of the works of Echeverría and founding member of the Generation of 1837. His patronising condescension was typical, at least in the River Plate region, of the times. Yet, paradoxically, his message (evidently with an eye on the market) was meant to encourage women to read; men should avoid the counterproductive defensive 'Paraguayan strategy' of restricting women to boring books. Women should be allowed to read poetry, but as long as it was written by men, 'un poeta'. Poetry (written by men, or possibly virile women such as Gómez de Avellaneda)[9] is urged as a controlling mechanism on women's minds and self-expression, as an instrument to enforce ideological and psychological repression. Volatile women, who are compared with fragile idiots, children and butterflies (and, by analogy, effeminate men, 'mariposas'), are self-destructive and need to be tutored. Gutiérrez may well have been writing tongue in cheek, but his words are symptomatic of discursive representations of sexual difference throughout the nineteenth century, particularly following Rousseau. As we have seen, his emphasis on feminine irrationality and dependence did not bode well for women still aiming (in the 1860s) to present themselves as rational individuals, patriots and citizens of the state.

The textual representation of the feminine in trope, its extrapolation to the generic category woman in public discourse, and the ambiguous inclusion of women in political discourse, rendered women's exclusion from the post-independence public-political sphere natural and acceptable. To challenge this state of affairs, it was crucial that women should sign, publish and claim ownership of their own writings, irrespective of political persuasion, means of publication or genre (poetry, essays, novels, articles, school books, histories, and memoirs). By publishing, women reminded the self-appointed producers of public culture that women, too, were culturally productive. Women's intervention changed the shape of public culture in that it had to acknowledge and respond to their presence. If women writers were mocked or criticised, so much the better; this way, the mechanisms of exclusion, the power relations of sexual difference, were made evident. Like the women studied here, the *letradas* had to test the limits in order to expose the gender injustice of their times.

Notes

1 Quoted by C.K. Ogden in *Militarism versus Feminism* (1915), in Marshall, Ogden and Sargant Florence 1987: 77.
2 Schaar contrasts the Natural Patriotism of older societies with the Covenanted Patriotism of the United States.
3 The list of caudillos/statesmen is long and includes: Alvear, Artigas, Belgrano, Bolívar, Carrera, Dorrego, Francia, Lavalle, O'Higgins, Oribe, Quiroga, Rivera, Rosas, San Martín, Santa Cruz, Santander, and Sucre.
4 As stated in the 1837 Constitution (González-Doria 1986: 350).
5 The sixth-century Salic Law, which forbade women to inherit land, was used in fourteenth-century France to bar them from the throne.
6 The anthology was published in Valparaíso in instalments and included fifty-three authors. Bello was impressed with Avellaneda's work and wrote to Gutiérrez referring to the anthology, 'Siento mucho que me haya tocado estar tan cerca de esta señora' (Auza 1992: 149).
7 'A la poetisa cubana Doña J.G. de Avellaneda, Soneto' (Marín 1874: 79).
8 The protagonists of Charlotte Brönte's *Jane Eyre* and *Villette*, and Elizabeth Gaskell's *Mary Barton*.
9 The anthology includes four poems by Cuban Gertrudis Gómez de Avellaneda and one religious poem by Silveria Espinosa de los Monteros (Nueva Granada).

Bibliography

Acevedo, Alfonso and Josefa Acevedo, 1850. *Biografía del General José Acevedo Tejada.* Bogotá: Imprenta del Neo Granadino.

Acevedo, Josefa, 1848. *Tratado sobre economía doméstica para el uso de las madres de familia y de las amas de casa.* Bogotá: Imprenta de José A. Cualla.

—, 1854a. *Biografía del Doctor Diego Fernández Gómez.* Bogotá: Imprenta de Francisco Torres Amaya.

—, 1854b. *Poesías de una Granadina.* Bogotá: n.p.

—, 1855. *Biografía del Teniente Coronel Alfonso Acevedo y Tejada.* Bogotá: Imprenta de Francisco Torres Amaya.

—, 1857. *Ensayo sobre los deberes de los casados. Dedicada a la juventud granadina.* 5th edn. Bogotá: Imprenta de Francisco Torres Amaya.

—, 1860. *Recuerdos nacionales. José Acevedo i Gómez.* Bogotá: Imprenta de Pizarro i Pérez.

Adams, Percy G., 1983. *Travel Literature and the Evolution of the Novel.* Lexington, KY: University Press of Kentucky.

Adelman, Jeremy (ed.), 1999. *Colonial Legacies. The Problem of Persistence in Latin American History.* New York: London Routledge.

Adie, Kate, 2003. *Corsets to Camouflage: Women and War.* London: Hodder and Stoughton.

Aguilar, José Antonio and Rafael Rojas, 2002. *El republicanismo en Hispanoamérica. Ensayos de historia intelectual y política.* Mexico, D.F.: Fondo de Cultura Económica

Aguirre, Gisela, et al., 1999. *Manuel Belgrano.* Buenos Aires: Editorial Planeta Argentina.

Aichinger, Wolfram, Marien Bidwell-Steiner, Judith Bosch and Eva Crescutti (eds), 2003. *The 'Querelle des femmes' in Romania. Studies in Honour of Friederike Hassauer.* Vienna: Verlag Turia und Kant.

Alazraki, Jaime, 1995. 'Sobre el género literario de "El Matadero"', in *Teoría e interpretación del cuento,* ed. Peter Fröhlich and Georges Güntert. Bern: Peter Lang, pp. 411–26.

Alberdi, Juan Bautista, 1942. *Bases y puntos de partida para la organización política de la República Argentina,* ed. Clodomiro Zavalia. Buenos Aires: Ediciones Estrada.

Album de Señoritas (Buenos Aires) 1854.

Almeida, Miguel Vale de, 2000. *Um Mar da Cor da Terra. Raça, Cultura e Política de Identidade*. Oeiras: Celta.

Alonso, Amado, 1951. 'Prólogo', in *Obras completas de Andrés Bello, IV: Gramática de la lengua castellana destinada al uso de los americanos*. Caracas: Ministerio de Educación, pp. ix–xciii.

Alvarez Saá, Carlos, 1995. *Manuela: Sus diarios perdidos y otros papeles*. Quito: Imprenta Mariscal, Quito.

Amunátegui, Miguel Luis, 1867. *D[a]. Mercedes Marín del Solar*. Santiago: Imprenta de la República.

Anderson, Benedict, 1991. *Imaginary Communities*, 2nd edn. London: Verso.

Andrews, George Reid, 1985. 'Spanish American Independence: A Structural Analysis', in *Latin American Perspectives*, 44.12: 105–32.

Anzaldúa, Gloria, 1999. *Borderlands/La Frontera. The New Mestiza*, 2nd edn. San Francisco: Aunt Lute Books.

Arambel Guinazu, María Cristina and Claire Emilie Martin, 2001. *Las mujeres toman la palabra: Escritura femenina del siglo XIX*, vol.1. Madrid: Iberoamericana.

Arciniegas, Germán, 1961. *América mágica: II Las mujeres y las horas*. Buenos Aires: Editorial Sudamericana.

Ardila, Hector M., 1984. *Hombres y letras de Colombia*. Bogotá: Gráficas Herpin Ltda.

Area, Lelia, 1997. 'El periódico *Album de Señoritas* de Juana Manso (1854): Una voz doméstica en la fundación de una nación', in *Revista Iberoamericana*, 63: 178–79: 149–71.

—, 2005. *'Album de Señoritas' de Juana Manso. Periodismo y frustración para un proyecto 'domestico' de fundar una nación*. Buenos Aires: Feminaria Editora.

Arenales, José I., 1920 [1832]. *Memoria histórica sobre las operaciones e incidencias de la división libertadora a las órdenes de Gen. D. J. Alvarez de Arenales, en su segunda campaña de la Sierra del Perú en 1821*. Buenos Aires: Vaccaro.

Arrom, Silvia Marina, 1985. *The Women of Mexico City, 1790–1857*. Stanford, CA: Stanford University Press.

Artilheiro, O. No. 1, July 22 1837; No. 8 September 9 1837; No. 11 September 30 1837; No. 13 October 14 1837; No. 19 November 24 1837; No. 52, July 21 1838. Museu de Comunicação Social José Hipólito da Costa, Porto Alegre.

Auza, Néstor Tomás, 1988. *Periodismo y feminismo en la Argentina 1830–1930*. Buenos Aires: Emecé.

—, 1992. '*América Poética*: primera antología americana', in *Cuadernos Hispanoamericanos*, 500: 141–51.

—, 2006. 'La condición social de la mujer rioplatense de la Revolución de Mayo a la Organización nacional', in *Hispanic Research Journal*, 7.1: 57–69.

Balibar, Etienne and Pierre Macherey, 1974. 'Sur la littérature comme forme idéologique: quelques hypothèses marxistes', in *Littérature*, 13: 29–48.

Balta Campbell, Aída, 1998. *Presencia de la mujer en el periodismo escrito peruano 1821–1960*. Lima: Universidad de San Martín de Porres.

Barandas, Ana Eurídice Eufrosina de, 1990 [1845]. *Ramalhete ou Flores Escolhidas no Jardim da Imaginação*, 2nd edn. Porto Alegre: Nova Dimensão e EDIPUCRS.

Barman, Roderick J., 1988. *Brazil: The Forging of a Nation 1798–1852*. Stanford, CA: Stanford University Press.

Basadre, Jorge, 1981. *Peruanos del siglo XIX*. Lima: Rikchay Perú.

Battersby, Christine, 1998. *The Phenomenal Woman: Feminist Metaphysics and the*

Patterns of Identity. Cambridge: Polity Press.

Bauzá, Hugo F., 2000. '*El Matadero*. Estampa de un sacrificio ritual', in *Revista de Crítica Literaria Latinoamericana*, 25.51: 191–98.

Becker, Marília Beatriz Cibils, 1991. *Delfina Benigna da Cunha: 200 Anos*. Porto Alegre: Evangraf.

—, 1993. 'Delfina Benigna da Cunha', in *50 Anos de Literatura: Perfil das Patronas*, ed. Academia Literária Feminina do Rio Grande do Sul. Porto Alegre: Instituto Estadual do Livro, pp. 19–27.

—, 1997. 'Delfina Benigna da Cunha', in *Presença Literária: Academia Literária Feminina do Rio Grande do Sul*. Porto Alegre: Nova Dimensão, pp. 91–9.

Belgrano, Manuel, 1914. *Documentos del Archivo de Belgrano*, vol. III. Buenos Aires: Imprenta de Coni Hermanos.

Bello, Andrés, [1823] 1881–93. 'Indicaciones sobre la conveniencia de simplificar y uniformar la ortografía en América', in *Obras completas de Andrés Bello*, vol. I, ed. M.L. Amunátegui Reyes. Santiago de Chile: Consejo de Instrucción Pública/Imprenta Cervantes, 15 vols.

—, 1928 [1847]. *Gramática de la lengua castellana destinada al uso de los americanos*, ed. José Rufino Cuervo, 23rd edn. Paris: Andrés Blot.

—, 1951 [1843]. 'Filosofía del entendimiento', in *Obras completas de Andrés Bello*, vol. III, *Filosofía*, 22 vols. Prologue by Juan David García Bacca. Caracas: Ministerio de Educación.

—, 1952. *Antología poética*, ed. Eugenio Orrego Vicuña. Buenos Aires: Angel Estrada.

—, 1976. 'Modo de escribir la historia', 'Modo de estudiar la historia', in *Antología de discursos y escritos*, ed. José Vila Selma. Madrid: Editora Nacional, pp. 181–93, 194–201.

—, 1981. *Gramática de la lengua castellana destinada al uso de los americanos*, ed. Rafael Trujillo. Tenerife: Cabildo Insular e Instituto Universitario Lingüístico Andrés Bello.

Bengoechea, Mercedes, 2000. 'Historia (española) de las primeras sugerencias para evitar el androcentrismo lingüístico', in *Revista Iberoamericana de Discurso y Sociedad*, 2.3: 33–58.

Bengoechea, Mercedes and María Luisa Calero Vaquera, 2003. *Sexismo y redacción periodística*. Valladolid: Junta de Castilla y León/Dirección General de la Mujer e Igualdad de Oportunidades.

Benhabib, Seyla, 1991. 'On Hegel, Women and Irony', in *Feminist Interpretations and Political Theory*, ed. Mary Lyndon Shanley and Carole Pateman. University Park, PA: Pennsylvania State University Press, pp. 129–45.

Bethell, Leslie (ed.), 1985. *Cambridge History of Latin America* (8 vols). Cambridge: Cambridge University Press.

— (ed.), 1985. *Spanish America after Independence c. 1820–c. 1870*. Cambridge: Cambridge University Press.

Bhabha, Homi K., 1994. *The Location of Culture*. London: Routledge.

Biblioteca de impresos raros americanos, 1951. *Descripción de las fiestas cívicas celebradas en Montevideo. Oración inaugural pronunciada por Larrañaga en la apertura de la biblioteca pública de Montevideo, mayo 1816*. Montevideo: Universidad de La República, Facultad de Humanidades y Ciencias, Instituto de Investigaciones Históricas.

Bishop-Sanchez, Kathryn, (n.d.). *Utopias Desmascaradas. O Mito do Bom Selvagem e a Procura do Homem Natural na Obra de Almeida Garrett.* Book manuscript based on PhD dissertation. University of California, Santa Barbara, 2000. Forthcoming 2005 with Imprensa Nacional/Casa da Moeda, Lisbon.

Blackman, H.J., 1968. *Humanism.* Harmondsworth: Penguin.

Blanchard, Peter, 1992. *Slavery and Abolition in Early Republican Peru.* Wilmington, DE: Scholarly Resources.

—, 2004. *Freedom and Family: Slave Women and the Wars of Independence.* Toronto: Toronto University Press.

Blom, Ida, Karen Hagemann and Catherine Hall (eds), 2000. *Gendered Nations: Nationalism and Gender Order in the Long Nineteenth Century.* Oxford and New York: Berg.

Boléo, Luísa V. de Paiva, 1995. 'Ana Pimentel. A Primeira Mulher à Frente de uma Capitania no Brasil', in *O Rosto Feminino da Expansão Portuguesa. Actas I,* ed. Maria Reynolds de Souza et al. Lisbon: Comissão para a Igualdade e para os Direitos das mulheres, pp. 541–57.

Bolívar, Simón and Manuela Sáenz, 1996. *Correspondencia íntima,* ed. Manuel Espinosa Apolo. Quito: Centro de Estudios Felipe Guamán Poma.

Bonilla, H., 1990. 'O Impacto da Revolução Francesa nos Movimentos de Independência da América Latina', in *A Revolução francesa e seu impacto na América Latina,* ed. Osvaldo Coggiola. Brasilia: Universidade de São Paulo.

Bourdieu, Pierre, 1977. *Outline of a Theory of Practice,* trans. Richard Nice. Cambridge: Cambridge University Press.

—, 1990. 'La domination masculine', *Actes de la Recherche en Sciences Sociales,* 84, September: 3–31.

—, 1992. *Language and Symbolic Power,* trans. John B. Thompson. Cambridge: Polity Press.

Boxer, C.R., 1975. *Mary and Misogyny. Women in Iberian Expansion Overseas 1415–1815. Some facts, fancies and personalities.* London: Duckworth.

Brading, D.A., 1983. *Classical Republicanism and Creole Patriotism: Simón Bolívar and the Spanish American Revolution.* Cambridge: Centre of Latin American Studies.

Brewster, Claire, 2006. 'Gendering Latin American Independence: Database and Image Bank', in *Hispanic Research Journal,* 7.1: 85–93.

Brown, Matthew, 2005. 'Adventurers, Foreign Women and Masculinity in the Colombian Wars of Independence', in *Feminist Review,* 79: 36–51.

—, 2006. 'Soldier Heroes and the Colombian Wars of Independence', in *Hispanic Research Journal,* 7.1: 41–56.

—, in press. *Adventuring through Spanish Colonies: Simón Bolívar, Foreign Mercenaries and the Birth of New Nations.* Liverpool: Liverpool University Press.

Bushnell, David, 1999. 'Independence Compared. The Americas North and South', in *Independence and Revolution in Spanish America: Perspectives and Problems,* ed. Anthony McFarlane and Eduardo Posada-Carbó. London: Institute of Latin American Studies, pp. 69–83.

Bushnell, David and Neil Macaulay, 1994. *The Emergence of Latin America in the Nineteenth Century,* 2nd edn. Oxford: Oxford University Press.

Butler, Melissa A., 2003. 'Early Liberal Roots of Feminism: John Locke and the Attack on Patriarchy', in *Feminist Interpretations and Political Theory,* ed. Mary Lyndon Shanley and Carole Pateman. University Park, PA: Pennsylvania State University Press, pp. 74–94.

Caicedo Torres, José María, 1863. *Ensayos biográficos.* Paris: Librería de Guillaumin.

Cameron, Deborah, 1985. *Feminism and Linguistic Theory.* London: Macmillan.

—, 1995. *Verbal Hygiene.* London: Routledge.

Campbell, Leon, 1985. 'Women and the Great Rebellion in Peru, 1780–83', in *The Americas,* 42: 2: 163–96.

Canovan, Margaret, 1996. '"Breathes there the man, with soul so dead...": reflections on patriotic poetry and liberal principles', in *Literature and the Political Imagination,* ed. John Horton and Andrea T. Baumeister. London: Routledge, pp. 170–97.

Carranza, Adolfo P., 1910. *Patricias Argentinas.* Buenos Aires: Sociedad Patricias Argentinas.

Carvajal Thoa, Morayma Ofyr, 1949. *Galería del espíritu, mujeres de mi patria.* Quito: Edit 'Fr. Jodoco Ricke'.

Castañeda, Fray Francisco de Paula, 2001. *Doña María Retazos,* ed. Néstor Tomás Auza. Buenos Aires: Aguilar, Altea, Taurus, Alfaguara.

Castro-Klarén, Sara and John Charles Chasteen (eds), 2003. *Beyond Imagined Communities: Reading and Writing the Nation in Nineteenth-Century Latin America.* Baltimore, MD, and London: The Johns Hopkins University Press.

Caulfield, Sueann, 2001. 'The History of Gender in the Historiography of Latin America', in *Hispanic American Historical Review,* 81, 3–4: pp. 449–90.

Centeno, Miguel Angel, 2002. 'The Centre did not Hold: War in Latin America and the Monopolisation of Violence', in *Studies in the Formation of the Nation State,* ed. James Dunkerly. London: Institute of Latin American Studies, pp. 54–76.

Cevallos-Candau, Francisco Javier, Jeffrey A. Cole, Nina M. Scott and Nicomedes Suárez Araúz (eds), 1994. *Coded Encounters. Writing, Gender and Ethnicity in Colonial Latin America.* Amherst, MA: University of Massachusetts Press.

Chambers, Sarah C., 1999. *From Subjects to Citizens: Honor, Gender and Politics in Arequipa, Peru 1780–1854.* University Park, PA: Pennsylvania State University Press.

—, 2001. 'Republican Friendship: Manuela Sáenz Writes Women into the Nation 1835–1856', in *Hispanic American Historical Review,* 81.2: 225–58.

—, 2002. '"My only crime ... is to carry the surname Bolívar": Loyalist María Antonia Bolívar during the period of Venezuela's independence', paper prepared for the 12th Berkshire Conference on the History of Women, University of Connecticut, Storrs, 8 June.

—, 2003. 'Letters and Salons: Women Reading and Writing the Nation', in *Beyond Imagined Communities: Reading and Writing the Nation in Nineteenth-Century Latin America,* ed. Sara Castro-Klarén and John Charles Chasteen. Baltimore, MD, and London: The Johns Hopkins University Press, pp. 54–83.

—, 2006. 'Masculine Virtues and Feminine Passions: Gender and Race in the Republicanism of Simón Bolívar', in *Hispanic Research Journal,* 7.1: 21–40.

Chaney, Elsa M., 1979. *Supermadre: Women and Politics in Latin America.* Austin, TX, and London: University of Texas Press.

Chasteen, John Charles, 1997. 'Maria A.M: Frontier Matriarch', in *The Human Tradition in Modern Latin America,* ed. William H. Beezley and Judith Ewell. Wilmington, DE: Scholarly Resources, pp. 27–35.

—, 2003. 'Introduction: Beyond Imagined Communities', in *Beyond Imagined Communities: Reading and Writing the Nation in Nineteenth-Century Latin America,* ed. Sara Castro-Klarén and John Charles Chasteen. Baltimore, MD, and London: The Johns Hopkins University Press, pp. ix–xxv.

Cherpak, Evelyn, 1978. 'The Participation of Women in the Independence of Gran Colombia 1780–1830', in *Latin American Women: Historical Perspectives*, ed. Asunción Lavrin, Westport, CT: Greenwood Press, pp. 219–34.

Chust, Manuel, 1999. *La cuestión nacional americana en las Cortes de Cádiz*. Valencia: Fundación Instituto Historia Social/UNAM.

Chust, Manuel and Ivana Frasquet (eds.), 2004. *La trascendencia del liberalismo doceañista en España y América*. Valencia: Generalitat Valenciana.

Civantos, Christina, 2002. 'Exile Inside (and) Out: Woman, Nation and the Exiled Intellectual in José Mármol's *Amalia*, in *Latin American Literary Review*, 30.59: 55–78.

Clément, Jean-Pierre, 1979. *Indices del Mercurio Peruano, 1790–1795*. Lima: Biblioteca Nacional de Cultura.

—, 1997. *El Mercurio Peruano 1790–1795*, vol. 1 *Estudio*; vol. 2 *Antología*. Frankfurt am Main: Vervuet; Madrid: Iberoamericana.

Clemente Travieso, Carmen, 1965. *Mujeres de la Independencia: seis biografías de mujeres venezolanas*. Mexico: Talleres gráficos de México.

Clissold, Stephen, 1968. *Bernardo O'Higgins and the Independence of Chile*. London: Rupert Hart-Davis.

Collier, Simon, 1967. *Ideas and Politics of Chilean Independence*. Cambridge: Cambridge University Press.

Collins, Jane-Marie, 1999. 'Slavery, Subversion and Subalternity: Gender and Violent Resistance in Nineteenth-Century Bahia', in *Brazilian Feminisms*, ed. Solange Ribeiro de Oliveira and Judith Still. Nottingham: University of Nottingham, pp. 35–56.

Connell, R.W., 1987. *Gender and Power: Society, the Person and Sexual Politics*. Cambridge: Polity Press.

—, 1992. *Gender*. Cambridge: Polity Press.

—, 1994. *Masculinities*. Cambridge: Polity Press.

Conway, Christopher, 2001. 'Gender, Empire and Revolution in "La Victoria de Junín"', in *Hispanic Review*, 69: 299–317.

Cook, Joanne, Jennifer Roberts and Georgina Waylen (ed.), 2000. *Towards a Gendered Political Economy*. Basingstoke and London: Macmillan.

Cornejo Bournoncle, J., 1949. *Sangre Andina, diez mujeres cuzqueñas*. Cuzco: H.H. Rozas.

Cortés, Hernán, 1963 [c. 1520]. *Cartas y documentos*, intro. Mario Hernández Sánchez-Barba. Mexico City: Editorial Porrua.

Cortés, José Domingo, 1875. *América Poética*. Paris and Mexico: Bouret e hijo.

Costa, Emília Viotta da, 2000. *The Brazilian Empire. Myths and Histories*. Chapel Hill, NC: University of North Carolina.

Craske, Nikki, 2005. 'Ambiguities and Ambivalences in Making the Nation: Women and Politics in 20th-Century Mexico', in *Feminist Review*, 79: 116–33.

Cúneo Vidal, Rómulo, 1978. *Precursoras y mártires de la independencia del Perú*. Lima: Gráfica Morsom, S.A.

Cunha, Delfina Benigna da, 1834. *Poesias oferecidas às senhoras rio-grandenses*, 1st edn. Porto Alegre: Tipographia Fonseca.

—, 1846. *Collecção de Varias Poesias Dedicadas à Imperatriz-Viúva como Tributo de Gratidão*. Rio de Janeiro: Typographia Universal de Laemmert.

—, 2001 [1838]. *Poesias.* Porto Alegre: Instituto Estadual do Livro.
Curia, B., 1989. 'Introducción', in *Amalia*, vol. 1. Cuyo: Cectla/Universidad nacional de Cuyo, pp. 7–42.
Cussen, Antonio, 1992. *Bello and Bolívar: Poetry and Politics in the Spanish American Revolution.* Cambridge: Cambridge University Press.

Davies, Catherine, 2003. 'Founding-fathers and Domestic Genealogies: Situating Gertrudis Gómez de Avellaneda', in *Bulletin of Latin American Research*, 22.4: 423–44.
Deas, Malcolm, 2002. 'The Man on Foot: Conscription and the Nation State in Nineteenth-Century Latin America', in *Studies in the Formation of the Nation State*, ed. James Dunkerley. London: Institute of Latin American Studies, pp. 77–93.
De Austria, J., 1960. *Bosquejo de la historia militar de Venezuela.* Caracas: Academia Nacional de Historia.
de Beauvoir, Simone, [1949] 1997. *The Second Sex*, trans. and ed. H. M. Parshley. London: Vintage Classics.
de Certeau, Michel, 1988. *The Practice of Everyday Life*, trans. Steven Randall. Berkeley, Los Angeles, London: University of California Press.
de Torres, María Inés, 1995. *La Nación tiene cara de mujer? Mujeres y nación en el imaginario letrado del siglo XIX.* Montevideo: Arca.
del Solar, Enrique, 1874. 'Dos palabras', in *Poesías de la señora Dª. Mercedes Marín de Solar.* Santiago: Imprenta Andrés Bello.
Deleis, Mónica, Ricardo de Titto and Diego L. Arguindeguy, 2001. *Mujeres de la política argentina.* Buenos Aires: Aguilar.
Demaria, Laura, 2002. 'La generación argentina de 1837: constructores, jueces y ... caudillos', in *Hispanófila*, 134: 63–74.
Denegri, Francesca, 1996. *El abanico y la cigarrera: la primera generación de mujeres ilustradas en el Perú.* Lima: Flora Tristan/Centro de la Mujer Peruana and Instituto de Estudios Peruanos.
'Despedida de las chilenas al egercito libertador del Perú', 1820. Biblioteca Nacional de Chile, Sala Medina.
Devoto, Fernando and Marta Madero (eds), 1999. *Historia de la vida privada en la Argentina*, vol. 1, *País antigüo. De la colonia a 1870.* Buenos Aires: Taurus.
Diario de Lima (Lima) 1790–92.
Díaz, Arlene J., 2004. *Female Citizens, Patriarchs and the Law in Venezuela, 1786–1904.* Lincoln, NE, and London: University of Nebraska Press.
Díaz del Castillo, Bernal, 1955. *Historia verdadera de la conquista de la Nueva España*, vol. I. Mexico City: Editorial Porrúa.
—, 1963. *The Conquest of New Spain*, trans. J.M. Cohen. London: Penguin Books.
—, 1968. *Historia verdadera de la conquista de la Nueva España*, vol. II. Mexico City: Editorial Porrúa.
Díaz y Díaz, Oswaldo, 1962. *Los Almeydas: Episodios de la resistencia patriota contra el ejército pacificador de tierra firme.* Bogotá: Editorial ABC.
Diccionario biográfico histórico y geográfico argentino, 1997. Buenos Aires: El Ateneo.
Didier, T. Jaén, 1966. 'El concepto de democracia en Esteban Echeverría', in *Cuadernos Americanos*, 25.148: 139–47.
Domenella, Ana Rosa and Nora Pasternac, 1997. *Las voces olvidadas: Antología crítica de narradoras mexicanas en el siglo XIX.* Mexico City: El Colegio de México.
Dore, Elizabeth, 2000. 'Property, Households and Public Regulation of Domestic

Life: Diriomo, Nicaragua, 1840–1900', in *Hidden Histories of Gender and the State in Latin America*, ed. Elizabeth Dore and Maxine Molyneux. Durham, NC, and London: Duke University Press, pp. 147–71.
— (ed.), 1997. *Gender Politics in Latin America. Debates in Theory and Practice.* New York: Monthly Review.
Dore, Elizabeth and Maxine Molyneux (eds), 2000. *Hidden Histories of Gender and the State in Latin America.* Durham, NC, and London: Duke University Press.
Duarte, Constância Lima, 1989. 'Posfácio', in Nísia Floresta Brasileira Augusta, *Direitos das Mulheres e Injustiça dos Homens*, ed. Constância Lima Duarte. São Paulo: Cortez, pp. 101–34.
—, 1999. 'Nísia Floresta e Mary Woolstonecraft (sic): Diálogo e Apropriação', in *Literatura e Feminismos. Respostas Teóricas e Reflexões Críticas*, ed. Christina Ramalho. Rio de Janeiro: Elo, pp. 85–96.
—, 2005. *Nísia Floresta. A Primeira Feminista do Brasil.* Florianópolis: Editora Mulheres.
Dudink, Stefan and Karen Hagemann, 2004. 'Masculinity in Politics and War in the Age of Democratic Revolutions, 1750–1850', in Stefan Dudink, Karen Hagemann and John Tosh, *Masculinities in Politics and War. Gendering Modern History*. Manchester: Manchester University Press, pp. 3–21.
Dudink, Stefan, Karen Hagemann and John Tosh, 2004. *Masculinities in Politics and War. Gendering Modern History*. Manchester: Manchester University Press.
Dueñas-Vargas, Guiomar, 2006. 'Constructing Patriarchy: Women and the Construction of Gender in 19th Century Colombia', paper delivered at the LASA conference, San Juan de Puerto Rico, March 15–18 2006.
Dunbar Temple, Ella, 1943. 'Periodismo del siglo XVIII, in *El Semanario Crítico*', supplement of *El Mercurio Peruano*, XXV, 198: 3–36.
Dunkerley, James (ed.), 2002. *Studies in the Formation of the Nation State in Latin America*. London: Institute of Latin American Studies.

Earle, Rebecca, 2000. 'Rape and the Anxious Republic: Revolutionary Colombia 1810–1830', in *Hidden Histories of Gender and the State in Latin America*, ed. Elizabeth Dore and Maxine Molyneux. Durham, NC, and London: Duke University Press, pp. 127–46.
—, 2001 '"Two Pairs of Pink Satin Shoes!!" Race, Clothing and Identity in the Americas (17th–19th centuries)', in *History Workshop Journal*, 52: 175–95.
—, 2002a. 'Padres de la Patria and the Ancestral Past: Celebrations of Independence in Nineteenth-century Spanish America', in the *Journal of Latin American Studies*, 34.4, pp. 775–805.
—, 2002b. 'The Role of Print in the Spanish American Wars of Independence', in *The Political Power of the Word*, ed. Iván Jaksić. London: Institute of Latin American Studies, pp. 9–33.
Echaque, Juan Pablo, 1947. 'La heroína Juana Azurduy', in *América*, XXIII, 87: 72–79.
Echeverría, Esteban, 1972 [1874]. *Obras completas de Esteban Echeverría*, 2nd edn., ed. Juan María Gutiérrez. Buenos Aires: Ediciones Antonio Zamora.
—, 1999. *El Matadero/La Cautiva*, ed. Leonor Fleming, 6th edn. Madrid: Cátedra.
Erauso, Catalina de, 1996. *Lieutenant Nun: Memoir of a Basque Transvestite in the New World.* trans. Michele and Gabriel Stepto. Boston: Beacon Press.
Espinosa Apolo, Manuel (ed.), 1996. Simón Bolívar and Manuela Sáenz,

Correspondencia íntima. Quito: Centro de Estudios Felipe Guamán Poma.
Estrada, Jenny, 1984. *Mujeres de Guayaquil, siglo XVI al siglo XX*. Guayaquil: Banco Central de Ecuador.
Etchart, Martha B., 1979. *Documentos de historia americana*. Buenos Aires: Cesarini Hnos. Editores.

Fachel, José Plínio Guimarães, 2002. *Revolução Farroupilha*. Pelotas: EGUFpel.
Feijóo, Benito Gerónimo, 1774. *Essay on the Learning Genius and Abilities of the Fair Sex Proving them Not Inferior to Man, from a Variety of Examples Extracted from Ancient and Modern History Translated from the Spanish of El Theatro Critico by Benito Geronimo Feijóo*. London: D. Steel, Bookfeller No.1, Union Row, The Lower End of the Minorities, Little Tower Hill.
Feliú Cruz, Guillermo, 1955. *La imprenta durante el gobierno de O'Higgins, Cuatro periódicos de 1818*. Santiago de Chile: Imprenta Cultura.
Felstiner, Mary Lowenthal, 1976. 'Kinship Politics in the Chilean Independence Movement', in *Hispanic American Historical Review*, 56.1: 58–80.
Fernández-Armesto, Felipe 1992. *Columbus*. Oxford and New York: Oxford University Press.
—, 2004. *The Americas. The History of a Hemisphere*. London: Weidenfeld and Nicolson.
Fernández Fraile, Máximo, 1994. *Historia de la literatura chilena*, vol. 1. Santiago: Editorial Salesiana.
Fernández Sarasola, Ignacio, 2004. 'La Constitución española de 1812 y su proyección europea e iberoamericana', Alicante: Biblioteca Virtual Miguel de Cervantes, 1–29, http://www.cervantesvirtual.com, accessed July 2005.
Fisher, John, 2003. *Bourbon Peru*. Liverpool: Liverpool University Press.
Fitzgerald, G.E., 1971. *The Political Thought of Bolívar. Selected Writings*. The Hague: Martinus Nijhoff.
Fletcher, Lea, 1994. *Mujeres y cultura en la Argentina del siglo XIX*. Buenos Aires:
Flores, Hilda Agnes Hübner, 1989a. *Sociedade, Preconceitos e Conquistas*. Porto Alegre: Nova Dimensão.
—, 1989b. 'Maria Clemência da Silveira Sampaio', in *Presença Literária: Academia Literária Feminina do Rio Grande do Sul*. Porto Alegre: Nova Dimensão, pp. 57–62.
—, 1990. 'Parte I, in Ana Eurídice Eufrosina de Barandas, *Ramalhete ou Flores Escolhidas no Jardim da Imaginação*. Porto Alegre: Nova Dimensão, pp. 11–50.
—, 1991. 'Ana Eurídice Eufrosina de Barandas', in *Travessia: Revista de Literatura Brasileira*, 23: 15–36.
—, 2000. 'Contribuição Feminina', in *No Contexto do Brasil*, ed. Lotário Neuberger, Porto Alegre: EDIPLAT, pp. 165–82.
Flores, Moacyr, 1990. *A Revolução Farroupilha*. Porto Alegre: UFRGS Editora.
—, 2002. *República Rio-Grandense: Realidade e Utopia*. Porto Alegre: EDIPUCRS.
—, 2003. *História do Rio Grande do Sul*. Porto Alegre: EDIPLAT.
Floresta, Nísia, 1989 [1832]. *Direitos das Mulheres e Injustiça dos Homens*, ed. Constância Lima Duarte. São Paulo: Cortez.
Foley, Barbara, 1986. *Telling the Truth. The Theory and Practice of Documentary Fiction*. Ithaca, NY, and London: Cornell University Press.
Folger, Robert, 1999. 'Fisuras del discurso liberal en "El Matadero"', in *Mester*, 28: 37–57.

Fontaine Aldunante, Arturo, 1981. 'Andrés Bello, formador de opinión pública', in *Atenea. Revista de Ciencias, Arte y Literatura*, Concepción, Chile, 443–44: 117–34.

Foucault, Michel, 1970. *The Order of Things. An Archeology of the Human Sciences.* London: Tavistock.

Fowler, Bridget, 1991. *The Alienated Reader: Women and Romantic Literature in the Twentieth Century.* Hemel Hempstead: Harvester Wheatsheaf.

Franco, Jean, 1989. *Plotting Women: Gender and Representation in Mexico.* New York: Columbia University Press.

Frigeri, Rosane and Francisco Ricardo Rüdiger, 1985. 'Mulher e Sociedade na Época Farroupilha', in *O Papel da Mulher na Revolução Farroupilha,* org. Diva Ione Silveira. Porto Alegre: Tchê, pp. 155–80.

Galindo de Ugarte, M., 1991. *Constituciones bolivianas comparadas 1826–1967.* La Paz: Los amigos del libro.

Galdames, Luis, 1941 [1926]. *A History of Chile,* trans. Isaac John Cox. Chapel Hill, NC: University of North Carolina Press.

García, Flavio A., 1954. 'Una poetisa de 1816', in *Revista Nacional,* Montevideo, 61.186: 379–88.

—, 1956. 'Crítica versificada a las fiestas mayas de Montevideo 1816', in *Boletín Histórico,* Montevideo, 69, April–June: 79–84.

García y García, Elvira, 1924. *La mujer peruana a través de los siglos.* Lima: Imp. Americana, Plazuela del Teatro.

Gatens, Moira, 1991. '"The Oppressed State of my Sex": Wollstonecraft on Reason, Feeling and Equality', in *Feminist Interpretations and Political Theory,* ed. Mary Lyndon Shanley and Carole Pateman. University Park, PA: Pennsylvania State University Press, pp. 112–28.

Gazmuri Riveros, Cristián, 1993. 'Libros e ideas políticas francesas y la gestación de la Independencia de Chile', in *América Latina ante la revolución francesa,* ed. Leopoldo Zea. Mexico, D.F.: UNAM, pp. 81–108.

Glassman Hersh, Blanche, 1979. '"Am I Not a Woman and a Sister?". Abolitionist Beginnings of Nineteenth-century Feminism', in *Antislavery Reconsidered. New Perspectives on the Abolitionists,* ed. Lewis Perry and Michael Fellman. Baton Rouge and London: Louisiana State University Press, pp. 252–83.

Glover, David and Cora Kaplan, 2000. *Genders.* London and New York: Routledge.

Goldman, Noemí, 'Morenismo y derechos naturales en el Río de la Plata', in *América Latina ante la revolución francesa,* ed. Leopoldo Zea. Mexico, D.F.: UNAM, pp. 151–68.

Goldstein, Joshua S., 2001. *War and Gender: How Gender Shapes the War System and Vice Versa.* Cambridge: Cambridge University Press.

Gómez de Avellaneda, Gertrudis, 1841. *Poesías de la señorita Da. Gertrudis Gómez de Avellaneda.* Madrid: Establecimiento tipográfico, Calle del Sordo, N° 11.

—, 1850. *Poesías de la excelentísima señora Da Gertrudis Gómez de Avellaneda de Sabater.* Madrid: Imprenta de Delgrás hermanos; reprinted 1852 by Mexico, D.F.: Imprenta de Juan R. Navarro.

—, 2001 [1841]. *Sab,* ed. Catherine Davies. Manchester: Manchester University Press.

Gómez Paz, Julieta, 1976. 'La mujer argentina en la poesía de ayer y hoy', in *La Mujer argentina (ensayos),* ed. Consejo de Mujeres de la República Argentina. Buenos Aires: Consejo de Mujeres de la República Argentina.

González, Adolfo Luis, 1993. 'Las Revoluciones atlánticas y los derechos del hombre: el caso argentino (1810–35)', in *América Latina ante la revolución francesa*, ed. Leopoldo Zea. Mexico, D.F.: UNAM, pp. 125–49.

González del Valle, Luis T., 2000. 'Iniquidad oficial y objeción individual de la España decimonónica a través de algunas cartas inéditas de Gertrudis Gómez de Avellaneda', *Bulletin of Hispanic Studies*, 57: 451–78.

González-Doria, F., 1986. *Historias de las constituciones españolas de Godoy a Suárez*. Madrid: Cometa.

González-Stephan, Beatriz, 2002. *Fundaciones: canon, historia y cultura nacional: la historiografía literaria del liberalismo hispanoamericano del siglo XIX*. Madrid and Frankfurt am Main: Iberoamericana Vervuert.

Graham, Maria, 1993. *The Captain's Wife. The South American Journals of Maria Graham 1821–23*, ed. Elizabeth Mavor. London: Weidenfeld and Nicolson.

Graham, Maria Callcott, n.d. *Life of Dom Pedro*. Typescript account of Maria Graham' s life in Brazil, dictated to the Hon. Caroline Fox in 1834–35 and copied by James Allen. MS. Eng. c. 2730. Bodleian Library.

Greenblatt, Stephen, 1991. *Marvelous Possessions: The Wonder of the New World*. Chicago: University of Chicago Press.

Grez, Vicente, 1966 [1878]. *Las mujeres de la independencia*. Santiago de Chile: Empresa Zigzag.

Guadarrama González, Pablo, 1995. 'Filosofía e ilustración en Simón Bolívar', in *Cuadernos Americanos*, Nueva época, 6.54: 32–45.

Guardia, Sara Beatriz, 1985. *Mujeres peruanas: El otro lado de la historia*. Lima: Empresa Editora Humboldt.

Guardino, Peter and Charles Walker, 1992. 'The State, Society and Politics in Peru and Mexico in the Late Colonial and Early Republic Period', in *Latin American Perspectives*, 73.19: 10–43.

Guerra, Francois-Xavier, 1999. 'De lo uno a lo múltiple. Dimensiones y lógicas de la Independencia', in *Independence and Revolution in Spanish America: Perspectives and Problems*, ed. Anthony McFarlane and Eduardo Posada-Carbó. London: Institute of Latin American Studies, pp. 43–68.

Guest, Harriet, 2000. *Small Change. Women, Learning, Patriotism 1750–1810*. Chicago and London: University of Chicago Press.

Guillaumin, Colette, 1996. 'The Practice of Power and the Belief in Nature', in *Sex in Question. French Materialist Feminism*, ed. Diana Leonard and Lisa Adkins. London: Taylor & Francis, pp. 72–108.

Gutiérrez, Juan María, 1941. 'La literatura de Mayo', *Los poetas de la revolución*, Buenos Aires: Academia Argentina de Letras, pp. 3–26.

— (ed.), 1866. *Poesía Americana: composiciones selectas escritas por poetas sud-americanos de fama, tanto modernos como antiguos*. Buenos Aires: Imprenta del Siglo.

Gutiérrez Chong, Natividad, 2004. *Mujeres y nacionalismo en América Latina: De la Independencia a la nación del nuevo Milenio*. Mexico, D.F.: UNAM.

Hagemann, Karen, 2004. 'Female Patriots: Women, War and the Nation in the Period of the Prussian-German Anti-Napoleonic Wars', *Gender and History*, 16.2: 397–424.

Hahner, June E., 1978. 'The Nineteenth-Century Feminist Press and Women's Rights in Brazil', in *Latin American Women. Historical Perspectives*, ed. Asunción Lavrin. Westport, CT, and London: Greenwood Press, pp. 254–85.

—, 1990. *Emancipating the Female Sex. The Struggle for Women's Rights in Brazil, 1850–1940*. Durham, NC, and London: Duke University Press.

Hall, Captain Basil, R.N., F.R.S., 1840. *Extracts from a Journal Written on the Coasts of Chili, Peru and Mexico in the years 1820, 1821, 1822*. London: Edward Moxton.

Hall, Catherine, 1985. 'Private Persons versus Public Someones: Class, Gender and Politics in England 1780–1850', in *Language, Gender and Childhood*, ed. Carolyn Steedman, Cathy Urwin and Valerie Walkerdine. London: Routledge, Kegan Paul, pp. 10–33.

—, 1992. *White, Male and Middle-Class: Explorations in Feminism and History*. Cambridge: Polity Press.

Halperín Donghi, Tulio, 1951. *El pensamiento de Echeverría*. Buenos Aires: Editorial sudamericana.

—, 1973. *The Aftermath of Revolution in Latin America*, trans. Josephine de Bunsen. New York, San Francisco, London: Harper and Row.

Haraway, Donna J., 1991. 'Gender for a Marxist Dictionary: The Sexual Politics of a Word', in *Simians, Cyborgs and Women. The Reinvention of Nature*, London: Free Association Books, pp. 127–48

Harvey Brown, Richard, 1987. *Society as Text*. London and Chicago: University of Chicago Press.

Hennessy, Rosemary, 1993. *Materialist Feminism and the Politics of Discourse*. London and New York: Routledge.

Hernández Sánchez-Barba, Mario, 1972. 'Las Indias en el siglo XVIII', in *Historia social y económica de España y América*, ed. J. Vicens Vives, vol. 4, 5 vols., Barcelona: Editorial Vicens-Vives, pp. 263–428.

Hincapie Borda, Alicia, 2000. *Tras la imagen y la presencia de Policarpa*. Bogotá: Lerner.

Hirsch, Marianne, 1989. *The Mother-Daughter Plot*. Bloomington, IN: Indiana University Press.

Hoffmann, Paul, 1976. *La femme dans la pensée des lumières*. Paris: Editions Ophrys.

Hufton, Olwen, 1992. *Women and the Limits of Citizenship in the French Revolution*. Toronto, Buffalo and London: University of Toronto Press.

—, 1997. *The Prospect Before Her. A History of Women in Western Europe*, vol. 1, *1500–1800*. London: Fontana.

Hull, K.E., 2002. 'Review of Bourdieu's *Masculine Domination*, trans. Richard Nice, Cambridge and Oxford: Polity and Blackwell, 2001', in *Social Forces*, 81.1: 351–52.

Humble, Nicola, 2000. 'Introduction', in *Mrs Beeton's Book of Household Management*. Oxford: Oxford University Press, pp. vii–xxx.

Humboldt, Alexander von, 1852. *Personal Narrative of Travels to the Equinoctial Regions of America during the years 1799–1804*, trans. Thomasina Ross, vol.1. London: Henry G. Bohn, York Street, Covent Garden.

Iglesia, Cristina (ed.), 1998. *Letras y Divisas. Ensayos sobre literatura y rosismo*. Buenos Aires: Eudeba/Universidad de Buenos Aires.

Iriarte, Tomás, 1863. *Biografia del Brigadier General D. José Miguel Carrera (dos veces Primer Magistrado de la República de Chile)*. Buenos Aires: Imprenta de Mayo.

Irigaray, L., 1985. *Speculum of the Other Woman*, trans. Gillian C. Gill. Ithaca and New York: Cornell University Press.

Iser, Wolfang, 1976. *The Act of Reading. A Theory of Aesthetic Response*. London and Henley: Routledge, Kegan Paul.

Jaksić, Iván, 2001. *Andrés Bello: Scholarship and Nation Building in Nineteenth-Century Latin America.* Cambridge: Cambridge University Press.

Janes, Cecil (ed.), 1960. *The Journal of Christopher Columbus.* London: A. Blond and Orion Press.

Jitrik, Noé, 1970. *Ensayos y estudios de literatura argentina.* Buenos Aires: Galerna.

Johnson, J.J., 1968. *Simón Bolívar and Spanish American Independence 1783–1830.* Princeton, NJ: D. Van Nostrand Co. Ltd.

Johnson, Julie Greer, 1983. *Women in Colonial Spanish American Literature: Literary Images.* Westport, CT, and London: Greenwood Press.

—, 1993. *Satire in Colonial Spanish America. Turning the New World Upside Down.* Austin, TX: University of Texas Press.

Johnson, Lyman L. and Sonya Lipsett-Rivera (eds), 1998. *Sex, Shame and Violence. The Faces of Honour in Colonial Latin America.* Albuquerque: University of New Mexico Press.

Jornal das Senhoras (Rio de Janeiro) 1852.

Kaplan, Caren, Norma Alarcon and Minoo Moallem (eds), 1999. *Between Woman and Nation: Nationalisms, Transnational Feminisms, and the State.* Durham, NC, and London: Duke University Press.

Karasch, Mary, 1988. 'Suppliers, Sellers, Servants and Slaves' in *Cities and Society in Colonial Latin America,* ed. Louisa Schell Hoberman and Susan Migden Socolow. Albuquerque: University of New Mexico Press, pp. 251–83.

Keane, Angela, 2000. *Women Writers and the English Nation in the 1790s: Romantic Belongings.* Cambridge: Cambridge University Press.

Keen, Benjamin, 1992. *A History of Latin America.* Boston: Houghton Mifflin Company.

Kelley, Mary, 1984. *Private Woman, Public Stage: Literary Domesticity in Nineteenth-Century America.* Oxford, New York and London: Oxford University Press.

Kerber, Linda K., 1980. *Women of the Republic: Intellect and Ideology in Revolutionary America.* Chapel Hill, NC: North Carolina University Press.

Kiesling, E.C., 2003. 'Review of J. Goldstein, *War and Gender*', in *War in History,* 10.4: 502–04.

Kinsbruner, Jay, 1973. *Chile: A Historical Interpretation.* London: Harper and Row.

Kirkpatrick, Susan, 1989. *Las Romanticas: Women Writers and Subjectivity in Spain 1835–1850.* Berkeley: University of California Press.

Klawe, Janina Z., 1995. 'O Papel das Mulheres nos Descobrimentos e na Expansão Portuguesa' in *O Rosto Feminino da Expansão Portuguesa. Actas I,* ed. Maroa Reynolds de Souza et al. Lisbon: Comissão para a Igualdade e para os Direitos das mulheres, pp. 253–58.

Knaster, Meri, 1977. *Women in Spanish America. An Annotated Bibliography from Pre-Conquest to Contemporary Times.* Boston: G.K. Hall.

Kristeva, J., 1986. 'About Chinese Women', trans. S. Hand, in *The Kristeva Reader,* ed. T. Moi. Oxford: Blackwell, pp. 138–59.

Kucich, Greg, 2000. 'Romanticism and the Re-engendering of Historical Memory', in *Memory and Memorials 1789–1914. Literary and Cultural Perspectives,* ed. Matthew Campbell, Jacqueline M. Labbe and Sally Shuttleworth. London: Routledge, pp. 15–29.

LaCapra, Dominick, 1985. *History and Criticism.* Ithaca, NY, and London: Cornell University Press.

Landes, Joan B., 1988. *Women and the Public Sphere in the Age of the French Revolution*. Ithaca, NY, and London: Cornell University Press.

—, 2001. *Visualizing the Nation: Gender, Representation and Revolution in Eighteenth-Century France*. Ithaca, NY, and London: Cornell University Press.

—, 2004a. 'Republican Citizenship and Heterosocial Desire: Concepts of Masculinity in Revolutionary France', in *Masculinities in Politics and War. Gendering Modern History*, ed. Stefan Dudink, Karen Hagemann and John Tosh. Manchester: Manchester University Press, pp. 96–115.

—, 2004b. 'Revolutionary Anatomies', in *Monstrous Bodies/Political Monstrosities in Early Modern Europe*, ed. Laura Lunger Knoppers and Joan B. Landes. Ithaca, NY, and London: Cornell University Press, pp. 148–76.

Lange, Lynda, 1991. 'Rousseau and Modern Feminism', in *Feminist Interpretations and Political Theory*, ed. Mary Lyndon Shanley and Carole Pateman. University Park, PA: Pennsylvania State University Press, pp. 95–111.

Lanuza, José Luis (ed.), 1941. *Cancionero del tiempo de Rosas*, 2nd edn. Buenos Aires: Emecé Editores.

Lasarte, Pedro, 1999. '"La Vieja y el Periquillo": Una aproximación a la Lima de Juan del Valle y Caviedes', in *Esta, de nuestra América pupila. Estudios de Poesía Colonial*, ed. Georgina Sabat Rivers. Houston, TX: Society for Renaissance and Baroque Hispanic Poetry, pp. 125–39.

Lavrin, Asunción (ed.), 1978. *Latin American Women: Historical Perspectives*. Westport, CT, and London: Greenwood Press.

—, 1978a. 'In Search of the Colonial Woman in Mexico', in *Latin American Women: Historical Perspectives*, ed. Asunción Lavrin. Westport, CT, and London: Greenwood Press, pp. 23–59.

—, 1978b. 'Some final considerations of trends and issues in Latin American women's history', in *Latin American Women: Historical Perspectives*, ed. Asunción Lavrin. Westport, CT, and London: Greenwood Press, pp. 302–32.

—, 1984. 'Women in Spanish American Colonial Society', in *Cambridge History of Latin America*, ed. Leslie Bethell, vol. 2. Cambridge: Cambridge University Press, pp. 321–55.

—, 1988. 'Female Religious', in *Cities and Society in Colonial Latin America*, ed. Louisa Schell Hobermann and Susan Migden Socolow. Albuquerque: University of New Mexico Press, pp. 165–95.

—, 1989. *Sexuality and Marriage in Colonial Latin America*. Lincoln, NE, and London: University of Nebraska Press.

—, 2006. 'Spanish American Women, 1790–1850: The Challenge of Remembering', in *Hispanic Research Journal*, 7.1: 71–84.

Lavrin, Asunción and Rosalva L. Loreto (eds), 2002. *La escritura femenina en la espiritualidad barroca novohsipana siglos XVII y XVIII*. México D.F.: Universidad de las Américas y Archivo General de la Nación.

Lecuna, Vicente, 1929. *Cartas del Libertador, Tomo IX, Julio de 1828 a diciembre de 1829*. Caracas: Lit. y Tip. del Comercio.

Lecuna, V. (ed.), 1947. *Simón Bolívar. Obras completas*, vol. 1. Caracas: Ministerio de Educación Nacional de los Estados Unidos de Venezuela; Havana: Editorial Lex.

— (ed.), 1975. *Documentos referentes a la creación de Bolivia*, vol. 2. Caracas: Gobierno de Venezuela, Imprenta Nacional.

Le Doeuff, Michèle, 1989. *Hipparchia's Choice. An Essay concerning Women,*

Philosophy, etc., trans. Trista Selous. Oxford and Cambridge, MA: Blackwell.

Leitner, Claudia, 2003. '*Querelle des femmes / Querelle d'Amérique*: Reinvindicaciones de la América española en la *Defensa de las mujeres* de Feijoo', in *The Querelle des femmes in the Romania. Studies in Honour of Friederike Hassauer*, ed. Wolfram Aichinger, Marien Bidwell-Steiner, Judith Bosch and Eva Cesscutti. Vienna: Verlag Turia und Kant, pp. 105–26.

Leonard, Diana and Lisa Adkins (eds), 1996. *Sex in Question: French Materialist Feminism*. London: Taylor & Francis.

Leonard, Elizabeth D. 1999. *All the Daring of a Soldier, Women of the Civil War Armies*. London and New York: W.W. Norton and Co.

Leonard, Irving, 1949. *Books of the Brave, Being an Account of Books and of Men in the Spanish Conquest and Settlement of the Sixteenth Century New World*. Cambridge, MA: Harvard University Press.

Lévi-Strauss, Claude, 2002 [1977]. *Myth and Meaning*. London and New York: Routledge.

Lewkowicz, Lidia F., 2000. *Juana Paula Manso (1819–1875). Una mujer del siglo XXI*. Buenos Aires: Corregidor.

Lichtblau, Myron I, 1959. *The Argentine Novel of the Nineteenth Century*. New York: Hispanic Institute.

Liddell, Charlotte, 2005. 'Brazil's First Feminist? Gender and Patriotism in the Works of Nisia Floresta'. Unpublished PhD thesis. University of Manchester.

Lievano Aguirre, Indalecio, 1983. *Bolívar*. Madrid: Ediciones Cultura Hispánica del Instituto de Cooperación Iberoamericana.

Lipsett-Rivera, Sonya, 2001. 'Marriage and Family Relations in Mexico during the Transition from Colony to Nation', in *State and Society in Spanish America during the Age of Revolution*, ed. Victor M. Uribe-Urán. Wilmington, DE: Scholarly Resources, pp. 122–48.

Lister, Ruth, 2000. 'Inclusión/exclusión: The Janus Face of Citizenship', in *Towards a Gendered Political Economy*, ed. Joanne Cook, Jennifer Roberts and Georgina Waylen. Basingstoke and London: Macmillan, pp. 98–117.

Lojo, María Rosa, 1991. '"*El Matadero*" de Esteban Echeverría. La sangre derramada y la estética de la "mezcla", in *Alba de América*', 9, 16–17: 41–63.

—, 1994. *La 'barbarie' en la narrativa argentina siglo XIX*. Buenos Aires: Corregidor.

López, J., 2003. *Society and its Metaphors*. New York and London: Continuum.

López Alves, Fernando, 1996. 'The Authoritarian Roots of Liberalism: Uruguay 1810–1886', in *Liberals, Politics and Power. State Formation in Nineteenth-century Latin America*, ed. Vincent C. Peloso and Barbara A. Tenenbaum. Athens and London: University of Georgia Press, pp. 111–33.

Lorenzo, Emilio, 1994. *El español de hoy, lengua en ebullición*, 4th edn. Madrid: Gredos.

Lynch, John, 1973. *The Spanish American Revolutions*. London: Weidenfeld and Nicolson.

—, 1985. 'The Origins of Spanish American Independence', in *The Cambridge History of Latin America*, vol 3, ed. Leslie Bethell. Cambridge: Cambridge University Press, pp. 3–50.

—, 1986. *The Spanish American Revolutions 1808–1826*, 2nd edn. New York and London: W.W. Norton and Co.

—, 1987. 'The River Plate Republics', in *Spanish America after Independence c.*

1820–c. 1870, ed. Leslie Bethell. Cambridge: Cambridge University Press, pp. 314–75.

—, 1992. *Caudillos in Spanish America 1800–1850*. Oxford: Clarendon Press.

—, 1999. 'Spanish American Independence in Recent Historiography', in *Independence and Revolution in Spanish America: Perspectives and Problems*, ed. Anthony McFarlane and Eduardo Posada-Carbó. London: Institute of Latin American Studies, pp. 13–42.

—, 2001. *Argentine Caudillo: Juan Manuel de Rosas*. Wilmington, DE: Scholarly Resources.

—, 2006. *Simón Bolívar: A Life*. New Haven, CT, and London: Yale University Press.

Macaulay, Neill, 1986. *Dom Pedro. The Struggle for Liberty in Brazil and Portugal, 1798–1834*. Durham, NC, and London: Duke University Press.

Macherey, Pierre, 1978. *A Theory of Literary Production*, trans. Geoffrey Wall. London and Boston: Routledge, Kegan Paul.

MacIntyre, Iona, 2005. 'Fraile Castañeda, *las matronas*, and the post-Independence Press in Buenos Aires', *Antes y Después del Quijote: en el cincuentenario de la Asociación de Hispanistas de Gran Bretaña e Irlanda*. Valencia: Biblioteca Valenciana, pp. 299–308.

—, 2006. 'Print Culture, Women and Statecraft in 1820s Buenos Aires'. Unpublished PhD thesis, University of Nottingham.

Macpherson, C.B., 1962. *The Political Theory of Possessive Individualism. Hobbes to Locke*. Oxford and New York: Oxford University Press.

Madariaga, Salvador de, 1947. *The Fall of the Spanish American Empire*. London: Hollis and Carter.

Madureira, Luís, 1994. 'Tropical Sex Fantasies and the Ambassador's Other Death: The Difference in Portuguese Colonialism', in *Cultural Critique*, 28: 149–73.

Maestri, Mário, 2003. 'As Sete Mulheres e as Negras sem Rosto', *Revista. Espaço Acadêmico* 29, Oct. 2003. http://www.espacoacademico.com.br/029/29maestri.htm. Accessed August 23 2005.

Maier, Linda S. and Isabel Dufano (eds), 2004. *Woman as Witness. Essays on Testimonial Literature by Latin American Women*. New York, Washington, Bern: Peter Lang.

Mansilla, Lucio V., 1904. *Mis memorias de infancia-adolescencia*. Paris: Garnier.

Manso, Juana, 1844. *Una Armonía. Homenage de Amistad al Sr. Don Juan Bautista Cuneo*. Montevideo: Imprenta del Nacional.

—, 1854. *La familia del Comendador*. Buenos Aires: Librería la Victoria.

Manso de Noroña, Juana, 1924 [1852]. *Los misterios del Plata. Episodios históricos de la época de Rosas escritos en 1846*, ed. Ricardo Isidoro López Muniz. Buenos Aires: Jesús Menéndez e hijo.

Marín del Solar, Mercedes, 1837. *Homenaje de gratitud a la memoria del benemérito Ministro Diego Portales*. Santiago: Imprenta de la Opinión.

—, 1874. *Poesías de la señora Dª. Mercedes Marín de Solar, dadas a luz por su hijo Enrique del Solar*. Santiago: Imprenta Andrés Bello.

Marshall, C., C.K. Ogden and M. Sargant Florence, 1987. *Militarism versus Feminism. Writings on Women and War*, ed. Margaret Kamester and Jo Vellacott. London: Virago.

Martin, Gerald, 1985. 'The literature, music and art of Latin America from

Independence to c. 1870', in *The Cambridge History of Latin America*, vol 3, ed. Leslie Bethell. Cambridge: Cambridge University Press, pp. 797–839.

Martín, Luis, 1983. *Daughters of the Conquistadores: Women of the Viceroyalty of Peru.* Albuquerque: University of New Mexico Press.

Martinez-Alier, Verena, 1974. *Marriage, Class and Colour in Nineteenth-century Cuba. A Study of Racial Attitudes and Sexual Values in a Slave Society.* Cambridge: Cambridge University Press.

Martínez Riaza, Ascención, 1985. *La prensa doctrina en la independencia de Perú, 1811–1824.* Madrid: Ediciones Cultura Hispanica.

Marvin, Garry, 1986. 'Honour, Integrity and the Problem of Violence in the Spanish Bullfight', in *The Anthropology of Violence*, ed. David Riches. Oxford: Basil Blackwell, pp. 118–35.

Masiello, Francine, 1992. *Between Civilization and Barbarism: Women, Nation and Literary Culture in Modern Argentina.* London and Lincoln, NE: University of Nebraska Press.

—, 1994. *La mujer y el espacio público: El periodismo femenino en la Argentina del siglo XIX.* Buenos Aires: Feminaria.

Mavor, Elizabeth (ed.), 1993. *The Captain's Wife. The South American Journals of Maria Graham, 1821–23.* London: Weidenfeld and Nicolson.

Maza Valenzuela, Erika, 1995. 'Catholicism, Anticlericalism, and the Quest for Women's Suffrage in Chile', Working Paper 214, Kellog Institute/University of Notre Dame. http://www.nd.edu/~kellog.

McClintock, Anne, 1995. *Imperial Leather. Race, Gender and Sexuality in the Colonial Context.* London and New York: Routledge.

McFarlane, Anthony and Eduardo Posada-Carbó (eds), 1999. *Independence and Revolution in Spanish America: Perspectives and Problems.* London: Institute of Latin American Studies.

Medina, J.T., 1923. *La literatura femenina en Chile.* Santiago: Imprenta Universitaria de Chile.

Mellor, Anne K., 1993. *Romanticism and Gender.* London: Routledge.

—, 2003. *Mother of the Nation. Women's Political Writings in England 1780–1830.* Bloomington and Indianopolis: Indiana University Press.

Mendelson, Johanna S.R., 1978. 'The Feminine Press: the View of Women in the Colonial Journals of Spanish America, 1790–1810', in *Latin American Women: Historical Perspectives,* ed. Asunción Lavrin. Westport, CT, and London: Greenwood Press, pp. 173–98.

Mendoza, Daniel, 1964. 'Gran Sarao' and 'Los muchachos a la moda', in *Antología de costumbristas venezolanos del siglo XIX.* Caracas: Ministerio de Educación, Dirección de Cultura y Bellas Artes, pp. 120–143, 107–120.

Menéndez y Pelayo, Marcelino, 1893. *Antología de poetas hispano-americanos*, vol. II. Madrid: Real Academia Española/Sucesores de Rivadeneyra.

—, 1895. *Antología de poetas hispano-americanos*, vol. IV, *Chile, República Argentina, Uruguay.* Madrid: Real Academia Española/Sucesores de Rivadeneyra.

Mercado, Juan Carlos, 1996. *Building a Nation: The Case of Echeverría.* Lanham, MD: University Press of America.

Mercurio Peruano (Lima) 1791–92.

Merrim, Stephanie, 1994. 'Catalina de Erauso: From Anomalie to Icon', in *Coded Encounters: Writing, Gender, and Ethnicity in Colonial Latin America*, ed. Francisco Javier Cevallos-Candua, Jeffrey A. Cole, Nina M. Scott and Nicomedes Suárez-

Araúz. Amherst, MA: University of Massachusetts Press, pp. 177–205.
Meznar, Joan E., 1997. 'Carlota Lucia de Brito: Women, Power and Politics in Northeast Brazil', in *The Human Tradition*, ed. William H. Beezley and Judith Ewell. Wilmington, DE: Scholarly Resources, pp. 41–52.
Midgely, Claire, 1995. *Women against Slavery: the British Campaigns 1780–1870*. London and New York: Routledge.
Miller, Nicola, 2006. 'The Immoral Educator: Race, Gender and Citizenship in Simón Rodríguez's Programme for Popular Education', in *Hispanic Research Journal*, 7.1: 11–20.
Millington, Mark, 2006. *Hombres in/visibles. La representación de la masculinidad en la literatura lationamericana 1920–1980*. Bogotá: FCE.
Mills, Sara, 1997. *Discourse*. London and New York: Routledge.
Miranda, Marta Elva, 1948. 'María Cornelia Olivares', in Emilia Romero de Valle, *Mujeres de América*. Mexico City: Secretaría de Educación Pública, pp. 56–57.
Mitre, Bartolomé, 1927 [1858]. *Historia de Belgrano*, vol. I. Buenos Aires: Editorial Científica y Literaria Argentina.
—, 1939. *Obras completas*, vol. IV. Buenos Aires: Guillermo Kraft.
—, 1940. *Obras Completas de Bartolomé Mitre*, vol. VI. Buenos Aires: Guillermo Kraft.
Mizraje, María Gabriela, 1999. *Argentinas de Rosas a Perón*. Buenos Aires: Biblos.
— (ed.), 2003. *Mariquita Sánchez de Thompson. Intimidad y política: diario, cartas y recuerdos*. Buenos Aires: Adriana Hidalgo.
Mohanty, Chandra Talpade, 1988. 'Under Western Eyes: Feminist Scholarship and Colonial Discourse', in *Feminist Review*, 30: 65–88.
Moi, Toril, 1999. *What is a Woman?* Oxford: Oxford University Press.
Molyneux, Maxine, 2000. 'Comparative Perspectives on Gender and Citizenship: Latin America and the former Socialist Sates', in *Towards a Gendered Political Economy*, ed. Joanne Cook, Jennifer Roberts and Georgina Waylen. Basingstoke and London: Macmillan, pp. 121–44.
Monsalve, José Donoso, 1926. *Mujeres de la independencia*. Bogotá: Imprenta Nacional.
Moreira, Maria Eunice (ed.), 2003. *Uma Voz ao Sul. Os Versos de Maria Clemência da Silveira Sampaio*. Florianópolis: Editora Mulheres.
Mosse, G.L., 1996. *The Image of Man: The Creation of Modern Masculinity*. Oxford: Oxford University Press.
Munizaga, G., 1988. *El discurso público de Pinochet: un análisis semiológico*. Santiago de Chile: CESOC/CENECA.
Muñoz Camargo, Diego, 1892 [c. 1576]. *Historia de Tlaxcala*. Mexico City: Oficina Tip. De la Secretaría de Fomento.
Murillo Rubiera, Fernando, 1982. 'Andrés Bello en Inglaterra', in *Cuadernos Hispanoamericanos*, 388, 2: 5–44.
Murray, Pamela, 2001. '"Loca" or "Libertadora"? Manuela Sáenz in the Eyes of History and Historians 1900–c. 1990', in *Journal of Latin American Studies*, 33.2: 291–310.
Murray, Stephen O., 2002. 'Review of Bourdieu's *Masculine Domination*, Cambridge and Oxford: Polity and Blackwell, 2001', in *The Journal of the Royal Anthropological Institute*, 8.2: 389–90.
Muzart, Zahidé Lupinacci (ed.), 2000. *Escritoras Brasileiras do Século XIX*, vol. 1. Florianópolis: Editora Mulheres.
Myers, Jorge, 1999. 'Una revolución en las costumbres: las nuevas formas de socia-

bilidad de la elite porteña, 1800–1860', in Fernando Madero and Marta Devoto, *Historia de la vida privada en la Argentina*, vol. 1, *País antigüo. De la colonia a 1870*, Buenos Aires: Taurus, pp. 111–45.

[N.A.] 1910. *Documentos de San Martín, vol. 3*. Buenos Aires: Imprenta de Coni Hermanos.

[N.A.] 1964. *Heroínas venezolanas*. Santiago de Chile: Publicaciones Embajada de Venezuela en Chile.

Nebrija, Antonio de, 1980 [1492]. *Gramática de la lengua castellana*, ed. Antonio Quilis. Madrid: Editora Nacional.

Neuhaus Rizo Patrón, Carlos, 1997. *Las Mariscalas*. Lima: Walkira Ediciones.

Neumann, E., 1963. *The Great Mother. An Analysis of the Archetype*, trans. R. Manheim, 2nd edn. Princeton, NJ: Princeton University Press.

Offen, Karen, 2000. *European Feminisms 1700–1950. A Political History*. Stanford, CA: Stanford University Press.

Operé, Fernando, 2003. '*La Cautiva* de Echeverría: el trágico señuelo de la frontera', in *Bulletin of Spanish Studies*, 80.5: 545–54.

O'Phelan Godoy, Scarlett, 1985. *Rebellions and Revolts in Eighteenth-century Peru and Upper Peru*. Köln: Böhlau Verlag.

Osório, Fernando, 1935. *Mulheres Farroupilhas*. Porto Alegre: Livraria do Globo.

Pagden, Anthony, 1990. *Spanish Imperialism and the Political Imagination*. New Haven, CT, and London: Yale University Press.

—, 1995. *Lords of All the World: Ideologies of Empire in Spain, Britain and France c. 1500–c. 1800*. New Haven, CT, and London: Yale University Press.

Palacio de Libarona, Agustina, 2004. 'Infortunios de la matrona santiagueña doña Agustina Palacio de Libarona la Heroína del Bracho (1840–42)', intro. Mary Berg, in *Woman as Witness. Essays on Testimonial Literature by Latin American Women*, ed. Linda S. Maier and Isabel Dufano. New York, Washington, Bern: Peter Lang, pp. 181–82, 183–200.

Pallares-Burke, Maria Lúcia Garcia, 1996. 'A Mary Wollstonecraft que o Brasil conheceu, ou a Travessura Literária de Nísia Floresta', in *Nísia Floresta, O Carapuceiro e outros ensaios de tradução cultural*. São Paulo: Editora HUCITEC, pp. 167–93.

Pallis, M., 1980. *Slaves of Slaves: The Challenge of Latin American Women*. London: Zed Press.

Parra de Riego, Carlos, 1935. 'La limeña conspiradora y patriota', in *Revista Chilena Zigzag*, 1555: 248–51.

Paz, Octavio, 1981 [1950]. *El laberinto de la soledad. Posdata. Vuelta a El laberinto de la soledad*. Mexico, D.F.: Fondo de Cultura Económica.

Pendle, George, 1990. *A History of Latin America*. Harmondsworth: Penguin.

Pérez Godoy, Manuel, 1948. 'Juana Azurduy', in *Mujeres de América*, ed. Emilia Romero de Valle. Mexico City: SEP, pp.33–37.

Pérez Vila, Manuel, 1983. *Gaceta de Caracas*, facsimile edn., 10 vols. Caracas: Biblioteca de la Academia Nacional de la Historia.

— (ed.), 1979. *Simón Bolívar: Doctrina del Libertador*, 2nd edn. Caracas: Biblioteca Ayacucho.

Piccirilli, Ricardo, 1957. *San Martín y la política de los pueblos*. Buenos Aires:

Ediciones Gure S.R.L.
Pierini, Margarita, 2002. 'Historia, folletín e ideología en *Los misterios del Plata* de Juana Manso', *Nueva Revista de Filología Hispánica*, 50.2: 457–88.
Pino Iturrieta, Elías, 1999. *Nueva lectura de la Carta de Jamaica*. Caracas: Monte Avila Editores.
—, 2003. *El Divino Bolívar: Ensayo sobre una religión republicana*. Madrid: Los libros de la Catarata.
Pitt-Rivers, J.R., 1965. 'Honour and Social Status', in *Honour and Shame. The Values of the Mediterranean*, ed. J.R. Peristiany. London: Weidenfeld and Nicolson.
Plato, *The Republic*, 1941, ed. and trans. Francis M. Cornford. Oxford: Clarendon Press.
Platt, Tristan, 1993. 'Simón Bolívar, the Sun of Justice and the Amerindian Virgin: Andean Conceptions of the *Patria* in Nineteenth-Century Potosí', in the *Journal of Latin American Studies*, 25, 1993: 159–85.
Poblete, Juan, 2003. *Literatura chilena del siglo XIX: Entre públicos lectores y figuras autoriales*. Santiago de Chile: Editorial Cuarto Propio.
Pontiatowska, Elena (ed.), 1993. *Patriota y amante de usted: Manuela Sáenz y el Libertador: diario inédito*. Mexico, D.F.: Editorial Diana.
Poulain de la Barre, François, 1990 [1673]. *The Equality of the Sexes*, trans. and intro. Desmond M. Clarke. Manchester and New York: Manchester University Press.
Pratt, Mary Louise, 1990. 'Women, Literature, and National Brotherhood', in *Women, Culture and Politics in Latin America*, ed. Emilie Bergmann et al. Berkeley: University of California Press.
—, 1992. *Imperial Eyes: Travel Writing and Transculturation*. London: Routledge.
Pupo-Walker, Enrique, 1973. 'Originalidad y composición de un texto romántico: *El Matadero* de Esteban Echeverría', in *El cuento hispanoamericano ante la crítica*, ed. Enrique Pupo-Walker. Madrid: Castalia, pp. 37–49.

Querejazu, R., 1987. *Chuquisaca 1539–1825*. Sucre: Imprenta Universitaria.
Quintana, Manuel José, 1958. *Poesías*. Madrid: Espasa Calpe.

Rama, Angel, 1996 [1984]. *The Lettered City*, trans. John Charles Chasteen. Durham, NC, and London: Duke University Press.
Ribeiro, Niamara Pessoa, 1985. 'Heroínas da Resistência Gaúcha', in *O Papel da Mulher na Revolução Farroupilha*, org. Diva Ione Silveira. Porto Alegre: Tchê, pp. 8–46.
Riches, David, 1986. 'The Phenomenon of Violence', in *The Anthroplogy of Violence*, ed. David Riches. Oxford: Basil Blackwell, pp. 1–27.
Roca, I.M., 2000. 'On the Meaning of Gender', in *Hispanic Research Journal*, 1.2: 113–28.
Rock, David, 1985. *Argentina 1516–1982. From Spanish Colonization to the Falklands War*. Berkeley and Los Angeles: University of California Press.
Rodríguez, Jaime E., 1998. *The Independence of Spanish America*. Cambridge and New York: Cambridge University Press.
Rodríguez Fernández, Mario, 1981. 'Bello, el poeta', in *Atenea. Revista de Ciencias, Arte y Literatura*, Concepción, Chile, 443–44: 41–52.
Roggiano, Alfredo A., 1977. 'Esteban Echeverría y el romanticismo europeo', in *Actas del Congreso de la Asociación Internacional de Hispanistas*. Toronto, 22–26 agosto, vol. VI, pp. 629–31.

Roldán Vera, Eugenia, 2003. *The British Book Trade and South American Independence*. Aldershot: Ashgate.
Romero de Valle, Emilia, 1966. *Diccionario manual de literatura peruana y materias afines*. Lima: Universidad Nacional Mayor de San Marcos.
Rosas Lauro, Claudia, 1999a. 'Educando al bello sexo: La mujer en el discurso ilustrado', in *El Perú en el siglo XVIII. La era Borbónica*, ed. Scarlett O'Phelan Godoy. Lima: Pontificia Universidad Católica del Perú, pp. 369–413.
—, 1999b. 'Jaque a la Dama. La imagen de la mujer en la prensa limeña de fines del siglo XVIII', in *Mujeres y género en la historia del Perú*, ed. Margarita Zegarra. Lima: Centro de Documentación sobre la Mujer, pp. 142–71.
Rotker, Susana, 2002. *Captive Women. Oblivion and Memory in Argentina*, trans. Jennifer French. Minneapolis, MN, and London: University of Minnesota Press.
Rumazo González, Alfonso, 1945. *Manuela Sáenz, La libertadora del Libertador*. Buenos Aires: Almendros y Nietos.

Sáenz Quesada, María, 2001. 'Prologue', in Mónica Deleis, Ricardo de Titto and Diego L. Arguindeguy, *Mujeres de la política argentina*. Buenos Aires: Aguilar, pp. 207–18.
Safford, Frank, 1985. 'Politics, ideology and society in post-Independence Spanish America', in *The Cambridge History of Latin America*, vol 3, ed. Leslie Bethell. Cambridge: Cambridge University Press, pp. 347–421.
Sánchez-Albornoz, Nicolás, 1984. 'The Population of Colonial Spanish America', in *The Cambridge History of Latin America*, vol 2, ed. Leslie Bethell, pp. 3–35.
Santomauro, Héctor, 1994. *Juana Manso y las luchas por la educación pública en la Argentina*. Buenos Aires: Corregidor.
Santos, Boaventura de Sousa, 2002. 'Between Prospero and Caliban: Colonialism, Postcolonialism and Inter-identity', in *Luso-Brazilian Review*, 39. 2: 9–43.
Sarmiento, Domingo Faustino, 1961. *Domingo Faustino Sarmiento. Epistolario Intimo*, vol. 2, ed. Bernardo González Arrili. Buenos Aires: Ediciones Culturales/Ministerio de la Educación y Justicia.
Schaar, John H., 1981. 'The Case for Patriotism', in *Legitimacy in the Modern State*, New Brunswick, NJ: Transaction Books, pp. 285–311.
Scheina, Robert L., 2003. *Latin America's Wars*, vol. I: *The Age of the Caudillo*. Washington, D.C.: Brassey's Inc.
Schmidt, Rita Terezinha, 2001. 'Introdução', in Delfina Benigna da Cunha, *Poesias*. Porto Alegre: Instituto Estadual do Livro, pp. 9–25.
Schmidt-Welle, Friedhelm (ed.), 2003. *Ficciones y silencios fundacionales. Literaturas y culturas poscoloniales en América Latina (siglo XIX)*. Madrid: Iberoamericana.
Schwartz, Stuart, 1997. 'The Landed Elite', in *The Countryside in Colonial Latin America*, ed. Louisa Schell Hoberman and Susan Migden Socolow. Albuquerque: University of New Mexico Press, pp. 97–121.
Scott, Joan Wallach, 1996. *Only Paradoxes to Offer: French Feminists and the Rights of Man*. Cambridge, MA, and London: Harvard University Press.
—, 1999. *Gender and the Politics of History*, 2nd edn. New York: Columbia University Press.
— (ed.), 1996. *Feminism and History*. Oxford and New York: Oxford University Press.
Semanario Crítico (Lima) 1791.
Seckinger, Ron L., 1976. 'South American Power Politics during the 1820s', in *The Hispanic American Historical Review*, 56.2: 241–67.

Shanley, Mary Lyndon and Carole Pateman (eds), 2003. *Feminist Interpretations and Political Theory*. University Park, PA: Pennsylvania State University Press.

Shumway, Nicolas, 1991. *The Invention of Argentina*. Berkeley, Los Angeles and London: University of California Press.

Silva, Maria Beatriz Nizza da, 1995. 'Mulheres Brancas no Fim do Período Colonial', in *O Rosto Feminino da Expansão Portuguesa. Actas II*, ed. Maria Reynolds de Souza et al. Lisbon: Comissão para a Igualdade e para os Direitos das mulheres, pp. 441–51.

Silva, Tony Simoes da, 2002. 'Raced Encounters, Sexed Transactions: "Luso-tropicalism" and the Portuguese Colonial Empire', in *Pretexts: literary and cultural studies*, 11.1: 27–39.

Silveira, Diva Ione (ed.), 1985. *O Papel da Mulher na Revolução Farroupilha*. Porto Alegre: Tchê Comunicações Lda.

Silverblatt, Irene, 1987. *Moon, Sun and Witches: Gender Ideologies and Class in Colonial Peru*. Princeton, NJ: University of Princeton Press.

Skidmore, Thomas E., 1999. *Brazil. Five Centuries of Change*. New York and Oxford: Oxford University Press.

Sluga, Glenda, 2004. 'Masculinities, nations and the new world order: peacemaking and nationality in Britain, France and the United States after the First World War', in *Masculinities in Politics and War. Gendering Modern History*, ed. Stefan Dudink, Karen Hagemann and John Tosh. Manchester: Manchester University Press, pp. 238–54.

Smith, B.C., 1989. *Changing Lives: Women in European History Since 1700*. London: D. Heath and Co.

Smith-Rosenberg, Carroll, 2000. 'Political Camp or the Ambiguous Engendering of the American Republic', in *Gendered Nations: Nationalism and Gender Order in the Long Nineteenth-century*, ed. Ida Blom, Karen Hagemann and Catherine Hall. Oxford and New York: Berg, pp. 272–92.

—, 2004. 'The Republican Gentleman: The Race to Rhetorical Stability in the New United States', in *Masculinities in Politics and War. Gendering Modern History*, ed. Stefan Dudink, Karen Hagemann and John Tosh. Manchester: Manchester University Press, pp. 61–76.

Soares, Pedro Maia, 1980. '*Feminismo no Rio Grande do Sul. Primeiros Apontamentos* (1835–1945)', in *Vivência, História, Sexualidade e Imagens Femininas*, ed. Maria Cristina A. Bruschini and Fúlvia Rosemberg. São Paulo: Brasiliense, pp. 121–50.

Socolow, Susan Migden, 1978. *The Merchants of Buenos Aires 1778–1810. Family and Commerce*. London and New York: Cambridge University Press.

—, 2000. *The Women of Colonial Latin America*. Cambridge: Cambridge University Press.

Solares-Larrave, Francisco, 2003. 'Texts, History and Narrative Discourse in Two Nineteenth-Century Spanish American History Novels', in *Latin American Literary Review*, 31.61: 58–80.

Soldevila, F. [Fernando], 1959. *Historia de España*, vol. IV. Barcelona: Ariel.

Sommer, Doris, 1991. *Foundational Fictions. The National Romances of Latin America*. Berkeley, Los Angeles and Oxford: University of California Press.

Sophia, A Person of Quality, 1975 [1739]. *Woman not Inferior to Man or A Short and Modest Vindication of the Natural Power of the Fair-Sex to a Perfect Equality of Power, Dignity, and Esteem, with the Men*. London: Bentham Press.

Sosa de Newton, Lily, 1986. *Diccionario biográfico de mujeres argentinas*. Buenos

Aires: Editorial Plus Ultra.

Sosnowski, Saúl, 1981. 'Esteban Echeverría: El intelectual ante la formación del estado', in *Revista Iberoamericana*, 47.117–15: 293–300.

Souza, Maria Reynolds de, et al. (eds), 1995. *O Rosto Feminino da Expansão Portuguesa. Actas I e II.* Lisbon: Comissão para a Igualdade e para os Direitos das Mulheres.

Spender, Dale, 1985. *Man Made Language*, 2nd edn. London, Boston and Melbourne: Routledge/Kegan Paul.

Stegagno-Picchio, Luciana, 2004. *História da Literatura Brasileira*, 2nd edn. Rio de Janeiro: Lacerda.

Stern, Steve, 1995. *The Secret History of Gender: Women, Men and Power in Late Colonial Mexico.* Chapel Hill, NC: University of North Carolina Press.

Stoner, K. Lynn, 1987. 'Directions in Latin American Women's History 1977–1985', in *Latin American Research Review*, 22.2: 101–34.

Suárez, Federico, 2002. *Las Cortes de Cádiz*, 2nd edn. Madrid: Ediciones Rialp.

Sutcliffe, Thomas, 1841. *Sixteen Years in Chile and Peru, From 1822 to 1839.* London and Paris: Fisher, Son, and Co.

Taylor, William 1979. *Drinking, Homicide, and Rebellion in Colonial Mexican Villages.* Stanford, CA: Stanford University Press.

Terralla y Landa, Esteban 1798. *Lima por dentro y fuera. En consejos económicos, saludables, políticos y morales que da un amigo a otro con motivo de querer dexar la ciudad de Mexico por pasar a la de Lima. Obra jocosa y divertida. En que con salados conceptos se describen, además de otras cosas, las costumbres, usos y mañas de las madamitas de allí, de acá y de otras partes.* Madrid: Villalpando.

Torres Caicedo, José María, 1863. *Ensayos biográficos y de crítica literaria.* Paris: Guillaumin.

Tosh, John, 2004, 'Hegemonic Masculinity and the History of Gender', in *Masculinities in Politics and War. Gendering Modern History*, ed. Stefan Dudink, Karen Hagemann and John Tosh. Manchester: Manchester University Press, pp. 41–58.

Tosta, Virgilio, 1987. *Historia de Barinas*, vol. II, *1800–1863*. Caracas: Fuentes Para la Historia Colonial de Venezuela, Academia Nacional de la Historia.

Trenti Rocamora, J. Luis, 1945. *Grandes mujeres de América.* Buenos Aires: Editorial Huarpes.

Tristan, Flora, 1979. *Memoires et pérégrinations d'une paria 1833–34.* Paris: Francois Maspero.

—, 1986. *Peregrinations of a Pariah 1833–34*, trans. Jean Hawkes. London: Virago.

'Una señora americana', 1824. *Cartas sobre la educación del bello sexo.* London: R. Ackermann.

Uribe-Urán, Victor M. (ed.), 2001. *State and Society in Spanish America during the Age of Revolution.* Wilmington, DE: Scholarly Resources.

Urquidi, José Macedonio, 1918. *Bolivianas ilustres, heroínas, escritoras, artistas.* Vol. 1. La Paz: Escuela Tipográfica.

Urzua, María and Ximena Adriasola, 1963. *La mujer en la poesía chilena. Antología 1784–1961.* Santiago de Chile: Editorial Nascimiento.

Vaillant, George C., 1950. *Aztecs of Mexico: Origin, Rise and Fall of the Aztec Nation.*

New York: Doubleday.

Van Young, Eric, 2001. 'Conclusion – Was there an Age of Revolution in Spanish America?', in *State and Society in Spanish America during the Age of Revolution*, ed. Víctor M. Uribe-Urán. Wilmington, DE: Scholarly Resources, pp. 219–46.

Vargas Martínez, G., 1992. 'Introducción a Feijóo, apologista de América', in *Cuadernos Americanos*, 1, 31: 214–29.

Vasconcellos, Eliane, 2000. 'Joana Paula Manso de Noronha', in *Escritoras Brasileiras do Século XIX*, vol. 1, ed. Zahidé Lupinacci Muzart. Florianópolis: Editora Mulheres, pp. 228–49.

Vergara Quiroz, Sergio, 1987. *Cartas de mujeres en Chile, 1630–1885*. Santiago de Chile: Editorial Andrés Bello.

Vergara y Vergara, José María, 1958. *Historia de la literatura en Nueva Granada*, vol. 3. Bogotá: Biblioteca de la Presidencia de Colombia, Editorial ABC.

Vicuña Mackenna, Benjamín, 1938 [1857]. *Obras completas, vol. IX, El ostracismo de los Carreras*. Santiago de Chile: Universidad de Chile.

Vidal, Hernán, 2004. *La literatura en la historia de las emancipaciones latinoamericanas*. Santiago de Chile: Mosquito Editores.

Vilaseca, Clara (ed.), 1952. *Cartas de Mariquita de Sánchez*. Buenos Aires: Peuser.

Villalba, Jorge (ed.), 1986. *Manuela Sáenz: epistolario*. Quito: Banco Central de Ecuador.

Viroli, Mauricio, 1995. *For Love of Country: An Essay on Patriotism and Nationalism*. Oxford: Clarendon.

Vogeley, Nancy, 1996. 'La figuración de la mujer. México en el momento de la Independencia', in *Mujer y cultura en la Colonia hispanoamericana*, ed. Mabel Moraña. Pittsburgh, PA: Biblioteca de América, pp. 307–26.

Weeks, Elsie, 1940. 'Great Chilean Women', in *Andean Monthly* 3: 4, June 1940: 174–81.

Weinberg, Felix, 1977. *El Salón Literario de 1837*, 2nd edn. Buenos Aires: Hachette.

Wenke, Silke, 2000. 'Gendered Representations of the Nation's Past and Future', in *Gendered Nations: Nationalism and Gender Order in the Long Nineteenth-century*, ed. Ida Blom, Karen Hagemann and Catherine Hall. Oxford and New York: Berg, pp. 63–77.

Whigham, Thomas L., 1997. 'Rosa Dominga Ocampos in Paraguay', in *The Human Tradition in Modern Latin America*, ed. William H. Beezley and Judith Ewell. Wilmington, DE: Scholarly Resources, pp. 53–61.

Whitford, M., 1991. *Luce Irigaray: Philosophy in the Feminine*. London and New York: Routledge.

Williamson, E., 1992. *The Penguin History of Latin America*. Harmondsworth: Penguin.

Wittig, Monique, 1986. 'The Mark of Gender', in *The Poetics of Gender*, ed. Nancy K. Miller. New York: Columbia University Press, pp. 63–73.

Wollstonecraft, Mary, 1992 [1792]. 'Author's introduction', in *A Vindication of the Rights of Woman*. Harmondsworth: Penguin.

Woolf, Virginia, 1984. *A Room of One's Own. Three Guineas*, ed. H. Lee. London: Chatto and Windus; The Hogarth Press.

Yuval-Davis, Nira, 1997. *Gender and Nation*. London: Sage.

Zabala, Rómulo, 1948. 'Policarpa Salavarrieta', in *Mujeres de América*, ed. Emilia Romero de Valle. Mexico City: Secretaría de Educación Pública, pp. 42–43.

Zavalía Lagos, Jorge A., 1986. *Mariquita Sánchez y su tiempo*. Buenos Aires: Plus Ultra.

Zea, Leopoldo (ed.), 1993. *América Latina ante la Revolución francesa*. Mexico D.F.: UNAM.

Zegarra, Margarita (ed.), 1999. *Mujeres y género en la historia del Perú*. Lima: Centro de documentación sobre la mujer.

Zilberman, Regina, 1991. 'Mulheres Sul-Rio-Grandenses: A voz por trás do gauchesco', in *Travessia*, 23: 37–53.

Zoraida Vásquez, Josefina, 1994. 'Women's Liberation in Latin America: Toward a History of the Present', in *Confronting Change, Challenging Tradition: Women in Latin American History*, ed. Gertrude M. Yeager. Wilmington, DE: Scholarly Resources, pp. 18–25.

Zuccotti, Liliana Patricia 1995. '*Los Misterios del Plata*, El fracaso de una escritura pública', in *Revista Interamericana de Bibliografía*, 45.3: 381–89.

—, 2004. 'La ficción documentada. *Amalia* y su difusión en *La Semana*', in *Letras y divisas. Ensayos sobre literatura y rosismo*, ed. Cristina Iglesia. Buenos Aires: Santiago Aros, pp. 111–24.

Index